LIBRARY OF NEW TESTAMENT STUDIES

402

formerly the Journal for the Study of the New Testament Supplement series

Editor
Mark Goodacre

THE PAUL-APOLLOS RELATIONSHIP AND PAUL'S STANCE TOWARD GRECO-ROMAN RHETORIC

An Exegetical and Socio-historical study of 1 Corinthians 1–4

CORIN MIHAILA

t&t clark

Published by T&T Clark International
A Continuum imprint
The Tower Building, 11 York Road, London SE1 7NX
80 Maiden Lane, Suite 704, New York, NY 10038

www.continuumbooks.com

British Library Cataloguing-in-Publication Data
A catalogue record for this book is available from the British Library

ISBN: 978-0-567-18382-8 (hardback)

Typeset by Data Standards Limited, Frome, Somerset, UK
Printed and bound in Great Britain by the MPG Books Group,
Bodmin and Kings Lynn

To my parents, Vasile and Elena Mihaila

Thank you for planting in my heart a love for God and his Word.

CONTENTS

The present work is a revision of my doctoral dissertation completed in December 2006 at Southeastern Baptist Theological Seminary under Dr Andreas Köstenberger. His scholarship, exegetical skills, guidance, and encouragement have made a great impact upon me throughout my studies, and have had a tremendous influence upon my development as a student of the Bible. I would also like to thank my second readers, Dr David Beck and Dr Scott Kellum, for their insightful suggestions during the defense. Dr David E. Garland, the external reader of the dissertation, has been a tremendous encouragement. His commentary on 1 Corinthians in the BENTC series has very much shaped my thinking and interpretation of the first four chapters of 1 Corinthians. Dr Garland has also been instrumental in publishing this dissertation by offering a positive evaluation of it and by encouraging me to seek out a publisher for it, and I am thankful for that.

The present work began as a desire to understand the biblical (Pauline) theology of preaching. What challenged me to think about this topic was the three weeks spent at Tyndale House, Cambridge, England, with other undergraduate students from Romania, under the leadership of my friend Dr Radu Gheorghita and in the company of Dr Bruce Winter, then the Warden at Tyndale House. It was the summer of 1996, when Dr Winter's monograph *Paul and Philo among the Sophists* was being published. His lectures during those weeks on 1 Corinthians 1–4 in light of Greco-Roman rhetoric fascinated me and influenced my thinking on biblical preaching. It was during those days that I started thinking about the relationship between Paul and Apollos in light of Paul's rejection of sophistic rhetoric, as can be gathered from the Corinthian correspondence.

Since then, I have come to appreciate the importance of studying the letter by also looking into its social background. Many authors have helped me in that direction, as will be seen throughout this work. So I am indebted to many scholars, both past and present, for their exegetical, rhetorical, and social analysis of the text of 1 Corinthians 1–4. They have influenced my thinking on this topic. Any deficiencies, however, are all my own. In this present work, then, I try to explain Paul's relationship to

Apollos in light of Paul's stance toward Greco-Roman rhetoric as most clearly seen in 1 Corinthians 1–4.

Soli Deo Gloria
Corin Mihaila
Brasov, Romania
September, 2008

ACKNOWLEDGMENTS

Growing up in the communist Romania, I never dreamed that I would ever have the blessing of studying the Scriptures in such depth. I learned from my parents to love the Word of God, study it, and memorize it. But the skills necessary to rightly divide the Word of truth were refined during my studies at Southeastern Baptist Theological Seminary, Wake Forest, NC. I benefited greatly from the wisdom and godliness of the professors at this seminary. Each contributed in some way to my getting where I am. First and foremost, my mentor, Dr Andreas Köstenberger, has been a model of scholarship to me. His encouragement throughout the program as well as his trust in giving me the opportunity to work as his research assistant as well as a doctoral fellow have motivated me to pursue excellence in my academic work. Professors such as Dr Maurice Robinson, who was the first to encourage me to pursue a Ph.D. while still working on my M.Div. at the same institution, and Dr David Beck, who trusted me with substitute teaching for him at numerous times and different courses, have made my experience at SEBTS a joyous one.

Aside from the academic support, I have been blessed to have the financial support of many people and churches, without which my studies would have been impossible. First I would like to thank my friend Dr Mark Harris who believed in me enough to motivate his church at that time, Center Grove Baptist Church, Clemmons, NC, to meet all my financial needs during my M.Div. years at SEBTS. Center Grove Baptist Church has continued its support through my Ph.D. studies, for which I will be forever indebted. Mark went to Pastor Curtis Baptist Church, Augusta, GA, and that church started to contribute to my financial needs during my Ph.D. studies. There other churches that have ministered to me in different ways, including financially, such as Command Baptist Church, Statesville, NC, and Second Baptist Church, Greer, SC. I have developed life-long friendships with these churches and many families in them, whose names would take the length of another dissertation to mention. But I would be wrong not to mention Jerry and Geraldine Houston, who have been like my American parents through the last few years. Their sacrificial giving and love are beyond words. Among the many things that they have done for me is to provide for me a very reliable means of transportation, that allowed me to travel in order to preach and speak at many church events throughought the eastern part of the US. Also the faithful support of Eric and Lisa Todd has been a great blessing. Pastor Hall Holliefied and his commitment to serve God even into his 80s has been an encouragement. Many others have provided me with a place to stay as I have moved from one place to another throughout the years or have fed me in numerous times. Thank you all for being a blessing to me. I will never be able to express fully how much I appreciate all of you. God knows your names and I pray that he may richly reward you according to his many riches in glory.

Above all, I would like to thank my God and Savior Jesus Christ for his grace through the whole time of my studies. Help me, Lord, to make good use of all you have taught me so that your Kingdom may benefit from it and the fame of your name be spread through me to all nations.

LIST OF ABBREVIATIONS

AB	Anchor Bible
ABD	Freedman, David Noel, ed. *Anchor Bible Dictionary*. New York: Doubleday, 1992
ABR	*Australian Biblical Review*
ADP	Advances in Discourse Processes
AGJU	Arbeiten zur Geschichte des antiken Judentums und des Urchristentums
AnBib	Analecta biblica
AsTJ	*Asbury Theological Journal*
ATR	*Anglican Theological Review*
AUSS	American University Studies Series
BCL	Biblical Classics Library
BDAG	Bauer, W., F. W. Danker, W. F. Arnt, and F. W. Gingrich. *Greek-English Lexicon of the New Testament and Other Early Christian Literature*. Chicago: Chicago University Press, 3rd edn, 1999
BDF	Blass, F., A. Debrunner, and R. W. Funk. *A Greek Grammar of the New Testament and Other Early Christian Literature*. Chicago: Chicago University Press, 1961
BETL	Bibliotheca ephemeridum theologicarum lovaniensium
BETS	*Bulletin of the Evangelical Theological Society*
BHT	Beiträge zur historischen Theologie
Bib	*Biblica*
BibInt	*Biblical Interpretation: A Journal of Contemporary Approaches*
BkNTC	Baker New Testament Commentary
BNTC	Black's New Testament Commentaries
BR	*Bible Review*
BSac	*Bibliotheca Sacra*
BTB	*Biblical Theology Bulletin*
BZNW	Beihefte zur *ZNW*
CBET	Contributions to Biblical Exegesis and Theology
CBQ	*Catholic Biblical Quarterly*
CC	Calvin's Commentaries

CJT	*Canadian Journal of Theology*
ConBNT	Coniectanea biblica, New Testament
CSPESPS	Cambridge Studies in Population, Economy and Society in Past Time
CTJ	*Criswell Theological Journal*
CurTM	*Currents in Theology and Mission*
DTT	*Dansk teologisk tidsskrift*
EBC	Expositor's Bible Commentary
EBib	Etudes bibliques
EDNT	Balz, H. and G. Schneider, eds. *Exegetical Dictionary of the New Testament*. ET. Grand Rapids: Eerdmans, 1990–1993
EKKNT	Evangelisch-Katholischer Kommentar zum Neuen Testament
ERT	*Evangelical Review of Theology*
ETL	*Ephemerides theologicae lovanienses*
ETSP	*Evangelical Theological Society Papers*
EvQ	*Evangelical Quarterly*
EvT	*Evangelische Theologie*
ExpTim	*Expository Times*
F&M	*Faith & Mission*
FCCGRW	First-Century Christians in the Graeco-Roman World
GNS	Good News Studies
GNTE	Guide to New Testament Exegesis
GTA	Göttinger theologische Arbeiten
HNT	Hondbuch zum Neuen Testament
HTR	*Harvard Theological Review*
ICC	International Critical Commentary
Int	*Interpretation*
JBL	*Journal of Biblical Literature*
JCEd	*Journal of Christian Education*
JETS	*Journal of the Evangelical Theological Society*
JOTT	*Journal of Old Testament Theology*
JRH	*Journal of Religious History*
JS	Judaic Studies
JSNT	*Journal for the Study of the New Testament*
JSNTSup	*Journal for the Study of the New Testament*, Supplement Series
JSOT	*Journal for the Study of the Old Testament*
JTS	*Journal of Theological Studies*
LCBI	Literary Currents in Biblical Interpretation
LCL	Loeb Classical Library
LEC	Library of Early Christianity
LPS	Library of Pauline Studies
MBPS	Mellen Biblical Press Series

MNTC	Moffatt New Testament Commentary
MSJ	*The Master's Seminary Journal*
NAC	New American Commentary
NCB	New Century Bible
NIB	The New Interpreter's Bible
NICNT	New International Commentary on the New Testament
NIDNTT	Brown, C., ed. *New International Dictionary of New Testament Theology,* 4 vols. Grand Rapids: Eerdmans, 1975–1985
NIGTC	New International Greek Testament Commentary
NIVAC	NIV Application Commentary
NovT	*Novum Testamentum*
NovTSup	*Novum Testamentum,* Supplements
NTG	New Testament Guides
NTS	*New Testament Studies*
NThT	*Nederlands Theologisch Tijdschrift*
NTT	New Testament Theology
ÖTK	Ökumenischer Taschenbuch-Kommentar
PFES	Publications of the Finnish Exegetical Society
PG	Migne, J.-P., ed. *Patrologia cursus completa … Series graeca,* 166 vols. Paris, 1857–1883
PHI-5	Packard Humanities Institute Latin Literary Texts up to AD 200
PRSt	*Perspectives in Religious Studies*
R&R	*Reformation & Revival*
ResQ	*Restoration Quarterly*
RevExp	*Review and Expositor*
RevQ	*Revue de Qumran*
RGG	*Religion in Geschichte und Gegenwart*
RSR	*Recherches de Science religieuse*
RTR	*Reformed Theological Review*
SBEC	Studies in Bible and Early Christianity
SBL	Society of Biblical Literature
SBLDS	SBL Dissertation Series
SBLNHS	SBL for the Nag Hammadi Seminar
SBLSP	SBL Seminar Papers
SBLSS	SBL Semeia Studies
SBLSymS	SBL Symposium Series
SE	*Studia Evangelica*
SEÅ	*Svensk exegetisk årsbok*
SHR	Studies in the History of Religions
SJT	*Scottish Journal of Theology*
SMBen	Series Monographique de Benedictina: Section paulinienne
SNT	Studien zum Neuen Testament

SNTSMS	Society for New Testament Studies Monograph Series
SNTW	Studies of the New Testament and Its World
SP	Sacra pagina
SR	*Studies in Religion/Sciences religieuses*
ST	*Studia theologica*
STAEKU	Schriftenreihe des Theologischen Ausschusses der Evangelischen Kirche der Union
TDNT	Kittel, G. and G. Friedrich, eds. *Theological Dictionary of the New Testament*, 10 vols.; trans. G. W. Bromiley. Grand Rapids: Eerdmans, 1964–1976
THKNT	Theologischer Handkommentar zum Neuen Testament
ThH	Théologie Historique
TLG	Berkowitz, L. and K. A. Squitier, eds. *Thesaurus linguae graecae: Canon of Greek Authors and Works,* Oxford: Clarendon, 3rd edn, 1990
TNTC	Tyndale New Testament Commentaries
TR	Theology and Religion
TWNT	Kittel, G. and G. Friedrich, eds. *Theologische Wörterbuch zum Neuen Testament.* 11 vols.; Stuttgart, Kohlhammer, 1932–1979
TynBul	*Tyndale Bulletin*
TZT	*Tübinger Zeitschrift für Theologie*
UBS	United Bible Society
USBHS	USB Handbook Series; Helps for Translators
WBC	Word Biblical Commentary
WTJ	*Westminster Theological Journal*
WUNT	Wissenschaftliche Untersuchungen zum Neuen Testament
ZNW	*Zeitschrift für die neutestamentliche Wissenschaft*

Ancient Sources

Aristide	*Or.*	*Oratoriae*
Aristotle	*Poet.*	*Poetica*
	Pol.	*Politica*
	Rhet.	*Rhetorica*
Augustine	*Doctr. Chr.*	*De Doctrina Christiana*
Cicero	*Acad.*	*Academicae quaestiones*
	Amic.	*De amicitia*
	Att.	*Epistulae ad Atticum*
	Fam.	*Epistulae ad familiars*
	Fin.	*De finibus*
	Inv.	*De inventione rhetorica*
	Off.	*De officiis*
	Part. or.	*Partitiones oratoriae*

	Sest.	*Pro Sestio*
	De or.	*De oratore*
	Quint. Fratr.	*Epistulae ad Quintum fratrem*
Dead Sea Scrolls	1QH	*Hodayot* or *Thanksgiving Hyms*
	11QT	*Temple Scroll*
Dio Chrysostom	*Achil.*	*Achilles (Or. 58)*
	Alex.	*Ad Alexandrinos (Or. 32)*
	Charid.	*Charidemus (Or. 30)*
	Cont.	*Contio (Or. 47)*
	Def.	*Defensio (Or. 45)*
	Dei. Cogn.	*De dei cognition (Or.12)*
	Dial.	*Dialexis (Or. 42)*
	Dic. Exercit	*De dicendi exercitatione (Or. 18)*
	Exil.	*De exilio (Or. 13)*
	Isthm.	*Isthmiaca (Or. 9)*
	De pace	*De pace et bello (Or. 22)*
	Pulchr.	*De Pulchritunide (Or. 21)*
	4 Regn.	*De regno iv (Or. 4)*
	Rhod.	*Rhodiaca (Or. 31)*
	2 Serv. Lib.	*De servitude et libertate ii (Or. 15)*
	Socr.	*De Socrate (Or. 54)*
	1 Tars.	*Tarsica prior (Or. 33)*
	Troj.	*Trojana (Or. 11)*
	Tumult.	*De Tumultu (Or. 46)*
	Tyr.	*De tyrannide (Or. 6)*
	Virt. (Or. 8)	*De virtute (Or. 8)*
Dionysius Halicarnassus.	*1–2 Amm.*	*Epistula ad Ammaeum i-ii*
	Ant.	*Antiquitates Romanae*
	Comp.	*De compositione verborum*
	Dem.	*De Demosthene*
	Is.	*De Isaeo*
	Thuc.	*De Thucydide*
Epictetus	*Diatr.*	*Diatribai (Dissertationes)*
	Ench.	*Enchiridion*
Eusebius	*Comm. Ps.*	*Commentarius in Psalmos*
	Hist. eccl.	*Historia ecclesiastica*
Isocrates	*Antid.*	*Antidosis (Or. 15)*
	Areop.	*Areopagiticus (Or. 7)*
	Demon.	*Ad Demonicum (Or. 1)*
	De pace	*De pace (Or. 8)*
	Paneg.	*Panegyricus (Or. 4)*
	Soph.	*In sophistas (Or. 13)*
John Chrysostom	*Exp. Ps.*	*Expositiones in Psalmos*

	Hom. 1 Cor.	*Homiliae in epistulam I ad Corinthios*
	Laud. Paul.	*De laudibus sancti Pauli apostoli*
	Sac.	*De sacerdotio*
Josephus	*A.J.*	*Antiquitates judaicae*
	J.W.	*De Bello judaico*
New Testament		
Apocrypha	*Gos. Thom.*	*Gospel of Thomas*
Old Testament		
Pseudepigrapha	*Apoc. El.*	*Apocalypse of Elijah*
	1 En.	*1 Enoch*
Philo	*Abr.*	*De Abrahamo*
	Aet. Mund.	*De aeternitate mundi*
	Agr.	*De agricultura*
	Cher.	*De cherubim*
	Flacc.	*In Flaccum*
	Jos.	*De Josepho*
	Leg. All.	*Legum allegoriae*
	Leg. Gai.	*Legatio ad Gaium*
	Migr. Abr.	*De migratione Abrahami*
	Mut. Nom.	*De mutatione nominum*
	Op. Mund.	*De opificio mundi*
	Plant.	*De plantatione*
	Poster. C.	*De posteritate Caini*
	Rev. Div. Her.	*Quis rerum divinarum heres sit*
	Sacr.	*De sacrificiis Abelis et Caini*
	Somn.	*De somniis*
	Spec. Leg.	*De specialibus legibus*
	Virt.	*De virtutibus*
	Vit. Cont.	*De vita contemplativa*
	Vit. Mos.	*De vita Mosis*
Philostratus	*Vit. soph.*	*Vitae sophistarum*
Plato	*Apol.*	*Apologia*
	Gorg.	*Gorgias*
	Leg.	*Leges*
	Phaedr.	*Phaedrus*
	Prot.	*Protagoras*
	Soph.	*Sophista*
	Theaet.	*Theaetetus*
	Tim.	*Timaeus*
Plutarch	*Aem.*	*Aemilius Paullus*
	Caes.	*Caesar*
	Cic.	*Cicero*
	Dem.	*Demosthenes*
	Frat. amor	*De fraterno amore*

	[*Lib. Ed.*]	*De liberis educandis*
	Mor.	*Moralia*
	Per.	*Pericles*
	Thes.	*Theseus*
Quintillian	*Decl.*	*Declamationes*
	Inst.	*Institutio oratoria*
Strabo	*Geogr.*	*Geographica*
Xenophon	*Cyr.*	*Cyropaedia*
	Mem.	*Memorabilia*
	Oec.	*Oeconomicus*

Other Sources

Friberg-Friberg — Friberg, Timothy, Barbara Friberg, and Neva F. Miller. *Analytical Lexicon of the Greek New Testament.* Grand Rapids: Baker, 20

Lampe, *Lexicon* — Lampe, G. W. H. *A Patristic Greek Lexicon.* Oxford: Clarendon, 13th edn, 20

Louw-Nida — Louw Johannes P. and Eugene A. Nida. *Greek-English Lexicon of the New Testament Based on Semantic Domains.* New York: UBS, 2nd edn, 1989

Miller, *Lexicon* — Miller, Neva F. *Analytical Lexicon of the Greek New Testament.* Grand Rapids: Baker, 20

LSJ — Liddell, H. G., R. Scott, and H. S. Jones, *A Greek-English Lexicon with Revised Supplement.* Oxford: Clarendon, 9th edn, 1996

LW — *Luther's Works.* J. Pelikan and H. Lehman, eds. Philadelphia: Fortress, 1966

Robertson, *Grammar* — Robertson, A. T. *A Grammar of the Greek New Testament in the Light of Historical Research.* London: Hodder & Stoughton, 3rd edn, 1919

Thayer — Thayer, J. H. *A Greek-English Lexicon of the New Testament.* New York: American Book Company, 1889

WDNTECLR — *The Westminster Dictionary of New Testament and Early Christian Literature and Rhetoric.* Westminster: John Knox, 2003

INTRODUCTION

Importance of the Topic

This work will be an exegetical and socio-historical investigation into the text of 1 Corinthians 1–4 in order to determine the relationship between Paul and Apollos in light of Paul's stance toward Greco-Roman rhetoric. The topic is important for several reasons. First, this passage is rightly assessed to be the clearest presentation of Paul's theology of preaching. The text of 1 Cor. 2.1-5, in particular, reveals Paul's intentional style of preaching as characterized by 'weakness' as contrasted with the rhetorical eloquence characteristic of the sophists. On the other hand, the Corinthians are portrayed in this section of the epistle as evaluating their teachers in light of worldly standards of what constituted persuasive speech. Consequently, the dissensions that existed in the church were caused by the Corinthians' preferences for different styles of delivery: some preferred Paul's, while others preferred Apollos'. In light of this situation, Paul gives theological reasons for his choice of style. But this raises a serious question: Is Apollos portrayed by Paul in 1 Corinthians 1–4 as one who adopts a sophistic rhetoric that Paul himself refutes? And if so, is Apollos an opponent of Paul? Is Paul competing against the more rhetorically gifted Apollos?

The topic is important, second, because it also addresses the issue of the social make-up of the Corinthian church, which is closely related to the issue of sophistic rhetoric. We know from 1 Cor. 1.26-28 that the Corinthian congregation was made up mostly of people of low status, though some in the congregation such as Erastus were from among the *nouveau riche* of Corinth. As a society driven by honor and shame, people sought to enhance their status and increase their honor by associating with people who could help them climb the social ladder. Among such people were the rhetors who would enter into a patron/client relationship with the rich. Thus, the social climbers knew what 'good' speech was and therefore evaluated and associated only with those who guaranteed them an increase in honor.

In light of these social values prevalent in the Corinthian society, it is not hard to see how the Corinthian Christians, upon their conversion, brought the same values into the church. This is seen especially in their preference for different teachers. Faced with such a situation, Paul insists on a re-socialization of the Christians which consisted in a change of values. This he does by means of reminding the Corinthians of the centrality of the cross. The cross, as a symbol of 'weakness' and 'shame', challenges the Corinthians' thirst for status and honor. But this raises another question: Has Apollos accepted to play along with the patron/client mold that Paul seeks to break? Or was Apollos someone who could help some of the Corinthian Christians to enhance their status by associating themselves with one who embodied the qualities of a rhetor?

Third, 1 Corinthians 1–4 gives us a picture of the proper role of a minister in the Christian *ecclesia* (cf. 1 Cor. 3.5-4.5). According to Paul, all the teachers are co-workers and servants in the church, while God alone holds the ultimate role. Paul, then, seems to challenge the Corinthians' preferences for different leaders by pointing to their equally insignificant role in the ministry in contrast to the centrality of God's role. Nevertheless, even in his presentation of the equal 'importance' of the ministers, some argue that Paul makes a distinction between the one who 'plants' and the one who 'waters' (1 Cor. 3.6) and between the one 'father' and the multiple 'guardians' of the Christian *ecclesia* (1 Cor. 4.15). This distinction seems to place an emphasis on order and therefore on authority. This raises yet another question: Is Paul seeking to restore his authority among the Corinthians, which had been diminished by the work of Apollos among them, by reminding them that he is the founder of the church? Is he claiming the authority inherent in the social concept of *paterfamilias*? If so, is Apollos seen as an opponent and a competitor rivaling Paul's authority?

All of these questions are raised by the text and are in need of an adequate answer, in keeping with the text. This work seeks to give such answers and then to synthesize them in order to present a description of Paul's stance toward rhetoric and how this sheds light on his relationship with Apollos, a description that we hope is coherent with an accurate reading of the text in light of socio-historical and exegetical research.

This work, in a sense, seeks to build upon previous research into the rhetorical background of the concept of σοφία as found in the monographs of Bruce W. Winter,[1] Duane Litfin,[2] Stephen Pogoloff,[3]

---

1   Winter, *Philo and Paul among the Sophists: Alexandrian and Corinthian Responses to a Julio-Claudian Movement* (Grand Rapids: Eerdmans, 2nd edn, 2002).

2   Litfin, *St. Paul's Theology of Proclamation: 1 Corinthians 1–4 and Greco-Roman Rhetoric* (SNTSMS, 79; Cambridge: Cambridge University Press, 1994).

3   Pogoloff, M. Stephen, *LOGOS AND SOPHIA: The Rhetorical Situation of 1 Corinthians* (SBLDS, 134; Atlanta: Scholars Press, 1992).

and Andrew D. Clarke.[4] We will also build upon the research into the social background of early Christianity, especially of Pauline congregations, done by Peter Marshall,[5] Wayne A. Meeks,[6] Gerd Theissen,[7] and most recently by C. K. Robertson.[8] We have decided to present a survey and evaluation of these previous studies in the body of the work, particularly at the beginning of each chapter, rather than, as is typically done, in the introduction. We will use the conclusions offered by these studies to discuss the relationship of Paul and Apollos in 1 Corinthians 1–4. This work will thus supplement them by an integration of the findings with exegesis of the passages and words relevant to Paul's relationship to Apollos.

Not much has been written on the Paul-Apollos relationship, at least not in the format of a monograph that takes into consideration all the recent research into the rhetorical and socio-historical background of the concept of σοφία in 1 Corinthians 1–4.[9] One dissertation may be considered an exception. Patrick Lynn Dickerson wrote his 'Apollos in Acts and First Corinthians' in order to reconstruct what can be known of Apollos, and we point to it as a good source for a detailed bibliography on the topic. His work is a historical research into the life of Apollos as can be gathered from the two canonical books. In ch. 2 of his dissertation, Dickerson argues that the relationship between Paul and Apollos was ambiguous: they were not quite allies, but not quite opponents either. While we agree with him that it is difficult to assess with precision the nature of Paul's relationship with Apollos, we will suggest here that, taken at face value, Paul's argument in 1 Corinthians 1–4 points to a harmonious relationship between the two. Any perceived tension between them is going beyond the evidence present in the text, and therefore should be looked upon with suspicion. Thus, we will attribute to Apollos a place between a positive and an ambiguous role.

---

4   Clarke, Andrew D., *Secular and Christian Leadership in Corinth: A Socio-Historical and Exegetical Study of 1 Corinthians 1–6* (AGJU, 18; Leiden: Brill, 1993).

5   Marshall, P., *Enmity in Corinth: Social Conventions in Paul's Relations with the Corinthians* (WUNT, 2; Tübingen: Mohr, 1987).

6   Meeks, Wayne, A.,*The First Urban Christians: The Social World of the Apostle Paul* (New Haven: Yale University Press, 1983).

7   Theissen, G., *The Social Setting of Pauline Christianity. Essays on Corinth by Gerd Theissen* (ed. and trans. by John H. Schütz; Philadelphia: Fortress, 1982).

8   Robertson, C. K., *Conflict in Corinth: Redefining the System* (SBL, 42; New York: Peter Lang, 2001).

9   For earlier monographs on Apollos see Patrick Lynn Dickerson, 'Apollos in Acts and First Corinthians' (Unpublished doctoral dissertation, University of Virginia, 1998).

Methodology

Much of the exegetical argument in this work is based on the study of important Greek words and their meaning as well as on the importance we give to certain socio-historical information behind the text. We will list here several guidelines for doing lexical analysis, which we will seek to follow in our study of different words throughout this work. These guidelines are based on our fundamental belief that meaning is the result of the combination of two factors: current usage and immediate context.[10]

First, we will pay close attention to the theme and details of the immediate context (i.e., the paragraphs and chapters) in which the word occurs. Second, we will look at other usages of the word in texts from the same author, in other texts in the Bible, and in extra-biblical material. We will focus, however, primarily on the *current* usage of the word. Therefore, we will analyze the occurrences of the word in the same period unless it can be shown that the word has not changed in its semantic value over time. In this sense, we will use the parallels distant in time with caution, though at times they may prove to be valuable to the study. For instance, an appeal to the Church Fathers may be legitimate, even if they are quite remote in time, especially if they interpret the text studied. Third, we will seek to be careful not to impose the meanings of the same word from a different context on the word in the context in case, even if the parallel context is contemporary with the time of the writing. The reason is that a language does not use words in an absolutely consistent way; neither does the same person. For this reason, we will select only that meaning to be relevant which is used in a context similar to the passage studied. Fourth, we will seek to be thorough in gathering the semantic range, since even a

---

10 For a thorough explanation of the methodology used in this work, see my dissertation with the same title (doctoral dissertation, Southeastern Baptist Theological Seminary, 2006), 5–18. For works that have helped us define our guidelines for word studies, see the following: D. A. Carson, *Exegetical Fallacies* (Grand Rapids: Baker, 1984); James Barr, *The Semantics of Biblical Language* (London: Oxford University Press, 1961); J. P. Louw, *Semantics of New Testament Greek* (SBLSS; Philadelphia: Fortress, 1982); Peter Cotterell and Max Turner, *Linguistics & Biblical Interpretation* (Downers Grove: InterVarsity, 1989); Jeffrey T. Reed, 'Modern Linguistics and the New Testament: A Basic Guide to Theory, Terminology, and Literature', in *Approaches to New Testament Study* (Stanley E. Porter and David Tombs, (eds); JSNTSup, 120, 36–62; Sheffield: Sheffield Academic Press, 1995); Moisés Silva, *Biblical Words and Their Meaning: An Introduction to Lexical Semantics* (Grand Rapids: Zondervan, 1983); Kevin J. Vanhoozer, *Is There Meaning in This Text? The Bible, The Reader, and the Morality of Literary Knowledge* (Grand Rapids: Zondervan, 1998); Ferdinand de Saussure, *Course in General Linguistics* (New York: McGraw-Hill, 1959); Anthony C. Thiselton, 'Semantics and New Testament Interpretation', in *New Testament Interpretation: Essays on Principles and Methods* (I. Howard Marshall, ed., 75–104; Exeter: Paternoster, 1977); E. A. Nida, 'The Implications of Contemporary Linguistics for Biblical Scholarship', *JBL* 91 (1972) 73–89; E. D. Hirsch, *Validity in Interpretation* (New Haven: Yale University Press, 1967).

rare meaning of a term is a possibility for the use of that term in the biblical context. We will be aware of the need to demonstrate discernment in this matter also, for although the gathering of all relevant parallels is a good indication of what a word can mean, the literature available should not be believed to exhaust all the possible meanings. The ancient literature available to us today is simply limited. Fifth, when dealing with a compound word, we will seek to avoid the root fallacy. In the case of a verb with a prepositional prefix such as μετασχηματίζω, we will seek to discern in which way (of the three) the prefix affects the meaning of the word. Sixth, in using dictionaries and lexicons, we will keep in mind that they are interpretative to a large degree. In other words, they offer the opinion of the author concerning the category of meaning and usage under which a word should fit. Their categories are not established facts. Moreover, all the lexicons and dictionaries build upon previous ones and therefore are bound to contain errors.

Besides word studies, the argument in support for our thesis relies also on background information.[11] Such information is necessary for interpretation since linguistically meaning is determined not only by the words themselves but also by the circumstances in which they were uttered. Thus, meaning is a combination of at least three factors: authorial intent, linguistic conventions, and shared assumptions. All these three factors are closely related to the author's and original readers' socio-historical context.

Our use of background information, however, will come with several qualifications. First, not all texts need an equal amount of extra-linguistic

---

11   For a thorough argument for the need of background information in understanding the biblical text as well as its limits, see my dissertation, pp. 18–33. For further study see the following, besides the ones mentioned in the previous note: Max Turner, 'Historical Criticism and Theological Hermeneutics for the New Testament', in *Between Two Horizons: Spanning New Testament Studies & Systematic Theology* (Joel B. Green and Max Turner, eds.; Grand Rapids: Eerdmans, 2000), pp. 44–70; Stephen E. Fowl, 'The Role of Authorial Intention in the Theological Interpretation of Scripture', in *ibid.*, pp. 71–87; Donald A. Hagner, 'The New Testament, History, and the Historical-Critical Method', in *New Testament Criticism & Interpretation* (David Alan Black and David S. Dockery, eds.; Grand Rapids: Zondervan, 1991), pp. 71–96; David E. Garland, 'Background Studies and New Testament Interpretation', in *ibid.*, pp. 347–76; Robert Mulholland, 'Sociological Criticism', in *ibid.*, pp. 295–316; Anthony C. Thiselton, *The Two Horizons: New Testament Hermeneutics and Philosophical Description with Special Reference to Heidegger, Bultmann, Gadamer, and Wittgenstein* (Grand Rapids: Eerdmans, 1980); Richard Freadman and Seamus Miller, *Re-thinking Theory: A Critique of Contemporary Literary Theory and an Alternative Account* (Cambridge: Cambridge University Press, 1992); Stephen C. Barton, 'Historical Criticism and Social-Scientific Perspectives in New Testament Study', in *Hearing the New Testament: Strategies for Interpretation* (Joel B. Green, ed.; Grand Rapids: Eerdmans, 1995), pp. 61–89; David A. deSilva, 'Embodying the Word: Social-Scientific Interpretation of the New Testament', in *The Face of New Testament Studies: A Survey of Recent Research* (Scott McKnight and Grant R. Osborne, eds.; Grand Rapids: Baker, 2004), pp. 118–29.

information for grasping the full meaning of the text. Some texts require more 'behind the text' information while for others an analysis of the context of the utterance – the literary context – may be sufficient to determine the author's intended meaning. Second, we must face the reality that we cannot acquire all the socio-historical 'givens' needed for an infallible interpretation, and therefore we must adjudicate between multiple options for the context of a text using an educated guess, while recognizing their limitations and provisional status.

Our belief in the importance of background studies will be reflected in our discussion in chapter two of this work, where we will seek to show that Paul has in mind the sophistic rhetoric when he speaks of σοφία in 1 Corinthians 1–4.

Approach to the Topic

In Chapter 1, we will seek to show the literary and thematic unity of 1 Corinthians 1–4, a necessary step in identifying the major issue(s) of this section of the epistle. This is particularly important in light of the fact that Paul intercalates a discussion on wisdom (i.e., 1 Cor. 1.17-2.16) in the middle of a discussion about parties. A demonstration of the unity of this section will point to the fact that the issue of parties is organically connected to the issue of wisdom and the Corinthians' high esteem of it.

Chapter 2 then will seek to show the kind of wisdom that the Corinthians appreciated. Here we will provide a short overview of different views on the background of σοφία (i.e., Gnosticism, Hellenistic Jewish Wisdom, and sophistic rhetoric) after which we will seek to show that the rhetorical background is the most likely. The Corinthians' appreciation of rhetorical eloquence, however, will prove to be closely related to certain social values and structures. Therefore, an investigation of the social background is necessary for a better understanding of Paul's argument in 1 Corinthians 1–4. The socio-rhetorical background will then shed light on the problem of the 'parties' in the Corinthian congregation, both their number and their nature.

In light of the discussion conducted so far, we will raise in Chapter 3 the issue of Paul's stance towards rhetorical eloquence. We will show from 1 Cor. 2.1-5 that Paul deliberately adopted a style of delivery that is consistent with God's *modus operandi* and at the same time in stark contrast with the sophistic rhetoric so much appreciated by the Corinthian Christians. We will also seek to question the idea that Paul's intention in this section is to re-establish his authority among the Corinthians and therefore to convince the Corinthians that they should obey him and not Apollos.

The fourth chapter will draw on the previous discussion by raising the question of Apollos' function in the argument. We will first provide an overview of different interpretations concerning Apollos. Then we will seek to determine Apollos' connection with rhetoric, both his training by a corroboration of information found in Acts 18.18-24 and his *modus operandi* among the Corinthians. An important text in determining Paul's attitude towards Apollos is 1 Cor. 3.5-17, which needs an in-depth analysis. However, the discussion in the first three chapters depends heavily on the meaning of μετεσχημάτισα in 1 Cor. 4.6, which will conclude Chapter 4.

The conclusion will summarize the findings and state that Apollos functions in 1 Corinthians 1–4 in a positive way. Taking Paul's argument and mention of Apollos at face value, one has only the choice of concluding that Apollos and Paul shared a harmonious relationship in ministry, though Apollos was most likely an independent missionary. Thus, the entire fault in the dissensions lies with the Corinthian Christians.

1 THE LITERARY AND THEMATIC UNITY OF 1 CORINTHIANS 1–4

Introduction

Anyone reading the Corinthian correspondence is confronted with the dilemma of the literary unity of the two canonical letters to the church in Corinth. Was some of Paul's correspondence with the Corinthians lost, the existence of which seems to be implied in places such as 1 Cor. 5.9 and 2 Cor. 2.3-4, 9?[1] Or is it possible that a later editor/compiler has pieced together fragments from more than two of Paul's letters of correspondence with the Corinthians resulting in the two canonical letters?[2] It is not within the scope of this work to defend the integrity of the Corinthian correspondence since it has no impact on the study at hand, but one should be aware that partition theories still find supporters among the students of the Corinthian epistles, with many options suggested.[3] However, we agree with Thiselton that 'partition theories are needed *only if exegesis fails to reveal a genuine coherence* within the epistle'.[4] What

---

1 Some scholars identify the 'Tearful Letter' with 1 Corinthians, e.g., Niels Hyldahl, 'Die Frage nach der literarischen Einheit des zweiten Korintherbriefes', *ZNW* 64 (1973) 289–306 (299); L. Aejmelaeus, *Schwachheit als Waffe: Die Argumentation des Paulus im Tränenbrief (2 Kor 10–13)* (PFES, 78; Göttingen: Vandenhoeck & Ruprecht, 2000), esp. pp. 16–26, identifies the 'Tränenbrief' with 2 Corinthians 10–13; also L. L. Welborn, 'The Identification of 2 Corinthians 10–13 with the "Letter of Tears"', *NTS* 37 (1995) 138–53.

2 The unity of the text of 1 Corinthians was basically uncontested until 1876 when H. Hagge first challenged the consensus. For a helpful chart representing the early contestants of the unity of 1 Corinthians see John C. Hurd, *The Origin of 1 Corinthians* (Macon: Mercer University Press, 2nd edn, 1983), p. 45. See also H. Merklein 'Die Einheitlichkeit des ersten Korintherbriefes', *ZNW* 75 (1984) 153–83 (154–56); and U. Schnelle, *The History and Theology of the New Testament Writings* (London: SCM, 1998), pp. 62–66.

3 For a synopsis concerning the controversy over the integrity of the first epistle to the Corinthians, see Anthony Thiselton, *The First Epistle to the Corinthians: A Commentary on the Greek Text* (NIGTC; Grand Rapids: Eerdmans, 2000), pp. 36–41. See also, John C. Hurd, 'Good News and the Integrity of 1 Corinthians', in *Gospel in Paul: Studies on Corinthians, Galatians, and Romans for Richard N. Longenecker* (L. A. Jervis and P. Richardson, eds.; JSNTSSup, 108; Sheffield: Sheffield Academic Press, 1994), pp. 38–62.

4 Thiselton, *First Corinthians*, p. 39 (emphasis by the author). See also John R. Lanci, *A New Temple in Corinth: Rhetorical and Archaeological Approaches to Pauline Imagery* (SBL, 1; New York: Peter Lang, 1997), p. 47. For the most recent defense of the unity of the

is more relevant to our study is the realization that the issue of unity and integrity is also discussed and debated at a micro-level, that is, the coherence of smaller discourse units within the individual canonical letters.

Such is the case with the unity of 1 Corinthians 1–4.[5] There are some who argue, for instance, that 1 Cor. 2.6-16 is a later interpolation[6] or that 1 Cor. 1.18–3.20 is a digression from the main theme that brings in irrelevant material.[7] This chapter, however, will seek to prove the literary and thematic unity of 1 Corinthians 1–4 by showing that Paul develops a coherent argument, despite the apparently unconnected themes found in these chapters. This we will seek to do in three steps.[8] First, we will identify and discuss the discourse units that make up Paul's argument in these chapters. Second, we will seek to identify the themes that are expounded in each unit. Third, we will seek to show how Paul brings apparently disjunctive themes together to form a coherent whole. We will thus look at elements of discourse analysis such as cohesion, prominence, and coherence, recognizing the interconnectedness of the themes.[9] As such, the interpretation of the discourse will be both bottom-up (beginning with morphology, moving up through words, phrases, clauses,

---

canonical Corinthian letters see, David Hall, *The Unity of the Corinthian Correspondence* (JSNTSS, 251; London: T&T Clark, 2003), especially chs 2 and 4. For a defense of the integrity of 1 Corinthians in particular, see H. Merklein, 'Die Einheitlichkeit des ersten Korintherbriefes', 153–83; and W. Schrage, *Der erste Brief an die Korinther (1 Kor 1,1–6,11)* (EKKNT, 7/1; Zurich: Bezinger/Neukirchen-Vluyn: Neukirchener Verlag, 1991), pp. 63–71. See also Kenneth E. Bailey, 'The Structure of 1 Corinthians and Paul's Theological Method with Special Reference to 4.17', *NovT* 25 (1983) 152–81 (153).

5 In his recent monograph, *Paul, the Fool of Christ: A Study of 1 Corinthians 1–4 in the Comic-Philosophic Tradition* (JSNTSup, 293; London: T&T Clark, 2005), p. 49, n. 1, Laurence L. Welborn reflects the view of other commentators concerning the two-fold division of the book: chapters 1–6 – subjects raised with Paul orally by messengers from Corinth, and chapters 7–16 – subjects about which the Corinthians have written. See, *inter alia*, William F. Orr and James A. Walther, *First Corinthians* (AB, 32; New York: Doubleday, 1976), pp. 120–22.

6 E.g., William O. Walker, Jr. '1 Corinthians 2.6-16: A Non-Pauline Interpolation?' *JSNT* 47 (1992): 75–94.

7 Cf. Wilhelm Wuellner, 'Greek Rhetoric and Pauline Argumentation', in *Early Christian Literature and the Classical Intellectual Tradition: In Honorem Robert M. Grant* (William R. Schoedel and Robert L. Wilken, eds.; ThH, 53; Paris: Beauchesne, 1979), pp. 177–88 (185).

8 Joop F. M. Smit, '"What is Apollos? What is Paul?" In Search for the Coherence of First Corinthians 1.10-4.21', *NovT* 44 (2002) 231–51 (231), follows H. Merklein, *Der erste Brief an die Korinther. Kapitel 1–4* (ÖTNT, 7/1; Gütersloh: Mohn, 1992), pp. 56–59, 99–114, in distinguishing three aspects of the coherence of a text: syntax, semantics, and pragmatics.

9 For this triumvirate that governs a text see John Beekman, John Callow, and Michael Kopesec, *The Semantic Structure of Written Communication* (Dallas: Summer Institute of Linguistics, 5th edn, 1981), pp. 20–21.

sentences, until reaching the discourse) and top-down (to show how the discourse as a whole influences the lower level structures).[10]

Determining the connection between the structure of the text and its meaning by the use of discourse analysis hopefully will reveal that Paul's purpose in this section is to effect unity among the Corinthian believers by pointing to the Corinthians' false perception of what true wisdom is.[11] Demonstrating the thematic unity of this section of the letter is particularly important in light of the fact that Paul intercalates a discussion on wisdom (i.e., 1 Cor. 1.18–2.16) in the middle of a discussion about parties. Proving the unity of this section will thus point to the fact that the σχίσματα question and the σοφία question are intertwined. It will then be necessary to show in the next chapter the nature of the wisdom that the Corinthians so highly esteemed.

Discourse Units in 1 Corinthians 1–4

We precede the discussion of the building blocks of Paul's argument in the first rhetorical unit with two assumptions: the boundaries of the unit and the roundness of its argument. Despite disagreements over the boundaries of the first rhetorical unit (i.e., whether 1 Cor. 4.14 [18]-21 belongs with 1 Cor. 1.10–4.13 [17] or with 1 Cor. 5.1–6.13),[12] the majority of commen-

---

10   On 'bottom-up' and 'top-down' analysis of a discourse see G. Brown and G. Yule, *Discourse Analysis* (Cambridge: Cambridge University Press, 2nd edn, 1983), pp. 234–36; R. de Beaugrande, *Text, Discourse and Process: Toward a Multidisciplinary Science of Texts* (ADP, 4; Norwood: Ablex, 1980), pp. 26–7.

11   There is an ongoing debate over the legitimacy of the use of the tools of discourse analysis in order to prove the literary unity of a text. For an evaluation of discourse analysis as a hermeneutical tool for the study of the New Testament, see Jeffrey T. Reed, 'Discourse Analysis as New Testament Hermeneutic: A Retrospective and Prospective Appraisal', *JETS* 39 (1996) 223–40. For a defense and application of discourse analysis to biblical texts in order to show the close link between the structure of a text and its meaning, see Reed's published dissertation, *A Discourse Analysis of Philippians: Method and Rhetoric in the Debate over Literary Integrity* (JSNTSup, 113; Sheffield: Sheffield Academic Press, 1997); David Alan Black, 'The Discourse Structure of Philippians: A Study in Textlinguistics', *NovT* 37 (1995) 16–49.

12   For arguments that 4.14-21 belongs with the subsequent rhetorical unit, see Ralph Bruce Terry, *A Discourse Analysis of First Corinthians* (SILUTAPL, 120; Arlington: University of Texas at Arlington Press, 1995), pp. 48–49; and Kenneth E. Bailey, 'The Structure of 1 Corinthians', 160–63. One argument relies on the assumption that the conjuctive δέ, marks the beginning of a new topic. See however, Kathleen Callow, 'The Disappearing δέ, in 1 Corinthians', in *Linguistics and New Testament Interpretation. Essays on Discourse Analysis* (David Alan Black and David S. Dockery, eds., Nashville: Broadman, 1992), pp. 183–93, who argues that in 1 Cor. 4.18 the conjuction operates with an intermediate span, introducing not a new topic, but a new aspect of an existing topic. See also M. M. Mitchell, 'Concerning περὶ δέ, in 1 Cor', *NovT* 321 (1989): 229–56. That these verses belong with the first rhetorical unit is usually taken as self-understood and in no need for

tators contend that 1 Cor. 4.14-21 constitutes not the introduction to the subsequent chapters, but the conclusion to the previous discussion. Schnelle thus voices the opinion of many commentators when he states that, 'Literary criticism has found no reason to question the unity of 1 Cor 1.1–4.21 as a coherent text . . . for which 1 Cor 4.14-21 is supposed to form the conclusion.'[13] We will take this view as we seek to prove the unity of the first rhetorical unit, without denying the fact that this last paragraph also looks forward, preparing the reader for what comes next.

Regardless of where one posits the end of the first thematic unit of the epistle, one aspect that most scholars agree on is that 1 Corinthians 1–4 should be treated as a unit. There are several pointers in the text that Paul uses to delineate this text as a rounded unit, of which we will mention two.[14] First, the text is marked off by at least two *inclusios*: the exhortation Παρακαλῶ (1.10 and 4.16) and the mention of the gospel (εὐαγγελίζεσθαι in 1.17 and τοῦ εὐαγγελίου in 4.15).[15] Secondly, important to notice is the prominence of the antithetical pair σοφία/μωρία which occurs frequently and almost exclusively in this part of the letter in 1 Cor. 1.17–2.16; 3.18-23; 4.10.[16]

---

argumentation. See Thiselton, *First Corinthians*, p. 345; C. K. Barrett, *The First Epistle to the Corinthians* (BNTC; Peabody: Hendrickson, 2nd edn, 1996), 114; and Andreas Lindemann, *Der erste Korintherbrief* (Tübingen: Mohr, 2000), 111.

13   Schnelle, *History*, p. 64. For Ben Witherington III, *Conflict & Community in Corinth: A Socio-Rhetorical Commentary on 1 and 2 Corinthians* (Grand Rapids: Eerdmans, 1995), p. 136, 1 Cor. 4.1-21 constitutes the fourth division of Paul's first argument.

14   Much of the discussion concerning the organization of the argument in the first rhetorical unit follows Smit, 'Search for Coherence', 231–40; and David W. Kuck, *Judgment and Community Conflict: Paul's Use of Apocalyptic Language in 1 Corinthians 3.5-4.5* (NovTSup, 66; Leiden: Brill, 1992), 154–5. Both Smit and Kuck present a structure of the unit following Benjamin Fiore's suggestion but with some modifications. See Benjamin Fiore, '"Covert Allusion" in 1 Corinthians 1–4'. *CBQ* 47 (1987) 85–102 (87–88), more fully argued in 'The Function of Personal Example in the Socratic and Pastoral Epistles' (unpublished doctoral dissertation, Yale Divinity School, 1982), 315–18.

15   This observation was made earlier by Nils A. Dahl, 'Paul and the Church at Corinth According to 1 Corinthians 1.10-4.21', in *Christian History and Interpretation: Studies Presented to John Knox* (W. R. Farmer, C. F. D. Moule, and R. R. Niebuhr, eds.; Cambridge: Cambridge University Press, 1967), pp. 313–35 (319). See also Victor Paul Furnish, 'Theology in 1 Corinthians', in *Pauline Theology. Vol II: 1 & 2 Corinthians* (David M. Hay, ed.; Minnesota: Fortress, 1993), pp. 59–89 (64).

16   The word group σοφία/σοφός appears 44 times in the first ten epistles; 28 of these are in 1 Corinthians, 26 in chs 1–3. This has also been noted earlier by E. E. Johnson, 'The Wisdom of God as Apocalyptic Power', in *Faith and History: Essays in Honor of Paul W. Meyer* (J. T. Carroll, C. H. Cosgrove, and E. E. Johnson, eds.; Atlanta: Scholars Press, 1990), pp. 137–38, who is followed by Richard B. Hays, 'Wisdom According to Paul', in *Where Shall Wisdom Be Found? Wisdom in the Bible, the Church and the Contemporary World* (Stephen C. Barton, ed.; Edinburgh: T&T Clark, 1999), p. 112. The word group μωρία/μωρός/μωραίνω occurs 13 times in the Pauline epistles, of which 10 are in the first four chapters of 1 Corinthians, while μωρία occurs only here in the entire NT.

One thus can see that 1 Cor. 1.10–4.21 forms a unit, with relatively clearly defined boundaries indicating that the passage begins and ends on the same issue. But alongside these discourse indicators that have been pointed out, the different sub-units in the text must be shown to cohere and form a thematic unity, otherwise we are left with a unit formed of disjointed themes.

The Building Blocks of the Argument in 1 Corinthians 1–4
In this section we will consider each building block that makes up the first unit of the letter and seek to determine whether its integrity can be proven exegetically and thematically. All commentators basically agree that 1 Cor. 1.1-9 is an introduction to the whole letter and that 1 Cor. 1.10-17 introduces the problem with which Paul was confronted in the Corinthian church: divisions. But even in the introduction to the whole letter, we find anticipated themes that will be developed in the first rhetorical unit.

Epistolary Salutation and Thanksgiving: 1 Cor. 1.1-9
Peter T. O'Brien's study, *Introductory Thanksgiving in the Letters of Paul*, has been the definitive work on the literary functions of the thanksgiving.[17] We may mention here that the thanksgiving section of a letter introduces major themes in the letter; it points to Paul's pastoral and apostolic concern; and prefigures one or more of the paraenetic purposes of the letter. These functions hold true to 1 Cor. 1.1 [4]-9 also. Several aspects are particularly important to notice in this introduction. First, by designating himself as 'an apostle of Christ Jesus through the will of God', Paul 'grounds his apostleship, beyond its historical realization in his "call", in its ultimate origins in the divine purposes.'[18] This emphasis is necessary in light of the Corinthians' challenge of Paul's leadership and authority in the church, relative to other teachers.[19] But it also highlights the theocentric note that will be noticed all throughout the unit, particularly in his own calling in 1 Cor. 3.10.

---

17 (SNT, 49; Leiden: Brill, 1977), 13–14. He challenges Paul Schubert's thesis, *Form and Function of the Pauline Thanksgivings* (BZNW 20; Berlin: Alfred Töpelmann, 1939), 13, that Paul's thanksgiving reports were mere literary devices.

18 G.D. Fee, *The First Epistle to the Corinthians* (NICNT; Grand Rapids: Eerdmans, (1987), p. 29.

19 The challenge to his authority will be discussed later, but suffice to mention here that such challenge is manifested in the party slogans: 'I am Paul's; I am Apollos'; I am Cephas'; I am Jesus', See Fee, *First Corinthians*, p. 30; and Barrett, *First Corinthians*, p. 31. Thiselton, *First Corinthians*, p. 55, however, denies that this terminology strikes an authoritarian note. So also David E. Garland, *1 Corinthians* (BECNT; Grand Rapids: Baker, 2003), p. 24.

Second, Paul points to the fact that the Corinthians form a single church body (τῇ ἐκκλησία).[20] The unity (*koinonia*) of the church is a theme reiterated over and over again throughout the epistle, but is particularly relevant to the first four chapters, as we will see, where Paul seeks to bring unity to a church plagued by divisions. The theme is further anticipated in the introduction as Paul talks about 'the church *of* God *in* Corinth', as opposed, for instance, to 'the church *of* the Thessalonians *in* God'. Fee is right to see in this slight change of address Paul's emphasis on the fact that the church belongs to God and not to them or to Paul or Apollos, a tendency brought out in the first section of the letter.[21] A further point concerning this church is that it is characterized by holiness (ἡγιασμένοις κλητοῖς ἁγίοις). Paul will bring this distinctive (or boundary marker) to the forefront in his discussion of the temple in 1 Cor. 3.16 as an argument against dissensions. Holiness (as the result of the indwelling of the Holy Spirit), Paul will argue, is what identifies the Christian church, distinguishes it from other temples in Corinth, and makes it into 'a new temple for Corinth.'[22]

Third, in the thanksgiving section (1 Cor. 1.4-9), Paul reminds the Corinthians of the spiritual gifts and blessings that they possess as a result of God's generous grace. Later, in 1 Cor. 3.12 Paul will speak of different people bringing gifts as they build the Christian community. The blessings mentioned in this introductory thanksgiving are those of λόγος and γνῶσις (1 Cor. 1.5). Paul says nothing negative about these gifts of 'speech' and 'knowledge' in this introduction, though later in his epistle he suggests that these gifts were greatly prized by the Corinthian believers and had become the basis for boasting and division in the Corinthian

20   Linda L. Belleville, 'Continuity or Discontinuity: A Fresh Look at 1 Corinthians in the Light of First-Century Epistolary Forms and Conventions', *EvQ* 59 (1987) 15–37 (17), points to the distinction of this formula in comparison to the other, more general, references such as 'to all the saints' (Phil. 1.1; Eph. 1.1; Col. 1.2). See also Garland, *1 Corinthians*, p. 27. Archibald Robertson and Alfred Plummer, *A Critical and Exegetical Commentary on the First Epistle of St. Paul to the Corinthians* (ICC; Edinburgh: T&T Clark, 2nd edn, 1914), p. 2, agree with Chrysostom who sees in the expression a protest against party-spirit.

21   Cf. Fee, First Corinthians, p. 31. See also Margaret Mitchell, *Paul and the Rhetoric of Reconciliation: An Exegetical Investigation of the Language and Composition of 1 Corinthians* (Tübingen: Mohr, 1991), 193.

22   See Lanci, *Temple*, 133; Demetrius K. Williams, 'Paul's Anti-Imperial "Discourse of the Cross": The Cross and Power in 1 Corinthians 1–4', *SBLSP* 39 (2000) 796–803 (807). 'Holiness of God's temple' is, we believe, the characteristic that Paul used in order to solve the double dilemma of conflict within and lack of conflict without. See Robertson, *Conflict in Corinth*, p. 28, and Craig S. de Vos, *Church and Community Conflicts: The Relationships of the Thessalonian, Corinthian, and Philippian Churches with their Wider Civic Communities* (SBLDS, 168; Atlanta: Scholars Press, 1999), p. 214.

ecclesia.[23] A. R. Brown is thus right to comment that, 'The Corinthians' greatest liabilities and greatest strengths lie in their gifts.'[24] Paul's criticism later in the epistle, however, is not against '*the gifts*, but people's *attitudes* toward them and their *misuse*.'[25] Thus, we agree with Thiselton that Paul's thanksgiving in the introduction on behalf of the Corinthians' blessings is sincere, without calling into question their riches in Christ.[26]

Fourth, in 1 Cor. 1.5-7, Paul portrays the community of the believers as a people waiting for 'the revelation of our Lord Jesus Christ' in that Day (τῇ ἀποκάλυψιν τοῦ κυρίου ἡμῶν Ἰησοῦ Χριστοῦ ... ἐν τῇ ἡμέρᾳ). In 1 Cor. 3.13, Paul picks up the motif of disclosure which will take place in that Day, but this time in reference to the quality of the teachers' works (ἡ γὰρ ἡμέρα δηλώσει, ὅτι ἐν πυρὶ ἀποκαλύπτεται).

Paul's sincere thanksgiving, however, raises the question of its paraenetic function. We have already mentioned that Paul's purpose in the introduction is not to criticize the Corinthians, but what does Paul seek to accomplish positively by reminding his readers of their gifts ἐν Χριστῷ Ἰησοῦ? An answer could be suggested by an application of rhetorical criticism to the analysis of 1 Corinthians, in which the opening section of an ancient letter (*exordium*) was designed to gain the goodwill of the audience.[27] Debate exists whether such an enterprise is legitimate

23 Cf. H. D. Betz, 'The Problem of Rhetoric and Theology According to the Apostle Paul', in *L'Apôtre Paul:Personalité, Style et Conception du Ministère* (A.Vanhoye, ed.; Leuven: Leuven University Press, 1986), p. 33.

24 A. R. Brown, *The Cross and Human Transformation: Paul's Apocalyptic Word in 1 Corinthians* (Philadelphia: Fortress, 1995), p. 71.

25 Thiselton, *First Corinthians*, p. 91 (emphasis by author). That γνῶσις is an issue in the Corinthian church is clear from statistics of word frequency: it occurs 10 times in 1 Corinthians, 6 times in 2 Corinthians and only 5 times in the other generally accepted Pauline epistles, and 8 times in the rest of the New Testament. We agree with Barrett, *First Corinthians*, p. 37, that the word 'does not necessarily point to the religious phenomenon described as Gnosticism ... it is most often used in a plain, non-technical sense.' Also λόγος can refer to a multitude of things in 1 Corinthians, either specific or general.

26 Thiselton, *First Corinthians*, p. 93. See also John B. Polhill, 'The Wisdom of God and Factionalism: 1 Corinthians 1–4', *RevExp* 80 (1983) 325–39 (326). Thiselton responds to J. Murphy-O'Connor's statement, *Paul the Letter Writer* (Collegeville: Liturgical, 1995), p. 62, that the introductory thanksgiving is 'remarkable for what it does not say.' See also Belleville, 'Continuity or Discontinuity', 18–19; Héring, *The First Epistle of Saint Paul to the Corinthians* (2nd ed. trans. A. W. Heathcote and P. J. Allcock. London: Epworth, 1962), p. 3; Barrett, *First Corinthians*, p. 36.

27 For an analysis of 1 Corinthians based on its rhetorical structure, see Witherington, *Conflict and Community*, pp. 44–48; Mitchell, *Reconciliation*, pp. 194–97; A. Eriksson, *Traditions as Rhetorical Proof: Pauline Argumentation in 1 Corinthians* (ConBNT, 29; Stockholm: Almqvist & Wiksell, 1998), pp. 48–53; Schrage, *Der erste Brief*, 1.110-11; George A. Kennedy, *New Testament Interpretation through Rhetorical Criticism* (Chapel Hill: University of North Carolina Press, 1984), p. 24, claims that the thanksgiving is aimed 'to secure their goodwill.'

and a justified concern is voiced that a strict advocacy of a rhetorical structure of Paul's letters may seem to be a Procrustean bed for Paul's way of argumentation.[28] But regardless of whether one believes that Paul, in writing 1 Corinthians, patterned his epistolary form according to the rhetorical conventions commended by Cicero, Quintilian, and other ancient writers of rhetorical handbooks, one thing is clear: '... if he was able to follow this rhetorical pattern in a nonmanipulative way which does not rely upon mere artifice, Paul might well adopt such a strategy. But he would do so only if this expresses his own genuine and sincere convictions.'[29] Thus, while Paul may intend to gain the audience's goodwill in this opening section, 'he does not praise the Corinthians [according to the ancient rhetorical technique], but pays tribute for what God has done, is doing, and will do in their midst through Christ.'[30] The theocentric element thus dominates this section.

Paul's concern, then, in this opening section is a pastoral concern. According to O'Brien, this section has a didactic function, teaching the Corinthians to celebrate God's undeserved 'rich' (ἐπλουτίσθητε) grace in including them among the community of believers.[31] Furthermore, 'it calls the readers to reconfirm their faith for which Paul gives thanks.'[32]

In summary, then, the mention of the gifts richly bestowed upon the Corinthians anticipates further development. Of interest here is Paul's discussion of the 'speech' about the cross in 1 Cor. 1.17-25, his preaching to the Corinthians in 1 Cor. 2.1-16 as contrasted with the Corinthians' false assessment of what 'wise speech' is, and the Corinthians' illegitimate boasting concerning their received gifts in 1 Cor. 1.26-31 and particularly the gift of teachers in 1 Cor. 3.5–4.13. But the opening section functions as more than just a prelude that introduces some of the themes and concerns of the letter. It also has a paraenetic function: to encourage the Corinthians to live up to their riches in Christ, anticipating thus the

---

28   For a recent evaluation, see Jeffrey T. Reed, 'Using Ancient Rhetorical Categories to Interpret Paul's Letters: A Question of Genre', in *Rhetoric and the New Testament: Essays from the 1992 Heidelberg Conference* (S. E. Porter and T. H. Olbricht, eds.; JSNTSup, 90; Sheffield: Sheffield Academic Press, 1993), pp. 292–324; and Stanley Porter, 'The Theoretical Justification for Application of Rhetorical Categories to Pauline Epistolary Literature', in *idem.*, 100–22. See also the more recent articles by Porter, 'Paul of Tarsus and His Letters', in *Handbook of Classical Rhetoric in the Hellenistic Period 330 B.C.-A.D. 400* (Leiden: Brill, 1997), pp. 531–85; and Reed, 'The Epistle', in *ibid.*, pp. 171–93.

29   Thiselton, *First Corinthians*, p. 94. He follows Pogoloff, *LOGOS AND SOPHIA*, 99–128.

30   Garland, *1 Corinthians*, p. 31.

31   O'Brien, *Introductory Thanksgiving*, pp. 108–20. He rightly compares the 'riches' of 1.5, with the boastful allusion to 'being rich' in 1 Cor. 4.8, and 'gifts' with 1 Cor. 4.7 and 12.4-11.

32   Garland, *1 Corinthians*, p. 32.

issue of spiritual immaturity among the Corinthians to which Paul will point in 1 Cor. 3.1-4.

If the introduction to the whole letter only subtly hints at some of the major themes and concerns that Paul will pick up and develop later in his epistle, 1 Cor. 1.10-17 is an overt introduction to the first major theme discussed in 1 Cor. 1.18–4.21, namely that of divisions. We will put off the examination of this passage till after the analysis of each individual segment that forms up the first rhetorical unit, for it will prove to be essential in showing its cohesion.

Agreement exists among scholars concerning the smallest building blocks of the first unit: 1 Cor. 1.18-25; 1.26-31; 2.1-5; 2.6-16; 3.1-4; 3.5-17; 3.18-23; 4.1-5; 4.6-13; 4.14-21. The consensus, however, dissipates when it comes to the question of how these small segments should be arranged into larger units. Nevertheless, there is an increasing agreement that Paul argues his case in four consecutive steps: 1 Cor. 1.18–2.5; 2.6–3.4; 3.5–4.5; 4.6-21.[33]

The First Section: 1 Cor. 1.18–2.5

The first section (1 Cor. 1.18–2.5) follows smoothly on the introduction as can be deduced from several verbal links between v. 18 and the preceding section.[34] Probably one of the most obvious links is that between the noun σταυροῦ (1 Cor. 1.18) and the verb ἐσταυρώθη (1 Cor. 1.13) in conjunction with the name of Christ (also in 1 Cor. 2.2). The Christological emphasis noticed in the introduction is continued throughout the first section, the cross being an abbreviation for the message of the crucified Christ.[35] Paul also uses the catchword λόγος in order to develop the theme of proclamation and wisdom. Whereas in 1 Cor. 1.5 Paul uses it in a positive sense, in this section, in juxtaposition with σοφία, 'the eloquent speech' has a negative connotation as it is contrasted with the discourse about the cross. The term σοφία also is taken up from the transitional v. 17 and becomes the major theme of the section, occurring both in positive and negative assessments as well as in paradoxical statements. Last but not least, the connective γάρ clearly is intended to continue the thought of (at least) v. 17 by means of explanation.

The first section consists of three small units: 1 Cor. 1.18-25; 1.26-31;

---

33   See among others Peter Lampe, 'Theological Wisdom and the "Word About the Cross." The Rhetorical Scheme in 1 Corinthians 1–4', *Int* 44 (1990) 117–31.

34   Cf. Ernest Best, 'The Power and the Wisdom of God. 1 Corinthians 1.18-25', in *Paolo A Una Chiesa Divisa (1 Corinthians 1–4)* (SMBen; Lorenzo De Lorenzi, ed.; Roma: Edizioni Abbazia di S. Paolo fuori le mura, 1980), p. 16. Apart from the verbal links, apparently there is no thematic continuity, and what follows (1.18-2.16) seems to be a digression. Furnish, 'Theology in 1 Corinthians', p. 64, calls this section 'a kind of excursus.'

35   Cf. Margaret M. Mitchell, 'Rhetorical Shorthand in Pauline Argumentation: The Functions of 'the Gospel' in the Corinthian Correspondence', in *Gospel in Paul*, p. 70.

2.1-5. The last segment is to be distinguished from the first two by its style. It is clear that Paul in 1 Cor. 2.1-5 is talking specifically about himself; he is applying the observations made in the previous segments to his own style of preaching. The three units, however, are stages in an argument predicated upon a series of antitheses, of which σοφία/μωρία and δύναμις/ἀσθένεια are prominent, though they are never juxtaposed in the text.[36]

In 1 Cor. 1.18-25 his main emphasis is on the contrast between God's power and wisdom manifested in the cross and the world's wisdom; the two are mutually exclusive. For Paul, the cross is the great divider, acting 'as an eschatological discernment', separating τοῖς ἀπολλυμένοις from τοῖς σωζομένοις (1 Cor. 1.18).[37] By means of citations and echoes (1 Cor. 1.19, 20, 21-24) from the Old Testament (Isa. 29.14; 33.18; 28.16),[38] Paul points to the failure of human wisdom in its quest for God, be it by means of σοφία (cf. Greeks) or δύναμις (cf. Jews). Charles B. Cousar rightly argues that, 'The problem of the world is that its norms for knowing have proved inadequate and have resulted in a not-knowing.'[39] In contrast to what the world deems as wise in regards to salvation, Paul declares God's salvation by means of the cross, which appears both as σκάνδαλον (for Jews) and as μωρίαν (for Greeks).[40] But what appears as foolish to those who are perishing is in fact a proof of the wisdom of God (1 Cor. 1.24). Luther thus is right in saying that God reveals himself *sub contraria specie*

---

36   Noted by Thomas W. Gillespie, 'Interpreting the Kerygma: Early Christian Prophecy according to 1 Corinthians 2.6-16', in *Gospel Origins & Christian Beginnings: In Honor of James M. Robinson* (James E. Goehring et al., eds.; Sonoma: Polebridge, 1990), p. 152.

37   Cf. Romano Penna, *Paul the Apostle: Wisdom and Folly of the Cross in a Theological and Exegetical Study* (trans. Thomas P. Wahl; Collegeville: Liturgical, 1996), 2.56. Barrett, *First Corinthians*, p. 51, following Kümmel also points to the fact that the distinction between the two groups is eschatological. See also Hays, 'Wisdom According to Paul', p. 113, who interprets the cross as 'an apocalyptic event.' For apocalyptic language in 1 Corinthians 1–4, see Williams, 'Paul's Anti-Imperial "Discourse of the Cross"', 796–823.

38   For the use of the Old Testament in these verses see H. H. Drake Williams III, *The Wisdom of the Wise: The Presence and Function of Scripture Within 1 Cor. 1.18-3.23* (AGAJU, 49; Leiden: Brill, 2001), 48–101.

39   Cousar, 'The Theological Task of 1 Corinthians: A Conversation with Gordon D. Fee and Victor Paul Furnish', in *Pauline Theology*, p. 95.

40   See Martin Hengel, *Crucifixion in the Ancient World and the Folly of the Message of the Cross* (trans. J. Bowden; Philadelphia: Fortress, 1977), 83. Recently, Welborn, *Paul, the Fool of Christ*, has argued that the semantic domain of the term 'fool' belongs to the theater background, more specifically, to that of the mime. Space does not allow us to evaluate this view. We will just mention here that the term 'foolishness' in this context conveys the idea of 'being ridiculous' or 'unacceptable' to the educated. Notice that the three categories of persons mentioned in 1.20 are perceived as professional experts whose 'intelligence' is mocked by the message of the cross. See Garland, *1 Corinthians*, p. 65.

('under a contrary appearance'), since 'the wisdom of God [is] hidden under the appearance of folly.'[41]

Thus, Paul is seeking to communicate in this segment that God's *modus operandi* in the world is to choose the cross, a symbol of weakness and a sign of foolishness according to the evaluation of the world, as the means to save those who believe. Paradoxically, the message about the cross which seems to be weak proves to be strong, and though seeming foolish in the end proves to be wise, since the cross accomplishes that which the wisdom and strength of man cannot achieve, namely salvation. The cross thus inverts and overthrows the worldly values of wisdom and power, for to the cross, recognized as the symbol of ultimate humiliation, is attributed power.[42] The cross forms the lens through which the world is perceived upside down or, more precisely, the right side up. In other words, the cross revolutionizes the perception of man, offering an alternate way of knowing to that of human wisdom. From the angle of the cross, the world's wisdom and God's involvement with the world will never look the same. Richard Hays thus rightly contends that, 'The cross becomes the starting point for an epistemological revolution, a *conversion of the imagination.*'[43] Thus, the cross becomes, in an ironic way, the means of the disclosure of God's wisdom and power. Moreover, through the cross the world's wisdom is disclosed and judged inadequate.

In 1 Cor. 1.26-31 Paul seeks to substantiate his argument about God's method of working for the salvation of those who believe by presenting an *ad hominem* argument. He reminds the Corinthians of the effect of the foolish message of the cross in their own lives. Having stated that the kerygma of the cross is 'power' unto salvation though it appears as 'weak', and 'wisdom' for those who are saved though it appears as 'folly' to those who are perishing, Paul points to the circumstances of the Corinthians' conversion.[44] Their 'call' was not the result of human wisdom, power, or

---

41   *Sapientia Dei abscondita sub specie stultitiae … Verbum Dei quoties venit, venit sub specie contraria menti nostrae.* Cited in Penna, *Paul the Apostle*, 54, n. 18. Fee, *First Corinthians*, p. 70, calls what happens in the cross the 'great reversal.'

42   Fee, 'Toward a Theology of 1 Corinthians', in *Pauline Theology*, p. 42, states that, 'Here God "outsmarted" the wise and "overpowered" the strong.' See also Demetrius K. Williams, 'The Terminology of the Cross and the Rhetoric of Paul', SBLSP 37 (1998) 677–99 (688).

43   Hays, 'Wisdom According to Paul', p. 113. The same argument is made by L. L. Welborn, 'On the Discord in Corinth: 1 Corinthians 1–4 and Ancient Politics', *JBL* 106 (1987) 85–111 (97); Cousar, 'Theological Task of 1 Corinthians', 94; and Fee, *First Corinthians*, p. 125.

44   Thiselton, *First Corinthians*, p. 180, states that 'κλῆσις alludes not simply to the act of call but to its attendance circumstance.' He follows Barrett, *First Corinthians*, p. 57; E.-B. Allo, *Saint Paul Première Épitre aux Corinthiens* (Paris: Gabalda, 2nd edn, 1956), p. 19; and Robertson and Plummer, *First Corinthians*, p. 24. *Contra*, Witherington, *Conflict and Community*, p. 113, who takes the meaning of 'socio-economic status' for κλῆσις apparently without supportive arguments.

status, but of God's choosing and working.[45] It has long been acknowledged that the three terms used by Paul in v. 26 (σοφοί, δυνατοί,
εὐγενεῖς) to describe the Corinthians' situation before conversion should
be understood in terms of social status: elite.[46] David DeSilva has recently
reminded us that the Greco-Roman society was built on values such as
honor and shame, and that these values went hand-in-hand with social
status.[47] In a society that prized honor, the Corinthians' lack of status at
the moment of their conversion was a clear illustration of the 'foolishness'
of God.[48] Yet this foolish choice in fact meant wisdom for the
Corinthians. Their election unto salvation, Paul argues, is a clear proof
that God works effectively contrary to the expected values of society.[49]
The result of their election was that their status was paradoxically

45 By underscoring what God has done on behalf of the Corinthians, Paul helps us to
hear the echoes that resound from the introduction (1.1-9): God called them (1.2), God
enriched them (1.5), God is saving them (1.18), God chose them (1.26-28), and God is the
source of their life in Christ Jesus (1.30). R. F. Collins, *First Corinthians* (SP, 7; Collegeville:
Liturgical, 1999), 109, rightly argues that the text 'underscores both the dynamic nature of
the call of God and God as the agent of the call.' See also, Victor Paul Furnish, 'Theology in
1 Corinthians', 65; Jan Lambrecht, 'The Power of God: A Note on the Connection Between 1
Cor. 1.17 and 18', in *Collected Studies on Pauline Literature and on The Book of Revelation*
(Roma: Editrice Pontificio Istituto Biblico, 2001), 36. Alexandra Brown, *The Cross and
Human Transformation*, p. 93, points to images of creation in the language of vv. 27–28,
similar to Rom. 9.25-26. Brown, 'Apocalyptic Transformation in Paul's Discourse on the
Cross', *Word & World* 16 (1996) 27–36(28), also makes a convincing argument in seeing the
discourse of the cross as an instance of 'performative utterance.' She takes over the
terminology from Austin, *How to Do Things with Words*, who defines performative utterance
as the capacity of some words to do what they say within certain cultural and linguistic
conventions that allow language to act in this way. For more on the power of the cross see
John Howard Schütz, *Paul and the Anatomy of Apostolic Authority* (SNTSMS, 26;
Cambridge: Cambridge University Press, 1975), esp. ch. 7.

46 Cf. Aristotle, *Rhet.* 2.12.2; Chrysostom, *Or.* 15.29-30; 31.74; Plutarch [*Lib. ed.*] 5c-d.
See, e.g., Gerd Theissen, *The Social Setting of Pauline Christianity*, pp. 69–120 (esp. pp. 70–
73); and Meeks, *The First Urban Christians. Contra* Justin J. Meggitt, *Paul, Poverty, and
Survival* (Edinburgh: T&T Clark, 1998), pp. 103–5.

47 DeSilva, ' "Let the One Who Claims Honor Establish That Claim in the Lord" ':
Honor Discourse in the Corinthian Correspondence', *BTB* 28 (1998) 61–74.

48 *Contra* Gail R. O'Day, 'Jeremiah 9.22-23 and 1 Corinthians 1.26-31: A Study in
Intertextuality', *JBL* 109 (1990) 259–67, who follows Wilhelm Wuellner, 'The Sociological
Implications of 1 Corinthians 1.26-28 Reconsidered' (E. A. Livingstone, ed.; *SE* VI; Berlin:
Akademie, 1973), 666–72; and the older translation of the *Jerusalem Bible*, punctuates v. 26
as an interrogative anticipating an affirmative answer: 'Look to your call, brothers and
sisters, were not many of you wise according to the flesh, were not many strong, were not
many of noble birth?' The result is the opposite of what is universally accepted among
commentators: the Corinthians *were* from among the social elite.

49 Leander E. Keck, in his article very suggestively entitled, 'God the Other Who Acts
Otherwise: An Exegetical Essay on 1 Cor. 1.26-31', *Word & World* 16 (1996) 437–43, rightly
concludes that Paul wrote this paragraph 'convinced that God is free to be the Other who
acts otherwise from prevailing wisdom', a conviction consistent with Isa. 55.8-9 (p. 442).

reversed – from 'nobodies' in a society that prized status to privileged status people in Christ. Thus, in Christ, a reversal took place, a reversal paradigmatic of God's paradoxical wisdom manifested in the cross.

But if such reversal was the result of God's choosing by means of the foolishness of the discourse about the cross, then Paul leaves no room for boasting. The cross (and its effect on the Corinthians) dissolves all fleshly boasting before God. The point that Paul is making in this segment of his argument is that God is consistent in his involvement on earth in that he saves by the 'weakness' and 'foolishness' of the cross, and saves those who are 'fools' and 'weak' according to worldly evaluation. Barrett rightly states that, 'It is not a plan that men would ever have thought of because it operates through Christian preaching which, since it is focused upon the cross, will inevitably be judged by worldly standards to be not wisdom but folly.'[50] We may add to this that no man could have come up with such a plan because it seeks to save the socially undeserving people. All this means, according to Paul's quotation of Jer. 9.22-23 [24-25], is that there is absolutely no room for boasting.[51] Since the Corinthians owe their Christian existence entirely to God, there is no room for human self-assertion; one can boast only in the Lord.[52]

Having shown thus God's foolish *modus operandi* in the world, Paul proceeds to show in 1 Cor. 2.1-5 how his own *modus operandi* as a herald[53] of the 'mystery'[54] of God is a reflection of God's *modus operandi*, in that

50　Barrett, *First Corinthians*, p. 53.

51　For a thorough analysis of the quotations see Williams, *The Wisdom of the Wise*, 104–32. He rightly argues that Jer. 9.22-23 provides a framework for 1.26-31 (p. 103).

52　Dahl, 'Paul and the Church at Corinth in 1 Cor. 1.10-4.21', 332, aptly observes that the Corinthians were upholding, using Lutheran terminology, a *theologia gloriae*, while Paul was preaching a *theologia crucis*. The former characterizes the Corinthians' self-perception while the latter Paul's view. See also Fee, *First Corinthians*, p. 176; and Thiselton, *First Corinthians*, p. 368.

53　Paul presents himself as a herald because 'the herald is not responsible for the content or the persuasiveness of the message he carries. The herald simply announces the message of another. A herald of the gospel proclaims the message of the cross faithfully, regardless of its incompatibility with human wisdom.' See Williams, 'Paul's Anti-Imperial "Discourse of the Cross"', 808. He follows Litfin, *Proclamation*, 248.

54　Whether the text of 2.1 should read μαρτύριον or μυστήριον is an issue of debate. For a detailed presentation of the history of reading see Veronica Koperski, '"Mystery of God" or "Testimony of God" in 1 Cor. 2,1: Textual and Exegetical Considerations', in *New Testament Textual Criticism and Exegesis: Festschrift J. Delobel* (A. Denaux, ed.; Leuven: Peeters, 2002), 305–15. We take μυστήριον as the preferred reading. Fee, among others, takes μαρτύριον as the original reading: 'Textual- Exegetical Observations on 1 Corinthinas 1.2, 2.1, and 2.10', in *Scribes and Scripture: New Testament Essays in Honor of J. Harold Greenlee* (David Alan Black, ed.; Winona Lake: Eisenbrauns, 1992), pp. 6–7; also C. Wolff, *Der erste Brief des Paulus an die Korinther* (THKNT, 7; Leipzig: Evangelische Verlagsanstalt, 1996). 47. Some who take the reading μυστήριον as the more probable reading are Schrage, *Der erste Brief*, 226–27; V. P. Furnish, *The Theology of the First Letter to the Corinthians* (NTT;

his proclamation is characterized by 'weakness' and 'foolishness.' The connection with the previous chapter is well expressed by Gordon Fee: Just as 'in the cross and in choosing you God in effect eliminated human boasting [...so] *I, for my part*, when I came to you, evidenced the same reality. I was totally stripped of self-reliance.'[55] The connection can also be gleaned from several lexical parallels that exist between 1 Cor. 1.18-31 and 2.1-5: λόγος and δύναμις θεοῦ are repeated from 1 Cor. 1.18 in 2.1 and 5;[56] Χριστὸν ἐσταυρωμένον, which is the focal point of 1 Cor. 1.18-25, is referred to in 1 Cor. 2.2 as the content of Paul's proclamation; the notion of τὰ ἀσθενῆ from 1 Cor. 1.27 is paradigmatic for Paul's own stage presence.

In this segment of Paul's argument, he contends that if the content of the message is 'Christ and him crucified', then the form which that message takes and the messenger who carries the message must be consistent with and correspond to the content of the message delivered (cf. Col. 1.24).[57] Since the essential character of the gospel is lack of impressiveness, according to what the world deems as impressive, then Paul deliberately adopted an unconventional mode of proclamation devoid of sophistication.[58] As such, Paul's self-characterization is self-effacement for the purpose of giving God the rightful place of honor in the creation of conviction by means of the Spirit's proof.[59] Paul proceeds to explain (γάρ) this position both in negative (1 Cor. 2.1-2, 4) and positive terms (1 Cor. 2.3, 4), concluding with the purpose for which he adopted a certain approach to preaching (1 Cor. 2.5).

His argument, then, is that adopting an eloquent style (presumably in

---

Cambridge: Cambridge University Press, 1999), p. 29; Collins, *First Corinthians*, 118; Thiselton, *First Corinthians*, p. 207. Hans Conzelmann, *1 Corinthians* (Hermeneia; trans. James W. Leitch; Philadelphia: Fortress, 1975), p. 53 n. 6, notes that it is 'impossible to decide' between the two readings.

55   Fee, *First Corinthians*, p. 90.

56   Lambrecht, 'The Power of God', 39, contends that 2.5 is intended to 'increase and complete the *Ringkomposition* which the expression ἐν δυνάμει Θεοῦ in 2.5 (cf. 1.18b) by itself brings about.'

57   Cf. Conzelmann, *1 Corinthians*, p. 53. See also Robertson and Plummer, *First Corinthians*, p. 29; Fee, *First Corinthians*, p. 93; Sigurd Grindheim, 'Wisdom for the Perfect: Paul's Challenge to the Corinthian Church (1 Corinthians 2.6-16)', *JBL* 121 (2002) 689–709 (692).

58   Robertson and Plummer, *First Corinthians*, p. 30, quote Wettstein: *Testimonium simpliciter dicendum est: nec eloquentia nec subtilitate ingenii opus est, quae testem suspectum potius reddit.*

59   For the idea that Paul seeks to point away from his own merits to God as the proper object of glory, as seen in 2.1-5, see, e.g., Fred G. Zaspel, 'The Apostolic Model for Christian Ministry: An Analysis of 1 Corinthians 2.1-5', *R&R* 7 (1998) 21–34. See also Peter John Dybvad, 'Imitation and Gospel in First Corinthians' (unpublished doctoral dissertation, Trinity Evangelical Divinity School, 2000), 125.

stark contrast to other public speakers, whether Christians or non-Christians) in his proclamation is only counterproductive to the gospel. Using in proclamation 'words of wisdom' so highly esteemed by the Corinthians is 'unsuitable for securing belief in the gospel.'[60] Barrett states: 'Preaching that depended for its effectiveness on the logical and rhetorical power of the preacher could engender only a faith that rested upon the same supports, and such a faith would be at the mercy of any superior show of logic and oratory, and thus completely insecure.'[61] True faith, Paul argues, is engendered not by rhetorical flourish (πειθοῖς σοφίας λόγοις), but by the work of the 'powerful Spirit'[62] as a result of the simple 'placarding' (*Bekanntmachung*) of the crucified Christ (cf. Gal. 3.1).[63] The work of the Spirit is the only means by which the Corinthians' faith can be safely anchored; and this is done by a 'plain' presentation of the cross.

In nuce, the first section of Paul's appeal for concord deals with three apparently disjunctive themes (the cross, the Corinthians' call, and Paul's adopted stage presence). Though apparently unconnected, these themes have at least three undeniable and interconnected aspects in common: weakness, reversal of values, and the undermining of any human basis for boasting.[64] By means of this attribute of weakness, Paul moves from contrasting wise speech with the kerygma of the cross, a symbol of weakness (1 Cor. 1.16-25), to illustrating the principle of reversal of values in the circumstances of the Corinthians' call while being of low status (1 Cor. 1.26-31), and by applying such a principle to his own ministry of proclamation in terms of 'unimpressive speech' (1 Cor. 2.1-5). By using the language of the world (i.e., 'weak' and 'foolish') to characterize these three areas, Paul seeks to remove any grounds for boasting in human wisdom (1 Cor. 1.18-25), social status (1 Cor. 1.26-31), and the preacher's cleverness (1 Cor. 2.1-5). In all these three segments, Paul seeks to help the

---

60   Winter, *Philo and Paul among the Sophists*, p. 164. See also Raymond Pickett, *The Cross in Corinth: The Social Significance of the Death of Jesus* (JSNTSup, 143; Sheffield: Sheffield Academic Press, 1997), 65.

61   Barrett, *First Corinthians*, p. 66. Likewise Robertson and Plummer, *First Corinthians*, p. 34.

62   The genitives πνεύματος and δυνάμεως probably form a hendiadys, cf. Colins, *First Corinthians*, 120. See also the discussion in Thiselton, *First Corinthians*, p. 222. It most likely refers not to miracle-working power that the apostles exercised in connection with preaching, as some Greek Fathers supposed, but it refers to that power by which the Spirit roughed faith unto salvation as a result of the proclamation of the Gospel (cf. 1 Thess. 1.5; 2.13).

63   Cf. Litfin, *Proclamation*, 247. Augustine, PL 4.12.28 states: 'The truth itself, when exhibited in its naked simplicity, gives pleasure, because it is the truth.'

64   Paul, in his Corinthian correspondence, regularly draws attention to his own weakness in order to demonstrate that his message was of divine, not human, origin. See 1 Cor. 4.9-13; 2 Cor. 4.7-12; 6.4-10; 11.30; 12.7-10. For a thorough study of these passages see John T. Fitzgerald, *Cracks in an Earthen Vessel: An Examination of the Catalogues of Hardships in the Corinthians Correspondence* (SBLDS, 99; Atlanta: Scholars Press, 1988).

Corinthians see things for what they are – adopt a divine perspective – and not take them as they seem to the world – human perspective.

Thus, in addressing his audience directly in 1 Cor. 2.1-5, Paul seeks to provide a theological justification of his own ministry of proclamation, by showing its consistency with the divine *modus operandi* and its incompatibility with the wisdom of the world.[65] In keeping with the paradoxical reversal effected by the discourse about the cross, Paul's own apparent weakness had a powerful effect as evidenced in the Corinthians' conversion when he first preached in Corinth. The effect shows that what he is preaching is in fact wisdom, but wisdom of a different order than that of the world. First Corinthians 2.1-5 is thus connected both verbally and thematically to the previous smaller segments, but it also anticipates the subject of the next section (1 Cor. 2.6-16) by the use of the phrase τὴν σοφίαν τοῦ κόσμου.

The Second Section: 1 Cor. 2.6–3.4

The second larger section (1 Cor. 2.6–3.4) is comprised of two smaller units: 2.6-16 and 3.1-4. This section follows in style the pattern that was seen in the first section: the first smaller unit is a general statement concerning some issue (in this case the contrast between two ways of responding to the revealed divine wisdom) followed by a unit in which Paul ('I') communicates directly with the Corinthians ('You'), seeking to apply the principle discussed in the previous segment.[66]

The style of 1 Cor. 2.6-16 is so much different than what we find in the surrounding sections that some scholars have argued that these verses are an interpolation.[67] The differences can be seen from a form-critical point

---

65   Smit, 'Search for Coherence', 248, rightly argues that, 'Paul here contends that his so-called inferior presentation actually meets the highest divine standards (*status qualitatis: constitution uiridicialis absoluta*).' See also Fee, *First Corinthians*, p. 90; Litfin, *Proclamation*, 204.

66   Cf. Smit, 'Search for Coherence', 236–37.

67   See Walker, '1 Corinthians 2.6-16: A Non-Pauline Interpolation?' 75–94, for three different views, of which he opts for the second: (1) it was composed by Paul, using ideas and terminology taken from his opponents; (2) it was composed by someone other than Paul but was incorporated into the letter by Paul, or (3) it is non-Pauline interpolation, both written by someone other than Paul and interpolated into the letter by someone other than Paul. To the same second group, who argue for Pauline authenticity, the most noticeable are J. Murphy-O'Connor, 'Interpolations in 1 Corinthians', *CBQ* 48 (1986) 81–94, and *Paul: A Critical Life* (Oxford: Clarendon, 1996), p. 283; and E. Earle Ellis, 'Traditions in 1 Corinthians', *NTS* 32 (1986) 481–502 (490). A major proponent for the third position is M. Widmann '1 Kor 2.6-16: Ein Einspruch gegen Paulus', *ZNW* 70 (1979) 44–53. Those who opt for the first position usually see in this text the theology of the opponents. Ulrich Wilckens, *Weisheit und Torheit: Eine exegetisch-religionsgeschichtliche Untersuchung zu 1 Kor 1 und 2* (BHT, 26; Tübingen: Mohr, 1959), 52–96, argues for a Gnostic background while Robin Scroggs, 'Paul: ΣΟΦΟΣ and ΠΝΕΥΜΑΤΙΚΟΣ', *NTS* 14 (1967–68) 33–55, for a Jewish Wisdom background.

of view in that there is an abrupt shift in v. 6 from singular to plural and that the catch-words (*Schlagwort*) κἀγώ and ἀδελφοί in 2.1 and 3.1 are an indication that the author is seeking to pick up again the threads of 2.1-5, acknowledging, according to some scholars, that what is in between is redactional. Semantically, Paul's employment of the language of wisdom to describe his own message seems to take a dramatic turn from his previous refutation of 'wise talk'. Some have argued based on this change that Paul takes back in this segment what he argued for in 1 Cor. 1.18–2.5.[68] From a linguistic point of view, the terminology of 1 Cor. 2.6-16 (e. g., τῶν ἀρχόντων τοῦ αἰῶνος τούτου, ψυχικὸς δὲ ἄνθρωπος, διδακτοῖς, πνευματικοῖς) differs from that found in the context, supporting thus, according to some, that the text is either pre- or post-Pauline.

Despite these stylistic peculiarities, there are, however, grounds to see this segment as an integral part of the argument of this section of the letter.[69] As already seen, this section elaborates on the concept of divine wisdom introduced in 1 Cor. 1.18-25. Thiselton rightly argues that, 'Paul has attacked their false "wisdom" in 1 Cor. 1.17–2.5, but now he wishes to make it clear that a true wisdom remains both part of his own teaching to Christian believers and an essential mark of a mature Christian community.'[70] In this sense, Paul reclaims the language of wisdom (and concepts associated with it such as mystery and hiddenness/unintelligibility) by redefining wisdom in light of the cross.[71] Paul, in other words, will use the

68   Cf. Rudolf Bultmann 'Karl Barth, "Die Auferstehung der Toten"', in *Glauben und Verstehen: Gesammelte Aufsätze* (Tübingen: Mohr, 1961), 1.42-44.

69   For a history of views concerning the connection of this segment with the context see Peter Stuhlmacher, 'The Hermeneutical Significance of 1 Cor. 2.6-16', in *Tradition and Interpretation in the New Testament: Essays in Honor of E. Earle Ellis for His 60th Birthday* (Gerald F. Hawthorne and Otto Betz, eds.; Grand Rapids: Eerdmans, 1987), pp. 330–32.

70   Thiselton, *First Corinthians*, pp. 224–25. See also Collins, *First Corinthians*, 122. That divine σοφία is the topic of this segment is evident from its emphatic first position that it occupies.

71   Cf. Thiselton, *1 Corinthians*, p. 224. This is not the same thing as saying that Paul takes over the (religious) language of his opponents in Corinth, cf. Charles B. Cousar, '1 Corinthians 2.1-13', *Int* 44 (1990) 171; Murphy-O'Connor, 'Interpolations in 1 Corinthians', 81–94; Fee, *First Corinthians*, 100. As Jeffrey S. Lamp, 'The Spiritual Christian: a Matter of Degree or Definition? (1 Cor. 2.6-3.4)', paper presented at the 48th National Conference (Jackson: Theological Research Exchange Network, 1997), 7, rightly argues that, 'the conjecture that Paul is drawing on Corinthian vocabulary is based on speculative reconstructions of theological backgrounds in Corinth.' Rather, it is simply stating that Paul, in his use of the language of wisdom, apparently seems to agree with the world's pursuit of wisdom manifested among the Corinthians, but immediately clarifies that the wisdom he proclaims is of a different order, inaccessible to those of 'this age.' In other words, Paul would see an oxymoron in the concept of 'wisdom of the world', since the world uses the concept of 'wisdom' in an illegitimate way.

There are basically three views when it comes to discerning whether Paul uses the religious language of his opponents. There are those like Wilckens, *Weisheit und Torheit*, 52–96, who

term wisdom in 1 Cor. 2.6-16 not in a pejorative way, by looking at it from a worldly perspective as in 1 Cor. 1.17-25 (a view from below), but in a positive sense as defined from God's perspective (a view from above). Moreover, Paul's concluding remarks in 1 Cor. 2.5 concerning the Spirit leads him to develop in this section the theme of the Spirit. The concept of μυστήριον also forms the verbal link between 1 Cor. 2.1 and 2.7. Thus, the concept of wisdom, the role of the Spirit, and the idea of mystery, found in the preceding segments, are elaborated in this section. Here Paul uses all these concepts to draw out a contrast described in terms of the discernment of the spiritual/mature and the fleshly person with regard to the revealed gospel.

The central theme of this section then can be summarized in the following way: the wisdom of God identified with the message of the cross[72] is perceived only by the 'mature' and 'spiritual' as a result of the revelation of God's Spirit and not as a result of human wisdom, and much less of the teachers' eloquence. Paul develops the argument in defense of divine wisdom in three stages.[73] First, he defines the character of this wisdom in terms of μυστήριον. God's wisdom remains hidden (τὴν ἀποκεκρυμμένην)[74] from the 'earthly rulers'.[75] Proof is, Paul contends,

---

argue that the views in this segment are not Paul's but they reflect the theology of the (Gnostic) opponents. On the other hand, there are those like Scroggs, 'Paul: ΣΟΦΟΣ and ΠΝΕΥΜΑΤΙΚΟΣ', 33–55, who take an opposite view arguing that nothing of the opponents' wisdom can be seen in this passage. A mediatory position is taken by Birger Albert Pearson, *The Pneumatikos-Psychikos Terminology in 1 Corinthians. A Study in the Theology of the Corinthian Opponents of Paul and Its Relation to Gnosticism* (SBLNHS, 12; Missoula: Scholars Press, 1973), 73–74, who argues that Paul 'presents his "wisdom" using the opponents' terminology and turning it back against them.' For more recent advocates of this view see Gregory E. Sterling, ' "Wisdom among the Perfect:" Creation Traditions in Alexandrian Judaism and Corinthian Christianity', *NTS* 37 (1995) 355–84; Christopher Tuckett, 'Jewish Christian Wisdom in 1 Corinthians?' in *Crossing the Boundaries: Essays in Biblical Interpretation in Honour of Michael D. Goulder* (BIS, 8; Stanley E. Porter, Paul Joyce, and David E. Orton, eds.; Leiden: Brill, 1994), 211–12; and Richard A. Horsley, 'Wisdom of Word and Words of Wisdom in Corinth', *CBQ* 39 (1977) 234–39 (238–39).

72   For arguments of identifying God's wisdom of 2.6-16 with the message of the cross from 1.18-2.5 rather than with some esoteric knowledge, see William Baird, 'Among the Mature: The Idea of Wisdom in 1 Corinthians 2.6', *Int* 13 (1959) 425–32; and Lamp, 'The Spiritual Christian', 3, following M. N. A. Bockmuehl, *Revelation and Mystery in Ancient Judaism and Pauline Christianity* (Tübingen: Mohr, 1990), p. 161.

73   See also Gillespie, 'Interpreting the Kerygma', p. 158.

74   τὴν ἀποκεκρυμμένην goes with σοφία and not with λαλοῦμεν and, given its perfect tense, it can convey the idea of 'remaining hidden', cf. Furnish, 'Theology in 1 Corinthians', 66, following Schrage, *Der erste Brief*, 251; *contra* Fee, *First Corinthians*, p. 105.

75   Commentators are divided over the reference of the expression οἱ ἄρχοντες. For an overview see Clarke, *Leadership in Corinth*, 114–8; and Wesley Carr, 'The Rulers of This Age-1 Cor. 2.6-8', *NTS* 23 (1976) 20–35. Some who take it to refer to spiritual powers are Barrett, 'Christianity at Corinth', in *Essays on Paul* (Philadelphia: Westminster, 1982), 1–27; idem, *First Corinthians*, p. 70; Conzelmann, *1 Corinthians*, p. 61; Schrage, *Der erste Brief*,

that they crucified Christ. In stark contrast (ἀλλὰ) to the imperceptibility of the gospel by the unspiritual is the other side of the coin – the revelatory or knowable nature of God's wisdom. While the hiddenness of the gospel is empirically verified, its perceptibility is scripturally illustrated.[76] By reference to the Old Testament Scriptures (Isa. 64.3 [4]; 65.17), Paul advances his argument from the character of God's wisdom to the medium of divine wisdom: the Spirit.[77]

In this second stage of the argument, then, Paul focuses on the role of τὸ πνεῦμα τοῦ θεοῦ. Since the unspiritual man does not know (and in 1 Cor. 2.14 καὶ οὐ δύναται γνῶναι) the things of God (i.e., the wisdom of God manifested in the cross), the role of the Spirit is to reveal them to the spiritual and mature (i.e., Christians).[78] The wisdom of God is not, Paul

---

250, 253–54; Collins, *First Corinthians*, 129. We agree here with those who believe that the reference is to earthly rulers. See Fee, *First Corinthians*, pp. 103–4; Wolff, *Der erste Brief*, 53–54; Lindemann, *Der erste Korintherbrief*, p. 63. One support for the latter view may be the larger context. Paul says about these rulers that, in crucifying Christ, they proved ignorance of divine wisdom. This idea of the divine wisdom escaping human wisdom was the theme of 1.18-25, 'wisdom' expressed in the cross. Williams, *The Wisdom of the Wise*, 202–8, sees in 2.6-8, 10–11, an echo from Dan. 2.19-23, which strengthens the view of earthly rulers as reference. Thiselton, *First Corinthians*, p. 238, seeks to bring together the two views (see his bibliography on the phrase [p. 228] and his extended discussion [pp. 233–39]). Gerd Theissen, *Psychological Aspects of Pauline Theology* (trans. John P. Galvin; Philadelphia: Fortress, 1987), pp. 369–70, argues similarly that the reference is to earthly rulers, though later he observes that these 'are heightened symbolically to demonic powers' (p. 378).

76 Lamp, 'The Spiritual Christian', 6 n.14, seems to agree with W. Harold Mare, *1 Corinthians* (EBC, 10; Grand Rapids: Zondervan, 1976), p. 201, that, based on the argument in this context, καθώς 'is more indicative of illustration, whereas ὅτι is more appropriate if proof were indicated.'

77 For a detailed discussion of the use of the Old Testament in this section see Williams, *The Wisdom of the Wise*, 159–65.

78 The identity of the 'spiritual' and 'mature' has been a matter of debate among commentators. Some scholars see in this terminology a distinction between two classes of Christians. According to this view, presumably Paul is speaking about some form of spiritual elitism. E.g., Conzelmann, *1 Corinthians*, p. 57 and Héring, *First Corinthians*, p. 15. This understanding is particularly advanced by those who believe that the background behind the concept of wisdom in 1 Corinthians is Gnostic. But Fee, *First Corinthians*, p. 120, rightly rejects such interpretation on the basis that it runs the risk of advocating that Paul adopts the exact view that the Corinthians were expounding and Paul was seeking to combat in this paragraph – wisdom devoid of the foolish message of the cross. See also Williams, *The Wisdom of the Wise*, 205; and Hays, 'Wisdom According to Paul', p. 120. Paul contradicting himself, of course, is not a problem for those who take this segment as an interpolation (the contrastive δέ, of 2.6 is regarded as introducing the words of Paul's opponents), and so they do not find it necessary to integrate Paul's apparent contradiction of himself. But, as we will see, the message of the text is that being spiritual and mature does not lead to Christian elitism, but to the understanding of the mystery of God – salvation through the cross. Thus, the 'mature' (rather than 'perfect' as a translation of τελείοις) and the 'spiritual' ones are to be identified simply with the believer. *Contra* Robin Scroggs, 'Paul: ΣΟΦΟΣ and ΠΝΕΥΜΑΤΙΚΟΣ', 47, n. 5. But see Garland, *1 Corinthians*, p. 92; and the helpful essay by Lamp, 'The Spiritual Christian', 1–20.

would argue, 'an innate property humans possess but a gift of God, a self-revelation taught by the Spirit.'[79] Paul's argument here is that only those who belong to the Spirit of God (himself given by God) can know or have access to God's wisdom;[80] those who have the world's wisdom are excluded from such knowledge. The reason is because the message of the cross has a logic that escapes human wisdom. The wisdom of God is incomprehensible to the world and can be judged and evaluated (συγ[άνα] κρίνω) only by those who have the Spirit of God.

With this, Paul moves to the last stage of his exposition of divine wisdom. Given the essential character of the divine wisdom – hiddenness – and the medium of the revelation of God's wisdom – the Spirit of God – Paul seeks to show that the transmission or proclamation (λαλοῦμεν) of such mystery must be done with a wisdom that conforms to the Spirit who reveals the mystery (διδακτοῖς πνεύματος).[81] For this reason, the

---

79   Cousar, 'Theological Task of 1 Corinthians', 96.

80   The adjective πνευματικός (with its ending -ικος) conveys the sense of 'belonging to or pertaining to'. See Gordon Fee, *God's Empowering Presence: The Holy Spirit in Paul's Letters* (Exeter: Paternoster, 1994), 28–32.

81   The referent of the first person plural form of the personal pronoun ἡμεῖς (i.e., 2.7, 10, 12, 16) and of the verbs occurring in the first person plural (i.e., λαλοῦμεν – 2.6, 7, 13, ἐλάβομεν – 2.12, ἔχομεν – 2.16) are a matter of debate. The tendency among commentators is to argue that it refers to all Christians. E.g., Barrett, *First Corinthians*, p. 69; Orr and Walther, *1 Corinthians*, 166; Collins, *First Corinthians*, 122. But Paul uses λαλέω in the next segment (3.1) as a reference to his proclamation when he first came to Corinth, which links it to καταγγέλλω in 2.1, where he refers to the same event in the past (see also Rom. 15.18; 2 Cor. 4.13; Phil. 1.14; 1 Thess. 2.2, 4, 16). This segment follows the one in which Paul argues for his *modus operandi* as a preacher and so the present segment continues it by way of contrast (probably including other teachers). Moreover, the verbal link in 2.6 (λαλοῦμεν) anticipates the occurrence of λαλοῦμεν in 2.13, where the reference is to teaching (διδακτοῖς). Also, Paul's use of the first person plural where he means ἐγώ is frequent in his letters (e.g., 1 Thess. 2.18). See Stauffer, *TDNT*, 4. 356ff. Thus, we may argue that λαλοῦμεν in this segment is Paul's way of speaking of himself and of other teachers as those who have been entrusted with the mystery of God. See Smit, 'Search for Coherence', 248, n. 50; *idem*, 'Epideictic Rhetoric in Paul's First Letter to the Corinthians 1–4', *Bib* 84 (2003) 184–202 (192); and Clarke, *Leadership in Corinth*, 117. Moreover, some of the terminology of this text is very similar to that of Jesus' address to the disciples who asked him about the reason why he speaks to the crowds in parables (cf. Matt. 13.10-17). Jesus' answer is that it has been given to the disciples to know the mystery (ὑμῖν δέδοται γνῶναι τὰ μυστήρια). Thus, we contend that Paul (and his companions) is the immediate referent, though certainly (as an application) all Christians have had access to this mystery – salvation through the cross. See Richard Gaffin, 'Some Epistemological Reflections on 1 Cor. 2.6-16', *WTJ* 57 (1995) 103–24 (113). Hence, Dybvad, 'Imitation and Gospel in First Corinthians', 132–33, is only partly right to contend, following R. W. Funk, 'Word and World in 1 Corinthians 2.6-16', in *Language, Hermeneutic, and Word of God: The Problem of Language in the New Testament and Contemporary Philosophy* (New York: Harper & Row, 1966), p. 300, that the language is 'inclusive-exclusive' when it comes to the Corinthians. It would be more precise to state that the language Paul uses in this segment is intentionally ambiguous (or open-ended). The ambiguity reflects the spiritual danger of the Corinthians' partisan spirit which Paul will

proclamation of God's wisdom lacks the σοφίας λόγοις (1 Cor. 2.13) so highly esteemed by the rulers of this age. In other words, Paul argues, the use of the wisdom of this world in proclaiming the cross will not make the gospel more effective and receptive, simply because it cannot. It is like trying to start a fire with water; it will never happen because it cannot happen. There is just no compatibility between the two ages; in fact, it is counterproductive to use σοφίας λόγοις to proclaim the hidden mystery of God (cf. 1 Cor. 1.17).

In light of these facts, Paul reminds the Corinthians once more how the wisdom of God (i.e., the cross) divides the ages, resulting in a separation between two distinct communities: οἱ τέλειοι/πνευματικοί and οἱ ψυχικοί. In this segment, then, Paul furthers his defense of his *modus operandi* introduced in 1 Cor. 2.1-5, by arguing that the problem is not with his *proclamation* in that it lacks wisdom; but that the wisdom that it does communicate can be *perceived* only by the τέλειοι and πνευματικοί and not by the ψυχικοί. To what group the Corinthians belong is not clear in this segment, though surely the Corinthians must have thought of themselves as mature and spiritual. Where Paul sees the Corinthians is clarified in the subsequent section, where Paul seeks to warn the Corinthians of their dangerous spiritual condition, given their partisan spirit.

The second sub-unit (1 Cor. 3.1-4) returns to the direct communication found in 1 Cor. 2.1 with the words κἀγώ and ἀδελφοί. The reference to Apollos and Paul also reminds the reader of the problem of dissensions of which we learn from the party slogans first mentioned in 1 Cor. 1.12, forming thus a kind of *inclusio* around 1 Cor. 1.18–2.16.[82] Nevertheless, the connection with the previous unit 1 Cor. 2.6-16 is of immediate importance. The primary link is the use of πνευματικοί in 1 Cor. 3.1. Paul, in 1 Cor. 2.6-16, distinguishes between the spiritual and the fleshly persons, a division reflecting their antithetical perception of the cross. Having already told the Corinthians that they have been chosen by God (1

---

address directly in the next segment. Thus, in light of the context, it would be more precise to state that the first person plural refers to Paul (and other teachers like Apollos) though all Christians experience the same revelation. Again, the Corinthians are made to think that they belong to the same 'privileged' group (the elect as contrasted with the fleshly) by the use of the first person plural; but Paul is using irony in order to shock them with his rebuke in 3.1-4. Therefore, the Corinthians are only *potentially* included, though in the next paragraph it proves that they are not *actually*. See Sterling, '"Wisdom among the Perfect"', 369, for a similar view; also Charles A. Wanamaker, 'A Rhetoric of Power: Ideology and 1 Corinthians 1–4', in *Paul and the Corinthians: Studies on a Community in Conflict. Essays in Honour of Margaret Thrall* (Trevor J. Burke and J. Keith Elliott, eds.; NovTSup, 109; Leiden: Brill, 2003), 129–30, n. 62. See Williams, *The Wisdom of the Wise*, 226–35, for a survey of opinions and his case for all Christians as 'potentially' having 'the mind of Christ' (2.16 quoting Isa. 40.13), a reference to the plan of salvation.

82   Cf. Kuck, *Judgment*, 161.

Cor. 1.26-31), it is only natural for the Corinthians to have thought that
Paul speaks of them when he mentions the spiritual and the mature. But in
the present segment of text Paul clarifies for the Corinthians a
misperception that they may have had concerning themselves: they were
not acting in accordance with their identity and therefore were in a
precarious spiritual condition.[83] Their communal dissension endangers
their status as chosen from among all people in order to be an illustration
of the wisdom of God. As a result, the Corinthians are to be blamed and
not Paul. Paul did teach 'wisdom', but the Corinthians were not able to
digest it and are still not able.[84] Paul, thus, gets to the root cause of their
partisan spirit – the inability to grasp the mystery of the cross and its
implication for the social life within their *ecclesia*.

In light of this spiritual condition expressed in an attitude of jealousy,
Paul characterizes the Corinthians as σαρκίνοις rather than
πνευματικοῖς, a characterization that may have come as a shock to
them.[85] Much has been written concerning the connotation of the
theological categories with which Paul operates in this context: τελείοις
πνευματικοῖς, ψυχικοῖς, νηπίοις, σαρκίνοις.[86] One important observa-

83 Smit, 'Search for Coherence', 237, is thus only partially right to see that the main link
between the two sections is the contrast between λαλοῦμεν ἐν τοῖς τελείοις in 2.6 and
λαλῆσαι ... ὡς νηπίοις in 3.1. The contrast (to be more precise) is between τοῖς τελείοις
and ὁ ψυχικός. Paul does not identify the Corinthians with the ψυχικός in this segment, but
he is also clear on refusing to address them as πνευματικοῖς and τελείοις, without denying
that they are spiritual. See Dybvad, 'Imitation and Gospel in 1 Corinthians', 137, following
Johannes Weiss, *Der erste Korintherbrief* (Göttingen: Vandenhoeck & Ruprecht, 2nd rev.
edn, 1910), p. 74. James Francis, '"As Babes in Christ" – Some Proposals Regarding 1
Corinthians 3.1-3', *JSNT* 7 (1980) 41–60 (43), rightly argues that Paul rebukes the
Corinthians not for lack of progress, 'but because they were in fact being childish, a condition
contrary to being spiritual.' This observation rightly argues against taking τελείοις (wrongly
translated as 'perfect' in this text) and νηπίοις as the extreme points on the axel of spiritual
development, a tendency present in certain theological systems. Sigurd Grindheim, 'Wisdom
for the Perfect: Paul's Challenge to the Corinthian Church (1 Corinthians 2.6-16)', *JBL* 121
(2002): 689–709 (708), for instance, wrongly forces categories from systematic theology and
meanings from other texts (e.g., Col. 1.28; Eph. 4.13 and Heb. 5.11–6.3) on this text. But
τελείοις here refers to the state of the believer in contrast to the unbeliever, not to 'some goal
for which every Christian must strive' or gradation in spirituality (as in other passages). See,
e.g., Fee, *First Corinthians*, p. 122. Thus, Paul is neither conferring nor denying to the
Corinthians the status of τελείοις and πνευματικοῖς. Rather, he is challenging them to
behave in a manner commensurate with a believer's status – one whose system of values has
been reversed by an understanding of the mystery of the cross. See especially Lamp's essay,
'The Spiritual Christian', and Furnish, *Pauline Theology*, 68. In this sense, -ικος indicates an
ethical relationship.

84 Cf. Smit, 'Epideictic Rhetoric in Paul's First Letter to the Corinthians 1–4', 194.

85 See Pickett, *The Cross in Corinth*, 41.

86 We have already pointed out that some see in these terms different degrees of
spirituality (i.e., the spiritual Christian, the infant Christian, and the carnal Christian). For a
critique of such an understanding present especially in the dispensational theology advocated

tion is that Paul works with antithetical pairs (e.g., τελείοις/πνευματικοῖς vs. ψυχικοῖς) throughout the first rhetorical unit of his letter, a dualism which continues in this section.[87] As such, νηπίοις and σαρκίνοις are not used to indicate a third possible spiritual category (i.e., carnal Christian as opposed to mature Christian and unbeliever) in which a Christian can persist, but that the Corinthians, by preferring one preacher over another, prove to be schizophrenics: they have the Spirit but they are not spiritual (i.e., do not belong to the Spirit).[88] Such a state is symptomatic of worldly behavior (κατὰ ἄνθρωπον περιπατεῖτε).[89] Fee rightly states that, 'The Corinthians are involved in a lot of unchristian behavior; in that sense they are "unspiritual", not because they lack the Spirit but because they are thinking and living just like those who do.'[90]

The paranaetic function of this segment is to warn the Corinthians that, by their assessment of preachers according to the worldly canons of wisdom, they place themselves in a dangerous spiritual condition, being more like the ones who crucified Christ rather than the ones who embraced him.[91] The reason is because this type of comparison and judging is characteristic of the ψυχικοί and not of the ones who have the νοῦν Χριστοῦ. In other words, Paul seeks to convince them of their misguided perception of preachers as evidenced in their quarreling and jealousy, a rather dangerous spiritual state. This warning leads into the next section (1 Cor. 3.5–4.5), which deals with the issue in a more direct manner.

The Third Section: 1 Cor. 3.5–4.5

In the third major section (1 Cor. 3.5–4.5), then, Paul seeks to show how the Christian teachers should be viewed properly. This is the key passage

---

by Lewis Sperry Chafer and Charles Ryrie based on this text, see Brian Borgman, 'Rethinking a Much Abused Text: 1 Corinthians 3.1-15', *R&R* 11 (2002) 71–93 (71–79). It is possible that Paul is not referring to their Christian life in its entirety, when he characterizes them as σαρκι,νοις; rather it is in their divisive behavior that they prove to be mere men.

87   For antithetical pairs in 1 Corinthians 1–4, see Grindheim, 'Wisdom for the Perfect', 705; he follows P. J. Du Plessis, ΤΕΛΕΙΟΣ: *The Idea of Perfection in the New Testament* (Kampen: Kok, 1959), p. 179. See also Clarke, *Leadership in Corinth*, pp. 101–2.

88   Paul's point is that there is an incompatibility between true spirituality and divisions. See Cousar, 'Theological Task of 1 Corinthians', 97; Sterling, '"Wisdom among the Perfect"', 370. Pickett, *The Cross in Corinth*, pp. 63–4, rightly interprets the difference between πνευματικοῖς and σαρκίνοις as epistemological, having to do with perception.

89   Cf. Winter, *Philo and Paul among the Sophits*, p. 173. For Paul's use of the metaphor of walking see R. Banks, '"Walking" as a Metaphor of the Christian Life: The origins of a Significant Pauline Usage', in *Perspectives on Language and Texts: Essays and Poems in Honor of Francis I. Andersen's Sixtieth Birthday* (E. W. Conrad & E. G. Newing, eds.; Winona Lake: Eisenbrauns, 1987), pp. 310–13.

90   Fee, *First Corinthians*, p. 123.

91   Cf. Grindheim, 'Wisdom for the Perfect'.

in understanding the issue behind dissensions. If up until now Paul has been arguing for the need of a new perspective in concordance with the reversals brought about by the cross, he now seeks to apply the new mindset to the particular problem plaguing the Christian community at Corinth, namely dissensions over preachers. The connection with the previous section is obvious by the use of the transitional particle οὖν in 1 Cor. 3.5 and the mention of the names of Paul and Apollos. That this is a new section is indicated by the introduction encoded in the rhetorical questions: 'What is Paul?' and 'What is Apollos?' This section is divided into three smaller units: 1 Cor. 3.5-17; 3.18-23; and 4.1-5. The unifying theme of these segments is the proper evaluation (i.e., judgment) of teachers. Each segment of text contains the idea of an assessment of teachers in terms of the quality of their labor (i.e., 1 Cor. 3.8b, 13–15, 17a, 19–20; 4.3-5). The paraenetic purpose of this section is to convince the Corinthians of their false assumption of the role as judges over the work of their teachers.[92] Paul argues that such a role is solely the prerogative of God as it will be carried out in the eschatological judgment.

The first segment (1 Cor. 3.5-17) properly defines the role of teachers as διάκονοι (servants; 3.5) under God's jurisdiction. Paul will illustrate this role by means of three analogies: the image of the field (3.5-9a); the image of the building (3.9b-15); and the image of the temple (3.16-17). Even from the start Paul emphasizes the particular role the teachers play in God's economy (τί) as opposed to the dignity of their status (τίς).[93] Andrew Clarke is therefore right to state that, 'Paul's language, and thus also his understanding of Christian leadership, are seen to be task-orientated. Paul deliberately plays down the role which the apostles fulfill: first, these leaders are to be considered more than servants who function under the Lord; and secondly, the focus is not on who they are, but rather on what their task is.'[94]

This is contrary to the personality cult and the foolish veneration of the apostles as heroes by the Corinthians (cf. 1 Cor. 1.10-17 and 3.1-4).[95] Paul, thus, seeks to point away from himself to God, to whom he assigns the key role; his is a menial one. This emphasis becomes even more

---

92 Dickerson, 'Apollos in Acts and First Corinthians', 117, also argues that the entire section is concerned with the issue of judgment.

93 One should be aware of the fact that, as Bruce M. Metzger observes, *A Textual Commentary on the Greek New Testament* (New York: UBS, 2nd edn, 1994), p. 482, 'the Textus Receptus, following P[46] C D F G and most minuscules, reads τίς ('Who?') in both instances [i.e., the questions τίς οὖν ἐστιν Ἀπολλῶς; τίς δε ἐστιν Παῦλος;].' Metzger, however, rightly points to the fact that, 'the implication of the neuter τι in v. 7 is decisive for τί in v. 5 (since the answer is "Nothing" the questions can scarcely have been "Who").'

94 Clarke, *Leadership in Corinth*, p. 119. Cf. Winter, *Philo and Paul among the Sophists*, p. 196.

95 Cf. Dybvad, 'Imitation and Gospel in First Corinthians', 147.

prominent by the use of the analogy from agriculture. The various tasks that the servants of God are to accomplish in the Corinthian community (i.e., 'planting' and 'watering') are all subordinated and inferior to God's ultimate role, as the one who makes it all happen.[96]

By means of the analogy from agriculture, Paul drives home (ὥστε) at least three important points. First, the Christian community is a theocentric community. Everything that pertains to the formation of the Christian community, of the people of God, from her constitution to her final glorification, depends on God.[97] The Corinthians therefore should focus on God and not his servants. He employs servants, each with different roles, in order to carry out his purposes, and so they have no independent importance. Paul's concern thus is to remove any ground for boasting in teachers, since all belong to God, regardless of their distinct individual gift/task.

In this respect, a second point becomes evident: the servants are one (ἕν εἰσιν), 'their equality [being] the equality of "nothingness" before the God whom they serve.'[98] They are insignificant and dispensable before God. This low-status self-perception of the apostles in relation to God leads Paul to classify the servants further as συνεργοί (1 Cor. 3.9) in relation to one another, as co-workers belonging to God.[99] Thus the emphasis falls on their equality as sub-servants to God; they together belong to God. This harmonious service of God undercuts the elevation of one over another. Therefore, Kuck argues, 'to latch onto the individual differences among the Lord's servants in an attempt to make the church a battleground for status is to overlook the fact that there is but one status in the church – servant of the Lord.'[100]

The implication of this fact brings out a third point evident in the

---

96   According to the Greco-Roman scale of values, the διάκονος was a function to which no honor was ascribed; it was rather a despised condition. See, e.g., Crysostom, *Or.* 14.1; 74.9; Plutarch, *Per.* 1.4-2.1. The contemptuous attitude toward serving is found in Plato, *Gorg.* 492b. Paul, by defining himself and the other teachers as 'servants', who work as one in the field, denies the Corinthians the opportunity of gaining honor by association with the teachers, since the 'servants' and the 'farmers' occupied a place in society deemed shameful, given their manual labor.

97   Williams, *The Wisdom of the Wise*, p. 243, sees in this analogy from agriculture an echo from Isa. 5.2, the song of the vineyard. The thrust of the text is thus that God is 'the chief worker within the Corinthian church and is the owner of it.'

98   Victor Paul Furnish, 'Fellow Workers in God's Service', *JBL* 80 (1961) 369.

99   Furnish, 'Fellow Workers in God's Service', 364–70; Thiselton, *First Corinthians*, p. 306; and Schrage, *Der erste Brief*, 1.292. *Contra* e.g., Donald P. Ker, 'Paul and Apollos–Colleagues or Rivals?' *JSNT* 77 (2000) 75–97 (87); and most of the Nineteenth and early-twentieth-century commentators, who take the phrase to mean 'co-workers with God'. But the only place where συνεργός refers to working together with God is 1 Thess. 3.2, though this reading has slim manuscript evidence.

100   Kuck, *Judgment*, p. 170.

analogy from agriculture: the Christian teachers are accountable to God, their Lord or employer, and not to the community for their work. Thus, the quality or worth of their effort (κόπον) will be left to God to evaluate; he will pass the final verdict and determine their pay and not the human public.[101]

The second metaphor of the building in 1 Cor. 3.10-15 enlarges on the concept of judgment introduced in verse 8b and continues the presentation of the servants and their various assigned roles.[102] With the use of this metaphor, as with the analogy from agriculture, Paul seeks to convince the Corinthians of the foolish distinction that they are making among teachers, since only God has such a prerogative in light of the future judgment. Ultimately, Paul seeks to achieve unity in the Christian community by eliminating any ground for human evaluation.[103]

As in the metaphor of the field where Paul presented himself as the instrument of God in bringing in the gospel to the Corinthians (ἐγὼ ἐφύτευσα of v. 6), so in the metaphor of the building Paul claims the pioneering role of laying the foundation ὡς σοφὸς ἀρχιτέκτων.[104]

---

101   Thiselton, *First Corinthians*, p. 304. See also Lamp, *First Corinthians 1–4 in Light of Jewish Wisdom Traditions: Christ, Wisdom, and Spirituality Spirituality* (SBEC, 42; Lewiston: Edwin Mellen, 2000), p. 180. One of the social conventions of Paul's day was that the assessment of the success of a speaker rested on the shoulders of the public audience. Some have rightly argued that the judgment that the Corinthians were directing to the teachers was the same as the audience's belief to be the final arbiter of rhetoricians (sophists) and their oratory. See, e.g., Witherington, *Conflict and Community*, p. 137, and Litfin, *Proclamation*, p. 130.

102   For links to previous metaphor see Harm W. Hollander, 'The Testing by Fire of the Builders' Works: 1 Corinthians 3.10-15', *NTS* 40 (1994) 89–104 (89); and David Kuck, 'Paul and Pastoral Ambition: A Reflection on 1 Corinthians 3–4', *CTM* 19 (1992) 174–83 (177–78). The two *topoi* of agriculture and architecture were commonly joined in the OT (Jer. 1.10; 18.9; 24.6; 31.28; 45.4; Ezek. 36.9, 10) and other Jewish literature (Sir. 49.7; Philo, *Leg.* 1.48; *Odes Sol* 38.16-22). The analogy with the temple also appears at times in conjunction with the building and field metaphors. See James E. Rosscup, 'A New Look at 1 Corinthians 3.12 – "Gold, Silver, Precious Stones"', *MSJ* 1 (1990) 33–51 (34, n. 4) who mentions Bertil Gärtner, *The Temple and the Community in Qumran and the New Testament* (Cambridge: Cambridge University Press, 1965), 27–29.

103   Welborn, *Politics and Rhetoric in the Corinthian Epistle* (Macon: Mercer University Press, 1997), pp. 61–2, argues that the architectural metaphor was an adequate symbol for the promotion of concord in Greco-Roman rhetoric especially in the political world. Likewise, Mitchell, *Reconciliation*, pp. 99–105; and Lanci, *Temple*, p. 78. Cf. Cicero *Amic.* 7.23; Aristide, *Or.* 23.31; Xenophon, *Mem.* 4.4.16. Nevertheless, Lanci argues, 'the maxim "a house divided against itself cannot stand" (Mk 3.25) articulates a sentiment which found wide application' (p. 79).

104   Some see in this a certain order which places Paul in higher and more authoritative position than Apollos. See for now Niels Hyldahl, 'Paul and Apollos: Exegetical Observations to 1 Cor. 3.1-23', in *Apocrypho Severini Presented to Søren Giversen* (Per Bilde, Helge Kjser Nielsen, and Jørgen Podemann Sørensen, eds.; Aarhus: Aarhus University Press, 1993): 68–82.

Though the phrase means 'skilled/experienced master-builder'[105] one cannot miss the semantic play on the word σοφός which recalls Paul's argument about preaching the wisdom of the cross (cf. 1 Cor. 1.18–2.16). The foundation thus is none other than Ἰησοῦν Χριστὸν καὶ τοῦτον ἐστουρωμένον. Paul did not undertake this role at his own initiative but he fulfilled it κατὰ τὴν χάριν τοῦ θεοῦ, pointing back to 5b ὡς ὁ κύριος ἔδωκεν.

With the use of this metaphor, Paul directs a stern warning to the teachers, picking thus up the theme of judgment from 8b based on the quality of their work.[106] The quality of their work is described in terms of the materials used for building; 'the builder must use fit materials and follow the plan of the architect and the building code.'[107] A σοφός builds in accordance and in compatibility with the value and stability of the foundation, which no one can replace.[108] Verse 13 then presents a list of various materials that builders use in construction.

Several points are important to grasp in order to bring out the full impact of Paul's warning. First, we must determine the nature of the variety of materials mentioned. There is general agreement among more recent commentators that though they seem to be presented in a scale of descending value, they do not have individual value.[109] Rather, the materials are best seen generally as different qualities of work.[110] Even so, it would not be pressing the metaphor too hard if we maintained that the materials could be grouped into two categories – perishable and imperishable – according to the outcome of judgment (1 Cor. 3.14-15).[111]

Second, we must determine the purpose for which these materials are

---

105   Lanci, *Temple*, p. 59, shows that the term ἀρχιτέκτων was 'a technical advisor, and usually not the designer of the building to be constructed ... the ancient equivalent of construction superintendents.' For a detailed analysis of the concept of master-builder see J. Duncan M. Derrett, 'Paul as Mater Builder', *EvQ* 69 (1997) 129–37. J. Shanor's study 'Paul as Master Builder: Construction Terms in First Corinthians', *NTS* 34 (1988) 461–71, also can shed light on the 'construction terms' used by Paul as compared to an inscription dated to the fourth century BC from Arcadian Tegea.

106   There are four views concerning the identity of the persons behind the indefinite pronouns: Peter, Apollos, all teachers, the entire Corinthian congregation. See Dybvad, 'Imitation and Gospel in First Corinthians', 150–52. It will be important to determine with more precision the referent in our discussion on the role of Apollos in the dissensions.

107   Garland, *1 Corinthians*, p. 114.

108   Cf. Fee, *First Corinthians*, pp. 139–40; and Lamp, *First Corinthians 1–4 in Light of Jewish Wisdom Traditions*, p. 181.

109   E.g., Fee, *First Corinthians*, p. 140. *Contra* Rosscup, 'A New Look at 1 Corinthians 3.12', 40–51, who concludes with saying that the various materials stand as symbols for a combination of things such as doctrine, character, activity, and motives.

110   Kuck, 'Paul and Pastoral Ambition', 177–78; Garland, *1 Corinthians*, p. 116.

111   Cf. Williams, 'Paul's Anti-Imperial "Discourse of the Cross"', 818; Schrage, *Der erste Brief*, 1.301; Hollander, 'The Testing by Fire of the Builders' Works', 93; and Thiselton, *First Corinthians*, p. 311.

mentioned.[112] Among the most often mentioned purposes is to remind people of the building of the tabernacle (cf. Exod. 25.3-7; 31.1-5; 35.32-33) and the temple (cf. 1 Chron. 22.14-16; 29.2; Pseudo-Philo *Bib. Ant.* 12.9: 11QT 3.5-7), anticipating thus the next imagery.[113] But the question is why would Paul wish the Corinthians to think of the materials that made up the tabernacle, for instance, and where do hay and straw fit in the construction? Likewise, Kuck's view that Paul seeks to emphasize the intrinsic value and durability of the 'construction materials' seems to be pressing the metaphor.[114] Most likely, the purpose for such a variety is simply to underscore the variety of qualities of work servants do and to advise the teachers to use wisdom so that their work may abide.[115]

Third, and most importantly, it is critical to determine the role of the fire as it relates to these materials and the reason Paul brings in his argument this image. Most commentators, rightfully so, detect in the terminology used by Paul in vv. 12–15 eschatological overtones. Ἡ ἡμέρα refers to the Old Testament 'Day of the Lord', which is characterized by 'public display' (φανερόν and δηλώσει), 'disclosure' (ἀποκαλύπτεται), 'fire' (τὸ πῦρ), 'reward' (μισθόν), and 'final salvation' (σωθήσεται). In the day of reckoning, the works of these teachers will become apparent by the instrumentality of the fire.[116] The fire will reveal the quality of their efforts.[117] Thus, the purpose of the fire is not to destroy (the normal effect of the eschatological fire cf. Jer. 43.12; *Sib Or* 3.53, 71–74, 618; *Apoc El.* 5.22-24; Jude 7; Rev. 18.8; 19.20; 21.8); nor to refine (cf. Isa. 1.24-26; Zech. 13.10; 1QH 5.15-16; Josephus, *A.J.* 20.166; *Herm Vis* 4.3.3-5), but to disclose. The result of this judgment is explained in negative and positive terms in the disjunctive εἰ clauses of vv. 14–15: the person whose works will remain will be rewarded and the person whose works will be destroyed will suffer loss and damage.[118]

---

112   See Garland, *1 Corinthians*, p. 116, for a summary of different view.

113   Esp. Fee, *First Corinthians*, pp. 140–1; also Lanci, *Temple*, p. 66.

114   Kuck, *Judgment*, p. 177; also Rosscup, 'A New Look at 1 Corinthians 3.12', 40.

115   Cf. e.g., Garland, *1 Corinthians*, p. 116.

116   Here we concur with Thiselton, *First Corinthians*, p. 313 who takes the 'works' as the subject of the middle/passive verb ἀποκαλύπτεται and not 'the Day' as Conzelmann, *1 Corinthians*, p. 76; Garland, *1 Corinthians*, p. 116; and Fee, *First Corinthians*, p. 142. This is not tautology, as some argue, for the second statement could function in an explanatory or epexegetical sense.

117   Thiselton, *First Corinthians*, pp. 312–13. Paul seems to have used the motif of the fire from Mal. 3.12-15. See J. Proctor, 'Fire in God's House: Influence of Malachi 3 in the NT', *JETS* 36 (1993) 9–14; also Williams, *The Wisdom of the Wise*, pp. 160–5. The idea of revelation of works and eschatological disclosure is a unique concept in Paul. Cf. Kuck, *Judgment*, pp. 179, 181.

118   Hollander, 'The Testing by Fire of the Builders' Works', 97, n. 35, interprets ζημιωθήσεται to mean 'he will be fined'. Fee, *First Corinthians*, p. 143, n. 43, however, argues that such a translation wrongly places the emphasis in the metaphor on works rather than on

What, then, is the purpose of Paul in using the analogy of the building combined with the eschatological fire which will test the work of each teacher? It seems that Paul aims primarily to warn these teachers to watch how they build, though more can be behind the use of the metaphor. He may be anticipating the clear injunction of 1 Cor. 4.1-5 not to judge. He may thus remind the Corinthians that only God's ultimate verdict will count, since only that Day will disclose the real quality of the work. Therefore any human evaluation is premature, or should we say with Paul, πρὸ καίρου (1 Cor. 4.5).

The third metaphor of the temple in 1 Cor. 3.16-17 particularizes the identity of the Corinthian community as God's building. It also carries forward the warning of watchfulness in regard to the quality of ministry found in the previous image, adding to it a sterner note. The sternness of the warning is due both to Paul's focus on the negative result of a ministry done for reasons of gaining honor and status (i.e., 'destruction') and also to his comparison of the church with the temple.[119] This analogy sets the Christian *ecclesia* apart from any secular and civic assembly, as being the only place on earth in which God dwells through his Spirit. The Christian community (not the individual as in 1 Cor. 6.19) is the *locus* of the Spirit's dwelling on earth making it a holy community.

The Spirit-ual identity of the Christian community prompts Paul to start with a serious question: Οὐκ οἴδατε. The question 'indicates both Paul's intensity of feeling and his belief that the principle at issue is axiomatic for the Christians and should not have escaped attention as a

---

fire. Paul does not mention the nature of the rewards though later (4.5) he does mention that it is in terms of praise or commendation, cf. Polhill, '"The Wisdom of God" and Factionalism', 335. Kuck, *Judgment*, pp. 169, 174, is right to argue against those who see in these verses a special level of judgment and rewards for apostolic laborers, though his intention is to show that these verses refer to all Christians. We think that though these verses do not teach special rewards for Christian teachers, we do believe that their immediate referent is the teachers. See also Ardel B. Caneday and Thomas R. Schreiner, *The Race Set Before Us: A Biblical Theology of Perseverance & Assurance* (Downers Grove: InterVarsity, 2001), for arguments against special rewards for teachers. As far as the loss, most commentators argue that it is not salvation though the idea of 'suffering loss' may be expanded on in the analogy of the temple as 'destruction.' This is however not likely since Paul does mention that such a man will escape 'by the skin of his teeth', cf. Witherington, *Conflict and Community in Corinth*, p. 134. The reward as well as the loss could be the praise received or denied, which will bring either honor or shame, in the Day of Judgment. For this possibility see 4.5, Phil. 2.14-16, 1 Thess. 2.19. More concretely, the praise for Paul would mean that those he invested in will be with him, and shame would conversely mean 'running in vain', his greatest fear (cf. Gal. 2.2; 4.11; 1 Thess. 3.5).

119 Some commentators seek to make a distinction between ναός (i.e., the inner sanctuary) and ἱερόν (i.e., the precincts of the temple). Thus, by choosing the term ναός, Paul seeks to amplify the seriousness of any act done against it. However, Lanci, *Temple*, pp. 91–2, rightly shows the ambivalence of ancient temple terminology, lending any narrowing of the meaning and reference improbable.

cardinal element in the community's thinking.'[120] This question seems to imply that the Corinthians have not thought through all the implications of their identity for life in the church. According to Pickett, 'The community of those who were "being saved" was counter-cultural inasmuch as its comprehension of reality and concomitant norms and values were expected to be at variance with those of the larger society.'[121] But they, who were supposed to be God's alternative to the secular city of Corinth, were in danger of reducing God's temple to nothing but a means of enhancing their personal status and increasing their own honor.[122] Such a thing God will not allow.

Thus, with the image of the church as God's temple, Paul picks up the issue of judgment, warning those who are in the process of destroying the church. Thiselton points to the play on words with the two uses of the verb φθείρω – defile/destroy, Paul seeking to emphasize the seriousness of the 'crime.'[123] In fact, Paul makes use here of the *lex talionis*, which communicates the idea of 'the destruction of the destroyer'.[124] The threat thus takes the warning of 1 Cor. 3.10-15 a step further.[125] Fee, however, is right to state that, 'The threat which is real is at the same time turned into an invitation for them to become what in fact they are by the grace of God: "God's holy temple in Corinth."'[126] But this would mean

---

120 Thiselton, *First Corinthians*, p. 316. Lanci, *Temple*, pp. 119–20, following Wilhelm Wuellner, 'Paul as Pastor: The Function of Rhetorical Questions in First Corinthians', in *L'apôtre Paul*, 71, argues that the question usually introduces a topic which is later developed throughout the rest of the letter.

121 Picket, *The Cross in Corinth*, pp. 66–7.

122 Garland, *First Corinthians*, p. 121, is right to observe that Paul does not mention how the temple is destroyed, but the context suggests the issues of division, boasting, personality allegiance, etc. See Mitchell, *Reconciliation*, p. 103, who cites as support Cicero, *Amic.* 7.23.

123 Thiselton, *First Corinthians*, p. 317. Lanci, *Temple*, pp. 67–68, has pointed out that the verb φθείρω cannot mean 'eschatological destruction' (at least not in regard to the temple) but damage or ruination (cf. 1 Cor. 15.33; 2 Cor. 7.2; 11.3 with the exception of 2 Pet. 2.12/Jude 10; see also the extra-biblical references he gives to support his view). The normal word for 'destruction', it is argued, is the compound verb διαφθείρω. Others claim that it refers to a destruction not of the church but of the church's unity, cf. e.g., Kuck, *Judgment*, pp. 187–8; Mitchell, *Reconciliation*, p. 103. Barrett, *First Corinthians*, p. 91, reminds us that there have been local churches that have gone out of existence for different reasons.

124 E. Käsemann, 'Sentences of Holy Law in the NT', in *New Testament Questions of Today* (London: SCM, 1969), 67. F. F. Bruce, *I and II Corinthians* (NCB; Grand Rapids: Eerdmans, 1971), p. 45, uses the terminology of 'the punishment fits the crime.'

125 Kuck, 'Paul and Pastoral Ambition', 179, rightly states that, 'Although work of varying quality will be accepted by God some kinds of work are out of bounds.' See also K. I. Yinger, *Paul, Judaism, and Judgment according to Deeds* (SNTMS, 105; Cambridge: Cambridge University Press, 1999), p. 220.

126 Fee, *First Corinthians*, p. 149.

readjusting their view of the church and of its teachers, which, in turn, would result in ceasing their boasting of teachers which led to dissensions.

This has been his aim all through this segment of text (1 Cor. 3.5-17) as he made use of the three metaphors: the field, the building, and the temple. The thinking of the Corinthians concerning teachers in the church was secular (1 Cor. 3.3-4). With the first metaphor Paul tries to take the focus off himself and the other teachers and to make God prominent. God chooses whom he uses; he creates the Christian community; and he is the one who will judge the quality of each teacher's work. The teachers are mere servants. With the second metaphor Paul warns the teachers to watch how they conduct their ministry, because there will come a Day of reckoning, when the quality of their work will be tested by fire to determine its compatibility with the enduring foundation, who is Jesus Christ. With the third metaphor, Paul pushes even further the issue of the accountability before God. Due to the identity of the church as God's holy temple, the Corinthians are in danger of being 'destroyed' because of their factionalism. Thus, the Corinthians must change their view concerning the teachers in the church, from people with status, who are a means to honor enhancement, to servants with a menial role. They also must take into account the true identity of the church. On the other hand, the teachers must take care to build in concordance with the foundation. Thus, at the root of the divisions were a worldly view of church leadership and an inadequate view of the nature of the church. Such an inadequate thinking precludes ecclesiastical unity.

The second unit (1 Cor. 3.18-23), Collins observes, forms a kind of *inclusio* to give a preliminary closure to the argument of 1 Cor. 1.10–3.23, alluding to Paul and Apollos, wisdom and folly, and boasting.[127] The emphasis is clearly on conveying to the Corinthians that they should beware of not glorying in men (i.e., preachers) under the guise of wisdom, not only because such wisdom proves to be foolishness, but also because the teachers belong to the church. In this segment, then, Paul brings together the twin towers of the Corinthians' problem: wisdom and dissensions caused by preferences for various teachers.[128]

Paul begins this unit with an exhortation to the Corinthians to beware of self-deception (Μηδεὶς ἑαυτὸν ἐξαπατάτω). He explains this danger in terms of what appears (δοκεῖ) as σοφία, recalling the central motif of 1 Cor. 1.18–2.16. Presumably he is referring to both the teachers who considered themselves 'wise' according to the wisdom τοῦ αἰῶνος τούτου using perishable materials to build upon the foundation, and, more precisely, to the Corinthians who thought of themselves as wise by their

---

127 Collins, *1 Corinthians*, pp. 162–3. See also Furnish, 'Theology in 1 Corinthians', 84; Kuck, *Judgment*, p. 188; and Fee, *First Corinthians*, p. 150.

128 Cf. Polhill ' "The Wisdom of God" and Factionalism', 335.

allegiance to teachers. Such wisdom is foolishness from God's perspective, for it will ultimately perish.[129] Therefore, if one is to be considered truly wise, Paul advises him to become first a fool, that is, to view things from God's perspective (i.e., from the perspective of the reversals created by the cross) and discard all worldly pretensions to wisdom.

Paul buttresses his exhortation with quotations of two Old Testament passages.[130] The first, from Job 5.13 (the only use of Job in the New Testament), communicates the same idea as 1 Cor. 3.17: God catches the crafty with their own craftiness. Ironically, Garland points out, 'this quotation proves its point, since it comes form Eliphaz, whose "wise" counsel is ultimately discredited.'[131] The second quotation from Ps. 94.11 asserts that God knows the thoughts τῶν σοφῶν; Paul adds, that they are futile. Both quotations thus function as a warning of the danger of self-deception.

Paul's advice to the Corinthians to become fools in order to become wise takes on a specific aspect (argument from general to specific): μηδεὶς καυχάσθω ἐν ἀνθρώποις. With this command, Paul reveals the nature of the Corinthians' wisdom: boasting of men (i.e., teachers). Such boasting is contrary to the identity of the Corinthians as chosen as a result of the 'foolishness of God', an experience that removes all grounds for boasting in people to the degree that the Corinthians are left with only one object of boasting: God (cf. 1 Cor. 1.29, 31).

Besides the quotations from the Old Testament, Paul brings in another reason that precludes any boasting in people: πάντα γὰρ ὑμῶν ἐστιν. Among the things which the Corinthians possess (reminiscent of 1 Cor. 1.5) are also the teachers over which they formed 'parties.' Thus, Paul turns on their head their allegiances to teachers expressed in their slogans 'I belong to Paul', for instance, by asserting that the truth is that 'I, Paul, and the other teachers belong to you.'[132] Teachers work in the service (διακονοί) of the church so that the Corinthians cannot claim to belong to them as if these teachers had been crucified for them (cf. 1 Cor. 1.16). Rather, Paul concludes by setting the right order in God's economy: the

---

129   Fee, *First Corinthians*, p. 152, rightly notices that Paul states here the reverse of 1.18-25. There Paul argued that the 'wisdom of God is foolishness to the world'; here 'the wisdom of this world is foolishness to God.' The same point is made but this time from God's perspective.

130   See Williams, *The Wisdom of the Wise*, pp. 321–30, for a thorough analysis of the citations in their original context and early Jewish literature.

131   Garland, *1 Corinthians*, p. 123. See also Fee, *First Corinthians*, p. 152, n. 7.

132   Thiselton, *First Corinthians*, p. 325. Bruce Winter has rightly observed that by reversing the concept of 'belonging', Paul was distancing himself from the cultural conventions that governed the relationship of secular disciples and their elitist teacher. See his *After Paul Left Corinth: The Influence of Secular Ethics and Social Change* (Grand Rapids: Eerdmans, 2001), esp. ch. 2.

teachers (and 'all things' enumerated in 1 Cor. 3.22) belong to the Corinthian church, and the church, in turn, is under the jurisdiction of God-in-Christ (as in 1 Cor. 3.9 – θεοῦ γεώργιον θεοῦ οἰκοδομή ἐστε). Thus Paul directs 'their focus one final time to the Creator, who is God over all.'[133] This should put an end to any divisions caused by glorying in people. Kuck concludes:

> The fact that they all together belong to Christ keeps their Christian liberty from pulling them apart in all sorts of individual directions through judging and boasting ... The factional strife in Corinth has been central at least in part by the desire of people to be judged as wise in the eyes of the culture, and to judge others in the church by that same worldly standard ... One theme stands out clearly: God as judge.[134]

Thus, as Kuck remarks, 'it all comes down to the question of who is competent to evaluate a servant of God ... Paul answers that question resoundingly and climactically in 1 Cor. 4.1–5. Only one has that right and ability, and that is the Lord.'[135] Thus, this third unit of the section seems to bring elements of the previous two smaller units together.[136] For instance, the ὑπηρέτας καὶ οἰκονόμους of 1 Cor. 4.1 describing the apostles surely reminds the reader of the διάκονοι of 1 Cor. 3.5 and the συνεργοί of 3.9. Also, the judgment theme in 1 Cor. 4.3-5 is a further elaboration of the judgment as discussed in 1 Cor. 3.12-17 and hinted at in 1 Cor. 2.14-16. The connection of this unit with previous discussion is also seen in the catch-word τὸ μυστήριον of 1 Cor. 4.1 as in 2.1, 7 and in the concessive οὕτως which indicates that this paragraph takes further the thought of the previous paragraph.

Paul dwells a little longer on the role of the teachers (ἡμᾶς) by describing them as ὑπηρέτας and οἰκονόμους. The first term means an assistant. Rengstorf makes the following useful distinction from the other terms Paul uses for servant: 'The ὑπηρέτης is distinguished from the δοῦλος, always used for slave, by the fact that he is free and can in some cases claim a due reward for his services', and from the διάκονος in that 'he willingly learns his task and goal from another who is over him.'[137] On the other hand, the second term, though still a servile term, is used for 'the chief household slave' who is entrusted with overseeing all the operations of the house and gives an account directly to the owner. He is also the

---

133 Fee, *First Corinthians*, p. 153.
134 Kuck, *Judgment*, p. 196. See also Thiselton, *First Corinthians*, p. 329.
135 Kuck, 'Paul and Pastoral Ambition', 179.
136 Smit, 'Search for Coherence', 238; also Fee, *First Corinthians*, p. 158.
137 K. H. Rengstorf, ὑπηρέτης, *TDNT* 8.532-33.

administrator of the affairs of the house and is expected to do his job with responsibility as instructed.[138]

By the use of these terms to describe the teachers and leaders of the church, Paul again challenges the Corinthians' worldly view of their teachers as free, high-status people, who bestow benevolences on those of lesser status.[139] Instead, Paul argues, they are mere administrators or stewards of the μυστηρίων θεοῦ (i.e., the gospel of Christ crucified as in 1 Cor. 2.6-16) who are accountable to God for the way they fulfill their God-assigned roles. Such a view of ministry as 'an inverted pyramid, where leaders are enslaved, belong to the community, and must serve it from below',[140] must have startled Paul's readers.

But Paul, in using these terms to describe the teachers as fulfilling servile roles, also brings out two other aspects of ministry. First, as an οἰκονόμος, he is accountable only to his master, God.[141] Paul will develop this idea in the remaining verses of this segment. Second, the only requirement of the servant of God is ἵνα πιστός τις εὑρεθῇ. The criteria of faithfulness or trustworthiness by which one such steward is to be judged is in stark contrast to the world's expectation of their teachers, that is, σοφία as eloquent speech, leadership skills, and so on.[142] With these criteria, Paul reintroduces the issue of the evaluation of the quality of teachers' workmanship, except that this time Paul focuses solely on himself. Speaking about his examination is almost like an afterthought;[143] it is as if Paul realized that, in warning the teachers (i.e., builders) of their accountability to God in that Day (1 Cor. 3.10-17), he excluded himself from that judgment since he was the one who laid the foundation.[144] He rectifies this by turning to the issue of the evaluation of his own ministry.

---

138   See, Thiselton, *First Corinthians*, p. 336; he translates the term 'estate manager.' For the religious background of οἰκονόμος see J. Reumann, 'Servants of God – Pre-Christian Religious Application of OIKONOMOS in Greek', *JBL* 77 (1958) 339–49; and *idem*, 'οἰκονομία-Terms in Paul in Comparison with Lucan *Heilsgeschichte*', *NTS* 13 (1966/67) 147–67.

139   It is possible that the two terms used by Paul in 4.1, and especially the second one, to refer to 'a person of elevated social status', in light of the fact that Erastus is described as οἰκονόμος τῆς πόλεως in Rom. 16.23. Cf. Theissen, *Social Setting*, pp. 75–83. What is important to keep in mind is that Paul is employing this terminology here not for the purpose of presenting himself as a high-status person, but as one working under the authority of another.

140   Witherington, *Conflict and Commuity*, p. 145. More on the social context follows in ch. 3.

141   Cf. Fee, *First Corinthians*, pp. 156, 158; and Polhill, 'The Wisdom of God and Factionalism', 336.

142   Thiselton, *First Corinthians*, p. 336.

143   Cf. Dickerson, 'Apollos in Acts and First Corinthians', 119, following Fee, *First Corinthians*, p. 154, who notes that 3.18-23 comes close to a doxology.

144   *Contra* Kuck, *Judgment*, pp. 175–6.

This emphasis on his ministry will continue throughout this chapter in spite of the use of plural personal pronouns.

He begins by underscoring the inadequacy of human judges, something at which he already hinted in the use of the three metaphors. According to Paul, both the humans and their courts (1 Cor. 4.3),[145] as well as one's own consciousness (1 Cor. 4.3a-4b)[146] are incompetent to pass a final verdict on the quality of the performance of his ministry. This argument bolsters his conclusion to which he has been building up starting with 1 Cor. 3.5, namely that God's judgment is the only judgment that counts, by which anyone is justified. The reason for this is that he is in the service of another, and what his master thinks is what counts. Thus Paul's concern is not so much with the results of human appraisal, because, even if they are positive, they do not definitively 'acquit' or 'vindicate' him (ἐν τούτῳ δεδικαίωμαι). They are of little or no consequence whatsoever, since 'the case is still pending.'[147] His concern is with how God will weigh his efforts, because only God will expose the 'individual's true colors.'[148] Thiselton asserts that, 'Paul does not therefore advocate a thick-skinned indifference to public opinion; his point is a different one, namely, its fallibility, relativity, and limits which make it an unreliable guide on which to depend', in comparison to God's penetrating judgment.[149]

The application is straightforward: ὥστε μὴ πρὸ καιροῦ τι κρίνετε ἕως ἂν ἔλθῃ ὁ κύριος.[150] Any human evaluation of one's ministry is premature (πρὸ καιροῦ)[151] and therefore should await the definitive verdict of God which he will give at his coming. Paul now specifies the reward alluded to in 1 Cor. 3.8 and 3.14 in terms of praise. Praise was one of the highest goals within Greco-Roman society, for praise bestows honor, which in turn enhances one's status in society. There were mutual benefits in terms

---

145   ἀνθρωπίνης ἡμέρας ('a day appointed by a human court') is contrasted with ἡ ἡμέρα ('the Day') of 3.13.

146   See Thiselton, *First Corinthians*, p. 340, for a discussion on human conscience. Paul does not reject the spirit of discernment and the role of the spirit-enlightened conscience, as he makes this clear in many places in his epistles. What he rejects is the right and ability to pronounce a definitive verdict. See Polhill, 'The Wisdom of God and Factionalism', 336.

147   Thiselton, *First Corinthians*, p. 341, quotes Jonathan Edwards.

148   Garland, *1 Corinthians*, p. 128.

149   Thiselton, *First Corinthians*, pp. 341–2.

150   Fee, *First Corinthians*, p. 163, suggests that in light of the Corinthians situation this injunction is best translated: 'So then, stop reaching a verdict on anything before the appointed time.' This strong imperative should not be taken to mean that on moral issues they should withhold judgment (cf. 5.12; 6.5).

151   See Thiselton, *First Corinthians*, p. 342, for translating πρὸ καιροῦ as 'the proper time' or 'favorable time' following O. Cullmann, *Christ and Time* (ET; 2d ed.; London: SCM, 1951), pp. 37–50.

of status and honor, when a disciple offered public praise to his master.[152]
Paul thus concludes his argument on the teachers' evaluation by
reinterpreting one of the values of the Corinthian society: the praising
of a teacher that counts is not from humans (i.e., the congregation) but
from God. With this Paul seeks to put an end to the Corinthians'
appraisal of teachers that led to boasting in preferred teachers, which in
turn led to dissensions in the church.

All through this section (1 Cor. 3.5–4.5) Paul has been laboring to
convince the Corinthians to give up any premature examination of
teachers that has led them to choose sides and have preferences. He set out
to show the inappropriateness of their allegiances in three steps. First, he
presents the menial role that God has assigned to these teachers by using
servile terms (διάκονος, συνέργος, ὑπηρέτης, and οἰκονόμος). Such a way
of describing their work takes the focus off the teachers and places the
emphasis on the importance of God. Their role is secondary to God, and
this is made clear in the use of the three metaphors (i.e., the field, the
building, and the temple). Second, the teachers belong to the Christian
community and not vice versa. God has set an order by which the
Corinthians occupy the middle position between the teachers and God-in-
Christ. Third, the teachers are responsible and accountable only to their
master, God, for the way in which they fulfill their assigned role. They are
to do so with faithfulness, seeking to build in accordance with the
foundation, who is Jesus Christ. This accountability to God implies that
the quality of their workmanship will be revealed in that Day, when the
only legitimate and valid verdict will be given by God. Allo concludes: if
Paul himself held reserve about his work 'in spite of his untroubled
conscience, his apostolic illumination, and heavenly revelations, how
much more should the Corinthians ... abstain from making precipitous
and imprudent judgments on a matter which certainly went beyond their
superficial spirits as "little infants in Christ" (1 Cor. 3.1-4)?'[153]

In all three steps of his arguments, Paul overtly or indirectly drives
home the point of the inadequacy of their evaluation of teachers. The
reasons are that they have too high a view of teachers (1 Cor. 3.5-17); that
their evaluation is done in accordance with the worldly standards of
wisdom (1 Cor. 3.18-23); and that the only appraisal that counts is that of
the divine tribunal at the appointed time (1 Cor. 4.1-5). Jouette Bassler is
thus right to state that:

> Paul had two serious problems to address – a general overvaluation of
> human leadership in the community and a criticism or undervaluation

---

152 See, David deSilva, *Honor, Patronage, Kinship, and Purity: Unlocking New
Testament Culture* (Downer Grove: InterVarsity, 2000), pp. 24–27; and Kuck, 'Paul and
Pastoral Ambition', 179. See Ch. 3 below:

153 Allo, *Première Épitre*, p. 70, quoted by Thiselton, *First Corinthians*, p. 344.

(by some) of his own ministry and gospel...Paul resolved this dilemma by focusing on the servant ministry of the apostles. As mere *servants* of God they are not to be evaluated above their master (3.5-9), but as servants *of God* they are answerable only to their master and not to human critics (4.1-5).[154]

The Fourth Section: 1 Cor. 4.6-21

The last major section (1 Cor. 4.6-21) of this first unit of the letter consists of two smaller units. The first unit, 1 Cor. 4.6-13, begins with a transitional verse in which Paul refers back to the previous discussion bringing it to a close. This verse contains some of the most notoriously difficult phrases to interpret in the Corinthian correspondence such as the meaning of the verb μετεσχημάτισα εἰς and of the phrase μὴ ὑπὲρ ἃ γέγραπται. Given the importance of unlocking the meaning of these statements (esp. of μετεσχημάτισα) for the entire argument that Paul has constructed up until this point, the challenge to interpret them will have to await resolution till the fourth chapter in this work.[155] For now it suffices to mention that regardless of how one interprets these statements, they say something about Paul and Apollos and the purpose for which their names were mentioned, particularly in 1 Cor. 3.5–4.5. In this respect, ταῦτα may refer to everything that has been said beginning with 1 Cor. 1.10, but no doubt points back to at least the previous major section where Paul discusses the role of the apostles and the inappropriateness of judging their ministry. Regardless of how far the reference should be pushed, it is clear that 1 Cor. 1.10–3.4, at least, lays the foundation for what is said in 1 Cor. 3.5–4.5, and therefore cannot be neglected.[156] In 1 Cor. 4.6 Paul gives the reason for such discussion: ἵνα μὴ εἷς ὑπὲρ τοῦ ἑνός φυσιοῦσθε κατὰ τοῦ ἑτέρου. Consequently, Paul's purpose of the discussion about himself and Apollos has been in order to deflate the Corinthians' puffed-upness

---

154 Bassler, '1 Cor. 4.1-5', *Int* 44 (1990) 179–83, esp. 80. See also Johannes Munck, 'The Church without factions: Studies in 1 Corinthians', in *Paul and the Salvation of Mankind* (London: SCM, 1959), p. 157; Thiselton, *First Corinthians*, p. 108; Garland, *1 Corinthians*, pp. 38–39; and Rupert Davies, *Studies in 1 Corinthians* (London: Epworth, 1962), pp. 41–8, quoted by Thiselton, *First Corinthians*, pp. 196–97.

155 For a detailed presentation of different views regarding the meaning of the two phrases see Thiselton, *First Corinthians*, pp. 348–56. For a survey of the meaning of μὴ ὑπὲρ ἃ γέγραπται see Ronald L. Tyler, 'The History of the Interpretation of μὴ ὑπὲρ ἃ γέγραπται in 1 Corinthians 4.6', *ResQ* 43 (2001) 243–52; and Garland, *1 Corinthians*, pp. 133–6.

156 Cf. Fitzgerald, *Cracks in an Earthen Vessel*, p. 120, n. 13; and Brian Dodd, *Paul's Paradigmatic "I": Personal Example as Literary Strategy* (JSNTSS, 177; Sheffield: JSOTPress, 1999), 45. Robertson and Plummer, *First Corinthians*, p. 80; Fee, *First Corinthians*, p. 165; Kuck, *Judgment*, pp. 210–11; J. S. Vos, 'Der μετασχηματισμός in 1 Kor 4.6', *ZNW* 86 (1995): 154–72; and Wolff, *Der erste Brief*, p. 84, limit the reference only to 3.5-4.5. Most commentators, however, extend the reference all the way to 1.10. See, *inter alia*, Thiselton, *First Corinthians*, p. 348; and Fiore, '"Covert Allusion"', 94.

with teachers, which was the result of comparing one teacher against the other. Such boasting and comparison were the cause of dissensions.

Beginning with v. 7, Paul explains the reason why they should not be puffed up. By a series of questions and by use of irony, the Corinthians are confronted with the roots of their dissensions: the desire for honor and status. Paul chains together three rhetorical questions that point one more time to their status as recipients of God's grace and not as inherently deserving or owning anything by right.[157] The Corinthians' boasting of teachers, Paul argues, has been based on a fundamentally defective perspective – viewing themselves as owners/patrons rather than recipients.

The Corinthians' inflated view of themselves is further characterized by Paul by means of hyperboles and irony in v. 8: ἤδη κεκορεσμένοι ἐστὲ ἤδη ἐπλουτήσατε, ἐκβασιλεύσατε.[158] Paul here characterizes the Corinthians as they saw themselves and not the way he views them (Rev. 3.17).[159] Thus, in their own view, the Corinthians have acquired a superior status (i.e., 'kings') giving them the right to be puffed up on behalf of their teachers. But in Paul's view their superior attitude is misguided. This is brought out not only by the use of the adverb 'already' (ἤδη) but also by

---

157   The first question–'Who differentiates you?'–can be interpreted both negatively and positively. Negatively, it would suggest a rebuke of the Corinthians for assuming the role as judges of someone's servant. See Marshall, *Enmity in Corinth*, p. 205; Kuck, *Judgment*, p. 215; Fee, *First Corinthians*, p. 171; Winter, *Philo and Paul*, p. 198. Positively, it would suggest that Paul argues that what makes the Corinthians special is attributable to God. See, e.g., Thiselton, *First Corinthians*, p. 356, who refers to the Church Fathers for this interpretation. It is probably best to view both aspects as being true and so hold them together, thus maintaining the ambiguity of the question as something intended by Paul. The second question, 'What do you have that you have not received?' would thus follow the train of thought, emphasizing God's grace in giving them everything (especially their teachers).

158   Fee, *First Corinthians*, p. 172, notices the argument of Paul in this verse constructed on staccato sentences seen in the use of asyndeton. See Smit, 'Search for Coherence', 239, for the stylistic figures in this segment, such as anaphora, homoioteleuton, polysyndetic enumeration, etc. 'Being satiated' was traditionally associated with ὕβρις, as were the other two terms. See Marshall, *Enmity in Corinth*, p. 208; Pogoloff, *LOGOS AND SOPHIA*, pp. 228–30. 'Being rich', as with the previous characteristic, was associated with the idea of a 'king'. The 'king' was the client's word for a rich patron, having thus a sociological connotation. See Dale B. Martin, *Slavery as Salvation: The Metaphor of Slavery in Pauline Christianity* (New Haven: Yale University Press, 1990), p. 210. See the discussion on *hybris* by Pickett, *The Cross in Corinth*, pp. 44–8. Garland, *1 Corinthians*, p. 138, however, claims that Paul's intention in the use of these terms is 'simply to censure the Corinthians' pride and arrogance' (cf. Philo, *Virt.* 30.161-74).

159   We have already mentioned that the verb πλουτέω is used in 1.5 in a positive sense. There Paul acknowledges the Corinthians' abundance in χαρισμάτα. Here Paul critiques the Corinthians for 'hav[ing] allowed the gifts [which include the teachers; cf. 12.27-31] to become a sign of status and a source of dissension. They should have humbly and gratefully received'. See Fee, *First Corinthians*, p. 170.

the use of ὄφελόν.[160] Paul rebukes the Corinthians that they too quickly want the glory, without understanding that glory comes in the form of the cross.

Thus the reason why their boasting is illegitimate is that they have forgotten one crucial aspect: glory is stamped by the cross.[161] This cruciform lifestyle and thinking have yet to characterize the Corinthians. Thus, again, Paul reminds the Corinthians of the necessity to adjust their thinking in accordance with the reversals brought about by the cross. That this has not yet happened is proven by the fact that the apostles, even if they wished, cannot share in their exalted position. Paul, in other words, confronts the Corinthians with the impossibility of being exalted while those through whom they have been enriched are so lowly. If the apostles cannot rise to the Corinthians' presumed status, then the Corinthians will have to assume the lowly status of the apostles. In what follows, then, Paul will contrast the Corinthians' exalted self-perception with the apostles' tribulations, which point to a low-status people. Garland asserts: 'By contrasting the cross-centered lifestyles of the apostles with the Corinthians' vainglory, Paul hopes to supplant their egotism with the wisdom of the cross.'[162]

160   According to Fee, *First Corinthians*, p. 174, n. 45; and Thiselton, *First Corinthians*, p. 359, ὄφελόν expresses and unfulfilled wish. Thiselton interprets Paul's critique of the Corinthians' self-perseption in terms of 'overrealized eschatology.' See his 'Realized Eschatology at Corinth', *NTS* 24 (1977–78) 510–26; *idem, First Corinthians*, pp. 358–9. He is followed in this interpretation, *inter alia*, by Schrage, *Der erste Brief*, pp. 338–40, who speaks of a premature triumphalism; Barrett, *First Corinthians*, p. 109. Against this view, Garland, *First Corinthians*, pp. 138–9, following Kuck, *Judgment*, pp. 214–19, argues that Paul counters the Corinthians arrogance not with eschatology but with ethics, the problem being 'not that they think that the judgment lies behind them, but that they have not given any thought to God's judgment at all' (p. 138). The concepts of wealth and reigning appear in contexts unrelated to eschatology (cf. Wis. 6.20; 7.8, 11; 8.14, 18; Philo, *Leg.* 1.13; 3.56; *Heir* 6.27; *Abr.* 44.261; *Virt.* 39: 212–19). In light of this, Garland translates ἤδη with 'so quickly', 'so easily', as opposed to 'slowly' and 'arduously', and not with 'already', as opposed to 'not yet'. See also Hall, *Unity*, p. 79ff; also Pickett, *The Cross in Corinth*, pp. 44–46; and Richard Hays, 'The Conversion of the Imagination: Scripture and Eschatology in 1 Corinthians', *NTS* 45 (1999) 396. For a distinct interpretation of the Corinthians' high status at the time of the writing of 1 Corinthians compared to their low status at the time of conversion see Christopher M. Tuckett, 'Paul, Scripture and Ethics: Some Reflections', *NTS* 46 (2000) 403–24, an interpretation based on the LXX text of the song of Hannah (1 Sam. 2.1-10).

161   This is not the same as saying, 'through cross to crown.' *Contra* W. Schrage, 'Das Verständnis des Todes Jesu Christi in Neuen Testament', in *Das Kreuz Jesu Christi als Grund des Heils* (E. Bizer et al., eds.; STAEKU, 3; Gütersloh: Mohn, 1967), 61, 65. See Ernst Käsemann, *Perspectives on Paul* (Philadelphia: Fortress, 1971), pp. 55–6.

162   Garland, *1 Corinthians*, p. 139. The comparison or σύγκρισις of people with illustrious examples is a standard rhetorical practice in epideictic rhetoric. See Mitchell, *Reconciliation*, 219. Scott Hafemann, *Suffering and the Spirit: An Exegetical study of II Cor. 2.14-3.3 within the Corinthian Correspondence* (Tübingen: Mohr, 1986), pp. 57–8, takes the first person plurals in 4.9-13 as literary or epistolary conventions with which Paul refers to himself alone.

Paul presents the apostles as being 'last' (ἐσχάτους) in their social ranking,[163] as 'near death' (ἐπιθανατίους) because of persecution, and 'a spectacle to the world' (θέατρον), that is, on display for the whole cosmos.[164] Each term seems to be developed by means of other sets of terms in the remaining verses. But what seems to be more obvious is Paul's intention to use these descriptions as a stark contrast to the Corinthians' exalted status. Fee rightly argues that the Corinthians were presumably embarrassed over Paul's lack of status (not to mention his lack of eloquence and wisdom). So for Paul to emphasize the cosmic proportions of his low status may have been a final blow to their pride.[165]

To bring in more clearly the contrast between the apostles and the arrogant Corinthians, Paul uses three more characteristics which recall the kind of people God chooses (1 Cor. 1.26) – μωροί, ἀσθενεῖς ἄτιμοι. Again, these terms have sociological connotations as the people of lowest status, and therefore the most despised among society.[166] Garland observes: 'If the Corinthians, however, are "wise", "strong," and "honored," they must be kowtowing to the world's standards, which brings into question whether they are truly Christ's.'[167]

Paul then, by means of a succinct enumeration, lists six hardships which the apostles endure on account of Christ: πεινῶμεν, διψῶμεν, γυμνιτεύομεν, κολαφιζόμεθα, ἀστατοῦμεν, κοπιῶμεν.[168] The first three

163   Cf. Fitzgerald, *Cracks in an Earthen Vessel*, p. 136, n. 58; Theissen, *Social Setting*, pp. 72–3.

164   Garland, *1 Corinthians*, p. 140, contends that these terms may draw on images from gladiatorial combats or from the procession of a conquering general at the end of which prisoners of war would be executed. See also Thiselton, *First Corinthians*, pp. 359–60, who refers to *Bel* 31 for the use of the word ἐπιθανατίους to mean those thrown to the lions. Welborn, *Paul, the Fool of Christ*, p. 3, however shows how each term used in this catalogue of hardships is taken from the world of the mime in which a person played the fool (cf. pp. 50–86). For a balanced view see Fee, *First Corinthians,* p. 175.

165   Fee, *First Corinthians*, p. 175.

166   Cf. Theissen, *Social Setting*, pp. 72–3.

167   Garland, *1 Corinthians*, p. 141.

168   Fee, *First Corinthians*, p. 178, rightly points to the unity of vv. 11–13, as they begin and end on the same note: ἄχρι τῆς ἄρτι/ἕως ἄρτι. In these verses (including v. 10) we have what some have termed a 'catalogue of hardships' or '*peristasis* catalogue.' Thiselton, *First Corinthians*, pp. 365–8, offers a good summary of three different views. The first is that of Fitzgerald, *Cracks in an Earthen Vessel*, esp. pp. 117–48, supplemented by the study of M. Schiefer Ferrari, *Die Sprache des Leids in den paulinischen Peristasenkatalogen* (Stuttgart: Katholisches Bibelwerk, 1991). Fitzgerald argues for a Cynic-Stoic background of this catalogue. In light of this, Paul borrows the rhetoric of the Hellenistic sage, whose trials befit his wisdom. By contrast, any claim to wisdom (such as that of the Corinthians) divorced from hardships is inappropriate. Power, thus, manifests itself in adversity. J. Ruef, *Paul's First Letter to Corinth* (Philadelphia: Westminster, 1971), p. 34, as referenced by William David Spencer, 'The Power in Paul's Teaching (1 Cor. 4.9-20)', *JETS* 32 (1989) 551–61 (54), also argues that the catalogue of hardships is Paul's means to establish his apostolic

images describe a destitute person, who has no food, no drink, and no clothes. This is in stark contrast to the Corinthians' self-perception as lacking nothing. The last three images build on the concept of poverty by describing the condition of a slave, who is abused, a wanderer, and one who does hard manual labor. This description is again meant to be contrasted to the Corinthians' self-perception as patrons, who have their own clients, and for whose status thus manual labor is unfitting.[169] All these six terms, together with the previous three, seem to expand on the concept of being 'last' in terms of social ranking. The last three also seem to make the transition to the next three terms that describe abuse.

Paul explains next how the apostles respond to different kinds of abuses, presumably insisting on the concept of 'near-death' experiences. Though reviled (λοιδορούμενοι), persecuted (διωκόμενοι), and slandered (δυσφημούμενοι), they respond with blessing (εὐλογοῦμεν), endurance (ἀνεχόμεθα), and conciliation (παρακαλοῦμεν). Commentators have rightly observed that the apostles' responses are parallel to Christ's.[170]

At last, Paul concludes this catalogue of hardships with two terms that sum up the world's opinion of apostles. These terms seem to explicate what Paul means by the concept of 'being on display before the whole cosmos' of v. 9 since he uses the same word κόσμος. He describes the apostles as 'the scum which clings to surfaces unwanted or the filthy residue' (περικαθάρμα) and as 'the scrapings from everyone's shoes' (περίψημα).[171]

Paul, in this section, then, seeks to contrast the self-exalted view of the Corinthians with the self-deprecated view of the apostles, which is more

---

authority. Karl Plank, *Paul and the Irony of Affliction* (Atlanta: Scholars Press, 1987), esp. pp. 33–70, represents a second opinion. He argues that in 4.8-13, Paul embarks on a 'rhetoric of irony' which discloses the absurdity of the Corinthians' claim to be reigning while the apostles are the 'scum of the earth'. Unlike Fitzgerald, Plank rightly relates power to the paradox of the cross. This last point is the main emphasis of a third view concerning the catalogue of hardships, represented by W. Schrage, 'Leid, Kreuz und Eschaton. Die Peristasenkataloge als Merkmale paulinischer theologia crucis und Eschatologie', *ET* 34 (1974): 141–75; and K. T. Kleinknecht, *Der leidende Gerechtfertigte: Die alttestamentlich-jüdische Tradition vom leidenden Gerechten" und ihre Rezeption bei Paulus* (WUNT, 2/13; Tübingen: Mohr, 1984), esp. pp. 208–304. Paul thus identifies himself with the afflictions of Jesus.

169 See E. Coye Still, III, 'Divisions over Leaders and Food Offered to Idols: The Parallel Thematic Structures of 1 Corinthians 4.6-21 and 8.1-11.1', *TynBul* 55 (2004) 17–46 (22–26), who argues for the structural prominence of Paul's manual labor in the hardship catalogue.

170 E.g., Fee, *First Corinthians*, pp. 179–80; Garland, *1 Corinthians*, p. 141.

171 Cf. Thiselton, *First Corinthians*, pp. 364–5. These are popular forms of self-deprecation, notices Garland, *1 Corinthians*, p. 141, alluding to Ignatius, *Eph* 8.1; 18.1; *Barn* 4.9. Some have argued that these terms in fact portray the apostles as scapegoats and despised sin-offerings. Cf. Barrett, *First Corinthians*, pp. 112–13; Marshall, *Enmity in Corinth*, p. 213. *Contra* Conzelmann, *First Corinthians*, p. 90, n. 49.

consonant with Jesus Christ (cf. Isa. 53.2b-3). Fee states well the lesson that Paul is seeking to teach the Corinthians in this segment of text: 'The irony is devastating: How they perceive themselves, masterfully overstated in vv. 8 and 10, is undoubtedly the way they think *he* ought to be. But the way he actually is, set forth in the rhetoric of vv. 11–13, is the way *they* all ought to be.'[172]

Paul anticipates that, by overexposing the Corinthians' misconceived self-perception by means of a stark contrast with the apostles' cruciform lifestyle, he would shame the Corinthians.[173] Paul's purpose in writing 'these things'[174] is not to bring about the shame understood as one of the social values of the world which affected the social status of the person shamed.[175] Though the Corinthians would unmistakably feel ashamed, his confrontation has aimed at bringing about a change in their attitudes that reflected the reversals of the cross.[176] Therefore he emphasizes in this second unit (4.14-21) the positive purpose of his catalogue of afflictions – to admonish them to imitate him. He will seek to turn ἐντροπῇ into νουθεσία by displaying fatherly concern for the Corinthians' well-being.

This segment is connected to the previous one by the use of the verb φυσιοῦσθε in 1 Cor. 4.18, 19 (cf. 4.6). The problem that Paul is seeking to correct is thus reiterated – the arrogance and pride that the Corinthians were taking in certain teachers. He seeks to correct the problem by calling them to imitate him, no doubt as he imitates Christ; otherwise he warns them that he will return to them with a disciplining rod.

Paul's admonition, however, is not imposing, as can be shown from his use of family language. He addresses them as a 'father' (πατήρ) addresses his 'beloved children' (τέκνα μου ἀγαπητά), thus with conciliatory intentions. His appeal to them is that of one who has had the unique role of parenting them, as contrasted to that of the 'myriads' of παιδαγωγοί ('caretakers/guardians').[177] In that unique role as the founding father (ἐγὼ ὑμᾶς ἐγέννησα), Paul goes on to spell out the point of the entire

---

172   Fee, *First Corinthians*, p. 165 (emphasis by author). For a similar evaluation, see Winter, *Philo and Paul among the Sophists*, pp. 196–200.

173   See Smit, 'Epideictic Rhetoric in Paul's First Letter to the Corinthians 1–4', 198, following, Merklein, *Der erste Brief*, p. 323. Thiselton, *First Corinthians*, p. 368, following Plank, *Paul and the Irony of Affliction*, argues that the irony is intended to achieve realism, not low self-esteem. Mitchell, *Reconciliation*, pp. 213–14, notes that epideictic elements of blame or praise are sometimes allowed in deliberative rhetoric (cf. Isocrates, *Or.* 4.130).

174   Garland, *1 Corinthians*, pp. 144–5, may be right in seeing in the phrase γράφω ταῦτα a reference not only to the immediately previous segment, but also to the 'the entire attack on their factions, beginning in 1.10 (cf. 4.6).'

175   See Witherington, *Conflict and Community*, pp. 8 and 24.

176   Cf. Thiselton, *First Corinthians*, p. 369.

177   For a correct understanding of παιδαγωγοί see N. H. Young, '*Paidagōgos*: The Social Setting of a Pauline Metaphor', *NovT* 29 (1987) 150–76. Thiselton, *1 Corinthians*, p. 370, makes a parallel with John 10.11-14 to explain the meaning as 'hired help.'

segment: μιμηταί μου γίνεσθε ('imitate me').[178] It is not very clear what Paul wishes the Corinthians to imitate in him, but based on contextual inferences, it is safe to assume that the content of imitation is living out the foolish wisdom of the cross.[179] This is particularly evident from the fact that Paul adds to the spiritual birth image the means of their salvation, that is, διὰ τοῦ εὐαγγελίου, whose content is evidently that described in 1 Cor. 1.18-31. Therefore, as Garland states, 'The ultimate aim is not to be Paul-like, but Christlike (11.1). The Corinthians are to imitate him only insofar as his behavior corresponds to the gospel.'[180] This is made clear by the fact that Timothy will 'remind them' of his ways (or 'patterns of life'). This means that both Timothy and Paul live in the same ὁδόν, a way characteristic of every Christian and taught in every church.[181]

Paul concludes this segment and the whole discussion on factionalism with a reminder of the main issue he has been confronting – arrogance on behalf of one teacher against the other. This arrogance apparently has been expressed by 'some' in talk against Paul. Therefore Paul warns the Corinthians of his soon face-to-face confrontation, in which their talk will prove to be devoid of power. The reason is because 'God's reign' will prove to be 'in power' ('effective'; cf. 1 Cor. 2.4-5), and not their worldly pretensions to wisdom and status reversed by the cross (cf. 1 Cor. 1.18-31). Regardless of this stern warning, Paul, as a father, wishes that he would not have to come with a disciplining rod (ἐν ῥάβδῳ),[182] but in 'love' and with a 'gentle spirit.' The matter is in their hands and not his.

With this concluding paragraph, then, Paul brings into focus the issue that underlies the dissensions in Corinth, namely puffed-upness on behalf of teachers. Paul answers such a spirit of jealousy, arrogance, and quarrelling, with his own example, as one who lives out the implications of the cross. In this regard, if the dissensions are to stop in Corinth, there is only one solution: to imitate Paul, for in imitating him they will live out the reversals implicit in the cross. Unity, then, is possible only if the

---

178 Fee, *First Corinthians*, p. 183, contends that Paul is seeking to reestablish his authority over them with this statement.

179 See Pickett, *The Cross in Corinth*, p. 158.

180 Garland, *1 Corinthians*, p. 147.

181 Cf. Robertson and Plummer, *First Corinthians*, p. 91; also Lindemann, *Der erste Korintherbrief*, p. 116 (cf. Acts 9.2; 18.25-26; 19.9, 23).

182 The 'rod' was an image of discipline (παιδεία), cf. Philo, *Post.* 28.97. With the mentioning of the rod, Paul brings into focus one more time the contrast between the father and the παιδαγωγοῖ. See Garland, *1 Corinthians*, p. 149.

Corinthians understand and accept the logic of the apostle's weakness as congruent with the logic of the cross.[183]

Major Themes in 1 Corinthians 1–4

The previous section of the chapter has focused primarily on identifying the discourse units and sub-units of 1 Cor. 1.18–4.21. Most of the discussion was descriptive, in that we sought to summarize the contents of each unit, making exegetical observations where it was necessary for grasping the general meaning of the text, but leaving for later more detailed discussions of crucial hermeneutical issues that have a bearing on the subject of this work. We have also sought to point to the lexical, syntactical, and thematic connections between the segments. We have noticed that each segment either builds upon and expands a certain topic introduced in the previous segment or picks up a theme already developed elsewhere in the first four chapters. It is now time to clearly define the main theme(s) of each segment, see how they combine at the level of each of the four major sections, and present possibilities of integrating all the themes in a unified whole. We will start with a summary of each individual segment and its theme. This will lead into investigating the flow of Paul's argument and the cohesion of the segments. Then we will seek to determine what major theme(s) the unit brings to the forefront. Lastly, we will evaluate a possible way of understanding the literary and thematic unity of this first rhetorical unit of the letter in terms of chiastic structure. We will end by seeking to show that 1 Cor. 1.10-17, which is the introduction to the first rhetorical unit, points to the same theme(s) and gives a preliminary explanation of the cohesion of Paul's argument in the first unit of the letter.

The Theme(s) of Each Segment

We have noticed above that there is a consensus among the students of the Corinthian correspondence over the smallest building blocks of Paul's argument in 1 Cor. 1.18–4.21. Our study has proceeded with the following divisions in mind: 1 Cor. 1.18-25; 1.26-31; 2.1-5; 2.6-16; 3.1-4; 3.5-17; 3.18-23; 4.1-5; 4.6-13; 4.14-21. In seeking to avoid repetition, we will point to key ideas in each segment without going into great details. These ideas can be charted in the following way:

---

183   See Dodd, *Paul's Paradigmatic "I"*, p. 51, who follows J. Bradley Chance, 'Paul's Apology to the Corinthians', *PRSt* 9 (1982) 145–55 (151). See also Pickett, *The Cross in Corinth*, p. 59.

Text	The Main Theme(s)
1.18-25	God's *modus operandi* in this world is to save by the preaching of Christ crucified. On the one hand, according to the 'wisdom' of this world such method is foolishness, since the cross is perceived both as a 'scandal' and a symbol of weakness. On the other hand, according to true wisdom – divine wisdom – the cross provides the epistemological lens through which things are perceived at their true value. In this sense, the 'wisdom' of the world proves to be inadequate for attaining to salvation, while the 'foolishness' of God proves to be both power and wisdom unto salvation.
1.26-31	The reversal of values inherent in the cross is seen the Corinthians' own experience of salvation. God did not choose to save those with a high social status in society (e.g., based on education, power, nobility), but mostly those deserving no honors according to the standards of the world. This is a clear proof that God works effectively contrary to the expected values of society. This removes any ground for boasting in man and any human self-assertion.
2.1-5	Paul has deliberately adopted an unconventional mode of proclamation, devoid of 'wisdom of words.' His stage presence and his speech however proved to be consistent with the nature of the message he preached – 'weakness'. Paul adopted such a *modus operandi* so that faith may be based not on human ability to persuade but solely on the work of the Holy Spirit.
2.6-16	The wisdom that Paul (and other teachers) preaches is one that divides the humankind into two groups: the mature/spiritual – who perceive the mystery of the gospel as a result of a revelation by means of the Spirit of God as opposed to the instrumentality of human 'wisdom' – and the fleshly – for whom the message of the cross remains imperceptible and therefore unacceptable.
3.1-4	The Corinthians are in a precarious spiritual condition, given their partisan spirit. Paul cannot identify them with the spiritual, but he also hesitates to call them fleshly. Rather, they are 'carnal', behaving as mere humans. In other words, they have failed to think through the ethical implications of belonging to the Spirit. Their preferences for different teachers show that their way of evaluating things is still worldly and not spiritual.

Text	The Main Theme(s)
3.5-17	Paul uses three analogies (i.e., the field, the building, and the temple) to prove the illegitimacy of human evaluation of teachers. In the process, he clarifies other points. First, the teachers are merely co-servants who perform their God-assigned roles under his jurisdiction. Second, teachers must fulfill their task with seriousness since the real quality of their work will be revealed by the test of the eschatological fire. Third, given the 'apart' (holy) identity of the church, the Corinthians by their factionalism are in danger of being destroyed.
3.18-23	Boasting in men is a fundamental characteristic of worldly wisdom. For one to have the wisdom of God must renounce such boasting in men, which leads to dissensions. In fact, Paul argues, such boasting is absurd since teachers belong to the church and the church to God-in-Christ.
4.1-5	The correct view of teachers is as stewards of the things entrusted to them by God. Their responsibility is thus to be faithful to their master who employed them. It is only God, their master, who can pass the final and valid verdict on their work. Any human judgment is inadequate and premature and must await the eschatological divine assessment.
4.6-13	Paul argues that the Corinthians' boasting with teachers has been based on a fundamentally defective perspective – viewing themselves as patrons rather than recipients. This is symptomatic of a theology of glory. Paul counters such a view with a catalogue of the apostle's hardships, which is a living out of a theology of the cross.
4.14-21	Paul admonishes the Corinthians to imitate his cruciform lifestyle as a solution to dissensions manifested in boasting in teachers. Their lack of obedience to his fatherly advice will force him to come with discipline.

A glance at the key ideas of each small segment will inevitably convince one that there are several themes that occur over and over again as Paul develops his argument throughout the first four chapters of 1 Corinthians. Themes that are prominent in this unit are: wisdom, preaching, cross, social status, boasting, Spirit, revelation, spiritual/fleshly/carnal persons, jealousy, divisions, Paul and Apollos (and Cephas), servanthood, judging and judgment, weakness, honor, hardships, imitation, etc. Despite Conzelmann's statement that the first rhetorical unit of the letter is a collection of individual topics such as these with no unity of style or content,[184] if we believe that Paul is a coherent speaker we must discover how he expresses these themes in an integrated whole to the extent that he makes sense to the Corinthians.[185]

The Cohesion of the Segments within Each Major Section
We have noticed that there is a lack of consensus over the way the small segments should be arranged into larger sections. At the same time, we have observed a certain direction in which recent scholarship is moving, a direction which sees Paul making his case in four consecutive steps: 1 Cor. 1.18–2.5; 2.6–3.4; 3.5–4.5; 4.6-21. This is based on the argument that each major section concludes with a direct address of Paul to the Corinthians (first person singular addressing second person plural or first person plural).[186] The question which we will seek to answer now is the contribution of the segments identified above to the argument of each larger section. The combination of the themes of each segment renders the following themes at the level of the larger sections:

Text	The Main Theme(s)
1.18–2.5	The cross brings a reversal of values, a reversal which renders the 'wisdom' of the world inadequate for salvation (1.18-25). The reversal is seen in the low-status Corinthians whom God chose for salvation (1.26-31) and in the unimpressive style of proclamation which Paul adopted (2.1-5).
2.6–3.4	The wisdom of God which overturns the values of the world is accessible only by the revelation of the Spirit (2.6-16). The Corinthians' partisan spirit reveals that they are still patterning their thinking according to the values of the world (3.1-4).
3.5–4.5	The Corinthians have no right to judge or to boast in teachers, for they are mere servants whose work will be tested by God (3.5-17), they belong to the church (3.18-21), and are accountable only to God (4.1-5).

184 Conzelmann, *First Corinthians*, p. 82.

185 We will assume here that Paul did make sense to the Corinthians in what he wrote. There are those, of course, who see an important distance between Paul and the Corinthians in that Paul's perception of the situation in Corinth was a complete misreading. This would make Paul's argument completely incoherent to the original readers. E.g., Wilckens, *Weisheit und Torheit*, p. 16. For a critique see Scroggs, 'Paul: ΣΟΦΟΣ and ΠΝΕΥΜΑΤΙΚΟΣ', 33–34, n 1; also Pogoloff, *LOGOS AND SOPHIA*, pp. 84–87.

186 The special placement and role of these sections (1.18-25; 2.1-4; 3.1-4; 3.16-23; 4.1-5; and 4.14-21) have been identified by Fiore '"Covert Allusion"', 87–88, but have been integrated into a coherent structure by Smit, 'Search for Coherence', 233, and Kuck, *Judgment*, pp. 154–5.

Text	The Main Theme(s)
4.6-21	The Corinthians' self-assessment reflects a theology of glory in contrast to the apostles' catalogue of hardships which reflects a theology of the cross (4.6-13). The only way to put an end to boasting is by imitation of the cruciform manner of life exemplified by Paul (4.14-21).

A look at these four major sections reveals a relative difficulty in combining the themes of each small segment. The first section is dominated by the topic of wisdom vs. foolishness/lack of impressiveness. The second section speaks of divine wisdom and dissensions. The third section speaks mainly of servanthood, judgment, and wisdom. The fourth section speaks of imitation and boasting vs. suffering. It is difficult at first to see the connection between all these themes, though the themes of wisdom and divisions certainly are prominent. However, some have sought to show the cohesion of all these themes by arranging the segments and sections into a chiastic pattern.

Chiastic Structure of 1 Corinthians 1–4

Commentators have assumed different chiastic structures for this unit.[187] Probably one of the most convincing chiastic structures is that suggested by Bruce Terry in his discourse analysis of 1 Corinthians.[188] He argues that the topics of division and wisdom, combined with the topic of servanthood, form a double chiasmus:

A	Division (1.10-17)
B	Wisdom (1.18–2.16)
A`	Division (3.1-4)
C	Servanthood (3.5-15)
D (A`` B`)	Wisdom and Division (3.16-23)
C`	Servanthood (4.1-17)

Terry's chiastic organization of the unit has some value in it, for it

---

187   See, e.g., Bailey, 'The Structure of 1 Corinthians', 156.
A (1.6) The Tradition
  B (1.10-16) Paul, Apollos and Cephas
    C (1.17-2.5) We preach: Christ crucified – not human wisdom
    C` (2.6-16) We preach: a hidden wisdom of God
  B` (3.1-4.15) Paul, Apollos and Cephas
A` (4.16) The Concluding Appeal
This chiasm is contested by Terry, *Discourse Analysis*, 101. See also Fee, *First Corinthians*, 50–51, for a less complicated chiastic structure (1.18-2.5/2.6-3.4/3.5-4.21) and Dickerson, 'Apollos in Acts and First Corinthians', 102, n. 48, for an evaluation.

188   Terry, *Discourse Analysis*, pp. 44, 101.

points to passages that discuss similar issues though at different stages in the argument. This we have noted throughout the exegesis of each individual segment by drawing attention to the effect of *inclusio*. However, Terry's chiastic structure does not adequately integrate the topic of divisions with the topic of servanthood, and we are not so sure that servanthood is a major topic in the designated sections. Rather, the topic of judgment/evaluation more adequately defines the content of these passages.

In conclusion, it may be necessary to give up the attempt to find a chiastic structure behind Paul's argument in these first four chapters of 1 Corinthians. Such structure may prove to be an imposition. We are thus left to accept a less homogeneous structure behind Paul's argument, but nonetheless a coherent one. A preliminary explanation of the cohesion of all these themes may be found in the introduction to the first rhetorical unit (1 Cor. 1.10-17).

The Introduction (1 Cor. 1.10-17)

It is generally accepted that 1 Cor. 1.10 constitutes the thesis statement at least for the first four chapters of 1 Corinthians.[189] In this verse Paul points to what the major problem is in the Corinthian church – ἔριδες and σχίσματα.[190] He also shows the purpose (ἵνα) for which he writes:to persuade the Corinthians to agree (τὸ αὐτὸ λέγητε πάντες) with one another[191] and work towards unity, particularly unity of mind (ἐν τῷ

189 Mitchell, *Reconciliation*, p. 1, interprets 1.10 as the major statement of the rhetorical thesis of the whole epistle emphasizing ecclesial unity. See also Witherington, *Conflict and Community*, p. 94; Johan S. Vos, 'Die Argumentation des Paulus in 1 Kor. 1.10-3.4', in *The Corinthian Correspondence* (Reimund Bieringer, ed.; Leuven: Leuven University Press, 1996), 87. For the function of the thesis statement in the ancient rhetorical writings see Aristotle, *Rhet*. 3.12.13; Quintilian, *Inst*. 4.4.2-5.28.

190 One should notice that σχίσματα was not something that was necessarily present in the church, but rather a possible outcome of the ἔριδες within the church, if they would not cease. Welborn, *Politics and Rhetoric in the Corinthian Epistle*, pp. 7–8, contends that Paul's goal in 1 Corinthians 1–4 is what Plutarch (*Mor*. 824 C-E) describes as the object of the art of politics as the prevention of [*stasis*]. The problem was nevertheless widespread in the Corinthian *ecclesia* to the point that 'the whole body [was] infected with the spirit of strife', as observed by J. B. Lightfoot, *Notes on the Epistles of Saint Paul from Unpublished Commentaries* (London: n.p., 1904), p. 153, and demonstrated by the use of the pronoun ἕκαστος in 1.12.

191 It is possible that Paul has in mind by this phrase the actual verbal nature of the Corinthian dissensions, expressed in slogans (cf. 1.12; 3.4), quarreling (cf. 1.11; 3.3), preaching (cf. 1.17; 2.4; 2.13; 4.19), and boasting (cf. 1.29; 1.31; 3.21; 4.7). See Kuck, *Judgment*, p. 156.

αὐτῷ νοΐ καὶ ἐν τῇ αὐςτῇ γνώμῃ).[192] Implicit here is the fact that the divisions are the result of various ways of thinking about teachers, as Paul will shortly point out. Thus, Paul urges (παρακαλῶ) concord in a divided

192   Given this purpose, these first four chapters of the letter have been categorized by some as deliberative rhetoric, according to rhetorical criticism. See, e.g., Witherington, *Conflict and Community*, p. 94; Elisabeth Schüssler Fiorenza, 'Rhetorical Situation and Historical Reconstruction in 1 Corinthians', *NTS* 33 (1987) 386–403; and Mitchell, *Reconciliation*, pp. 20–64. This view has been challenged recently by Smit, 'Epideictic Rhetoric in Paul's First Letter to the Corinthians 1–4', 184–201, though see Wuellner, 'Greek Rhetoric and Pauline Argumentation', 184, who quotes Perelman and L. Olbrechts-Tyteca, *A New Rhetoric: A Treatise on Argumentation* (Notre Dame: University of Notre Dame Press, 1971), 54, in arguing for epideictic rhetoric. See also Wuellner's 'Where is Rhetorical Criticism Taking Us?' *CBQ* 49 (1987) 41–54645) Kennedy, *New Testament Interpretation*, p. 87, claims that parts of the letter employ a forensic or judicial rhetoric. See also M. Bünker, *Briefformular und rhetorische Disposition im 1 Korintherbrief* (GTA, 28; Göttingen: Vandenhoeck & Ruprecht, 1983), pp. 50–1.
    One must beware of drawing a too strict parallel between the rhetorical form of Paul's epistles and the structure of argument as prescribed in the ancient Greek rhetorical handbooks. See Lanci, *Temple*, pp. 49–50, for a balanced view. One danger, pointed out by Pogoloff, *LOGOS AND SOPHIA*, pp. 87–95, is to focus primarily and exclusively on formal parallels (e.g., terms employed) to the neglect of differences in situations (e.g., political vs. ecclesiastical) and therefore in functions. Thus, he rightly argues that 'one would have to demonstrate that these terms and topoi were used *exclusively* for such purposes' (p. 90). As a result, a more probable assessment of the first rhetorical unit is that it contains terms and topoi from all three types of rhetoric. This, however, does not prove that Paul is dependent upon these types of argumentation. The most that can be argued is that Paul may have adopted them. If that is the case, he certainly adapted them to fit his situation. See Jeffrey Reed, 'Using Ancient Rhetorical Categories to Interpret Paul's Letters', 307–8, and David E. Aune, *The New Testament in its Literary Environment* (LEC, 8; Philadelphia: Westminster, 1987), pp. 49, 159, 203. For a recent negative evaluation of rhetorical genre analysis of Paul's epistles see R. Dean Anderson Jr., *Ancient Rhetorical Theory and Paul* (CBET, 18; Kampen: Kok Pharos.; 1996: rev. edn. 1996), esp. pp. 255–65 for a critique of Mitchell's thesis and pp. 96–107 for an evaluation of rhetorical criticism and Paul's epistles in general. For the relation of rhetoric to epistolography, see esp. pp. 109–27. For a positive evaluation of rhetorical criticism as applied to Paul's letters see Frank W. Hughes, 'The Rhetoric of Letters', in *The Thessalonians Debate: Methodological Discord or Methodological Synthesis?* (Karl P. Donfried and Johannes Beutler, eds.; Grand Rapids: Eerdmans, 2000), pp. 194–240. To support his approach he makes reference to 'Demetrius's' handbook *Eloc.* 223–35, which compares letters to dialogues in their styles, Cicero's *De or.* 2.49, where he argues that when official messages were sent to or from the Senate no other genus of rhetoric is needed, 'since the ability acquired by a ready speaker, form the treatment of his other subjects and topics, will not fail him in situations of that description', and to Demostenes' *Epistle 1* as an example of the use of rhetoric in ancient letters by the greatest Greek orator. See also Charles A. Wanamaker, 'Epistolary vs. Rhetorical Analysis: Is a Synthesis Possible?' in *idem*, 255–86. More will be said on the pre-Christian Paul in Chapter 4.

church.[193] He does this both positively and negatively in the form of a simple chiastic structure ABA[194]:

Παρακαλῶ δὲ ὑμᾶς ἵνα
  A τὸ αὐτὸ λέγητε πάντες
    B μὴ ᾖ ἐν ὑμῖν σχίσματα
  A ἦτε δὲ κατηρτισμένοι ἐν τῷ αὐτῷ νοΐ καὶ ἐν τῇ αὐτῇ γνώμῃ

Also in this introductory paragraph, Paul makes clear that the divisions are occasioned by Christians comparing and evaluating preachers which resulted in preference of one teacher over another, as seen in the party slogans of v. 12: Ἐγὼ μέν εἰμι Παύλος, Ἐγὼ δὲ Ἀπολλῶ, Ἐγὼ δὲ Κηφᾶ, Ἐγὼ δὲ Χριστοῦ. The nature of the preferences is alluded to in the transitional v. 17 – preference for preaching with σοφία λόγου. Scholars have interpreted the meaning of σοφία in different ways, but it is obvious that this 'wisdom' is mentioned in association with Christian proclamation. In this sense, Paul sees an incompatibility between the wisdom esteemed by the Corinthians and the preaching of Christ crucified (cf. 1 Cor. 2.1-5). Verse 17, then, provides the transition into the main body of the first section, a transition from the issue of divisions to the issue of the proclamation of the cross devoid of σοφία λόγου. Such a change of topic may seem rather abrupt and awkward in light of the fact that Paul has said nothing so far about σοφία, unless the explanation is that Paul regards the factions to be a symptom of a worldly understanding of what wisdom is.[195] The Corinthians' preference of certain teachers over others, based on worldly criteria for wisdom, then, seems to be the root of divisions in the church. In other words, the topics of wisdom and divisions are organically connected. The former is the theological root, while the latter is the ethical symptom.

But there is one more issue that Paul brings into the discussion as he introduces the problem of divisions, which should shed some light on the main issue discussed in 1 Corinthians 1–4, namely baptism (1 Cor. 1.13-17). Paul's insistence on the topic of baptism, and his apparent lessening of its importance in comparison to that of preaching, indicates the

193 For a discussion of the verb παρακαλῶ as having an illocutionary (on the basis of apostleship or friendship) or perlocutionary (on the basis of rhetorical persuasion) force, see Thiselton, *1 Corinthians*, pp. 109, 111–14. Here he challenges the view of Mitchell, *Reconciliation*, p. 1, and Witherington, *Conflict and Community*, pp. 94–95, that the verb introduces a rhetorical argument. The distinction between illocutionary and perlocutionary speech-acts was introduced by J. L. Austin, *How to Do Things with Words*.

194 Cf. Fee, *First Corinthians*, p. 53.

195 So also John D. Herman, 'Paul's Rhetoric of the Cross in 1 Corinthians 1–4' (unpublished MST. dissertation, Trinity Lutheran Seminary, 1993), 20. Among the few commentators who believe Paul starts a new topic at 1.18 is Lightfoot, *Unpublished Commentaries*, p. 157. *Contra* Best, 'The Power and the Wisdom of God', 10.

probability that the Corinthians overemphasized the importance of the person performing the rite, of the ministerial agency, and missed the message of the cross. [196] Raymond Pickett, as others, has rightly assessed that baptism in the Corinthians congregation may have been a way of identifying with the baptizer, attitude which resulted in allegiances and ultimately to discord. [197]

In light of this misconception of leadership and baptism, Paul seeks to de-emphasize the importance of the role of the teacher and to maximize the importance of Christ and the word about the cross. He does this by means of a series of three rhetorical questions which constitute a *reductio ad absurdum*.[198] The point he seeks to make is that placing of human teachers on the same level as Christ is ludicrous and, worse, idolatrous.

In the introduction (1 Cor. 1.10-17) to his first rhetorical unit, then, Paul foreshadows themes that he will develop in the rest of his argument for unity: wisdom (1 Cor. 1.18–3.4) and divisions (1 Cor. 3.5–4.21). It is in this introduction that we discover a basic way of integrating them. The cohesion of these themes can be stated in the most basic way: Paul seeks to put an end to divisions by admonishing the Corinthians to give up the worldly way of evaluating their teachers. Each part of this statement can then be amplified: the divisions were based on preferences as expressed in slogans of allegiance; the importance placed on teachers ran the risk of diminishing the crucial place of the cross of Christ in the formation of the Christian community; what seems to have been the criteria for differentiating between teachers is a misconceived notion of wisdom; the solution to the divisions was the adoption of the same perspective.

The introduction, then, helps us see how Paul combines the themes of the first rhetorical unit of the epistle. It remains, then, to prove that Paul was coherent in the way he argued his case against divisions and that the topics discussed in this first unit of the letter are not randomly and dissimilarly placed.

Coherence of 1 Corinthians 1–4

Thus far we have analyzed the syntax and structure of 1 Corinthians 1–4 to see the building blocks in Paul's argument. We have concluded that

---

196   See Thiselton, *First Corinthians*, pp. 140, 142. He quotes Chrysostom (*Hom. 1 Cor.* 3.6). See also Richard B. Hays, *First Corinthians* (Interpretation; Louisville: John Knox, 1997), p. 24; Best, 'The Power and the Wisdom of God', 13; and Robertson, *Conflict in Corinth*, p. 123.

197   Pickett, *The Cross in Corinth*, p. 60. See also Winter, *Philo and Paul among the Sophists*, pp. 185–7; Clarke, *Leadership in Corinth*, pp. 92–3.

198   Thiselton, *First Corinthians*, p. 134. Garland, *1 Corinthians*, pp. 40, 49, claims that Paul uses sarcasm in posing these questions. See also Hays, *First Corinthians*, p. 23.

Paul develops his argument in four major sections, which together address the themes of divisions and wisdom, themes that Paul introduces in 1 Cor. 1.10-17. We have already anticipated a certain connection between these two themes, a connection however that we need to investigate a little deeper, since both the coherence and the main theme of this first discourse unit is dependent upon the connection between the two themes.[199] Once we establish the function of the wisdom theme in Paul's argument against divisions, we will offer a brief summary of the logical flow of Paul's thought process in 1 Cor. 1.10–4.21.

The Rhetorical Scheme of 1 Corinthians 1–4

The connection between the topic of divisions and the wisdom theme does not become obvious from a first reading of the text. In fact, a *prima facie* reaction is that there is no connection between the two. One should be aware that after the first mention of the problem of divisions in 1 Cor. 1.13, there is no other mention of it until 3.2. Just as the modern reader is puzzled at the reason of the 'insertion' of the wisdom talk in the middle of a text dealing with divisions (1 Cor. 1.18–2.16), so the Corinthians must have wondered about the silence concerning the divisions between 1 Cor. 1.17 and 3.2. Is it only the interesting digression of an absent-minded apostle? More likely, however, the so-called digression has a deliberate and specific rhetorical purpose. It is its purpose as a building block within the flow of Paul's argument that we must determine.

A number of scholars have pointed out the fact that Paul uses the rhetorical device of *schēma* throughout the first four chapters.[200] Noticing this device, they argue, is important for establishing the coherence of the first rhetorical unit of the letter. Joop Smit, for instance, has argued that Paul uses covert speech by his use of four names in the slogans of 1 Cor. 1.12, of the verb ἀπόλλυμι in 1 Cor. 1.18-19, and of the indefinite pronoun in 3.10, in order to establish his authority before the Corinthians (particularly before the followers of Apollos). What gives coherence to the first rhetorical unit, he argues, is Paul's confrontation of the followers of Apollos, confrontation disguised in certain phrases.[201]

Though without reference to the rhetorical device *schēma*, Demetrius K.

---

199 Gerhard Sellin, 'Das "Geheimnis" der Weisheit und das Rätsel der "Christuspartei" (zu 1 Kor 1–4),'' *ZNW* 73 (1982) 69–96(69), rightly sees the issue of how wisdom is regarded by Paul as the cause of the dissensions as the crucial question. Barrett, *First Corinthians*, p. 40, discusses 1 Cor. 1.10-4.21 under the heading 'Wisdom and Division at Corinth.'

200 *Schēma* can have the general meaning of 'figures of speech' such as irony and hyperbole, and the narrower, technical meaning of 'covert allusion'.

201 Smit, 'Search for Coherence', 247. See also Ker, 'Paul and Apollos', 75–97. They see these chapters as Paul's attempt to reestablish his authority by subtly downplaying Apollos and his followers. This claim however may be doubtful in light of the fact that Paul never

Williams, in a 1998 SBL paper entitled 'The Terminology of the Cross and the Rhetoric of Paul', has addressed the function of the discourse about the cross (and implicitly of wisdom) within Paul's argument against divisions in similar ways. He points to Paul's use of the cross as 'the rhetorical *terminology of argumentation* ...' In other words, 'the "terminology of the cross" functions as a rhetorical *tool of argumentation*.'[202] Applied to the first rhetorical unit of 1 Corinthians, 'Paul employs cross terminology to establish his ethos as truly the wisest leader and founder of the Corinthian community and to show that true wisdom, the wisdom he proclaims, is to be found in the cross of Christ.'[203] Thus, according to Williams, Paul introduces the speech about the cross in order to defend his own rejection of eloquent speech (i.e., wisdom), which the Corinthians so much appreciated. In other words, the exposition on the cross and the reversals inherent in it provide Paul with the tools he needs to reestablish his authority before the Corinthians.

Such a claim, both by Smit and Williams, will have to await more detailed discussion in Chapter 3, where we will evaluate the suggestion that 1 Corinthians 1–4 is an *apologia*. Nevertheless, one should not lose from sight the fact that Paul's intent, at least in 1 Cor. 3.5–4.5, is to convince the Corinthians that any desire to place one teacher above another is a reflection of worldly wisdom. Therefore it would be hard to believe that Paul advises against such practice while at the same time engaging in it.

More relevant for our discussion of covert speech are the articles by Benjamin Fiore and Peter Lampe.[204] Fiore argues that the rhetorical meaning of σχηματίζειν is 'using an artifice of dissimulation or fiction, of making an oblique reference to a delicate subject, which thereby became covered or hidden by "color" (another rendering of *schēma*) so as not to offend the listeners ... to compose a speech with veiled meaning'.[205] Thus, the allusive way of speaking was particularly used when addressing people of certain social status (i.e., elite) and therefore used for the purpose of avoiding direct confrontation and public shaming of such people. In the Corinthians' case, Paul uses this device in order to avoid shaming (cf. 1

---

mentions any of his opponents or enemies by name, as was the standard Greco-Roman rhetorical convention. Cf. Plutarch, *Aem.* 31.5; Cicero, *Fam.* 1.9.20; Chrysostom, *Or.* 46.6. But Paul does mention Apollos several times in his argument against dissensions.

202   Demetrius K. Williams, 'The Terminology of the Cross and the Rhetoric of Paul' 677 (emphasis by author). He follows Käsemann, *Perspectives on Paul*, p. 36, who argues that the 'theology of the cross is a polemical theology'.

203   Williams, 'The Terminology of the Cross', 692.

204   Fiore, '"Covert Allusion"', 85–102; Lampe, 'Theological Wisdom and the "Word About the Cross"', 117–31.

205   Fiore, '"Covert Allusion"', 89. For a discussion of this rhetorical device, see Quintilian, *Inst.* 9.1-2.

Cor. 4.14) the high-status Corinthians who were seeking honor by association with different teachers, while at the same time condemning factionalism.[206]

The weakness, however, of such a claim is that Paul uncovers the meaning of his discourse and he does it not just in 1 Cor. 4.6 where he uses the term μετεσχημάτισα,[207] but becomes very direct and condemning of the Corinthians especially in 1 Cor. 3.1-4 and 4.7-13. Fiore is thus forced to admit that 'Paul's concern is for the good of the community, and not for the purity of rhetorical forms'.[208] If such is the case, then, Paul cannot be using this rhetorical device, since in using *schēma*, according to Quintilian, the speaker leaves the hidden meaning to the hearer to discover (*aliud latens et auditori quasi inveniendum*).[209] This fundamental difference between Paul's argument and the rhetorical device *schēma* does not warrant the use of the device. *Schēma* is by definition disguise, and to say that Paul uses *schēma* at first and then exposes his intention is to deny the very nature of such a device. Paul may be indirect in 1 Cor. 1.18–2.16, but he is not using *schēma*.[210]

This critique applies also to Lampe who has argued that Paul used the rhetorical device called *schēma* in order to address indirectly the issue of divisions.[211] His insight into the use of this rhetorical device by Paul in 1 Corinthians 1–4 merits quoting here in full:

> Thus, as the rhetoric suggests, the *schēma* of 1 Corinthians 1.18-2.16 hides a 'ticklish' message behind a seemingly 'harmless' text. The seeming harmlessness of *emphasis* and *schēma* usually is attained by replacing a specific thought which is potentially dangerous in the situation with a general thought (*infinitum*) not necessarily related to the situation. Paul fulfills this rhetorical rule exactly. The two main *general* thoughts (*questio infinita*) of 1 Corinthians 1.18-2.16 are: (1) All human wisdom of the world is about to perish (1.18-25), and (2) all Christian wisdom is exclusively *God's* gift through the spirit (2.6-16). The specific issue (*questio finita*), however, is the parties' adoration of the apostles and their wisdom. Applying both general thoughts to the specific issue, one arrives at the following conclusion: Either the wisdom of the

---

206 Ibid., 95. More on the social organization of the Corinthian community follows in Chapter 3.

207 Notice, however, the difference between Paul's use of μετασχηματιζω and the word for 'covert allusion' σχηματίζω. It would be unique for Paul's term to be used as 'covert allusion'. Cf. BDAG 641–42.

208 Fiore, ' "Covert Allusion" ', 96.

209 Quintilian, *Inst.* 9.2.65.

210 For points at which Fiore's thesis is susceptible to criticism, see Anderson, *Ancient Rhetorical Theory and Paul*, pp. 245–46.

211 Lampe, 'Theological Wisdom and the "Word About the Cross" ', 117–31. He also uses Quintilian's writings for the definition of schēma.

apostles is a human quality and therefore a reason for praising them –
but then it is also bound to perish – or the wisdom of the apostles is
exclusively a spiritual gift from *God*, justifying God alone as the object
of praise. In both cases, the way is obstructed for praising apostles,
which sums up the whole thought figure of 1.18-2.16.[212]

So, even though at first blush there is no apparent connection between the
topic of divisions and the wisdom theme, a careful reading of the text will
reveal a strategy that Paul is using in order to persuade the Corinthian
believers to work toward unity. This strategy is implied in the movement
from general foreground (i.e., wisdom) to specific background (i.e.,
parties). Thus, Lampe would say, Paul addresses the wisdom theme in 1
Cor. 1.18–2.5, but the whole time he is referring to the topic of divisions.

Lampe argues that Paul's strategy can be seen in 1 Cor. 1.18–2.5. Here,
Paul draws his audience into condemning the 'Jews and the Greeks' for
their human wisdom, only later (1 Cor. 3.18-23) to condemn them for the
same thing – their high esteem of human wisdom. Lampe hints at the
rhetorical device *captatio benevolentiae* when he states that,

> At first, the Corinthian readers probably enjoyed this, listening to a
> criticism of 'Jews and Greeks', until they are surprised to discover (3.18-
> 19) that they, too, with their partisan boasting about Christian wisdom,
> had already been denounced in 1.18-2.5. In other words, by criticizing
> 'Jews and Greeks', Paul at the same time accused a Christian
> misbehavior in Corinth... Like a Trojan horse, it at first pleases its
> listeners until they are shocked to discover that they themselves are
> criticized by the same text.[213]

According to Lampe, then, Paul uses the discourse about wisdom as a
kind of a smoke screen, making the Corinthians think that he is talking
about one thing when in fact he aims at something else. Such a device may
seem deceptive and dishonest, but was received with favor in Paul's day,
since it assumed wisdom on the part of the audience to be able to 'crack
the code.'[214] Unlike Fiore, who argues that Paul seeks to avoid shaming
the high status Corinthians, Lampe argues that Paul used such a device to
'avoid stepping openly on the toes of these two other apostles [Apollos
and Peter]. In other words, criticizing the Corinthians' praise of Apollos
and Cephas, Paul nevertheless avoids hurting the feelings of these two
with any direct statement – a genuine masterpiece.'[215] Unlike Fiore,
however, he fails to notice that Paul does seem to uncover his intentions in
1 Cor. 4.6, though, as we have already noticed, Paul does not shy away

---

212   Ibid., 130.
213   Ibid., 128.
214   Cf. Quintilian, *Inst.* 9.2.68, 78. He also states that the use of such device was *en vogue*
in his day (9.2.65).
215   Lampe, 'Theological Wisdom and the "Word About the Cross"', 130.

from censuring the Corinthians at least in his direct address in 1 Cor. 3.1-4 and by the use of irony in 1 Cor. 4.8-13, which inevitably must have brought shame to them. That is the reason why Paul seeks to point to the main intention of the 'things' spoken: imitation (1 Cor. 4.14).

We may conclude, then, that despite similarities between Paul's way of argumentation in the first rhetorical unit and the ancient rhetorical device *schēma*, the fundamental differences render the claim of Paul using such device as improbable. Nevertheless, especially Lampe's study rightly underscores the importance of looking at the rhetorical function of Paul's use of the wisdom motif in his argument against dissensions. What is the purpose of bringing in a discussion on wisdom and the cross, when the main issue in the Corinthian church is dissensions? Both Fiore and Lampe contend that the reason Paul uses such a device is to avoid a direct confrontation in an already volatile situation, which would only aggravate the problem.[216] But, as a skilled rhetor, they would argue, Paul masterfully makes his point indirectly, avoiding thus the shaming of the Corinthians. Since we have already argued that such a function does not stand in light of the fact that Paul discloses his intentions, defeating thus the purpose of his assumed covert speech, we must look for another function of the wisdom discourse. It is here that we will suggest that Paul's discourse on wisdom does not serve just rhetorical purposes (e.g., establishing authority, avoiding shame), but it is an integral and necessary building block in his argument against divisions. The discourse on the cross and wisdom lays the theological foundation for his ethical exhortation against dissensions. Thus we turn last to an examination of the way Paul structures his argument logically in order to deal with dissensions, which should point to the coherence of the first rhetorical unit.

The Logical Arrangement of the Building Blocks in 1 Corinthians 1–4
At this point it is necessary to bring in some of the observations made along the way as we discussed each segment of text and identified their major theme(s). Three in particular are relevant for our argument for coherence. First, we must see the place of 1 Cor. 3.1-4 as transitional between the discourse on wisdom and the main theme of divisions.[217] This text functions as the liaison between the two major issues. We have argued that in his discussion of wisdom (1 Cor. 1.18–2.16), Paul underscores the reversal of values performed by the cross. The cross turns upside down the values of the world and reinterprets what true wisdom is. The cross stands between two ages, characterized by two opposite sets of values and two

---

216 See also Smit, 'Search for Coherence', 242–43; and Ker, 'Paul and Apollos', 84.
217 Cf. Kuck, *Judgment*, pp. 154–55.

contrastive ways of perception. It is at this point that Demetrius Williams'
observation that the cross is for Paul a rhetorical tool employed in
polemical contexts is useful. The λόγος τοῦ σταυροῦ demolishes worldly
wisdom and power by interpreting them as foolishness. Pickett agrees: 'In
this context the critical function of Paul's theology of the cross comes to
the fore inasmuch as it serves as the basis for denouncing those cultural
values according to which the cross is rejected as foolishness.'[218] The
Corinthians' salvation and Paul's own preaching devoid of worldly
wisdom form a convincing proof of the reversal inherent in the cross,
juxtaposed with the inability of the world through its wisdom to attain to
salvation. But while the cross condemns human wisdom, it also points to
true wisdom – God's mysterious plan of salvation – which is perceived
only by the one who belongs to the Spirit. The cross thus not only reverses
values but also divides people according to the way they relate to these
values. This being Paul's basic argument in 1 Cor. 1.18–2.16, he proceeds
in 1 Cor. 3.1-4 to make the connection and application to the divisive
situation in the Corinthian church. By their preferences for various
teachers expressed in their slogans, the Corinthians still have the mind of
the world rather than the mind of Christ. In other words, they still
evaluate their teachers according to the standards and values of the world
rather than the values implicit in the reversals created by the cross. 'But in
what light should the teachers be viewed?' the Corinthians would ask as
they hear 1 Cor. 3.1-4 read to them. We could almost hear Paul
responding: 'I am glad you asked.' He goes on to explain what values are
associated with teachers in light of the cross, which is the wisdom of God.
Thus, the most basic connection between wisdom and divisions is seen in
this transitional paragraph: the wisdom of the world is the value that the
Corinthians appreciated in their teachers and that divided them into
parties formed around preferred teachers.

Another paragraph that is crucial in determining the connection
between the discourse on wisdom and the theme of divisions is 1 Cor.
3.18-23. This paragraph fulfills a paraenetic function as an application of
the discussion about the proper role of the teachers in God's economy.
But more than that, it connects it with the first major theme of this unit,
wisdom. Obviously, the Corinthians' problem was boasting in men (i.e.,
teachers) by claiming each to be the follower of one or another, and in so
doing they thought that they were wise. They were, but only according to
the standards of the world. Consequently, Paul admonishes them to
become fools, that is, to stop allegiances to men, to remember that
teachers are their possession, and that together they belong to God.

Thus, from 1 Cor. 3.1-4 we learn that the Corinthians evaluated their
teachers according to the wisdom of the world, while from 1 Cor. 3.18-23

218 Pickett, *The Cross in Corinth*, p. 69.

we learn that the Corinthians considered not only their teachers to be wise but also themselves by association with various ones of these teachers. Both of these ideas are brought together in 1 Cor. 4.6, in the second purpose clause where Paul discloses the Corinthians' fundamental problem – boasting of one teacher (the Corinthians' wisdom) over against another (the teachers' wisdom). In the remainder of the argument, then, Paul seeks to point again, but more emphatically and contrastively, to the way the apostles are adequately viewed in light of the cross.

A third observation we have made which will help us integrate the two major themes is the introductory paragraph 1 Cor. 1.10-17. As we have already underscored, this paragraph presents us with the purpose for which Paul wrote (at least) this first rhetorical unit – to bring about unity. We have also mentioned that the cause of divisions in the Corinthian *ecclesia* was preferences for different teachers, based in part on the value they placed on the one performing the act of baptism and on proclamation ἐν σοφίᾳ λόγου. Thus in 1 Cor. 1.17, a transitional verse, Paul seems to allude to what exactly the Corinthians appreciated in their teachers – wisdom related to proclamation. It is this wisdom which he expounds on in 1 Cor. 1.18–2.16. Thus Paul saw the problem of divisions as merely symptomatic of a much deeper problem – the Corinthians' fascination with σοφίᾳ λόγου.[219]

With these observations made, we can now more easily understand the logical flow of Paul's argument in the first rhetorical unit of the letter and the connection between the discourse on wisdom and the theme of divisions. Paul introduces the issue of dissensions in 1 Cor. 1.10-17 by mentioning that at its roots is the Corinthians' appreciation of 'wisdom of words' in their teachers' proclamation. In 1 Cor. 1.18–2.16, then, Paul sets out to prove the inadequacy of worldly wisdom to attain to salvation and therefore the inappropriateness of 'wisdom of words' in the proclamation of the good news of salvation. Both are based on the nature of the gospel as hidden and unacceptable to the world. In 1 Cor. 3.1-4 Paul warns the Corinthians that by their evaluation of teachers according to worldly wisdom places them in a dangerous spiritual state, as people who still think as mere men. The solution to divisions and their precarious spiritual state is for the Corinthians to view the apostles as mere servants of God, whose work will be tested (1 Cor. 3.5-17). This Paul follows with two climactic applications: 1 Cor. 3.18-23 admonishes the Corinthians to cease considering themselves wise, because such deception is based on an inadequate evaluation of teachers and their role, opposing thus worldly wisdom to servanthood; and 1 Cor. 4.1-5 warns against assuming the role as judges who pronounce the final verdict on someone else's servants, since such prerogative belongs only to God. After this double high point,

---

219 Cf. Cousar, '1 Corinthians 2.1-13', 170.

Paul connects the themes of divine wisdom with servanthood, seen in the cruciform lifestyle of the apostles in antithesis with the Corinthians' high esteem of themselves. After driving home thus one more time how teachers should be viewed in light of the reversals of the cross, Paul concludes his argument for concord by admonishing the Corinthians to imitate him, that is, to adopt the values introduced by the cross. Thus, Paul begins his speech on concord by a discourse on the cross and rounds it off with similar emphasis. For Paul, then, the solution to the problem of dissensions was an adaptation to the values proclaimed by the cross, which destroys the wisdom of the world esteemed by the Corinthians.

This way of viewing the logical flow of Paul's argument, then, leaves the obvious impression of a coherent argument. The discourse about the cross and wisdom forms the theological foundation upon which Paul can build his ethical case and exhort the Corinthians to behavioral change within the Christian *ecclesia*.

Conclusion

One of the basic assumptions of effective speech is that it makes sense and is clearly articulated. Without clarity, a speech is bound to fail to persuade the audience to follow a certain course of action. This is true of any speech, especially inspired speech such as that of Paul in 1 Corinthians 1– 4. By means of his written speech in the first four chapters of 1 Corinthians, Paul seeks to persuade the Corinthians to work towards unity. He will succeed in it only if his communication makes sense to his audience.

This chapter has sought to show that Paul's speech in 1 Corinthians 1–4 forms a rounded and unified argument. We have sought to prove the unity of his argument by looking at three main aspects of speech: cohesion, prominence, and coherence. In the process of determining the unity we have pointed to the way the individual smaller units relate to each other lexically, syntactically, and thematically. We have also pointed to two prominent themes in the discourse: divisions and wisdom. At last, we have shown how Paul integrates the two themes in his speech on concord.

This analysis has sought to show that Paul's purpose in 1 Corinthians 1–4 was to bring about unity among the Corinthian believers by pointing to their false estimation of preachers done in light of human wisdom. In the second chapter of this work we will investigate the nature of the wisdom that was at the root of the divisions in the Corinthian *ecclesia*.

2 THE SOCIAL AND RHETORICAL BACKGROUND OF 1 CORINTHIANS 1–4

Introduction

In the first chapter of this work we have sought to prove the literary and thematic unity of the first rhetorical unit of 1 Corinthians. There we have identified and then attempted to integrate the discourse on wisdom with the major theme of dissensions. We have concluded that by his discourse on the cross and wisdom (1 Cor. 1.18–2.16) Paul laid the necessary theological foundation for his ethical exhortation against divisions (1 Cor. 3.4–4.21). In other words, Paul has sought to show how the Corinthians' behavior characterized by a partisan spirit was reflective of a fundamental failure to grapple with the reversals implicit in the cross in terms of what constitutes true wisdom. This means that the solution that Paul offers to dissensions is a way of understanding and viewing things (particularly teachers) in a way radically impacted by the cross. This means renouncing 'the wisdom of the world' and all the social values attached to it.

But what is this 'wisdom of the world' that the Corinthians so highly esteemed and that caused them to have preferences among teachers? This chapter will seek to identify the nature of this wisdom, so that we may be able to see more clearly the root cause of the divisive spirit in the Corinthian *ecclesia*. In other words, we will discuss issues related to the background of 1 Corinthians 1–4. The discussion will be carried out in several stages. First, we will seek to provide a brief history of interpretation of the term σοφία and its background, seeking to show that sophistic rhetoric is the best candidate for the meaning of σοφία. This will prove to be important for understanding what Paul so adamantly rejects as antithetical to the cross. Second, we will provide an overview of the social structures and networks of the city of Corinth and the influence they seem to have had upon the life of the Christian *ecclesia*. We will observe here that Paul calls for a resocialization of the Corinthians Christian in conformity with the values implicit in the cross. In light of the socio-rhetorical description of the situation behind 1 Corinthians 1–4, we will conclude with a brief discussion of the 'parties' represented by the slogans of 1 Cor. 1.12.

This investigation into the social and rhetorical background of the dissensions is necessary for a clear understanding of the wisdom so much esteemed by the Corinthians. Without this understanding, important details of Paul's argument remain obscure, hidden to the reader for lack of contrast.[1] It also prepares the ground for the next two chapters of the work where we will investigate the implications of the method and content of Paul's argumentation in 1 Corinthians 1–4, especially as related to Paul's theology of preaching and Apollos' function in Paul's argument.

The Background of Σοφία in 1 Corinthians 1–4

Over the past century, there have been three main hypotheses concerning the background of the language of wisdom which Paul employs in the first rhetorical unit of 1 Corinthians: Gnosticism, Hellenistic-Judaism, and Rhetoric. In this section of the chapter we will provide an overview of the ideas of each hypothesis, the main advocates of each position, and a critical evaluation of these ideas. We will sift through the arguments of each view with the purpose of determining which of these views is most faithful to the text. The reason for adopting one solution and not another will be because it will offer the most *probable* explanation and context for the *cumulative* data that have been gathered in the study conducted in the first chapter.[2]

Gnosticism

The claim that the Corinthians held to a Gnostic belief is a by-product of the *religionsgeschichtliche Schule* as represented particularly by Bultmann and the discoveries of the Nag Hammadi texts in the late 1940s.[3] The works of two scholars in particular have shaped subsequent debate over the origins of Gnosticism and its influence especially in Corinth: Ulrich Wilckens and Walter Schmithals.

Wilckens' position is argued in his monograph *Weisheit und Torheit*,[4] where the discussion revolves around the development of the Gnostic Sophia myth. This myth was the main tenet of Valentinian Gnosticism, but Wilckens argues that it had roots that predate Christianity (e.g., *1 Enoch* 42). He sees this myth as underlying Paul's discussion in 1 Cor. 2.6-

---

1   Cf. Litfin, *Proclamation*, p. 206.

2   See, e.g., Dahl, 'Paul and the Church at Corinth According to 1 Corinthians 1.10-4.21', 317, 318.

3   James D. G. Dunn, *First Corinthians* (NTG; Sheffield: Sheffield Academic Press, 1995), p. 34.

4   See also his article 'σοφία', in *TDNT*, 465–528. He significantly revised his view in 'Das Kreuz Christi als die Tiefe der Weisheit Gottes: Zur 1 Kor. 2,1–16', in *Paolo a una Chiesa Divisia*, 43–81.

16. This text, according to Wilckens, presents the idea of the descent of the heavenly Redeemer through the realms of the *archons* who gives spiritual wisdom to God's people. The most provocative aspect of his argument is that in this text Paul seeks to critique the Corinthians' Gnostic wisdom by using their terminology, but ironically, in exposing his own view he actually puts forth the Corinthians' own position with which he essentially agrees.[5] In other words, Paul got too carried away with his Gnostic parody to the point of sounding Gnostic himself, and for good reasons, argues Wilckens: Paul actually shared many ideas with the Gnostics.

Schmithals brought the Gnostic thesis to its full expression in his dissertation *Die Gnosis in Corinth*, written under Bultmann.[6] Like Wilckens, Schmithals sees a developed Jewish Gnosticism behind the Corinthian wisdom and an appropriation by Paul of the Corinthians' Gnostic terminology.[7] In distinction from Wilckens, Schmithals describes the Christ as a suffering revealer rather than as a redemptive Messiah.[8] Both, however, base their arguments especially on the terminology in 1 Cor. 2.6-16, so that any evaluation of a Gnostic background must begin with an explanation of these terms.[9]

Some of the terminology that presumably provides prime evidence of early Gnostic thought in 1 Corinthians is as follows. First, the advocates of a Gnostic background tend to associate γνῶσις with σοφία. In this regard, the Gnostic Corinthians, it is argued, were boasting of a higher knowledge and wisdom against those lacking them (cf. 1 Cor. 8.1ff).[10] The term γνῶσις, thus, is taken in a technical sense, referring both to form and content. Second, it is argued that this esoteric knowledge belonging to an elite group of Christians is clearly seen in the distinction between two

5 Wilckens, *Weisheit und Torheit*, pp. 60, 216f.

6 (Göttingen: Vandenhoeck & Ruprecht, 1956); ET *Gnosticism in Corinth: An Investigation of the Letters to the Corinthians* (trans. John E. Steely; Nashville: Abingdon, 2nd edn, 1971).

7 Ibid., 152–55. See also Wilckens, *Weisheit und Torheit*, pp. 52–60.

8 Ibid., 138–41.

9 For a critique of Wilckens see Robin Scroggs, 'Paul: ΣΟΦΟΣ and ΠΝΕΥΜΑΤΙΚΟΣ', pp. 33–5; and Judith L. Kovacs, 'The Archons, the Spirit and the Death of Christ: Do We Need the Hypothesis of Gnostic Opponents to Explain 1 Cor. 2.6-16?' in *Apocalyptic and the New Testament: Essays in Honor of J. Louis Martyn* (Joel Marcus and Marion L. Soards, eds.; JSNTSup, 24; Sheffield: JOST Press, 1989), 217–18. For a thorough critique of the hypothesis of Gnosticism or proto-Gnosticism in Corinth see Robert McLachlan Wilson, 'How Gnostic Were the Corinthians?' *NTS* 19 (1972–73) 65–74; *idem*, 'Gnosis at Corinth', in *Paul and Paulinism: Essays in Honour of C. K. Barrett* (Morna D. Hooker and S. G. Wilson, eds.; London: Alden, 1982), pp. 102–14.

10 Schmithals, *Gnosticism in Corinth*, 229. See also Richard A. Horsley, 'Gnosis in Corinth: 1 Corinthians 8.1-6', *NTS* 27 (1980): pp. 32–51.

classes of Christians – τέλειοι/πνευματικοί and νήπιοι.[11] This distinction,
it is argued, is supported by the use of the term μυστήριον.[12] Thus, only
the upper echelons of Christians have the capacity to apprehend deeper
and more mysterious teaching, something that the Gnostics also
preached.[13] Thirdly, it is argued that πνευματικοί is a key term of
identification in later Gnosticism which presumably proves that the
Corinthians regarding themselves as πνευματικοί is evidence that they
held to a Gnostic teaching.[14] *In nuce*, the constellation of these terms in 1
Cor. 2.6-16, terms used also by Gnostics, seemingly proves that the
Corinthians (and Paul by his appropriation of them) were holding to
Gnostic teaching. The argument that the background of this passage is
Gnostic is apparently strengthened by the use of 1 Cor. 2.9 in the
seventeenth saying of the Gnostic *Gospel of Thomas*, as if to suggest that
the authors of such Gnostic writings regarded 1 Corinthians as a source of
Gnostic teachings.[15]

To this use of these terms in an allegedly Gnostic sense in 1 Cor. 2.6–3.1
two types of response are in order. First, the literary context is
determinative of meaning.[16] The context and not the presuppositions of
the *religionsgeschichtliche Schule* must guide one's exegesis and search into
the meaning of these terms as used by Paul in this passage. Just because
many terms used by Paul are also present in Gnostic writings, does not
guarantee that these different contexts give the terms similar meanings.[17]
Terms do not have meanings in isolation but in relation to each other,
their semantic content being dependent on their context and frame of
reference. Thus, while Hans Conzelmann favors a distinction of classes in
1 Cor. 2.6-3.1, he rightly states that, 'The position in Corinth cannot be
reconstructed on the basis of the possibility of the general history of
religion. ... Certainty attaches only to what we can learn from the text.'[18]
The Gnostic hypothesis will prove to be an imposition upon the text that
distorts the natural meaning of these terms in their context. But what is
the natural meaning of these words as determined by the literary context?

---

11 Wilckens, *Weisheit und Torheit*, pp. 52–96. See also Scroggs, 'Paul: ΣΟΦΟΣ and
ΠΝΕΥΜΑΤΙΚΟΣ', 35.

12 Wilckens, *Weisheit und Torheit*, p. 206. See for this interpretation also Conzelmann, *1
Corinthians*, p. 63; Barrett, *First Corinthians*, pp. 71–2.

13 Wilckens, *Weisheit und Torheit*, pp. 70–80.

14 For Gnostic evidence see John Painter, 'Paul and the Πνευματικοί at Corinth', in *Paul
and Paulinism*, p. 247, n. 21.

15 Cf. Collins, *First Corinthians*, p. 17.

16 See the introduction to my dissertation for principles of word studies.

17 Cf. Samuel Laeuchli, *The Language of Faith: An Introduction to the Semantic Dilemma
of the Early Church* (Nashville: Abingdon, 1962), pp. 19; also 16. Thiselton, *First Corinthians*,
pp. 226, 240, and 269, follows Laeuchli in critiquing the Gnostic hypothesis.

18 Conzelmann, *1 Corinthian*, p. 15. See also Cousar, '1 Corinthians 2.1-13', 169.

According to our study in the previous chapter, the passage that allegedly contains a constellation of Gnostic terms (i.e., 1 Cor. 2.6-16), seeks to explain two ways of relating to the wisdom proclaimed by Paul. Since from the beginning of his argument Paul has been working with contrasts between the world and Christians, it is hard to see Paul switching to distinctions between Christians in this passage, as the advocates of a Gnostic background argue.[19] Paul is still speaking about divine wisdom, which is unacceptable to the world. As such, he speaks of mystery, which we have identified with the wisdom of God and the cross, *vis-à-vis* the world. It is the world with its system of values that cannot and will not accept the wisdom of God. The reason Paul gives is because such mystery can be known only by revelation through the agency of God's Spirit. Only those who have the Spirit of God (i.e., οἱ πνευματικοί) can perceive the wisdom of God. But, as Fee argues, 'The gift of the Spirit does not lead to special status among believers; rather, it leads to special status *vis-à-vis* the world.'[20] Therefore, while it may be correct to associate γνῶσις with σοφία and to argue that σοφία in this passage refers to both form and content, σοφία refers not to a Gnostic, esoteric knowledge that differentiates between classes of Christians, but to the proclamation of the cross that makes an eschatological distinction between Christians and unbelievers. In this respect, the context clearly shows that the unbelieving Jewish leaders (i.e., οἱ ἄρχοντες; cf. Acts 13.27) were the paradigmatic example of the rejection of Christ by the world as a result of their ignorance in reference to the mystery of God. Given this literary context and the continuity of Paul's argument, this explanation of these terms seems to be the most natural reading, rendering a Gnostic interpretation unnecessary.[21]

In summary, then, the insight gained from the exegesis of these terms in their immediate context shows that they are not used in a Gnostic sense, but that another explanation is more probable. We will corroborate this conclusion with a second response to the Gnostic hypothesis which derives from a short analysis of Gnosticism, allegedly Gnostic technical terms, and its assumed influence on the Corinthians (and Paul). The question that must be answered and has been answered definitively is whether it is legitimate to speak of Gnosticism in Paul's time.

It is generally accepted today that a distinction must be made between Gnosticism as it defines the Gnostic systems which first emerged in the second century and the 'gnosis' or 'proto-gnosticism' with its trends and tendencies in a Gnostic direction which should be used for the earlier

---

19   Cf. Fee, *The First Epistle to the Corinthians*, pp. 99–100.
20   Ibid., p. 120.
21   Cf. Conzelmann, *1 Corinthians*, p. 15.

period.[22] Therefore, 'the continued use of the term "gnosticism" (or "Gnosticism") with reference to the Corinthian church may simply be anachronistic and misleading'.[23] Robert McLachlan Wilson, who is known for his early critique of a Gnostic hypothesis behind 1 Corinthians, agrees by stating that what is happening in postulating a Gnostic background for 1 Corinthians is a 'reading [of the] first-century documents with second-century spectacles.'[24] In order to see clearly that a Gnostic hypothesis is unnecessary to explaining 1 Cor. 2.6–3.1, he points to the distinction between two directions of approaching the issue. He explains:

> Those who begin with the developed Gnosticism of the second century and go back to Paul's letters have no difficulty in identifying 'gnostic motifs' – terms, concepts and ideas which may legitimately be described as Gnostic because they are used as technical terms in the context of Gnostic systems. This usage however may be question-begging, since there is no way of showing that these terms and concepts are *already* Gnostic in an earlier context. ... Those who begin at the other end can interpret such terms and concepts without reference to Gnosticism – only to find themselves at a loss to explain how and why this new significance should so suddenly be given to them.[25]

This quotation from Wilson points to two important aspects that do away with an assumed necessary Gnostic background behind 1 Corinthians. First, the mere use by Paul of terms that later became technical terms in Gnosticism does not betray a Gnostic presence in 1 Corinthians. C. K. Barrett's statement that γνῶσις 'is most often used in a plain, non-technical, sense', has been universally accepted in most recent scholarship.[26] Thus, even a proto-gnostic hypothesis is improbable in light of the fact that the terms are used in a non-technical way by Paul.[27]

Second, just because a Gnostic book such as *Gospel of Thomas* quotes

---

22   Cf. Dunn, *1 Corinthians*, p. 36. This consensus was reached at Messina. The papers for the Messina conference were published in *Le originin dello gnosticismo: Colloquio di Messina, 13–18 aprile 1966* (U. Bianchi, ed.; SHR, 12; Leiden: Brill, 1970).

23   Dunn, *1 Corinthians*, p. 36.

24   Wilson, 'Gnosis at Corinth', p. 109. W. Schrage, *Der erste Brief*, p. 250, also holds to a proto-gnostic hypothesis. For a more recent evaluation of current views on Gnosticism see Michael Williams, *Rethinking "Gnosticism": An Argument for Dismantling a Dubious Category* (Princeton: Princeton University Press, 1996).

25   Wilson, 'Gnosis at Corinth', p. 103. See also Dunn, *1 Corinthians*, pp. 38–40.

26   Barrett, *First Corinthians*, 37. See also Thiselton, *First Corinthians*, 226, 233; Cf. Pearson, *Pneumatikos-Psychikos*, 27–81; and Dunn, *First Corinthians*, 37.

27   In fact, to define the Corinthians' theology as proto-Gnostic is not to define it at all, since it is a too general category. Dale Martin, *The Corinthian Body* (New Haven: Yale University Press, 1995), p. 71, rightly states that the proto-Gnostic hypothesis only begs the question.

from 1 Corinthians, this does not render 1 Corinthians (or Paul) Gnostic. In fact, as Painter rightly states, 'The use of this language does not in itself prove gnostic influence as it is possible that Paul's language influenced the development of later Gnosticism'.[28] Wilson expounds on this idea:

> The similarities are certainly present, but when we examine each in its context, in Paul on the one hand and in the Gnostic literature on the other, then the differences emerge. Since the Gnostics admittedly appealed to Paul, the inference is that they are the borrowers [not the other way around], and that the material has undergone some *Umdeutung* at their hands. To prove Gnostic influence on Paul (or his opponents) we should require to find independent evidence for the existence of something which could be clearly recognized as Gnosticism in the background of Paul's ministry.[29]

The analysis of both the immediate context and of (proto-) Gnosticism in Paul's day has shown that a Gnostic hypothesis is not viable. And if this is the case, then one also cannot claim that Paul speaks as a Gnostic in 1 Cor. 2.6-16. As Scroggs argues, such a claim would 'reduce the first two chapters to an argument which would have been completely incoherent to the Corinthians.'[30] Therefore, another background to the language of σοφία must be sought that gives a more plausible explanation of the data.

Hellenistic-Jewish Wisdom

Another candidate for the background of σοφία esteemed by the Corinthians is that of Hellenistic Jewish wisdom traditions. As with the advocates of a Gnostic background, so also those who see Jewish wisdom traditions behind the language of σοφία in the first three chapters of 1 Corinthians start with the terminology of 2.6–3.4, more precisely with the contrast πνευματικοί vs. ψυχικοί and its relation to wisdom. It is argued that these two terms are labels for two distinct spiritual classes of Christians, not much different from what the Gnostic hypothesis claims. And this is not a surprise, since the category of proto-Gnosticism is very general, covering various early theological systems, and there are parallels between Philo's exegesis, for instance, and that of the later Gnostics.[31] Among those who maintain such levels of spirituality based on the pair

---

28   Painter, 'Paul and the Πνευματικοί at Corinth', p. 240. See also Wilson, 'Gnosis at Corinth', p. 104, who quotes Robert Law, *The Tests of Life* (Edinburgh: n. p., 1909), p. 28, as saying that 1 Corinthians shows 'into how congenial a soil the seeds of Gnosticism were about to fall.' See also Collins, *First Corinthians*, p. 17; and Conzelmann, *1 Corinthians*, p. 15.

29   Wilson, 'Gnosis at Corinth', p. 109.

30   Scroggs, 'Paul: ΣΟΦΟΣ and ΠΝΕΥΜΑΤΙΚΟΣ', 33.

31   See, e.g., Sterling, '"Wisdom among the Perfect"' 383–84; Wilckens, *Weisheit und Torheit*, pp. 192–7; and R. M. Wilson, 'Philo of Alexandria and Gnosticism', *Kairos* 14 (1972) 213–19.

πνευματικοί vs. ψυχικοί as evidenced in the Jewish wisdom traditions are Birger A. Pearson, Richard A. Horsley, and James A. Davis.

Pearson, in his monograph *The Pneumatikos-Psychikos Terminology in 1 Corinthians*, seeks to locate the source of the Corinthians' theology embedded in the contrast of πνευματικοί with ψυχικοί in Hellenistic Jewish exegesis of Gen. 2.7. This dualism brings out the sharp distinction between the higher and heavenly πνεῦμα or πνευματικός nature of man, and the lower and earthly ψυχή or ψυχικός nature of man.[32] In consequence, according to the Jewish wisdom traditions represented by Philo and the Wisdom of Solomon, σοφία is the determinative factor in establishing one's level of spirituality – πνευματικός or ψυχικός.[33] Paul's task, then, was to redefine the meaning of πνευματικός and its relation to σοφία. Pearson summarizes his investigation in this way:

> It has been determined that Paul, in 1 Corinthians 2.1-16, has skillfully used the language of his opponents, and has turned it back against them by interpreting their language in an apocalyptic fashion. In doing so, Paul has not succumbed to the theology of his opponents, but has substituted his own concept of 'wisdom' for that of his opponents. Using their terminology, he has robbed them of their claim to *sapientia propria*, and has stressed in contrast that the true wisdom, which is 'foolishness' for men governed by the values of this world, is a *sapientia aliena*, given by God to man by the Spirit, and whose content is simply: the word of the cross. Thus, there is no ground for boasting at all. The Christian is *simul sapiens et stultus*.[34]

Horsley in several articles has attempted to refine the earlier thesis of Pearson arguing that, 'It is possible to determine with some degree of precision the nature and the background of the "proto-gnosticism" in Corinth: Hellenistic Jewish religiosity focused on Sophia and *gnosis*.'[35] He challenges Pearson by noting that there is no distinction between the higher and lower parts of the soul in Wisdom of Solomon and Philo. More importantly, he argues that, 'For this distinctive language [πνευματικός vs. ψυχικός] so important for understanding the

---

32 Pearson, *Pneumatikos-Psychikos*, 19–20, 82. He cites the following references to exegesis of Gen. 2.7 in conjunction with 1.27 in Philo, *Opif.* 135; *Leg.* 3.161; *Somn.* 1.34; *Her.* 55ff; *Spec.* 4.123; *Plant.* 18; and in Wis. 2.1-5. See also Lamp, *First Corinthians 1–4 in Light of Jewish Wisdom Traditions*, pp. 37–43.

33 Pearson, *Pneumatikos-Psychikos*, 39.

34 Ibid., 41–42.

35 Horsley, 'Pneumatikos vs. Psychikos: Distinctions of Spiritual Status among the Corinthians', *HTR* 69 (1976) 269–88; *idem* 'Wisdom of Word and Words of Wisdom in Corinth', 224–39; *idem* ' "How Can Some of You Say that There Is no Resurrection?" Spiritual Elitism in Corinth', *NovT* 20 (1978) 203–31; *idem*, 'Gnosis in Corinth: 1 Corinthians 8.1-16', *NTS* 27 (1981) 32–51, quote from p. 32.

Corinthian situation there is no convincing terminological parallel whatsoever in contemporary comparative material.'[36]

Nevertheless, Horsley contends that this contrast is parallel, on the one hand, to the fundamental contrast between the heavenly (immortal) and earthly (mortal) man of 1 Cor.15.44-54, and on the other hand to two other contrasts in the context of 1 Corinthians 2: mature vs. infant and wise vs. foolish.[37] Thus, Horsley argues, though the πνευματικός vs. ψυχικός terminology is missing in Philo, the conceptual parallels are there, particularly in Philo's exegesis of Gen. 1.27 and 2.7a.[38] This means that the Philonic theology is present in Corinth. He states: 'It would appear that the Corinthians used *pneumatikos-psychikos* along with the rest of these terms to make the same basic contrast between people of different levels of spiritual ability and attainment, different religious types of people, for whom the heavenly *anthrōpos* and the earthly *anthrōpos* were paradigmatic symbols in Philo.'[39] For both the distinction is determined by the possession of σοφία, as both the content and the agent of salvation.[40] This Philonic theology, Horsley contends, was mediated through an eloquent interpreter, such as Apollos, based on his Alexandrian origin (cf. Acts 18.24-28).[41]

While both Pearson and Horsley focus essentially on finding linguistic and conceptual parallels between the Corinthians' wisdom and Hellenistic Jewish Wisdom traditions as found in Philo and Wisdom of Solomon, James Davis, in his monograph *Wisdom and Spirit,* provides a more comprehensive treatment of the background behind the wisdom language. He includes Palestinian Jewish wisdom traditions as found in Sirach and Qumran in seeking to reveal the relation between σοφία and πνευματικός.[42] Two aspects distinguish Davis from his predecessors: the identification of the Corinthian wisdom with Torah meditation and the significant role of the Spirit's assistance in attaining wisdom via Torah

---

36 Horsley, 'Pneumatikos vs. Psychikos', 270.

37 Ibid., 274–80 and 280–84, respectively. This argument has been conceded, e.g., by Murphy-O'Connor, *Paul*, p. 281.

38 Horsley, 'Pneumatikos vs. Psychikos', 288.

39 Ibid., 280.

40 Ibid., 288.

41 Horsley, 'Wisdom of Word and Words of Wisdom in Corinth', 231; *idem*, 'Building an Alternative Society: Introduction', in *Paul and Empire: Religion and Power in Roman Imperial Society* (Richard Horsely, ed.; Harrisburg: Trinity, 1997), p. 212. The same was argued earlier by Pearson, *Pneumatikos-Psychikos*, 18; *idem, Gnosticism, Judaism, and Egyptian Christianity* (Minneapolis: Fortress, 1990), p. 171.

42 James Davis, *Wisdom and Spirit: An Investigation of 1 Corinthians 1.18-3.20 against the Background of Jewish Sapiential Traditions in the Greco-Roman Period* (Lanham: University Press of America, 1984), p. 142. For a helpful summary, see Lamp, *First Corinthians 1-4 in Light of Jewish Wisdom Traditions*, pp. 100–1.

study.[43] According to Davis, three features of Jewish wisdom traditions were present in Corinth: (1) a nomistic emphasis seen in the identification of spiritual wisdom with the investigation of the meaning of Torah[44]; (2) a tendency to distinguish between individuals at different levels with respect to the acquisition and attainment of wisdom[45]; and (3) a stress upon eloquence as a quality of the πνευματικοί.[46] These three features are tied together by the role of the Spirit. The Spirit is regarded as the source of higher wisdom and assists the ones who are part of an elite group to become pneumatics as they study the Torah. Davis concludes:

> In both Hellenistic and Palestinian Judaism we found that the content of wisdom is defined with respect to the Torah; there is discussion about levels of attainment with regard to the acquisition of wisdom; the mediation of wisdom at the highest level of sapiential achievement is consistently attributed to a spirit sent by God, or to God's own Spirit; and qualities such as eloquence and perfection are throughout our sources assigned to the person who has successfully attained to the wisdom and understanding brought by divine assistance.[47]

Like Pearson and Horsley, Davis argues that the Corinthians had embraced a Philonic type of wisdom, perhaps under the influence of Apollos. In light of this reconstruction of the background, Paul critiques this nomistic wisdom for the reason of its low estimate of the cross and argues that the Torah-wisdom is inadequate and therefore superseded by the wisdom given by the Spirit as a result of the Christ-event.[48]

From the succinct presentation of the Jewish wisdom hypothesis, it is evident that the various linguistic and conceptual parallels from chronologically plausible sources recommend this hypothesis over Gnosticism. Moreover, it provides a possible answer to the question of the avenues by which such theological traditions may have been introduced in the Corinthian church: Apollos.[49] But the claim that Apollos was the

43 Davis, *Wisdom and Spirit*, pp. 7–62, 122.
44 Ibid., pp. 103, 124.
45 Ibid., p. 75.
46 Ibid., pp. 128, 143.
47 Ibid., p. 142.
48 Ibid., pp. 104, 106, 143.
49 There is another branch of the Jewish wisdom hypothesis that identifies Peter with the person who introduced such theology in Corinth, either by a personal visit to Corinth or by a strong Judaizing party in Corinth who considered Peter to be its apostle. Such theory was first exposed by Schmidt and made famous by F. C. Baur, 'Die Christuspartei in der korinthischen Gemeinde, der Gegensatz des petrinischen und paulinischen Christenthums in der ältesten Kirche', *TZT* 4 (1831) 61–206. See recently Gerd Lüdemann, *Opposition to Paul in Jewish Christianity* (Minneapolis: Augsburg, 1977); also Michael Goulder, 'Σοφία in 1 Corinthians', *NTS* 37 (1991) 516–34; and *idem, Paul and the Competing Mission in Corinth* (LPS; Peabody: Hendrickson, 2001). For a critique of Goulder's thesis see Tuckett, 'Jewish

expositor of Jewish wisdom based on study of the Torah is going beyond the evidence found in Acts 18.24-28 and represents a very improbable theory in light of the fact that the Corinthian correspondence lacks any indication in that direction.[50] Litfin is right to state that 'the easy relationship between Paul and Apollos would have been inconceivable if Apollos had taught Philonic doctrines to the Corinthians and thereby become the source of Paul's problems in Corinth.'[51] In fact, the argument concerning the connection of Apollos with the Hellenistic Jewish wisdom background in 1 Corinthians seems to be based on a circular argument: it seeks to prove (i.e., Apollos introduced Torah-wisdom in Corinth) that which it assumes (i.e., Apollos embraced a Hellenistic Jewish teaching).

G. Robert Wynne, in his 1912 monograph on Apollos, very aptly remarks: 'There is no reason to think that the teaching of St. Paul and of Apollos varied seriously. . . . The censure of St. Paul was not addressed to any false doctrine taught by his successor [Apollos], but to those who recklessly endangered unity by this blind favoritism.'[52] That this is so is evidenced by what Luke tells us in Acts about Apollos. First, he "was instructed in the way of the Lord', that is, in the way of Jesus (Acts 18.25). Second, Aquila and Priscilla completed whatever was lacking in his Christian knowledge (Acts 18.26), so that if he did use to teach a different doctrine (though this is seriously doubtful) he received proper instructions in theology. Third, he was sent with letters of recommendation to Corinth (Acts 18.27), something the 'brothers' (including Aquila and Priscilla) would not have done had they suspected him to teach differently from Paul. And fourth, Luke tells us that he 'helped them [i.e., the Corinthians] much which had believed through grace' (Acts 18.27), something Luke would not have written had Apollos introduced in Corinth a teaching different from Paul's gospel of Christ crucified. All these suggest strongly that Apollos did not have a different doctrine or teaching than that of the church, and consequently of Paul, much less one based on Jewish wisdom traditions. That he was δυνατὸς ἐν ταῖς γραφαῖς (cf. Acts 18.24) does not single him out necessarily, since preaching in the early church (viz. Acts) implied great knowledge of the Old Testament which served for proving the messianic character of Jesus. Similarly, his origin from

---

Christian Wisdom in 1 Corinthians?' 201–20. The Petrine party in Corinth has been also advocated in a modified theory by C. K. Barrett, 'Christianity at Corinth', and 'Cephas in Corinth in Essay on Paul (Philadelphia: Weshuinster, 1982), 1–27 and 28–39 respectively.

50 See Ker, 'Paul and Apollos', 79.

51 Litfin, *Proclamation*, p. 231. The suggestion that Apollos may have introduced false doctrine in the church begs the question of why Paul does not confront him directly, since he is not afraid to openly denigrate others, even in the face of opposition (Gal. 1.6-9; 2.11; 5.10-12; 6.12-13; Phil. 3.2; 2 Cor. 11.4, 13–15). Cf. Pogoloff, *LOGOS AND SOPHIA*, 101.

52 Wynne, *Apollos or Studies in the Life of a Great Layman of the First Century* (London: SPCK, 1912), pp. 59–60; also 69.

Alexandria, and presumably an acquaintance with Philonic exegesis, does not require that he indeed was influenced by Jewish wisdom traditions or that, had he been, he continued to use it after his 'discipleship training' under Aquila and Priscilla.[53]

Nevertheless, the hypothesis of Hellenistic Jewish wisdom is not dependent upon this conjecture about Apollos, and thus other weaknesses must be explored. Moreover, if the main pillars upon which the hypothesis rests are proven weak, the speculation concerning Apollos will also crumble, remaining at the stage of being a mere conjecture.

The Jewish wisdom background seems to rely heavily upon two premises that need evaluation. First, all advocates argue that the distinction between πνευματικός and ψυχικός finds its linguistic and conceptual parallel particularly in Philo and Wisdom of Solomon, which allegedly proves that the Corinthians adopted a Jewish Wisdom theology. Similar distinctions in levels of spirituality were observed concerning the Gnostic hypothesis, and we do not need to repeat the critique lodged there based on contextual considerations and on the logical flow of the argument.[54] One issue, however, still needs to be addressed, namely the degree to which it is legitimate to read the Corinthians' theology into Paul's terminology.[55] Various positions have already been briefly mentioned, but a preference needs to be identified.

It is quite obvious that the Corinthians' thinking was characterized by worldly values as identified in the phrase σοφία τοῦ κόσμου or τοῦ αἰῶνος τούτου. They even considered themselves σοφοί. Paul seeks to challenge this wisdom by presenting a different wisdom, represented by the cross, a wisdom he preaches to the πνευματικοί. Pearson's distinction between two levels of Christians forces him to argue '[t]hat Paul here states that this "wisdom" is reserved for the "perfect" is pure irony, for in fact Paul elsewhere stresses that the secrets of God's salvific plan belong to the entire congregation of the elect' (cf. 2 Cor. 4.3f).[56] The context, however, does not require that we see in Paul's statement an irony but a fact, considering our arguments that Paul identifies the πνευματικοί with all Christians (cf. 1 Cor. 12.1-3) and that the wisdom/mystery he preaches is

---

53   Barrett, 'Christianity at Corinth', 4, rightly states that 'there is no ground for supposing that every Alexandrian Jew was a potential Philo (although some writers seem to think so).' See also Kuck, *Judgment*, p. 162; Munck, *Paul and the Salvation of Mankind*, pp. 143–4, 154.

54   See Pickett, *The Cross in Corinth*, p. 51, and Hurd, *The Origin of 1 Corinthians*, p. 107.

55   One important aspect of the issue here is that of 'mirror-reading'–how much of Paul's (negative) statements can be interpreted as responses to the Corinthians' theology. For guidelines and a test case of mirror-reading see John Barclay, 'Mirror-Reading a Polemical Letter: Galatians as a Test Case', *JSNT* 31 (1987) 73–93. See also, Cousar, 'Theological Task of 1 Corinthians', 93.

56   Pearson, *Pneumatikos-Psychikos*, p. 32.

Christ crucified (not a 'mystery' for any believer). That the Corinthians might have regarded themselves πνευματικοί, a term carrying a theological baggage different than the one Paul implies by its use, is a moot point in this text. In this respect, we believe that the terminology used by Paul is not something that he borrowed from his opponents, since it is part of his vocabulary in describing believers (cf. Gal. 6.1). E. A. Judge states:

> Whereas in other respects (for example in the field of personal relations and the ministries in church) Paul is very ready to forge his own vocabulary, here he by no means concedes their terms to his opponents. Wisdom (*sophia*), reason (*logos*), and knowledge (*gnosis*) are all ideals central to his own position. He stigmatizes what is invalid in the case of others by qualifying the terms with phrases such as 'of the world' or 'according to the flesh'.[57]

Thus, as we have argued, what Paul challenges in 1 Cor. 2.6–3.4 is not a certain theology but a worldly mindset. Scroggs rightly argues, 'I think it doubtful that very much evidence of the *content* of the opponents' wisdom can be found anywhere in chapters 1–4.'[58] Paul uses the contrast between πνευματικός and ψυχικός not for the purpose of classifying the Corinthians as second-class Christians, maintaining the class distinctions present in Jewish wisdom traditions, but to warn them of their precarious spiritual state given their worldly thinking concerning Christian leadership.

A second major premise of this hypothesis is that the σοφία against which Paul polemicizes should be identified with the Torah interpretations of the Jewish wisdom traditions. In other words, Paul challenges the Corinthians' alleged theology based on the study of Torah. This reconstruction, however, is questionable, not the least because the Corinthian *ecclesia* was predominantly a Gentile congregation.[59] Also, William Baird, in his review of Davis' monograph, rightly asks, 'If the real distinction between Paul and his opponents is their stress on the Torah and his focus on Christ and the cross, how are we to explain the shape of the apostle's argument? Why, for instance, does Paul fail completely to mention the law in 1 Cor. 1.18–3.17,' and why other vocabulary he uses elsewhere to denigrate reliance on the law (such as 'works of the law') is missing?[60] Thus, it is difficult to detect any diatribe against the law in 1 Corinthians 1–4 or anywhere else in 1 Corinthians. On the contrary, Paul

57 Judge, 'Early Church against Classical Education', *JCEd* 77 (1983) 11. See also Kovacs, 'The Archons, the Spirit and the Death of Christ', 225, 229.
58 Scroggs, 'Paul: ΣΟΦΟΣ and ΠΝΕΥΜΑΤΙΚΟΣ', 34 (emphasis by author).
59 Ker, 'Paul and Apollos', 80.
60 William Baird, 'Review: *Wisdom and Spirit: An Investigation of An Investigation of 1 Corinthians 1.18–3.20 against the Background of Jewish Sapiential Traditions in the Greco-*

seems to regard the requirements of the Law as neutral (cf. 1 Cor. 9.19-23).[61] More importantly, the Corinthians do not seem to be overly concerned with Torah-morality, given their immoral behavior.[62]

Given these weaknesses, the hypothesis of Jewish wisdom traditions behind the σοφία language in 1 Cor. 1.18–3.4 remains at the level of a hypothesis. Moreover, the linguistic and conceptual parallels do not seem to suggest that their presence in our text necessarily means an importation of the theology of the Jewish wisdom context. The argument of this hypothesis is much too limited for a discussion of these affinities, and there is virtually no mention of other background issues such as social and cultural factors that would contribute to its validity.[63] Such issues have been taken into consideration by the Greco-Roman hypothesis for the background of the σοφία language.

Greco-Roman Rhetoric

The rhetorical hypothesis is the oldest proposal for the background of the σοφία language, although in modern times it had been eclipsed for a time by the two aforementioned hypotheses. We should not lose sight of the fact, however, that even in the Jewish wisdom interpretation rhetorical eloquence was conceded as highly esteemed by the Corinthians, but it has not received the central place that it seems to hold in Paul's argumentation.[64] The last two decades, thus, have sought to revive the proposition of Paul's relation to rhetoric investigated by the Church Fathers, applied by Calvin, and advanced by Johannes Weiss and Hans Windisch at the beginning of the twentieth century.[65] Probably the impetus toward the revival of this hypothesis has been given in the 1960s by E. A. Judge with his insistence on the Greco-Roman social context of

---

Roman Period by James A. Davis', *JBL* 106 (1987) 149–51 (150). See also Schrage, *Der erste Brief*, p. 47; and Dahl, 'Paul and the Church at Corinth according to 1 Corinthians 1.10-4.21', pp. 41–2.

61   Tuckett, 'Jewish Christian Wisdom in 1 Corinthians?' 209.

62   Cf. Lamp, *First Corinthians 1–4 in Light of Jewish Wisdom Traditions*, pp. 101–2; and Tuckett, 'Jewish Christian Wisdom in 1 Corinthians?' 213.

63   Cf. Clarke, *Leadership in Corinth*, p. 102, n. 68.

64   Winter, *Philo and Paul among the Sophists*, pp. 60–112, has read Philo as a source of information concerning the Second Sophistic. He shows how Philo himself is a critic of rhetorical eloquence.

65   For research into the question of Paul's rhetorical skills by the Early Church Fathers see E. A. Judge, 'Paul's Boasting in Relation to Contemporary Professional Practice', *ABR* 16 (1968) 37–50. On the history of research concerning Paul and rhetoric see Betz, 'The Problem of Rhetoric According to the Apostle Paul', pp. 16–21. See Weiss, *Der erste Korintherbrief*, xxxiii; Heinrici, G., *Der erste Brief an die Korinther* (Göttingen: Vandenhoeck, 1896), pp. 65–6.

the early church.[66] Since then, there have been a number of scholars who have interpreted 1 Corinthians 1–4 within the framework of Greco-Roman rhetoric, such as Duane Litfin, Stephen Pogoloff, Bruce Winter, L. L. Welborn, and Margaret Mitchell. This interpretation has unmistakably become generally accepted among the commentators of the Corinthian correspondence and thus needs to be evaluated.

If the focus passage for the Gnostic and Jewish Wisdom hypotheses is 1 Cor. 2.6-16, the Greco-Roman rhetoric hypothesis rests on the terminology found in 1 Cor. 2.1-5. It is in this passage, it is believed, that one finds Paul's anti-rhetorical stance concerning his theology of preaching as he rejects σοφία λογοῦ in proclamation. Litfin wrote his monograph *St. Paul's Theology of Proclamation* in order to substantiate such a claim.[67] In the first part of his study he seeks to prove the importance of σοφία as rhetoric in first-century Corinth and to describe its nature with reference to sophists such as Plato, Isocrates, Aristotle, Cicero, Quintilian, and lesser writers of the first-century AD. Several characteristics of the sophists arise from the study, which then form the backdrop against which, it is believed, Paul constructs his theology of preaching couched in σοφία language. First, the sophists, defined as 'professional educators who gave instructions to young men and public displays of eloquence for fees',[68] employed rhetoric in order to succeed, holding to the belief that persuasion was the goal of rhetoric.[69] It was the task of the orator to create belief. Everything depended upon *his* skill. Second, the key to persuasion was rhetorical adaptation 'to the exigencies of the rhetorical situation so as to achieve a predetermined result.'[70] In this sense, the successful speaker always appealed to certain social values such as honor in order to persuade his audience. Third, despite pejorative words used to refer to sophists such as 'flatterers' or 'crowd pleasers', there was an intimate association between eloquence and wisdom. One could not be eloquent without possessing wisdom and vast knowledge.[71] Fourth, eloquence was a means to wealth and honor.[72] These characteristics point to one important fact, which Litfin so adequately summarizes: 'The orator

66   Judge, 'Early Christians as a Scholastic Community: Part II', *JRH* 1 (1960–61) 4–15; 125–37; *idem*, 'Paul's Boasting in Relation to Contemporary Professional Practice', 37–50; *idem, The Social Pattern of Christian Groups in the First Century: Some Prolegomena to the Study of the New Testament Ideas of Social Obligations* (London: Tyndale, 1960).

67   Litfin, *Proclamation*, p. 17.

68   Ibid., p. 38.

69   Ibid., pp. 41, 81, 91. See, e.g., Cicero, *Inv.* 1.6, *Part. Or.* 5; Quintilian, *Inst.* 2.15.5.

70   Ibid., pp. 55, 92, 105, 115. See, e.g., Plato, *Phaed.* 270B-271B; *Gorg.* 452D-453A; Quintilian, *Inst.* 2.13.2; 10.1.3-6.

71   Ibid., pp. 44, 95, 120. See, e.g., Cicero, *Inv.* 1.9; *De or.* 3.22.82; 3.60-61; *Part. or.* 23.79; 79. So also Judge, 'Early Christians as a Scholastic Community', 126.

72   Ibid., pp. 57, 129.

played the crowd but the crowd called the tune.'[73] It depended upon the deliberation of the crowd whether the speaker succeeded or not. The audience was in a sense the judge of the speaker who was on trial.[74]

Against this background of σοφία as rhetoric, it is argued that Paul presents his theology of preaching (especially in 1 Cor. 2.1-5). The Corinthians functioned as arbiters of his preaching in contrast to that of other preachers, much like the audience of the Greco-Roman orators, disapproving his *modus operandi* as a result of measuring his 'performance' against the standards and characteristics of an accomplished speaker in first-century Greco-Roman culture.[75] As a result, 'Paul was eager to vindicate his approach to public speaking against the complaints of his critics'.[76] He does this by taking an anti-rhetorical stance.[77] The theological aspects of his defense in 1 Corinthians 1–4 form the rationale for his behavior, which means that the core issue of the dissensions was over matters of form and not theology.[78] Litfin, thus, by referring to the rhetorical background is able to identify the cause of the dissensions without ascribing heretical doctrinal positions to the parties. Paul's argument, then, is that the *content* of his message forced him to adopt a correspondent *form* of presentation. As such, Paul describes his task as that of a herald – to announce rather than to persuade by means of σοφία λογοῦ.[79] This means that Paul believed that his responsibility was not to create πίστις nor to adapt to the rhetorical situation but simply to explain the gospel. His audience, in turn, had no right to judge his rhetorical ability, for in doing so they were acting in a worldly fashion and were presuming that the gospel needed human assistance (i.e., rhetoric) in order to result in faith. Litfin concludes: 'Hence, the true contrast in Paul's argument is between two different ways of demonstrating the truthfulness of the Gospel, and therefore between two different bases of belief'.[80]

73 Ibid., pp. 58; see also 133.
74 Ibid., pp. 86, 130–31.
75 Ibid., p. 153.
76 Ibid., p. 155.
77 Michael A. Bullmore, *St. Paul's Theology of Rhetorical Style: An Examination of 1 Corinthians 2.1-5 in Light of First Century Greco-Roman Rhetorical Culture* (San Francisco: International Scholars Publications, 1995), p. 16, thinks that Litfin's thesis is too general and argues that Paul rejects not something essential to Greco-Roman rhetoric, but reacts only against 'a particular rhetorical embodiment in which stylistic virtuosity [i.e., the flashy Asian style of oratory] was the dominant feature'. Litfin, 'Review: *St. Paul's Theology of Rhetorical Style: An Examination of 1 Corinthians 2.1-5 in Light of First Century Greco-Roman Rhetorical Culture* by Michael A. Bullmore', *JBL* 116 (1997) 569, responds by arguing that Bullmore's 'treatment is vulnerable to the charge that it is reductionistic in that it portrays first-century rhetoric focusing on style exclusively'.
78 Litfin, *Proclamation*, pp. 171–2.
79 Ibid., pp. 196–201.
80 Ibid., p. 249.

Winter, in his monograph *Philo and Paul among the Sophists*, provides a more comprehensive picture of first-century sophistry, seeking to show in the first part that the Second Sophistic was a movement 'already flowering if not flourishing'[81] in the Corinth of Paul's time. In the second part, he suggests that Paul's argument in 1 Corinthians 1–4 is directed against the values and practices of the sophists which have infiltrated and marked the thinking of the Corinthian believers.[82]

Winter seeks to prove the first point from literary and non-literary Alexandrian (e.g., Philo, Dio Chrysostom) and Corinthian sources (e.g., Favorinus, Epictetus, Paul). The sophists are presented in these sources as 'rhetoricians whose ability in oratory was such that they could both secure a public following and attract students to their schools.'[83] Rhetoric was tertiary education, so that those who benefited from training under a sophist were preparing for professional and political life.[84] It is within this context of a sophist seeking pupils and young men seeking education that would secure them a high standing in society that one can perceive the most telling conventions and practices of the Second Sophistic, which allegedly form the background to the problems in the Corinthian church.[85] First, among the primary concerns of the sophist was fame and wealth.[86] They charged excessive fees from those who sought their rhetorical training (cf. *P. Oxy* 2190). Despite this fact, the public was ready to give them the due respect and ascribe to them honor. Thus, sophists were numbered among the elites of society. Second, the means to attracting students to their schools and gaining recognition was public declamation, which sought to impress.[87] Public declamations were prepared with great fanfare, emphasis being placed during the declam-

---

81 Winter, *Philo and Paul among the Sophists*, p. 4. An important source for Second Sophistic is Philostratus, *Vit. soph.*

82 See also his *After Paul Left Corinth*, ch. 2; *idem*, 'Philodemus and Paul on Rhetorical Delivery (ὑπόκρισις)', in *Philodemus and the New Testament World*, (John T. Fitzgerald, Dirk Obbink, and Glenn S. Holland, eds.; NovTSup 111; Leiden: Brill, 2004), 323–42.

83 Winter, *Philo and Paul among the Sophists*, p. 4.

84 Ibid., p. 5. Isocrates established the first rhetorical school in Athens in 390 BC. Thereafter rhetoric formed the curriculum of the most advanced of the three stages of Greco-Roman education. See D. L. Clark, *Rhetoric in Greco-Roman Education* (New York: Columbia University Press, 1957), esp. ch. 3, 'The Schools', pp. 59–66. For information on training in rhetoric for politics see, e.g., Chrysostom, *Or.* 4.108; 6.12; 13.22-23; 21.1-5. The students were called μαθηταί, cf. Chrysostom, *Or.* 9. See also E. A. Judge, 'The Reaction against Classical Education in the New Testament', *JCEd* 77 (1983) 7–14 (7).

85 Most of the characteristics that will be presented are present in Philo, *Contempl.* as he compares the sophists to *Therapeutai* elder; cf. Winter, *Philo and Paul among the Sophists*, pp. 63–7.

86 Ibid., p. 59; see, e.g., Chrysostom, *Or.* 6.21; 22.2-5; 32.10; Philo, *Mos.* 11.212; Protagoras 313c-d; Plato, *Soph.* 213–35.

87 Ibid., pp. 31–2; see, e.g., Chrysostom, *Or.* 11.

ation particularly upon ὑπόκρισις – stage presence (cf. Epitectus Περὶ καλλωπισμοῦ III) – and form. Third, the pupils, in their commitment to their teachers often engaged in *synkrisis* with the teachers of other pupils, which inevitably led to factionalism.[88]

Winter believes that these and other conventions form the background of the σοφία language in 1 Corinthians 1–4. Thus, in regard to the second point of his monograph, Winter argues that Paul takes a deliberate and 'calculated' anti-sophistic stance particularly in 1 Cor. 2.1-5, where one finds a constellation of rhetorical terms and concepts which Paul rejects as incompatible with proclamation,[89] and in 1 Cor. 3.18-23, where Paul seeks to reverse the sophist/disciple boasting and imitation.[90] Confronted with the Corinthians' valuation of wisdom (i.e., sophistic rhetoric) manifested in their dissensions over teachers and their rhetorical ability, Paul seeks to defend his anti-sophistic *modus operandi*. That his rhetorical ability as far as his delivery (ὑπόκρισις) is concerned did not measure up to that of the sophists is seen, Winter argues, from self-characterization (ἰδιώτης τῷ λόγῳ cf. 2. Cor. 11.6) and from the assessment of his opponents (ἡδὲ παρουσία τού σώματος ἀσθενὴς καὶ ὁ λόγος ἐξουθενημένος cf. 2 Cor. 10.10).[91]

Winter's approach differs from Litfin's in that he narrows the background of Paul's use of the language of wisdom from a general rhetorical one emphasizing the key role of the speaker and audience in the success of a communicative act to the sophistic background that encompasses a whole worldview expressed in speech. At the same time, the two approaches have many points of contact, among which two are essential for our discussion. First, they both focus on the rhetorical background of the σοφία language in 1 Corinthians 1–4, which suggests that Paul was an anti-rhetor. The question of how this claim comports with the idea that his epistle(s) seems to be rhetorically structured and to contain rhetorical devices will be discussed in the next chapter of this work. Suffice it to state here that the cumulative evidence presented by both Litfin and Winter have convinced us (and most recent commentators) that what caused divisions in the Corinthian church was a worldly evaluation of their teachers' delivery wedded to the cultural values of secular Corinth. Thus their reconstruction of the background seems to give the best explanation to the causes of divisions and to fit best with Paul's argument in 1 Corinthians 1–4 as explained in the first chapter of this work. The Corinthians evaluated their teachers based on worldly σοφία (i.e., rhetoric) leading to boasting and ultimately to dissensions

---

88 Ibid., p. 55; see, e.g., Chrysostom, *Or.* 6.21; 8.9.
89 Ibid., pp. 148–50; 155–64.
90 Ibid., pp. 195–6.
91 Ibid., pp. 213–28.

while Paul seeks to defend his *modus operandi* devoid of worldly wisdom by pointing to the reversal of values implicit in the cross, namely, that God works contrary to the expectations the world has of an eloquent speaker. Likewise, authentic faith is engendered by simply 'placarding' the gospel, while human eloquence renders the cross ineffective.

Secondly, as with the Jewish Wisdom hypothesis, both Litfin and Winter attribute to Apollos a certain (indirect) role in the dissensions, based on his alleged rhetorical prowess (cf. Acts 18.24-28).[92] If that is the case, then this raises serious questions. Is Apollos portrayed by Paul in 1 Corinthians 1–4 as one who adopts a sophistic rhetoric that Paul himself refutes? And if so, is Apollos an opponent of Paul? Is Paul competing against the more rhetorically gifted Apollos? We will seek to answer these questions in the fourth chapter of this work. Until then, it is not too much to say that Apollos does seem to be a prominent figure in Paul's argumentation in 1 Corinthians 1–4, and that the information found in Acts 18.24-28 must be used corroboratively.

Pogoloff's focus is not so much on the historical development of Greco-Roman rhetoric but on the parallels between the social value system of rhetoric (i.e., σοφία) and that of the Corinthians.[93] He argues that σοφία as rhetoric is skill in preaching plus a whole world of social status. In this sense, 'σοφία tends to describe educated or cultured characteristics of persons of high social standing.'[94] Not only did rhetoric prepare one for the professional and political life, but rhetoric itself was the mark of an educated person, σοφία λογοῦ, according to Pogoloff, meaning 'cultured speech'.[95] Thus, 'the "wise speaker" was one who employed language in a manner which suited him to an upper class station.'[96]

Rhetoric, however, was not only something that reflected the social status of the one who employed it, but at the same time the rhetorical ability of a person was a reason for preferences and dissensions.[97] Individuals were attracted to rhetors whose styles reflected the character-istics of their social standing. This was so in light of the fact that Corinth was inhabited mostly by the *nouveau-riche* who, being in the shadow of Rome and Athens, were competing for status, seeking to increase their honor.[98] In such a society, Pogoloff claims, the sophists 'were sought by

92 Ibid., pp. 177–9. See also Litfin, *Proclamation*, p. 253.
93 In fact Pogoloff, *LOGOS AND SOPHIA*, 65, strongly rejects the use of evidence from the period of the Second Sophistic, *contra* Winter.
94 Ibid., p. 113; also 132–36. See, e.g., Plutarch, *Mor.* 146F-58B, 801D-2E; Chrysostom, *Or.* 18.1-3; Petronius, *Sat.* 48.
95 Ibid., pp. 110–11.
96 Ibid., p. 119. See, e.g., Cicero, *Fin.* 3.22.75; 3.17.56-57, for the connection between σοφία and the values of fame and honor.
97 Ibid., pp. 173–96.
98 Ibid., pp. 121–6.

all status seekers as prizes',[99] that is as means to enhance their own status.

These social values attached to rhetoric, argues Pogoloff, were what the Corinthian Christians desired for themselves and that led to dissensions. He contends that the Corinthian believers, hungry for status just like those of the larger society, were comparing their teachers based on their rhetorical ability, with adherence to one or the other conferring them a certain rank in society.[100] Paul, in turn, responds to this type of thinking by overthrowing the cultural values wedded to rhetoric. Pogoloff states:

> In Paul's narrative world, the normal cultural narratives of eloquence and status are radically reversed. What persuades is speech about what is ordinarily unfit for contemplation: not a life which is cultured, wise, and powerful, but one marked by the worst shame and the lowest possible status. Paul's rhetoric of the cross thus opposes the cultural values surrounding eloquence.[101]

Based on these observations, Pogoloff writes a narrative of the rhetorical situation seeking to establish the specific exigencies that prompted Paul's specific response.[102] The value of his study lies in the fact that he goes beyond merely cataloging linguistic and conceptual parallels to the social networks and cultural values wedded to rhetoric. However, as Anderson notes, 'Pogoloff's emphasis that Paul is only concerned with the social status of rhetoric, and not rhetoric (or some characterization thereof) *per se* is not persuasive ... The point of the text [1 Cor. 2.1-4] is that Paul is not superior (or a superior person) *in terms of speech or wisdom*, not that he does not have a superior social status *per se*.'[103] Regardless, Pogoloff's emphasis on the social world of Paul's day that influenced the Corinthians is well taken, and we will return to it later in this chapter after analyzing one more perspective that may enrich our understanding of σοφία as rhetoric.

This perspective is represented by Welborn and Mitchell. Both understand the language Paul uses in his argument against dissensions as well as the Corinthian slogans as characterizing conflict within city-states.[104] Welborn, for instance, argues that 'Paul's advice in 1 Corinthians 1–4 has [much] in common with speeches on concord (περὶ

---

99   Ibid., p. 160.

100   Cf. Ibid., p. 172; see also Witherington, *Conflict and Community*, p. 94.

101   Ibid., pp. 120; see also 203–24, for the opposite values which Paul underscores such as suffering, servanthood, etc. See also Judge, 'The Reaction against Classical Education', 7–14, for an earlier view on the values associated with rhetoric, the tertiary education.

102   See also Fiorenza, 'Rhetorical Situation', 386–403.

103   Anderson, *Ancient Rhetorical Theory and Paul*, p. 271.

104   E.g., σχίσματα (1.10) cf. Herodotus, *Hist.* 7.219; Diodorus Siculus, *Bib. Hist.* 12.66.2; ἔριδες (1.11) cf. Plutarch, *Caes.* 33; ζῆλος (3.3) cf. Lysias 2.48; Philo, *Flacc.* 41; μερίς (1.13) cf. Polybius 8.21.9; φυσιοῦσθε (4.6) cf. Xenophon, *Mem.* 1.2.25; Philo, *Leg.* 86.154;

ὁμόνοιας) by ancient politicians and rhetoricians.'[105] As a consequence, he sets out to prove, by investigating Paul's beginning argument in the context of ancient politics, that 'Paul's goal in 1 Corinthians 1–4 is not the refutation of heresy but what Plutarch describes as the object of the art of politics–the prevention of στάσις.'[106] In other words, according to Welborn, the real problem in the Corinthian church is not theological but one of partisanship, rendering it impossible to differentiate between parties based on doctrine.[107]

Welborn goes on to argue that political parties, just like the Corinthian parties, formed in accordance with social and economic differences.[108] Paul, then, Welborn argues, seeks to discuss the issue of dissensions in 1 Corinthians 1–4 in the context of social and economic differences (1 Cor. 1.26) by denying 'that the Corinthians are distinguished in the true, spiritual sense' and by 'stressing the reversal of status brought about by divine election.'[109] Thus Paul addresses 'those whom he regards as the prime movers in faction, the social and political elite.'[110] But in doing so, he expresses solidarity with the despised and oppressed in order to 'bring the δῆμος into his faction' (cf. Cicero, *Sest.* 96–98 and Herodotus 5.66).[111]

Within this political and economic understanding of discord, Paul's disavowal of σοφία λογοῦ as 'cleverness in speaking' (i.e., rhetoric) comes naturally into play, since it was believed that language and rhetoric played an important role in creating discord and exacerbating conflict.[112] Welborn argues that 'Paul's opponents in Corinth, who sought to lead the new movement by "persuasive words of wisdom," might have answered the apostle as the democratic rhetor, Diodotus, answered Cleon: it is the duty of the good citizen to be a good speaker, to employ fair argument, whatever eloquence, to advise the people responsibly.'[113] 'Wisdom' thus was a claim by the rhetors to possess higher knowledge, which led to an elitism that reflected itself in political struggles. As a result, according to Welborn, Paul had to claim 'wisdom' so that he may

Chrysostom, *Or.* 30.19; 58.5. See Welborn, 'On the Discord in Corinth', 86–88, 91–92. See also Mitchell, *Reconciliation*, pp. 65–111, for political terms and *topoi* in 1 Cor. 1.10-4.21 paralleling the rhetorical handbooks and actual speeches and letters from antiquity.

105 Welborn, 'On the Discord in Corinth', 89. He recalls *1 Clement* 46.5 in support of his thesis.

106 Ibid., pp. 89–90.

107 Ibid. p. 89, following Calvin.

108 Ibid., p. 96, cf. Aristotle, *Pol.* 5.1.3 1301b3, 5.1.6 1301b27; Plato, *Gorg.* 502e-19d, 576a; Cicero, *Sest.* 100–2. See also Dale Martin, *The Corinthian Body*, p. 40.

109 Ibid., pp. 96 and 93.

110 Ibid., p. 98.

111 Ibid., p. 101.

112 Ibid., p. 102, he states: 'The σοφία which Paul fears will undermine the community is nothing other than rhetoric'; cf. Aristotle, *Pol.* 5.7.2 1301a1.

113 Ibid., p. 103.

regain his position as teacher, in order to put an end to factions (1 Cor. 2.6-16).[114] This was forced upon him by circumstances, since, just like 'the ancient world parties engaged in strife regularly made use of the courts as a means of attacking their political opponents', so also the Corinthians 'sought to "examine" his credentials in quasi-judicial proceedings.'[115] Paul, however, denies them such prerogatives (cf. 1 Cor. 4.1-5), seeking 'to turn the Corinthian Christians away from politics.' He does this, Welborn concludes, by reminding them that, 'The fate of the community does not rest upon precepts of statecraft, but upon the word of the cross. Thus, its members need not look to political leaders, but can await redemption from God.'[116]

Welborn's (and Mitchell's) study is a helpful reminder that church politics will always have some originating cause in ecclesiastical disputes.[117] However, despite the numerous terminological parallels to the political arena that he adduces, he does not show from the text that what was going on in the Corinthian church was political dispute. This relative neglect of the literary context of Paul's argument requires two observations. First, although he states that, 'We can still recognize the phenomenon [i.e., στάσις], though the apostle withholds the name,'[118] it is still surprising that Paul would not name the phenomena. The fact that *1 Clement* 46.9b names it ('...And your στάσις *continues*') does not necessarily mean that that is what was going on at the time of 1 Corinthians even if both letters address the same church, since the two letters discuss different situations or different levels of discord at two different times in history.[119] Christof W. Strüder rightly contends that there is a discontinuity between the two situations, the dissensions having a different character and nature, which can be seen in Clement's depiction of the church of Paul's time as positive, functioning 'as a positive counterpart to later developments' (cf. *1 Clement* 47.1-6).[120] Thus, στάσις characterizes the more serious dissensions during Clement's time, but not that of Paul's time. Moreover, the στάσις in Clement's time, as the σχίσματα of Paul's time, has nothing to do with politics.

Second, Pogoloff rightly observes that Welborn 'fails to notice the

---

114   Ibid., pp. 103–9.

115   Ibid., p. 107.

116   Ibid., p. 109.

117   Welborn, ibid., p. 110, reminds us that the repercussion of such separation can be heard in Augustine's negative valuation of the *civitas terrena*.

118   Ibid.

119   See Davorin Peterlin, 'Clement's Answer to the Corinthian Conflict in AD 96', *JETS* p. 39 (1996) 57–69; *idem* 'The Corinthian Church Between Paul's and Clement's Time', *ATJ* 53 (1998) 49–57.

120   Christof W. Strüder, 'Preferences not Parties: The Background of 1 Cor. 1.12', *ETL* p. 79 (2003) 431–55 (436–38). More on the issue of parties follows later in this chapter.

obvious *differences* in Paul's situation [than that of the political arena] which dictate different functions for similar forms.'[121] In other words, for instance, the slogans are for teachers and not for political leaders. Mitchell, ironically, parts ways with Welborn by stating that, 'Welborn has not produced one example of an ancient political slogan which has the same formula (personal pronoun + εἰμι [or ellipsed] + genitive of a proper name).'[122] This leads us to a further observation: both Welborn and Mitchell assume too much from mere parallels in terms and *topoi*. Pogoloff aptly comments that they have not demonstrated that 'the vocabulary and *topoi* were used *exclusively* for such purposes ... and that such terms were not used in a new, metaphorical sense.'[123]

Third, as Dale Martin remarks, 'The ideological purpose of *homonoia* speeches was to mitigate conflict by reaffirming and solidifying the hierarchy of society.'[124] If that is the primary purpose of such speeches, Welborn (*et al.*) has not proven the claim that Paul seeks to reestablish his authority in 1 Corinthians 1–4 by reaffirming the hierarchy. That this is not what Paul does in this first rhetorical unit will become evident throughout this work, especially in Chapter 2.

Fourthly, Welborn is too quick to dismiss any theological dimension to the problems in the Corinthian church, limiting it strictly to political and sociological causes.[125] This, in fact, is the case with most of the advocates of the Greco-Roman rhetoric hypothesis which we have mentioned above and of the sociological interpretation which we will survey next.[126] Although we have argued against the Gnostic and Jewish Wisdom hypotheses' claim for σοφία as content, we have not done so to the point of denying what we have concluded in our examination in Chapter 1, namely, that the dissensions were symptomatic of a fundamental misperception of Christian ministry and leadership, which in turn proves that the Corinthians have not thought through the implications of the *theologia crucis*. They have not denied the validity of the cross, but they have not grappled with its implications for ecclesiastical life. This placed them in a precarious spiritual state.

But regardless of the points at which Welborn's thesis is subject to criticism, his understanding of σοφία as rhetoric agrees with the other

121 Pogoloff, *LOGOS AND SOPHIA*, p. 89.

122 Mitchell, *Reconciliation*, p. 84.

123 Ibid., 90. Here we are dealing with the exegetical fallacy called 'parallelomania.' See also Anderson, *Ancient Rhetorical Theory and Paul*, p. 263.

124 Martin, *The Corinthian Body*, p. 40.

125 Cf. Ker, 'Paul and Apollos', 83. See Dunn, *1 Corinthians*, p. 43.

126 E.g., Pogoloff, *LOGOS AND SOPHIA*, p. 105 quoting Scroggs, 'Paul: ΣΟΦΟΣ and ΠΝΕΥΜΑΤΙΚΟΣ', 36. See also Clarke, *Leadership in Corinth*, p. 91. All basically follow Munck, *Paul and the Salvation of Mankind*, pp. 135–6, who underscores that the divisions occurred 'for non-theological reasons.' Munck follows John Chrysostom, PG 61.23.

scholars we have presented under the Greco-Roman rhetoric hypothesis. The rhetorical background seems to best account for the terminology Paul uses in his argument against dissensions. Evidently, the critique that we have raised against the Gnostic and Jewish Wisdom traditions regarding the danger of parallelomania could apply also to the Greco-Roman hypothesis.[127] Winter, in the revised edition of his monograph, aptly responds to such critique by appealing to the *Sitz im Leben* of the passage, i.e., the pervasive features of public declamations of sophists.[128] Complementary to this is the literary context. First Corinthians 1–4, as we have argued, makes best sense when read against this background, rather than another. But before one embraces wholeheartedly the rhetorical background, at least one important qualification is in order.

One should not too quickly assume that every time Paul uses the word σοφία in 1 Corinthians 1–4 he is referring to rhetoric. Rather, a subtle distinction must be maintained between the larger semantic domain that σοφία covers (including rhetoric) and the phrase σοφία λογοῦ ('eloquence in speech' – rhetoric). Smit has attempted to argue that σοφία λογοῦ does not mean 'rhetorical skill' (lit. *ars rhetorica*) but 'logical wisdom', because Paul's argument in this first rhetorical unit 'belongs to the most rhetorical parts . . . proclaiming the crucified Christ in a highly rhetorical fashion.'[129] We will return to the issue of Paul's disavowal of rhetoric in the next chapter, but suffice it to say here that Paul is nowhere rejecting reason by claiming anti-intelectualism (*sacrificium intellectus*).[130] Moreover, the evidence adduced by Litfin and Winter is overwhelmingly in favor of understanding σοφία when used in juxtaposition with λόγος as rhetoric (i. e., cleverness in speaking), not the least because when the two are used together they appear in the context of preaching (cf. 1 Cor. 1.17; 2.1, 4, 13).[131]

Having said that, σοφία still acquires several senses in 1 Corinthians 1–4 as opposed to just one: rhetoric. Barrett rightly asserts that, 'It is scarcely an exaggeration to say that there is a different shade of meaning in the word σοφία (and σοφός) every time it occurs.' He goes on to state that 'the occurrences of the word may be grouped into two categories, good and bad, each with two subdivisions. Any attempt to draw the lines too sharply would lead to error; there are close relations between all four

---

127 See Anderson, *Ancient Rhetorical Theory and Paul*, pp. 275–6. The question is whether the terminology Paul uses in these introductory chapters are 'standard' or 'technical.'

128 Winter, *Philo and Paul among the Sophists*, pp. 150–63, esp pp. 160–1. See also 'The Entries and Ethics of Orators and Paul (1 Thess. 2.1-12)', *TynBul* 44 (1993) 55–74 for the same *Sitz im Leben* for Paul's *apologia* in 1 Thess. 2.1-12.

129 Smit, 'Search for Coherence', 245.

130 Cf. Litfin, *Proclamation*, p. 249.

131 Cf. BDAG, 'σοφία', 759; also Tuckett, 'Jewish Christian Wisdom in 1 Corinthians?' 212–13. *Contra* Anderson, *Ancient Rhetorical Theory and Paul*, p. 274.

groups.'[132] In the negative sense, when σοφία is used in combination with λόγος it refers to rhetoric, that is, to speech.[133] What Paul rejects, then, on the one hand, is preaching that relies on human skill to persuade. On the other hand, σοφία also refers to philosophy, in the sense of humanly devised ways of attaining salvation (cf. 1 Cor. 1.18-31; 2.6–3.4).[134] Lampe calls this type of wisdom *theo*logical wisdom.[135] This is the sense of σοφία when it is qualified as τοῦ κόσμου (1 Cor. 1.20), ἀνθρωπίνης (1 Cor. 1.25; 2.13), and τοῦ αἰῶνος τούτου (1 Cor. 2.6). In this sense, the unregenerate places emphasis on signs (i.e., the Jews) and arguments (i.e., Greeks) to attain to salvation. As Conzelmann states, the Jews and Greeks alike 'set themselves up as an authority that can pass judgment upon God ... They expect God to submit himself to their criteria [i.e., signs and arguments]. This, however, would mean that revelation would have to present itself as a factor belonging to the world.'[136] Thus, 'God would become a mere object of human, worldly thoughts. God would be in our pocket.'[137] But Paul rejects any soteriological scheme that starts with man (*sapientia propria*). Lampe states: 'Such wisdom is not a possession that human beings can get hold of, manipulating it, and being proud of it. Rather, this Logos itself takes possession of human beings.'[138]

Thus Paul responds to both wisdom as persuasive speech (e.g., καθ' ὑπεροχὴν λόγου ἢ σοφίας) and wisdom as human theology, with the wisdom of the cross as *divine revelation* that can be accepted only by the conviction brought about by the powerful work of the Holy Spirit. The kerygma of the cross shatters the human expectations, God effecting salvation by means of the work of the Holy Spirit as a result of the simple placarding of Christ crucified. Such a positive understanding of wisdom has a crucial role in Paul's argument against dissensions. Lampe explains it in this way: 'When the cross is proclaimed and through this act a community is founded, human wisdom and strength do not contribute anything to it. God rejects them as legitimate tools. Therefore, this is the

132   Barrett, 'Christianity at Corinth', 7–8; *idem, First Corinthians*, pp. 67–8. See also Tuckett, 'Jewish Christian Wisdom in 1 Corinthians?', 212, and Dunn, *1 Corinthians*, p. 41.

133   Of course, we must guard against confusing σοφία λογοῦ with λογος σοφίας as Conzelmann, *1 Corinthians*, p. 37, reminds us. Here we are strictly referring to the combination σοφία λογοῦ.

134   See, e.g., Schrage, *Der erste Brief*, p. 152.

135   Lampe, 'Theological Wisdom and the "Word About the Cross"', 121 (emphasis by author).

136   Conzelmann, *1 Corinthians*, p. 47.

137   Lampe, 'Theological Wisdom and the "Word About the Cross"', 123, following the quotation from Conzelmann.

138   Ibid., 124.

final point of this argument – the Corinthian parties cannot praise any apostle for these qualities'.[139]

From these various senses in which Paul uses the term σοφία one can see that rhetoric is only one of them, though we should add, a central one. Thus, to assert, as Anderson does, that 'Paul uses σοφία in this whole passage in terms of content, not form' and that 'these chapters in themselves say virtually nothing concerning Paul's views on rhetorical theory and practice',[140] is reductionistic. It would also be reductionistic to assert that σοφία always refers to rhetoric in 1 Corinthians 1–4. A faithful reading of the term in context would recognize that σοφία used in the negative senses refers to both rhetoric and philosophy; to both human eloquence and human efforts. Barrett, however, is right to argue for an intricate connection between the two negative senses of wisdom: 'σοφία is more than technique; it has come to be a way of estimating and assessing life'.[141]

We may thus conclude this evaluation of the Greco-Roman hypothesis by asserting that Paul starts and ends his discussion about σοφία (1 Cor. 1.18-31 and 2.6-16) by attacking the σοφία τοῦ κόσμου understood in general as a way of perception about salvation: human theology. In this sense, Paul opposes the wisdom of the world with the word about the cross, to show that God works salvation contrary to the expectations of the world. While the world evaluates things in light of her values and focuses on man, God imparts salvation through revelation in the cross. From this general sense, Paul moves to the more particular and pertinent sense of the term σοφία – eloquence in speech (1 Cor. 2.1-5). With this use, Paul seeks to oppose two different ways of persuasion: the human way by means of rhetoric and the divine way by means of the work of the Spirit. These two senses, then, are shown their relevance for the Corinthian situation especially in 1 Cor. 3.1-4. By evaluating their teachers according to their ability to speak 'persuasively' – the second sense of σοφία, the Corinthians actually proved to have a worldly perception of things, the first sense of σοφία.[142] With these things in mind we can move next to the social values associated with worldly wisdom, which the cross overturns.

The Social Background of 1 Corinthians 1–4

Timothy Lim has rightly observed that, 'It is difficult not to recognize that a sociological interpretation, not to the exclusion of but complementing the theological exegesis, is also needed, for Paul in this passage [2.1-5] employs terminology which traditionally belongs to rhetoric and appears

---

139   Ibid., 127.
140   Anderson, *Ancient Rhetorical Theory and Paul*, p. 276.
141   Barrett, 'Christianity at Corinth', 8.
142   *Contra* Anderson, *Ancient Rhetorical Theory and Paul*, p. 275.

to be distinguishing himself from the other preachers who were circulating in the Corinthian church'.[143] Moreover, we have also pointed out that Pogoloff was right in associating rhetoric with status and in reminding us that rhetoric was a common cause for dissensions. Given these factors, it is necessary to investigate the social background of the dissensions in the Corinthian church. Much has been written on 'the social setting of Pauline Christianity', to borrow the title of Gerd Theissen's foundational and influential book, and therefore we will seek to paint only in broad stokes the sociological factors at work in the Corinthian church.[144] In this regard, we will discuss briefly issues such as the social structure of the city of Corinth and of the Corinthian church, the social networks extant in the Corinthian society at large and to which the Corinthian Christians belonged, and Paul's response to the Corinthians' confusion of the identity of the church with other networks which led to dissensions. An investigation of the social dimension of the dissensions will hopefully shed more light on the rhetorical situation of 1 Corinthians 1–4.

Corinth was re-founded as a Roman colony in 44 BC after its destruction in 146 BC. The new settlers belonged mostly to the *liberti* (i.e., freedmen) who were seeking to move upwardly in a culturally heterogeneous society that offered opportunities for social advancement.[145] Upward mobility in terms of social status was achieved by means such as wealth, family lineage, and cultural sophistication.[146] As such, the members of the *nouveau riche* sought to increase their honor and esteem in at least two ways.[147] First, they sought to enter into a patronage/client relationship with those of unequal status, which involved the offering of *beneficia* to their clientèle and the receiving of praise in return from the recipients of such *beneficia*,[148] and the invitation of sophists to entertain their guests at a meal (i.e., *symposium*) with an *encomium* or other form of

143 Lim, ' "Not in Persuasive Words of Wisdom, but in the Demonstration of the Spirit and Power" ', *NovT* 29 (1987) 137–46.

144 For details see esp. Theissen, *Social Setting*; Marshall, *Enmity in Corinth*; and Meeks, *The First Urban Christians*.

145 Cf. Robertson, *Conflict in Corinth*, p. 88; Timothy L. Carter, ' "Big Men" in Corinth', *JSNT* 66 (1997) 45–71 (53). For details of the history, demographic and political features of the Roman Corinth, see esp. De Vos, *Church and Community Conflicts*, 179–95; also Clarke, *Leadership in Corinth*, pp. 9–21.

146 Cf. Witherington, *Conflict & Community in Corinth*, pp. 22–4; also Clarke, *Leadership in Corinth*, pp. 23–39.

147 For a discussion of the social values of honor and shame evident in 1 Corinthians see David A. deSilva, 'Let the One Who Claims Honor Establish That Claim in the Lord: Honor Discourse in the Corinthian Correspondence', *BTB* 28 (1998) 61–74; *idem. Honor, Patronage, Kingship & Purity*, esp. ch. 2.

148 Cf. Clarke, *Leadership in Corinth*, pp. 31–2. On patronage, see esp. John K. Chow, *Patronage and Power: A Study of Social Networks in Corinth* (JSNTSup, 75; Sheffield: JSOT Press, 1992), esp. chs 2 and 3.

epideictic rhetoric.[149] Second, the upwardly mobile persons also sought to
advance socially by seeking to enter into friendships with persons equal
status, which entailed certain established social expectations such as gift
exchange.[150] Such a focus on enhancing one's status and increasing one's
honor in the Roman Corinth led not only to competition for status and
honor among people, which most often than not was associated with
ὕβρις (i.e., pride),[151] but it also led to a clearer distinction among social
classes evident in the conventional social relationships and networks.[152]

Such a social stratification seems to characterize the Corinthian church
as well. At the beginning of the twentieth century, Adolf Deissmann
concluded, based on his analysis of the Greek used in the New Testament,
that the early Christians belonged to the middle and lower social
classes.[153] Since then a 'New Consensus'[154] has formed which defends the
idea that the Pauline congregations reflected a fair cross-section of urban
society, including people from a relatively high social strata.[155] At least
three pieces of evidence are set forth to support this assessment. First, it is
argued that most of the people in the Corinthian congregation mentioned
by Paul by name are of 'high status inconsistency'.[156] Hans Dieter Betz
may be correct to assess that at Corinth 'the Pauline mission had
succeeded – for the first time, it seems – in winning converts from the
better educated and cultured circles'.[157] Second, the terminology of 1 Cor.
1.26 used to describe the Corinthians at the time of their conversion carry
indubitable social connotations and point to the fact that though the
majority of the members were of low status, a few were from among the

149   Witherington, *Conflict & Community in Corinth*, pp. 191–95; 243–47.

150   On friendship and enmity see esp. Marshall, *Enmity in Corinth*, esp. chs 1 and 2. See
also Judge, 'The Social Identity of the First Christians: A Question of Method in Religious
History', *JRH* 11 (1980) 201–17 (214–15).

151   See, e.g., Clarke, *Leadership in Corinth*, p. 96; also Marshall, *Enmity in Corinth*, pp.
182–219.

152   Cf. Theissen, *Social Setting*, p. 102.

153   Deissmann, *Light from the Ancient East: The New Testament Illustrated by Recently
Discovered Texts of the Graeco-Roman World* (trans. L. R. M. Strachan; London, 1927), p. 9.
This is similar to Celsus' remarks about the scruffy background of the Christians as quoted
by Origen, PG 3.44.

154   A term coined by Abraham Malherbe, *Social Aspects of Early Christianity* (Baton
Rouge: Louisiana State University Press, 1977), p. 31, whose views concords with those of
the ones we will make reference to in the discussion that follows.

155   Cf. Theissen, *Social Setting*, p. 106, who draws on the earlier investigations by Judge,
Social Pattern, esp. p. 60. *Idem* 'The Social Identity of the First Christians', pp. 201–17. See
also Meeks, *The First Urban Christians*, p. 73; De Vos, *Church and Community Conflicts*, p.
203; and David W. J. Gill, 'In Search of the Social Elite in the Corinthian Church', *TynB* 44
(1993) 323–37.

156   Cf. Meeks, *The First Urban Christians*, p. 73; Theissen, *Social Setting*, pp. 73–96; De
Vos, *Church and Community Conflicts*, pp. 197–203.

157   Betz, 'The Problem of Rhetoric and Theology according to the Apostle Paul', p. 24.

elite of society.[158] Third, some of the Corinthian Christians regarded themselves as people who have acquired wealth and status since their conversion (cf. 1 Cor. 4.10).[159] That this is the case is evident from the fact that Paul expects the Corinthians to participate in the collection for Jerusalem (cf. 1 Cor. 16.2),[160] from the fact that some were involved in litigations against other brothers (cf. 1 Cor. 6.1-8) – presumably the rich against poor brothers, since the poor, on the one hand, had no financial means to take the rich to court, and on the other hand it was socially improper and disadvantageous for the poor to do so[161] – and from the fact that Christians met for worship in house-churches, which had to be large enough to accommodate a congregation of 50 to 100 people.[162]

Based on these observations, it is argued that the social stratification of the Corinthian congregation was in part the cause of dissensions in the church. This is supported by reference, among others, to the conflict at the Lord's Supper between the 'have' and the 'have-nots' (cf. 1 Corinthians 11),[163] to the disagreements between the 'weak' and the 'strong' concerning the food offered to idols (cf. 1 Corinthians 8–10),[164] to the litigations between the rich and the poor (cf. 1 Corinthians 6),[165] and to the dissensions of chs 1–4 allegedly between the local leaders who competed for honor by offering food and lodging to different teachers

158   See, e.g., Theissen, *Social Setting*, pp. 70–3, and Clarke, *Leadership in Corinth*, pp. 41–57.

159   Cf. Tuckett, 'Paul, Scripture and Ethics: Some Reflections', *NTS* 46 (2000) 403–24. There is a general agreement that the terms used by Paul in 1 Cor. 4.10 to describe the Corinthians' present status carry social connotations and reflect the consciousness of the whole congregation. See Theissen, *Social Setting*, pp. 72–3; and John M. G. Barclay, 'Thessalonica and Corinth: Social Contrasts in Pauline Christianity', *JSNT* 47 (1992) 49–7 (57). See also Pickett, *The Cross in Corinth*, p. 42. *Contra*, Fee, *First Corinthians*, pp. 176–7; Schrage, *Der erste Briefe*, p. 343; and Hall, *Unity*, p. 58, *et al.* These later scholars take the terms to refer to spiritual rather than social status.

160   Theissen, *Social Setting*, pp. 96–7, and Hall, *Unity*, pp. 76, 79.

161   Cf. Clarke, *Leadership in Corinth*, pp. 59–71. He follows Bruce W. Winter, 'Civil Litigation in secular Corinth and the Church: The Forensic Background to 1 Corinthians 6.1-8', *NTS* 37 (1991) 559–72. Consider Petronius, *Satyricon* 14 quoted by Robertson, *Conflict in Corinth*, 102, n. 61.

162   Hall, *Unity*, pp. 53, 75–6. The size of a house-church is debatable, with some arguing for smaller than 40 to 50 people and others for up to 100. For more details see De Vos, *Church and Community Conflicts*, pp. 203–5.

163   Cf. Theissen, *Social Setting*, pp. 96, 151; *idem* 'Social Conflicts in the Corinthian Community: Further Remarks on J. J. Meggitt, Paul, Poverty and Survival', *JSNT* 25 (2003) 371–91 (377–81); Meeks, *The First Urban Christians*, pp. 67–8. *Contra* Lindemann, *Erste Korintherbrief*, p. 252.

164   Cf. Theissen, *Social Setting*, pp. 121–43; *idem*, 'Social Conflicts in the Corinthian Community', pp. 381–9; De Vos, *Church and Community Conflicts*, pp. 222–3. *Contra* Hall, *Unity*, pp. 59–64.

165   Cf. Clarke, *Leadership in Corinth*, pp. 59–71.

who could enhance their status by entering into a patronage and/or friendship relationships.[166]

This New Consensus has been recently challenged by Justin J. Meggitt, particularly in his book *Paul, Poverty and Survival*, arguing that the Corinthians were from among the 'poor' of the first century.[167] Thus, he argues against the claim that there were any among the Corinthian Christians who were of the elite of society.[168] However, while his criticism of the claim that Christianity was actually an elite movement is correct, few have embraced Meggitt's attempt to revive the Old Consensus.[169] It is not the place here to rehearse the arguments and reactions to his claims, but suffice it to say that there is clear evidence in Paul's epistles, including 1 Corinthians, to support the claim that the Corinthian congregation was heterogeneous, numbering among its members people from all social strata, even though we agree with David Hall that 'any estimate of the social composition of the Corinthian church, or of the city of Corinth as a whole [...] is bound to be speculative'.[170]

Moreover, it is undeniable that the heterogeneous composition of the Corinthian congregation inevitably caused tensions in the church. However, it would be reductionistic to speak of a single 'fault line' (i.e., socio-economic) separating the Christians in Corinth.[171] C. K. Robertson is thus right to characterize such an understanding as static, when in fact

166   Cf. Theissen, *Social Setting*, pp. 54–7, 64; Meeks, *The First Urban Christians*, pp. 177–225; Pogoloff, *LOGOS AND SOPHIA*, pp. 197–231; De Vos, *Church and Community Conflicts*, pp. 220–1. See also Welborn, 'On the Discord in Corinth', 96. *Contra* Hall, *Unity*, p. 79.

167   Meggitt, *Paul, Poverty and Survival* (Edinburgh: T&T Clark, 1998), p. 179. By 'the poor', Meggitt means the 'destitute', people who live 'at or near subsistence level' (p. 5), who existed in 'abject poverty' (p. 50).

168   Advocates of the New Consensus agree that at least Erastus was among the middle-high status Christians. See, e.g., Clarke, *Leadership in Corinth*, pp. 41–57. *Contra* Meggitt, 'The Social Status of Erastus (Rom 16.23)', *NovT* 38 (1996) 218–23.

169   See the three articles discussing Meggitt's thesis in *Paul, Poverty and Survival* in *JSNT* 84 (2001) Dale B. Martin, 'Review Essay: Justin J. Meggitt, Paul, Poverty and Survival' (51–64); Gerd Theissen, 'The Social Structure of Pauline Communities: Some Critical remarks on J. J. Meggitt, Paul, Poverty and Survival' (65–84); and Justin J. Meggitt, 'Response to Martin and Theissen', (85–94); also Gerd Theissen, 'Social Conflicts in the Corinthian Community', 371–91. Another discussion was carried in the same journal [26.3 (2004)] around Steven J. Friesen's thesis of a poverty scale, which in many ways agrees with Meggitt's assessment of the Corinthian church and the Greco-Roman society at large. See Steven J. Friesen, 'Poverty in Pauline Studies: Beyond the So-called New Consensus' (323–61); John Barclay, 'Poverty in Pauline Studies: A Response to Steven Friesen' (363–66); and Peter Oakes, 'Constructing Poverty Scales for Graeco-Roman Society: A Response to Steven Friesen's "Poverty in Pauline Studies"' (367–71).

170   Hall, *Unity*, p. 77; also D. G. Horrell, *The Social Ethos of the Corinthian Correspondence: Interests and Ideology from 1 Corinthians and 1 Clement* (Edinburgh: T&T Clark, 1996), p. 94.

171   See Martin, *The Corinthian Body*, p. 69.

'there were more factors at work in Corinth than simply economic ones'.[172] Thus, there is need of a more dynamic picture of the conflict in Corinth, which takes into consideration the multiple overlapping networks to which many in the church already belonged. As such, we concur with Robertson that 'the interpersonal disputes in Corinth resulted from "an even more fundamental problem concerning perception" of the church itself, as the Christian ἐκκλησία became seen as one more relational system among other associations and networks.'[173] That this is so is hinted at in Paul's accusation against the Corinthians that κατὰ ἄνθρωπον περιπατεῖτε (cf. 3.4) and his stress on the unique identity of the church – ἐν Χριστῷ. This contrast can be fully grasped only when we compare the Christian ἐκκλησία with other (secular) networks to which the Corinthians belonged and with which they presumably confused the new social entity – ἡ ἐκκλησία τοῦ θεοῦ.[174] Following Wayne Meeks and C. K. Robertson, we will explore four models which resemble the Pauline *ecclesia* in order to determine how belonging to any of these networks might have shaped the (worldly) thinking of the Christian Corinthians in regard to belonging to the Christian *ecclesia*.[175]

The first model comparable to that of the Christian community is that of the household. Although the οἶκος was considered the 'element from which a πόλις is made, so to speak the seed-bed of the πολιτεία',[176] some of the rights that women, slaves, and clients enjoyed in the household make the οἶκος a unique social network. One aspect that will be explored in more detail in the next chapter is that of the concept of *paterfamilias* and the related concept of *patria potestas*. We will only mention here that, contrary to some who believe that the father of a household acted like a tyrant, wielding power and discipline indiscriminately throughout the household, according to recent studies it has been shown that the father related to his children differently than to the slaves of his household.[177]

172 Robertson, *Conflict in Corinth*, p. 23. See pp. 5–34 for an evaluation of Theissen, Meeks, Martin and others, evaluation with which we agree.

173 Ibid., pp. 54; 55–57. He follows Pickett, *The Cross in Corinth*, p. 41, who uses the terminology of Mary Douglas, *Natural Symbols: Explorations in Cosmology* (New York: Pengin, 2nd edn, 1973), p. 46.

174 See Judge, 'The Social Identity of the First Christians', 216.

175 See Meeks, *The First Urban Christians*, esp. pp. 74–110: and Robertson, *Conflict in Corinth*, esp. pp. 51–113. For a more balanced view of the parallels between the Christian ecclesia and the society at large, esp. the parallel with the voluntary associations, and an evaluation of Meeks, see Philip A. Harland, *Associations, Synagogues, and Congregations: Claiming a Place in Ancient Mediterranean Society* (Minneapolis: Fortress, 2003), esp. pp. 177–264.

176 Cicero, *Off.* 1.54, quoted by Robertson, *Conflict in Corinth*, p. 58.

177 See Robertson, *Conflict in Corinth*, p. 62. For more on this see Andrew D. Clarke, *Serve the Community of the Church: Christians as Leaders and Ministers, First-Century Christians in the Greco-Roman Word* Grand Rapids: Eerdmans, 2000), esp. ch. 5.

This will prove to be crucial in understanding Paul's use of the language of the οἶκος in 1 Corinthians 1–4 for his purposes. Moreover, we have already mentioned that the Pauline congregations met in the 'οἶκος of X' (see 1 Cor. 1.11, 16, 16.15-16; Rom. 16.5, 23),[178] which carried with it the danger of confusing the structures of a household with those of the Christian *ecclesia*. Meeks explains:

> The adaptation of the Christian groups to the household had certain implications both for the internal structure of the groups and for their relationship to the larger society. The new group was thus inserted into or superimposed upon an existing network of relationships, both internal – kinship, *clientele*, and subordination – and external – ties of friendship and perhaps of occupation. The house as meeting place afforded some privacy, a degree of intimacy, and stability of place. However, it also created the potential for the emergence of factions within the Christian body of a city ... The household context also set the stage for some conflicts in the allocation of power and in the understanding of roles in the community ... there were certain countervailing modes and centers of authority in the Christian movement that ran contrary to the power of the paterfamilias, and certain egalitarian beliefs and attitudes that conflicted with the hierarchical structure.[179]

Among the ways in which the Christian *ecclesia* may have been perceived by some of the wealthier people as a household network, was as an avenue for status advancement by means of patron-client ties. It was not unusual for literary men (e.g., poets, rhetors, etc.) to be the clients of rich people and some of the Corinthians may have perceived, for instance, Paul's rejection of financial support as a declaration of enmity, since his decision would have hindered their possibility for acquiring more honor.[180]

---

178   For details see, J. M. G. Barclay, 'The Family as the Bearer of Religion in Judaism and Early Christianity', in *Constructing Early Christian Families: Family as Social Reality and Metaphor* (H. Moxnes, ed.; London: Routledge, 1997), p. 73.

179   Meeks, *The First Urban Christians*, p. 76. See also Clarke, *Serve the Community of the Church*, pp. 160–6. One example of the conflict created by the overlapping of the Christian ecclesia with the household network is the dissensions at the Lord's Supper. For more details see Theissen, *Social Setting*, pp. 145–74; Pogoloff, *LOGOS AND SOPHIA*, ch. 8. It is easy to see how in the context of the Christian worship it would be hard, for instance, for the master of a household to recognize equality with the slaves of his household, and even more to listen to them if a word of prophecy was given through them (cf. 1 Cor. 14.30). Jennifer A. Glancey, 'Obstacles to Slaves' Participation in the Corinthian Church', *JBL* 117 (1998) 481–501, has explored the specific difficulties that slaves encountered (cf. 1 Corinthians 7) in their desire to become members of a Christian congregation, given the fact that they were the sexual objects of their (non-Christian) masters. See also H. Moxnes, 'What is Family? Problems Constructing Early Christian Families', in *Constructing Early Christian Families*, pp. 13–41.

180   See Chow, *Patronage*, pp. 68–75. That Paul used the household as the usual context for preaching and teaching is discussed in detail by S. K. Stowers, 'Social Status, Public

The second model is that of the *collegia*, or of the voluntary associations. Robertson rightly argues that 'the association was like a miniature πόλις in an era when the πόλις of old had been swallowed up by the empire'.[181] Membership in these associations was often based on ethnic connection, rank, office, and professions. Meeks and others have pointed out that the *collegia* were characterized by several elements: (1) they often incorporated persons who shared a common trade or craft being thus more homogeneous in terms of status; (2) they engaged in common meals which were graced with the oratory of guest rhetors and provided the necessary context for socio-economic advancement; (3) they participated in rituals and cultic activities; and (4) they were able to function because of the beneficence of wealthier persons who acted as patrons.[182] It is not difficult to see from this characterization how the Christian ecclesia could have easily been regarded as another *collegium*.[183] This can be seen, Robertson has pointed out, in the conflict between the 'strong' and the 'weak' in 1 Corinthians 8–10 over participation at certain banquets.[184] It can also be inferred from the fact that the Christians belonging to these *collegia* were used to a homogeneous, relatively equal status, gatherings, but when joining the Christian *ecclesia* some have presumably found difficulty with its heterogeneous composition, that is, fellowship with people of lower status. Moreover, some of the wealthier in the church may have sought to function as patrons or sponsors of different teachers for the purpose of enhancing their status and increasing their honor.[185]

The third model is that of the secular (political) ἐκκλησία. The ἐκκλησία was the place were citizens assembled together to deliberate the needs and problems of the city. Robertson observes that, 'In the πολιτεία itself or, more specifically, in the secular ἐκκλησία or council, fellow citizens could

---

Speaking and Private Teaching: The Circumstances of Paul's Preaching Activity', *NovT* 26 (1984) 59–82 (64–73). The household context of preaching thus could have carried with it the danger of regarding Paul as a client rhetor for the patron of the household.

181 Robertson, *Conflict in Corinth*, p. 66. He also points out the fact that in Paul's time these *collegia* were suspect organizations since in earlier times, 'there were often connections between *collegia* and various political upheaval and campaigns for change' (p. 65). See the Senatorial ban in 64 BC: 'collegia quae adversus rem publicam videntur esse [constituta]' (Aconius, *In Senatu contra L. Pisonem* 8).

182 Meeks, *The First Urban Christians*, pp. 78–9. For more on voluntary associations, see Clarke, *Serve the Community of the Church*, esp. ch. 4.

183 For details on the extent to which the early Christian communities might have been classified among the voluntary associations by outsiders, see John S. Kloppenborg & Stephen G. Wilson, eds., *Voluntary Associations in the Graeco-Roman World* (London: Routledge, 1996). For a summary of the discussion see Clarke, *Serve the Community of the Church*, pp. 153–60.

184 Robertson, *Conflict in Corinth*, pp. 88–9.

185 Cf. Malherbe, *Social Aspects of Early Christianity*, pp. 88–9. Concerning patronage and the *collegia* see Chow, *Patronage*, pp. 64–8.

(and often did) vie with one another for power and primacy. . . . The same ἐκκλησία which provided a channel for possible κοινωνία between fellow citizens also acted as the battleground for their rivalries, disputes and mutual enmity'.[186] We have already evaluated Mitchell's and Welborn's proposition that Paul's attempt to promote concord in the Christian assembly resembles the *homonoia* speeches delivered in the context of a political conflict. Despite the criticism presented against a political background to the disputes in 1 Corinthians 1–4, it appears, as Robertson argues, that 'several members brought with them some of the patterns of the secular ἐκκλησία, elevating Paul and other Christian leaders to something like demagogues'.[187] This may not be surprising given the fact that, as Clarke points out, 'It is apparent that, from earliest times, the widely adopted designation of the Christian communities was that of "church" (ἐκκλησία). . . . This choice of word may have raised problems for those Christians who, by virtue of their comparative wealth and social standing, were "naturally" leaders in the local community and were expected to adopt similar positions of honor and respect within the Christian ἐκκλησία.'[188] The Corinthians' complaint about Paul's apparent lack of eloquence in speech resembles the importance placed on oratory in the secular ἐκκλησία.[189]

The fourth model that could provide some parallel (the most natural parallel) to the Christian ἐκκλησία is that of the Jewish συναγωγή. Two things are relevant to our discussion of the social background of the Corinthian disputes. First, 'the linkages between Jews in a city like Corinth were grounded in family or household relationships.'[190] Second, 'like their collegial counterparts, synagogues usually were composed of men only, although there was far greater diversity in the latter, both in terms of occupations and social status'.[191] There are thus evidences that 'Jewish synagogue organization was significantly influenced by surrounding Graeco-Roman culture, albeit maintaining some distinction.'[192] At any rate, the fact that at first the Christian communities intersected with the Jewish synagogues as far as organization, points to the fact that, 'for some of the first believers their long-standing continuity with Jewish tradition will certainly have suggested to them that elements of synagogue

186   Robertson, *Conflict in Corinth*, p. 64. For a thorough analysis of secular ἐκκλησία see Clarke, *Serve the Community of the Church*, esp. ch. 3.
187   Ibid., p. 86.
188   Clarke, *Serve the Community of the Church*, p. 152.
189   Ibid., p. 153.
190   Robertson, *Conflict in Corinth*, p. 68.
191   Ibid.
192   Clarke, *Serve the Community of the Church*, p. 167. For details see esp. ch. 6. See also Meeks, *The First Urban Christians*, p. 80, where he states that, 'the synagogue incorporated features of both . . . the association and the household.'

community life provided an appropriate model to adopt and modify.'[193] Among such aspects could be distinctions among persons of different class, gender, and economics.

From this survey of the four relational networks extant in parallel to the Christian *ecclesia*, it is plausible to claim that there was not only acquaintance with (in the sense that some of the Corinthians were members of these organizations), but also varying degrees of influence upon the Corinthian Christians as they thought about the new network they entered in as a result of conversion to Christ. The similarities between the Christian *ecclesia* and other networks may have been emphasized to the point of creating dissensions among the members of the newly formed social entity. It is for this reason that Paul felt the need to emphasize the unique identity of those ἐν Χριστῷ. Meeks has suggested that the early Christian *ecclesia* 'was all the old things that observers in the first century might have seen in it: a Jewish sect, a club meeting in a household, an initiatory cult, a school. Yet it was more than the sum of those things, and different from the mere synthesis of their contradictory tendencies.'[194] Thus, the fundamental problem of the dissensions in Corinth was the confusion of the Christians concerning the unique identity of their ἐκκλησία. This unique identity is stressed by Paul throughout his Corinthian correspondence, including 1 Corinthians 1–4.

We have already pointed out some of the aspects that distinguished the Corinthian *ecclesia* from the various social networks to which some of the Corinthian Christians belonged, such as heterogeneity vs. homogeneity, equality vs. hierarchy, and inclusivism vs. exclusivism. In addition to these, the unique identity of the Christian church can be gleaned from the terminology Paul uses to characterize the 'insiders', the church. David Horrell rightly states that, 'What seems clear is that the frequent use of ἀδελφός language reflects both an established designation for the members of the Christian assemblies and Paul's efforts to ensure that social relationships ἐν ἐκκλησίᾳ are structured in a manner appropriate to their description as groups of equal siblings.'[195] This equality is further emphasized by other designations of the members of the church such as κλητοῖς ἁγίοις (1 Cor. 1.2), without any differentiation of status implied

---

193 Ibid., p. 167. Jewish ethnicity and religious specificity clearly produced some disputes in the early church which was not ethnically homogeneous.

194 Meeks, *The First Urban Christians*, p. 120. See also Robertson, *Conflict in Corinth*, p. 17, for similarities and dissimilarities between the Christian church and the other models illustrated in fig. 1.c.

195 David G. Horrell, 'From ἀδελφόι to οἶκος θεοῦ: Social Transformation in Pauline Christianity', *JBL* 120 (2001) 293–311 (303). See also Robertson, *Conflict in Corinth*, p. 142.

in the terms.[196] Moreover, the characterization of the leaders of the church as διακονόι (and ὑπηρέτας Χριστοῦ καὶ οἰκονόμους μυστηρίων θεοῦ cf. 1 Cor. 4.1) has no parallel in the hierarchical structure of other relational networks.[197] That Paul uses the term ἐκκλησία to refer to the Christian church is no indication that Paul thought of the Christian assemblies as modeled after the political assemblies. Rather, its background is most likely the Old Testament concept of the *q ᵉhal yhwh* as a sanctified assembly.[198]

It is for these reasons that Theissen characterized Paul's relationship to his members as 'love-patriarchalism', a term that preserves a certain stratified system in the church while distinct from that of the larger society by love.[199] Dale Martin has modified the term to 'benevolent-patriarchalism', in order to reflect the reality that Paul

> maintained social hierarchy by urging the lower class to submit to those in authority and the higher class to rule benevolently and gently, accommodating its own demands in order to protect the interests of those lower down the social scale. Those of higher status might sometimes be encouraged to yield to those of lower status on a particular point; but within the context of benevolent patriarchalism this yielding was not to result in any actual status reversal or confusion. The upper class must continue to rule from a higher position of benevolent but firm strength.[200]

Thus, benevolent patriarchalism 'was opposed, on the one hand, to the radicalness of democracy, which would dangerously turn the natural status hierarchy upside-down, and, on the other, to tyranny, which would endanger itself by inflexibility.'[201] More will be said below about the cross as the means by which Paul 'redefines the system' and in the next chapter concerning Paul's use of the *paterfamilias* language with the alleged purpose of re-establishing his authority. Suffice to say here that Paul's emphasis on the uniqueness of the Christian *ecclesia* must have meant more than the imposition of love or benevolence over the hierarchy characterizing the other relational networks. In Paul's view, it seems, the Christian church is a completely new entity, with new structures and

196   For more terms see Meeks, *The First Urban Christians*, pp. 79, 85. He rightly subsumes these terms under the 'language of belonging'. See also Robertson, *Conflict in Corinth*, pp. 123–6.

197   For details see Clarke, *Serve the Community of the Church*, pp. 233–43.

198   Meeks, *The First Urban Christians*, p. 79. Also Robertson, *Conflict in Corinth*, 117–35.

199   Theissen, *Social Setting*, p. 107. For a critique see David Horrell, *The Social Ethos of the Corinthian Correspondence:Interests and Ideology from 1 Corinthian and 1 Element (SNTCW; Edinburgh: T. T Cloth, 1996)*, esp. pp. 126–98. See also Dale Martin, *Slavery as Salvation*, pp. 26–30, 88–91, 126–9.

200   Martin, *The Corinthian Body*, p. 42.

201   Ibid., p. 43.

relationships. In fact, as we will see, Paul's concern was that the Corinthians were thinking of the church in terms of another relational network. For Paul to preserve some of the hierarchical structures of the other relational networks in the church would render his argument for the uniqueness of the Christian *ecclesia* ineffective.

Besides the unique terms that Paul uses to characterize the 'insiders', he also designates the 'outsiders' in such a way that a distinction is clearly drawn between believers and non-believers. According to Meeks, terms such as ἀπολλυμένοις (1 Cor. 1.18), ὁ κόσμος (1 Cor. 1.21), τοὺς ἔξω (1 Cor. 5.12), etc., are used by Paul as a 'language of separation', distinguishing thus the Christians from the non-believers.[202] Both ideas of 'belonging' and 'separation' perhaps can be best seen in the phrase 'baptized εἰς Χριστόν', alluded to in 1 Cor. 1.13. Robertson argues that a

> 'fence' for the church was Christian baptism, which distinguished those who 'were being saved' from 'the perishing' (1.18). At the same time, baptism served as an 'entrance gate' into this Christian community. The key for Paul was that through this gate, one would enter a *new* and unique network in which distinctions of gender, ethnicity and socio-economic status were no longer relevant ... The movement of a believer 'toward a new orientation' through Christian baptism at the same time meant 'movement away from an old orientation' such as societal distinctions of ethnicity and status.[203]

While all this terminology is used by Paul to clearly differentiate between the Christian church and the other relational networks, what gives the Christian church its unique identity is the cross (ὁ σταυρός). We have already pointed to the coherence between the two major themes of wisdom and dissensions in 1 Corinthians 1–4, worldly wisdom (i.e., rhetoric) being at the root of dissensions, and that through the cross, God proved it ineffective in regards to acquiring salvation. We have also noted the opinion of some that the cross functions rhetorically in order for Paul to re-establish his authority, which will be discussed in detail in chapter three. But a more certain way of seeing the reason for Paul introducing the discourse on the cross is that the cross points to a new system with new values. Robertson again is right to note that,

> The cross – ὁ σταυρός – was offered here as the primary identity marker for those in the Christian ἐκκλησία .... In essence, this 'digression' on ὁ σταυρός answered the unspoken query, 'If Christians were the set-apart ones, from what were they set apart?' For Paul, the cross created a new, all-encompassing dichotomy that effectively reconstituted the

202 Meeks, *The First Urban Christians*, p. 94.
203 Robertson, *Conflict in Corinth*, p. 119. See also Meeks, *The First Urban Christian*, p. 79.

Corinthians' relational universe, replacing the more familiar dichoto-
mies of Jew and Greek (1.22-24), foolish and wise (1.26-27), weak and
strong. Instead of multiple *overlapping* networks, now there were only
two *mutually-exclusive* ones: 'those who are perishing' (ἀπολλυμένοι)
and 'those who are being saved' (σῳζομένοι). The message of the cross
was the instrument of 'second-order change', as it were, by which these
two networks were distinguished one from another.[204]

He continues:

The cross stood, as it were, at the crossroads of their relational world:
they continue to cling to a world and a *Weltanschauung* that was known
and acceptable to them, or they could embrace the identity of those for
whom Christ had died. The cross, therefore, served as a *divider*, marking
those who looked to the crucified Christ as 'the power and wisdom of
God' (1.24) as wholly set-apart from those whose faith still rested on
σοφία ἀνθρώπων (2.5) ... The cross was also a *unifier* for those within
the Christian network.[205]

By using the cross as an identity marker, then, Paul would remind the
Corinthians of the re-socializing effect of the cross. As already underscored, the Corinthians were still marked by the social values of the
surrounding culture, therefore Paul must emphasize again that the church
is a 'community whose rules govern all departments of life and he expects
the members to find in it their primary and dominant relationships.'[206]
But how did the Corinthians view their new identity in light of the social
background described above?

John Barclay, in a study on the social contrasts between the Christian
assemblies in Thessalonica and Corinth, has rightly pointed out that
whereas in Thessalonica the Christians suffered social conflict with the
surrounding society, 'there are plenty of signs suggesting the social
acceptability of the Corinthian Christians.'[207] Given their apparent lack of
understanding of the impact of the cross and conversion upon their social
relationships, they seemed to have continued to be fully integrated in
society, being in good terms with the wider community. They saw no
reason to break with the values and conventions of the larger society,

204 Robertson, *Conflict in Corinth*, pp. 136–7. Much of what he says about the cross is
dependent upon Pickett's *The Cross in Corinth* in which he analyzes the social significance of
the cross.
205 Ibid., pp. 138–9.
206 Barclay, 'Social Contrasts in Pauline Christianity', 60. See also Witherington,
Conflict and Community, p. 8. In Robertson's words, what was needed was 'a new paradigm
in which the church's members would view themselves together ἐν Χριστῷ as a unique and
primary system with clear boundaries', *Conflict in Corinth*, p. 54. See also deSilva, 'Let the
One Who Claims Honor', p. 64.
207 Ibid., p. 58. See also De Vos, *Church and Community Conflicts*, pp. 206–14, for
evidences in 1 Corinthians for this harmony with the 'outsiders'.

presumably because they considered the Christian *ecclesia* as one among other relational networks.[208] Thus, according to Robertson, 'the chief problem facing Paul was [...] the tendency on the part of many Corinthians to give priority to the claims and roles of their other, pre-existing networks rather than to those of the Christian ἐκκλησία.'[209]

It is not as if Paul denied the Corinthians any contact with the society; the issue was rather that the Corinthians felt too much at ease and were too friendly to the larger society to the point of neglecting any boundaries or identity markers that separated them from the outsiders and united the insiders.[210] Meeks rightly characterizes the Christian community's inter-action with others in society with the phrase 'boundaries with gates', the gates opening both ways. In other words, the gates were opened from the church toward the world in that the Corinthians remained part of the society but were also opened from the world toward the church through baptism. It is not surprising, then, that a tension existed 'between measures needed to promote a strong internal cohesion, including rather clear boundaries separating it from the larger society, and the intention to continue normal and generally acceptable interactions with outsiders.'[211]

From Paul's perspective, then, 'the Corinthians' boundaries were overly permeable or, using Meeks' terminology, the "gates" were open far too wide.'[212] The same conclusion is reached by the sociological exploration of the situation in Corinth by Timothy Carter as he reacts to J. H. Neyrey's conclusions.[213] Carter states that '[t]he community in Corinth suffers from porous boundaries.'[214] Both Carter and Neyrey use Mary Douglas' 'Grid and Group' matrix to compare and contrast Paul's and the Corinthians' attitudes regarding the boundaries of the Christian commu-nity.[215] According to Douglas, the horizontal 'group' axis measures the level of participation in a bounded social unit: low group indicates a high degree of individualism; high group indicates a high level of participation in a group. The vertical 'grid' axis measures the extent to which an individual accepts or rejects the prevailing symbol system of the

208 Both Chow, *Patronage and Power*, p. 110, and Witherington, *Conflict and Community*, pp. 30–1, 114–15, argue that the Corinthians regarded the church as another *collegium*. See also Barclay, 'Social Contrasts in Pauline Christianity', 71.

209 Robertson, *Conflict in Corinth*, p. 97.

210 Cf. ibid., p. 98.

211 Meeks, *The First Urban Christians*, p. 107. Here Meeks is influenced by Mary Douglas' description of a social group as a human body, with boundaries carefully guarded against impurity. See her *Natural Symbols*, p. 98.

212 Robertson, *Conflict in Corinth*, p. 28.

213 Neyrey, 'Body Language in 1 Corinthians: The Use of Anthropological Models for Understanding Paul and his Opponents', *Semeia* 35 (1986) 129–70.

214 Carter, ' "Big Men" in Corinth', 50.

215 M. Douglas, *Natural Symbols*.

surrounding culture: high grid means the individual shares the public system of classification; low grid means that this is rejected in favor of a private system of classification.[216] Contrary to Neyrey's conclusions, Carter rightly locates Paul in the 'high-group/low-grid' quadrant, while the Corinthians are in the 'high-grid/low-group' quadrant of competitive individualism.[217] In other words, while Paul proves to be highly involved in the Christian *ecclesia* and is determined to subvert the cultural values of the larger society by means of discourse of the cross, the Corinthians seem less concerned for the unity of their Christian community and all too ready to continue their comfortable integration within the πόλις. The distinction between Paul and the Corinthians, then, can be described in terms of 'two incompatible ways of perceiving and judging ... It is important to note, however, that perception and judgment always presuppose values (i.e., criteria) in terms of which the perceptions and judgments are made, and these values are always, to some extent anyway, socially determined.'[218]

The situation among the Corinthian Christians can then be described as characterized by presence of conflict within the Christian community and a relative absence of conflict between that community and its larger social environment.[219] Paul, on the other hand, sought to bring unity among those belonging to the Christian community and separation from the cultural values of the surrounding society. The contrast between Paul's stance and the Corinthians' is aptly described by Robertson: 'Theirs was a world of multiple networks ... but Paul was calling them to something not of this world.'[220]

More precisely, what distinguishes Paul's and the Corinthians' perceptions concerning unity and identity is the degree of the impact of the cross upon culture and its values. Clearly for Paul, the cross and the cultural values are at odds, and that is why one may speak of the 'scandal of the cross' as characteristic of Paul's discourse on the cross in 1 Cor. 1.18-25. Pickett is thus right to assess that 'Paul's argument in 1.18-25 is in substance a criticism of culture.'[221] Thus, by means of the discourse on the cross Paul addresses both the surface issue of unity and the more basic issue of identity – the boundaries of the Christian community. The function of the cross in Paul's argument, then, can bee seen as both deconstructive and constructive.[222]

---

216   See Carter, '"Big Men" in Corinth', 46, 70.

217   Ibid., 47–48. Neyrey locates Paul in the high-grid/high-group quadrant and the Corinthians in the low-grid/low-group quadrant of the matrix.

218   Pickett, *The Cross in Corinth*, p. 64.

219   Cf. Robertson, *Conflict in Corinth*, p. 27.

220   Ibid., p. 98.

221   Pickett, *The Cross in Corinth*, p. 70.

222   Ibid., p. 214.

The investigation of the social background of 1 Corinthians 1–4 has pointed out some important features that may shed more light on the dissensions in the Corinthian congregation. First, the Corinthian congregation was heterogeneous, consisting of people of various socio-economic status, though the majority were of lower status, at least at the inception of the Corinthian ecclesia. Second, the Corinthian Christians were confusing the Christian ecclesia with other relational networks to which they concomitantly belonged, behaving thus according to the cultural values of the larger society. Third, by means of the discourse on the cross, Paul seeks to complete the Corinthian Christians' resocialization into the new entity – ἐν Χριστῷ – by presenting the cross as the identity marker for the Christian assembly. According to Paul, the cross, a symbol of weakness and foolishness, has a countercultural effect, overturning the social values of the πόλις.

Though an investigation into the social background of 1 Corinthians 1–4 proves to be helpful in explaining the dissensions in Corinth, it must be kept in mind that it sheds light only from one angle, and must be corroborated with the information gathered in our investigation of the rhetorical-political background and especially with the exegesis of the text performed in the first chapter. Only this multifaceted approach will guard us from a reductionistic reconstruction of the rhetorical situation.

The Number and Nature of Parties in 1 Corinthians 1–4

Before we discuss and evaluate the various views on the number and nature of parties, we should mention that there is general agreement concerning at least two issues pertaining to the dissensions in Corinth, issues that we have already addressed throughout this chapter. First, the names associated with the slogans of 1 Cor. 1.12 are not *directly* responsible for the divisions in the Corinthian church.[223] Two reasons support this statement. On the one hand, Paul does not blame Apollos, for instance, for the presence of factions in the church anymore than he blames himself. His critique is thus addressed against the whole church (i.e., against the party spirit), not against a particular group.[224] On the other hand, Paul seems to be more critical of his own group than of any other one (cf. 1 Cor. 1.13), and in no way does he seek to identify himself with the Pauline group.[225] Thus, the text does not seem to support the

223 See Pickett, *The Cross in Corinth*, p. 49; Kuck, *Judgment*, p. 157; and Fee, *First Corinthians*, p. 55.

224 Cf. Kuck, *Judgment*, p. 163; Dunn, *Fist Corinthians*, p. 32; Pogoloff, *LOGOS AND SOPHIA*, p. 102; Collins, *First Corinthians*, p. 73; Munck, *Paul and the Salvation of Mankind*, p. 150.

225 Cf. Pogoloff, *LOGOS AND SOPHIA*, p. 101.

claim that Paul makes any of the persons behind the slogans directly responsible for the divisions. What is less certain, however, and this will necessitate more investigation, is whether Apollos, for instance, was *unintentionally* the source of divisions due to his *modus operandi,*[226] or whether Paul *indirectly* presents a critique of Peter or Apollos.

Second, the investigation into the socio-rhetorical background of the dissensions and of the concept of σοφία has revealed that, although Paul argues theologically against dissensions, there is no basis for claiming that the dissensions were over doctrine.[227] Rather, the dissensions were caused by the Corinthians' continued involvement with their former social networks whose values and conventions were carried over into the Christian *ecclesia*. Thus, the Corinthians' behavior was marked by worldly thinking to the point that their intra-church relationships did not present any signs of being impacted by the cross. Paul's solution to this problem was to remind the Corinthians of the cross and its eschatological effect of separating the world into two distinct groups delimited by boundaries, each with its own values, relationships, and ways of thinking about the cross, salvation, and teachers.

The certainty of these issues, however, is paralleled by at least a similar level of uncertainty concerning the number of parties in the Corinthian church.[228] There are proposed variants anywhere from four identifiable parties to no parties, and everything in between.[229] Others even question the existence of parties, and, as we will see, prefer other terminology to describe what was going on in the Corinthian church.

Few today maintain that there were four distinct parties in the Corinthian church and that we can speak of an actual schism or *stasis*. The 'classical' approach is most clearly expressed in H. A. W. Meyer's

---

226   Cf. Dodd, *Paul's Paradigmatic "I"*, p. 38; Pogoloff, *LOGOS AND SOPHIA*, p. 196; and Schrage, *Der erste Brief*, pp. 142–8.

227   This is the main thesis of Munck's essay, 'The Church Without Factions: Studies in 1 Corinthians 1–4', in *Paul and the Salvation of Mankind*, esp. pp. 138, 152; see also Kuck, *Judgment*, p. 157; Pickett, *The Cross in Corinth*, pp. 39–40; Clarke, *Leadership in Corinth*, p. 91; Welborn, 'On the Discord in Corinth', 88; Schrage, *Der erste Brief*, p. 144; Strüder, 'Preferences not Parties', 434. This view goes back to John Chrysostom, PG 61.23.

228   For the history of research up until 1991 see Schrage, *Der erste Brief*, pp. 142–8; and Merklein, *Der erste Brief*, pp. 115–18; For a more recent and comprehensive survey see Thiselton, *First Corinthians*, pp. 120–33.

229   Hall, *Unity*, p. 6, presents the variants into three possible interpretations: literal – four parties, semi-literal – less than four parties, and cryptic – unnamed leaders. His adoption of the third variant is dependent upon his interpretation of the verb μετεσχημάτισα in 4.6, so it will have to await our discussion in Chapter 5.

bold statement that 'there can be no reduction of parties below *four*.'[230] James Dunn rightly comments that the existence of four parties is the 'normal deduction' from 1 Cor. 1.12, though he also acknowledges that identifying the exact doctrinal profile of each group is problematic.[231] The 'classical' view has been seriously contested to the point that some have swung to the other extreme by claiming that there were no parties or factions within the Corinthian church, denying not only the existence of parties but also redefining the nature of the problem.

The best-known representative of this view is Johannes Munck. In questioning F. C. Baur's thesis of a Petrine/Pauline conflict in the early church, Munck proceeds to argue for a non-theological character of the problem in Corinth, which leads him to conclude that the issue was only 'disunity and bickerings', not factions, at least not yet.[232] Several arguments are adduced in support of this view. First, it is argued that, 'If it is factions that are referred to in chapters 1–4, they appear there only to disappear completely later.'[233] Second, Strüder notes that no word for "party" (e.g., αἵρεσις or μέρος) is used in 1 Cor. 1.12.[234] Third, lack of agreement in reconstructing the historical background must mean that there were no real factions.[235]

This state of the problem has led commentators to replace the term 'parties' with other words that reflect the non-theological and therefore the non-schismatic nature of the problem. Munck, for instance, argues for the less schismatic term 'bickerings',[236] while Strüder claims that it is inappropriate to speak of the existence of actual parties, only of 'competing preferences.'[237] Mitchell, however, though reluctant to use the term 'parties' to describe the problem in the Corinthian church, still argues, against Munck, that there were factions. She states:

230 Meyer, *Epistles to the Corinthians*, 1.26 (emphasis by author); He is followed by Robertson and Plummer, *First Corinthians*, p. 12; Barrett, 'Christianity at Corinth', pp. 4–6 seems to admit it also. See also Fee, *First Corinthians*, pp. 58–9. For more details see Thiselton, *First Corinthians*, p. 125.

231 Dunn, *First Corinthians*, p. 28. Most of those who argue for four distinct parties attribute parts of the letter to criticism of the theology behind the names.

232 See Munck, *Paul and the Salvation of Mankind*, p. 136. He is followed, among others, by Fee, *First Corinthians*, pp. 5, 59; Hays, *First Corinthians*, p. 22; Collins, *First Corinthians*, pp. 16, 73.

233 Munck, *Paul and the Salvation of Mankind*, p. 140. See also Collins, *First Corinthians*, p. 73.

234 Strüder, 'Preferences not Parties', 431.

235 Ibid., 435. See also Dunn, *First Corinthians*, p. 31; and Hurd, *The Origin of 1 Corinthians*, p. 107.

236 Munck, *Paul and the Salvation of Mankind*, p. 136.

237 Strüder, 'Preferences not Parties', 432.

The lack of theological content to the factions would make them no less factions! ... It is also methodologically problematic ... to deny the existence of Corinthian factions because scholars cannot reconstruct from 1 Corinthians the coherent and distinct positions of each of the groups named by the slogans in 1.12. ... We cannot conclude from our inability to reconstruct them that there weren't factions.[238]

Moreover, Conzelmann has rightly argued that 'it will not do to dismiss the group question as being merely a matter of harmless squabbles. The energy Paul expends upon it is too great for that.'[239]

For the advocates of this view, however, a more fundamental problem is raised: What about the slogans in 1 Cor. 1.12? The answer to this question varies from being 'an illustration of the quarrels in the community',[240] to 'Paul's fictive creation for the sake of argument',[241] 'exaggerated caricatures',[242] 'a forceful piece of rhetoric on the part of Paul rather than a statement about the specific situation at Corinth',[243] or a mention of the groups 'for the sake of completeness' when only one group is dominant.[244] At least three arguments support these interpretations of the slogans. First, as Mitchell observes, 'the four phrases are preceded by λέγω δὲ τοῦτο, which introduces Paul's commentary on the report of Chloe's people.'[245] Second, Conzelmann is probably right to state that, 'The word ἕκαστος, "each", must not of course be pressed to the effect that every single member has associated himself with one of the groups mentioned.'[246] And lastly, the word σχίσματα may be, according to Schrage, 'möglicherweise überspitzt.'[247]

What all these descriptions have in common then is that they all basically argue against schisms into parties. In fact, Paul seems to construct his argument in order to prevent such logical outcome suggesting thus that the schism had not yet taken place.[248] Therefore, we believe that a more appropriate description of the problem in Corinth is represented by the word 'preferences', though these preferences for different teachers certainly

---

238 Mitchell, *Reconciliation*, p. 71. She follows in this argument Welborn, 'On the Discord in Corinth', 88–89.

239 Conzemann, *1 Corinthians*, p. 34. He follows Wilckens, *Weisheit und Torheit*, p. 5, n. 1. *Contra* Fee, *First Corinthians*, p. 59, n. 56.

240 Strüder, 'Preferences not Parties', 432, 447.

241 Dodd, *Paul's Paradigmatic "I"*, p. 37.

242 Mitchell, *Reconciliation*, p. 86. Also Schrage, *Der erste Brief*, p. 139.

243 Collins, *First Corinthians*, p. 73. Also Pogoloff, *LOGOS AND SOPHIA*, p. 178.

244 Litfin, *Proclamation*, pp. 185, 230, referencing Gerhard Sellin, 'Das "Geheimnis" der Weisheit und das Rätsel der "Christuspartei".

245 Mitchell, *Reconciliation*, p. 86. Similarly, Strüder, 'Preferences not Parties', 448.

246 Conzelmann, *First Corinthians*, p. 33.

247 Schrage, *Der erste Brief*, p. 139.

248 Cf. Barrett, 'Christianity at Corinth', 3–4; and Wynne, *Apollos*, p. 47.

had begun to express themselves in a competing behavior. Moreover, it does seem that the slogans are not the *ipsissimae voces* of the Corinthians, but are Paul's own rhetorical creation for the sake of argument. This seems to be true, given the lexical and syntactical arguments listed above. But a more definite answer will have to be postponed until the further discussion of the Christ and Cephas parties.

The most problematic of the slogans is the one associated with Christ.[249] The basic view is that 'the existence of a Christ-party at Corinth is extremely doubtful',[250] which leaves only three possible parties in Corinth. The question that the advocates of this view must answer is the presence of the slogan 'I am Christ's.'[251] Of the various opinions put forward, two in particular present a higher probability. First is the view that this slogan is Paul's corrective to the party spirit, thus being his own confession or prescription.[252] In support of this view may be the fact that the Christ party is never named again even when the other three are.[253] Moreover, 1 Cor. 3.21-23 lists again three of the 'parties', but uses 'of Christ' as 'the umbrella over all three.'[254] Not least, the immediate following argument of Christ being indivisible as well as the larger context of 1 Corinthians 1–4 with its theocentric/Christological emphasis seems to point to the fact that the declaration 'I am Christ's' should be the confession of every Christian.[255] Fee and others, however, have pointed out that the grammatical pattern of the text (i.e., μέν, δὲ, δὲ, δὲ) does not set this slogan off from the others. For this to be the case, it is argued, a stronger adversative (i.e., ἀλλά) would be expected.[256] Despite this grammatical construction, Garland rightly concludes with a question: 'What is wrong with saying "I belong to Christ"? Is this not the confession of every Christian? There is no hint in the text that some Corinthians are claiming a unique relationship to Christ.'[257]

---

249 For a detailed discussion of the 'Christ-party' see Christof W. Strüder, *Paulus und die Gesinnung Christi: Identität und Entscheidungsfindung aus der Mitte von 1Kor 1–4* (BETL, 190; Leuven: Leuven University Press, 2005).

250 Hurd, *The Origins of 1 Corinthians*, p. 105.

251 For a summary of opinions and evaluation see ibid., pp. 101–7; Barrett, *First Corinthians*, pp. 43–6; and Thiselton, *First Corinthians*, pp. 129–33.

252 See, e.g., Hurd, *The Origins of 1 Corinthians*, p. 105; Garland, *1 Corinthians*, p. 49.

253 Cf. Mitchell, *Reconciliation*, p. 82, n. 101. See Dunn, *1 Corinthians*, pp. 31–2 for the arguments. This is somewhat supported by its absence from *1 Clem.* 47.3, though this has also been used by others to argue for this slogan to be a gloss. See Heinrici, *Der erste Brief*, p. 60; Weiss, *Der erste Korintherbrief*, pp. 15–16.

254 Dodd, *Paul's Paradigmatic 'I'*, pp. 39–40; see also Dunn, *1 Corinthians*, p. 30.

255 Garland, *1 Corinthians*, p. 49; also Mitchell, *Reconciliation*, p. 82 n. 101.

256 Fee, *First Corinthians*, pp. 58–9, n. 54; Collins, *First Corinthians*, p. 72; Schrage, *Der erste Brief*, pp. 146–8, though he does not consider this argument conclusive. See also W. O. Fitch, 'Paul, Apollos, Cephas, Christ', *Theology* 74 (1971) 20.

257 Garland, *1 Corinthians*, p. 49. See also Dodd, *Paul's Paradigmatic "I"*, p. 40.

The second possible view is a variant of the aforementioned view. Schrage gives it an ironic twist while V. P. Branick views it in terms of sarcasm, both arguing that the slogans could be extended *ad absurdum* to show that the competitive spirit behind human names are just as absurd as claiming that Christ could become the exclusive property of one group.[258]

It is difficult to reach a definite conclusion concerning the function of the fourth slogan,[259] but the context seems to point to the latter interpretation given above, namely that the slogan 'I am Christ's' is Paul's own rhetorical invention for the purpose of showing the absurdity of claiming allegiance to human teachers. Such a view then reduces the actual parties to only three in number. The great majority of scholars, however, go even further claiming that there were only two probable parties. The identity of these two parties is divided between Paul vs. Peter and Paul vs. Apollos.

The hypothesis that the Corinthians were divided into a Pauline (Paul and Apollos) and Petrine (Cephas and Christ) groups finds its source in F. C. Baur's reconstruction of early Christianity based on Hegel's dialectical philosophy of thesis-antithesis-synthesis.[260] Among the more recent advocates of Pauline and Petrine competing missions are C. K. Barrett and Michael Goulder.[261] Barrett identifies Peter (or someone acting in his name) as the unnamed person in 1 Cor. 3.10-17, for instance, whom the Petrine party wrongly identified with the foundational rock (cf. Matt. 16.18).[262] But since Peter and those sent by the 'pillars' in Jerusalem were rightly held in high regard, Paul had to conduct his critique against them in a covert way (cf. μετεσχημάτισα in 1 Cor. 4.6).[263]

The presumed conflict between Paul's and Peter's missions in early

---

258 Schrage, *Der erste Brief*, p. 148; and Branick, 'Source and Redaction Analysis of 1 Corinthians 1–3', *JBL* 101 (1982) 260, respectively. Pauline sarcasm would be interpreted as 'All of you want to belong to particular groups. I belong to Christ!' See also Merklein, *Der erste Brief*, p. 147. Both Schrage and Merklein follow E. Käsemann who states that the fourth slogan "[ist] als ironisierender Überbietung der anderen umlaufenden Parolen, also aus spezifisch paulinischer Rhetorik zu begreifen" (quoted by Smit, ' "What is Apollos?" "What is Paul?" ', 240, n. 31).

259 Cf. Strüder, 'Preferences not Parties', 440.

260 See Baur, 'Die Christuspartei', 61–206. For a critique of Baur's hypothesis see Munck, *Paul and the Salvation of Mankind*, p. 135; Strüder, 'Preferences not Parties', 432–33; Dunn, *1 Corinthians*, pp. 28, 31; Collins, *First Corinthians*, p. 71.

261 Barrett, 'Christianity at Corinth', and 'Cephas in Corinth', 1–27 and 28–39 respectively; Goulder, *Paul and the Competing Mission in Corinth*, which is an extended version of his earlier article 'Σοφία in 1 Corinthians', 516–34. The reconstruction is dependent on Galatians 2, associating Peter with Judaizing tendencies. For a critique see Munck, *Paul and the Salvation of Mankind*, pp. 142–3.

262 Barrett, 'Cephas in Corinth', 32–33. Barrett sees in every passage (in 1 and 2 Corinthians) where there are possible Jewish elements as evidence of Peter's theology.

263 Ibid., 37–38; Goulder, 'Σοφία in 1 Corinthians', 519.

Christianity being reflected in the disputes in 1 Corinthians, however, has been largely discarded. Though Peter must have been known to the Corinthians, since Paul mentions him, it is rather doubtful that he ever visited Corinth. It is possible that Paul added the name of Cephas not only to avoid narrowing the conflict to an alternative between Paul and Apollos,[264] but also to point to the absurdity of claiming allegiance to the baptizer, since Cephas did not baptize anyone in the Corinthian congregation.[265] Moreover, it is highly doubtful that Cephas had theological differences with Paul to the scale this hypothesis claims. Munck rightly states, 'It can hardly be imagined that Paul would have merely touched the surface of this matter if a false doctrine of that kind had existed. It is therefore probable that the criticism in 1 Cor. 3.10-17 is directed, as is the whole context, at the church and its bickerings.'[266] As a result, most commentators agree today that if there was any conflict in the Corinthian *ecclesia*, it was between the followers of Paul and those of Apollos.[267]

Several arguments seem to support the idea that the Apollos party was an actual party. First, it is certain that Apollos visited Corinth (cf. Acts 18; 1 Corinthians 3), while support for Peter's visit is lacking.[268] Secondly, as Winter argues, 'In 1 Cor. 1.12 Paul uses ἕκαστος to describe the groupings, but his choice of ἕτερος δέ in 3.4 and his inclusion of the additional term ζῆλος could suggest that the allegiance of members of the church is now in effect divided between two former teachers, himself and Apollos.'[269] Moreover, the name of Apollos clearly emerges as the central personality, particularly in chs 3 and 4.[270] These arguments have led most scholars today to see various degrees of conflict between Paul (i.e., his party) and Apollos (i.e., his party) and argue that the first rhetorical unit of 1 Corinthians is directed primarily against an Apollos faction.[271]

Thus, the dissensions were presumably the result of Apollos' different *modus operandi* from Paul's.[272] On the one hand, it is argued that Apollos possessed the qualities that Paul lacked as a public speaker such as

---

264 Smit, 'Search for Coherence', 242–43, 248. See quotations below.

265 Strüder, 'Preferences not Parties', 451.

266 Munck, *Paul and the Salvation of Mankind*, p. 142.

267 See Hurd, *The Origins of 1 Corinthians*, pp. 97–9, for authors who favor this view.

268 Ibid., p. 97, considers this as the reason why Apollos' party has had the advantage with scholars over the other two parties. See also Kuck, *Judgment*, p. 157.

269 Winter, *Philo and Paul among the Sophists*, pp. 176–7.

270 Cf. Pickett, *The Cross in Corinth*, p. 50.

271 E.g., Litfin, *Proclamation*, pp. 228–9. *Contra* Munck, *Paul and the Salvation of Mankind*, p. 144.

272 Cf. Winter, *Philo and Paul among the Sophists*, p. 141; Ker, 'Paul and Apollos', 84; Smit, ' "What is Apollos?" "What is Paul?" ', 242.

eloquence, which, we have seen, was a symbol of status. Such a conclusion is usually drawn from the information one finds in Acts 18.24-28 concerning Apollos' persuasiveness in speech. Given his abilities as a speaker (cf. ἀνὴρ λόγιος, δυνατός, ἐπιδείκνυμι), Apollos was perceived by some as a person who could enhance their status and increase their honor by associating with him.[273] Thus it is not difficult to infer that a cordial relationship developed between Apollos and some of the socially superior Corinthians. On the other hand, Apollos may have played into the social conventions of the day by accepting financial support from the Corinthians, while Paul refused patronage in Corinth as a dependent network (cf. 1 Corinthians 9), seeking to dissociate himself from the resident sophist.[274] The result of such refusal was, according to Marshall, an open rejection of friendship.[275] The 'enmity' with the higher status Christians in Corinth was also heightened by Paul's manual labor. Paul's decision to work with his hands was a sign of status inconsistency, a person of high status taking on a low status.[276] Thus, given their different approaches to ministry in Corinth, one could see how Paul and Apollos were esteemed differently by the Corinthians, Apollos' *modus operandi* aggravating the situation.

Before one agrees with this hypothesis, however, several observations are in order. First, one should notice that Luke describes Apollos' use of the Jewish Scriptures in Acts 18.28 in much the same way as he describes its use by Paul in Acts 17.3, though the issue of the use or rejection of rhetoric will have to be discussed in more detail later.[277] Secondly, Paul speaks positively of Apollos in 1 Cor. 3.5-9.[278] Thus, one may safely conclude with Kuck that 'in 1 Corinthians 1–4 there is no evidence that Paul regarded Apollos personally as an antagonist or rival.'[279] But the

---

273   *Contra* Pogoloff, *LOGOS AND SOPHIA*, pp. 184, 189.

274   Cf. Winter, *Philo and Paul among the Sophists*, pp. 167–9.

275   Marshall, *Enmity in Corinth*, pp. 1–34, 133–64; also Theissen, *Social Setting*, p. 127; Pogoloff, *LOGOS AND SOPHIA*, pp. 192–3; and Ker, 'Paul and Apollos', 83. Ker follows Chow, *Patronage and Power*, pp. 104–7, who develops this possibility. *Contra*, Winter, *Philo and Paul among the Sophists*, p. 166, n. 112.

276   Cf. Martin, *Slavery as Salvation*, pp. 77–82; also Ronald F. Hock, 'Paul's Tentmaking and the Problem of His Social Class', *JBL* 97 (1978) 555–64; *idem, The Social Context of Paul's Ministry: Tentmaking and Apostleship* (Philadelphia: Fortress, 1980), pp. 60–4; Pogoloff, *LOGOS AND SOPHIA*, p. 152. Bruce W. Winter, ' "If a man does not wish to work ...": A Cultural and Historical Setting for 2 Thessalonians 3.6-1', *TynBul* 40 (1989) 303–15.

277   Cf. Munck, *Paul and the Salvation of Mankind*, p. 144, n. 4; Litfin, *Proclamation*, p. 242.

278   Cf. Dunn, *1 Corinthians*, p. 32; Schrage, *Der erste Brief*, pp. 143–4. *Contra* Horsley, 'Wisdom of Word and Words of Wisdom', 231–32.

279   Kuck, *Judgment*, p. 163; *contra*, e.g., Ker, 'Paul and Apollos', who concludes that they were rivals. More on this issue in Chapter 5.

question still remains as to why Paul chose to speak of Apollos in 1 Cor. 3.5–4.5, and only Apollos? We will have to wait for an answer until after the discussion in Chapters 3 and 4 on Paul's and Apollos' relation to sophistic rhetoric, but for now the least we can say is that two slogans containing Paul's and Apollos' names are probably authentic or at least reflect the real conflict.

It is clear, then, that the only group that is the least difficult to identify is Paul's.[280] As a result, some have argued that the divisions were really only around Paul's name: some were for Paul, while the others were against Paul. Therefore, Paul fights only on one front, namely against those complaining of his *modus operandi* including his lack of rhetorical skill as well has his refusal to play the game of social conventions.[281] This hypothesis is heavily dependent upon Dahl's argument that 1 Corinthians 1–4 is an *apologia* for his authority and will have to await discussion in Chapter 3.[282] Suffice it to say here that the first rhetorical unit is a combination of rhetorical genres – epideictic, deliberative, and judicial. Thus, besides passages that have more of an apologetic emphasis, there are passages that have hortatory force. Therefore, as Winter argues, 'His *apologia* must be seen as his critique of the Corinthians and not simply a justification of his *modus operandi*.'[283]

In light of this succinct investigation into the nature and number of parties in the Corinthian church, several initial facts have come to the surface. First, concerning the nature of parties, it would be more true to the evidence to state that there were no actual parties in the church, at least not in the sense we use the word today. The church had not yet experienced schism. It is thus better to think of the problem as more of a matter of preferences for teachers, preferences that were formed based on worldly criteria of persuasive speech wedded to cultural values such as status and patronage. Second, it is doubtful that there were four distinct groups represented by the four slogans. Rather, at least the slogan 'I am Christ's' can be regarded as Paul's rhetorical creation in order to

280 Cf. Dunn, *1 Corinthians*, p. 28.

281 E.g., Litfin, *Proclamation*, pp. 184–5; Fee, *First Corinthians*, p. 156; De Vos, *Church and Community Conflicts*, pp. 218–19; William Baird, '"One against the Other": Intra-Church Conflict in 1 Corinthians', in *The Conversation Continues: Studies in Paul & John in Honor of J. Louis Martyn* (R. T. Fortuna and B. R. Gaventa, eds.; Nashville: Abingdon, 1990), p. 130.

282 Dahl, 'Paul and the Church at Corinth according to 1 Corinthians 1.10-4.21', pp. 321, 329. He modifies his argument in a later edition of his article which appeared in *Studies in Paul: Theology for the Early Christian Mission* (Nils Alstrup Dahl, ed.; Minneapolis: Augsburg, 1977), p. 61, n. 50. The section is better said to contain 'apologetic elements.' Litfin, *Proclamation*, p. 183, seems to place a heavy emphasis on the apologetic nature of the first rhetorical unit. *Contra* Pogoloff, *LOGOS AND SOPHIA*, p. 75.

283 Winter, *Philo and Paul among the Sophists*, p. 182.

emphasize the absurdity of claiming allegiance to human teachers. In a similar way, the slogan 'I am Cephas'' does not seem to point to a faction in the Corinthian church that followed Peter. It could be that Paul used this slogan in order to diffuse the tension in the church between the Paul and Apollos parties. Third, therefore, it is most likely that the dissensions in the church were actually represented by two groups and reflected in the two probably authentic slogans: 'I am Paul's' and 'I am Apollos''. Their distinct *modus operandi*, judged against the backdrop of social values characterizing the larger society, has caused the Corinthians to esteem the two apostles in different ways. Thus, with Pickett, one could legitimately advance the argument that '[t]here is a correlation between the content of the Corinthians' criticisms of Paul and the basis of their commitment to Apollos in that the social values in terms of which they rejected Paul served at the same time as the criteria in terms of which they revered Apollos.'[284] It remains, then, to be seen what was Paul's relation and response to sophistic rhetoric in the next chapter, and what was Apollos' connection to the same rhetoric in Chapter 4. This will allow us to determine with more precision the role of Apollos in the Corinthian dissensions.

Conclusion

This chapter has followed logically the conclusion of the first chapter. There we have argued for the coherence of Paul's argument in 1 Corinthians 1–4 by pointing out that Paul seeks to bring about unity in the Corinthian church by critiquing the worldly wisdom that the Corinthians used as a criterion for judging their teachers. This chapter has sought to answer the question of the nature of this worldly wisdom. We have shown that the best background against which we can feel the full impact of Paul's argument is that of the sophistic rhetoric.

We have also argued that rhetoric implied social values and conventions, which the Corinthians carried over into the church from the social networks to which they were still belonging, thus causing dissensions in the church. This is clearly seen in the slogans, which were Paul's creation, but which reflected the situation in the Corinthian church. An analysis of these slogans has led us to conclude that Paul and Apollos were the two most influential teachers in the community and inadvertently represented the two main competing groups, Paul's opponents and the Apollos party being one and the same. It remains to determine in the next chapter Paul's stance toward the worldly wisdom which we have defined as rhetoric.

---

284 Pickett, *The Cross in Corinth*, 52.

3 PAUL AND SOPHISTIC RHETORIC IN 1 CORINTHIANS 1-4

Introduction

So far we have concluded that at the root of dissensions in the Corinthian congregation lies an evaluation of teachers according to the values of the world (i.e., rhetorical eloquence), which resulted in viewing the Christian *ecclesia* as one association among other relational networks. Paul's response to such exigencies, then, is, among other things, to make a clear theological statement about preaching as related to sophistic rhetoric. Litfin rightly notes that '1 Cor. 2.1-5 provides the clearest and most detailed statement both positive and negative of the apostle's manner of preaching to be found anywhere in his writings.'[1] The question that we will seek to answer in this chapter is Paul's stance toward sophistic rhetoric in his proclamation of the gospel. The necessity of discussing such an issue has already been noticed in the questions raised by previous scholarship. Hans Dieter Betz, for instance, asks the following: 'Which kind of rhetoric corresponds positively, and which rhetoric clashes with the preaching of the gospel?' He continues: 'This for Paul is a theological problem of primary importance, especially in his correspondence with the Corinthians.'[2] Timothy Lim raises a more pertinent question: 'Is Paul inconsistent in his word and action to have refused persuasive speech here [2.1-5], but to use rhetorical devices and strategies elsewhere in his epistles, especially in 1 and 2 Corinthians?'[3] Or is Paul practicing that against which he has been preaching?[4] Do his letters betray the use of rhetoric which he so forcefully denounces in his preaching?

Such questions arise inevitably from an apparent discrepancy between the style of his writings, to which Augustine referred as having the finest rhetorical style in the Bible, a true marriage of *sapientia* and *eloquentia*,[5] and his belief that 'persuasive words of wisdom' are antithetical to the

---

1 Litfin, *Proclamation*, p. 204.
2 Betz, 'The Problem of Rhetoric and Theology According to the Apostle Paul', p. 16.
3 Lim, '"Not in Persuasive Words of Wisdom"', 137.
4 Horsley, 'Wisdom of Word and Words of Wisdom in Corinth', 230, n. 14.
5 Cf. Frank W. Hughes, 'Rhetorical Criticism and the Corinthian Correspondence', in *The Rhetorical Analysis of Scripture: Essays from the 1995 London Conference* (S. E. Porter &

'demonstration of the powerful Spirit' – they empty the cross (1 Cor. 1.17; 2.5). This disparity between *what* Paul states about his method of preaching and *how* he actually presents his message has been a *crux interpretum* in Pauline studies. In fact, even Paul's opponents in 2 Corinthians – the 'super-apostles' – have used this apparent inconsistency between how Paul came across in his letters and the kind of person he was as a means of challenging his authority in the Corinthian church: 'His letters are strong and weighty, but his presence weak and his speech contemptible' (2 Cor. 10.10).

The task of assessing Paul's stance toward rhetoric is made difficult in part by the fact that there is no information in Scripture concerning Paul's actual 'performance' of his sermons to serve as a comparison between his theory and practice of proclamation. Most of what is found in the New Testament relates to either Paul's statements about his style of preaching (i.e., 1 Cor. 1.17b; 2.1-5; 2 Cor. 11.6; and 1 Thess. 1–2), the statements made against Paul's delivery by those who attempted to undermine his authority in the Corinthian church (i.e., 2 Cor. 10.10), or to Paul's messages in letter form. In order to answer the issue at hand, then, we will start with a survey of the various opinions concerning Paul's stance toward rhetoric, followed by a more detailed exegesis of 1 Cor. 2.1-5, particularly with emphasis on the rhetorical aspects of the text. This, in turn, will raise the issue of written versus oral communication – to what degree they are similar and how they differ in Paul's culture. We will conclude this chapter with a discussion of Paul's alleged apologetic purpose in his stance toward sophistic rhetoric.

The conclusions of this chapter will prove to be foundational to the investigation of Paul's relationship to Apollos and Apollos' approach to sophistic rhetoric, which will be discussed in the last chapter. Does Paul claim authority over Apollos? Is Apollos guilty for adopting a preaching style that Paul rejects? That is, do Paul's presumed theological arguments against the use of rhetoric in proclamation imply a repudiation of Apollos' more refined style of preaching? Ultimately, we will seek to determine Apollos' role in the dissensions in light of Paul's stance toward rhetoric.

A Survey of Various Views on Paul, Preaching, and Rhetoric

There have been different attempts to unlock the conundrum of Paul's view concerning rhetoric and preaching. We have decided to group the views into three rough categories for the sake of clarity: Paul opposed to

---

T. H. Olbricht, eds.; JSNTSup, p. 146; Sheffield: Sheffield Academic Press, 1997), p. 336. See Augustine, PL 4.7.12. An ideal rhetoric was regarded as combining these two, cf. Cicero, *Inv.* 1.1-5; *De or.* 3.142-43, 2.33, 3.125.

rhetoric, Paul does not oppose rhetoric, and Paul is ambivalent toward rhetoric.

Paul Is Opposed to Rhetoric

As early as Origen, it was believed that rhetorical art is not able to persuade people to believe.[6] Therefore, any employment of such art in proclamation of the gospel is regarded as contradictory to the nature of the gospel as a mystery.

As a result, more recently, the classicist George Kennedy unambiguously states that Paul 'rejects the whole of classical philosophy and rhetoric',[7] thus making Paul into a kind of anti-rhetor.[8] Litfin argues along similar lines when he states that 'Paul repudiates entirely the dynamic of rhetoric for the purposes of preaching and opts instead for its diametrical opposite [i.e., the dynamic of the cross].'[9] The two dynamics of persuasion are mutually exclusive, because the dynamic of rhetoric attributes the speaker the key role in persuasion, while the dynamic of the cross rests on the conviction brought by the Spirit.[10] Thus, the reason Paul rejects rhetoric in preaching is because its use implies that more is needed than the cross for persuasion. Winter, in line with his research into the Second Sophistic, is more specific in his evaluation of Paul's theology of preaching, stating that 'Paul deliberately adopts an anti-sophistic stance.'[11]

This view is based on several assumptions. First, it is believed that 1 Corinthians 1–4 (esp. 2.1-5) contains terminology at home with Greek rhetoric. More will be said about this in the next section of this chapter, but it is enough to point here to the fact that Timothy Lim, even though does not fully agree with this position, correctly assesses that for the proponents of this view, 'It [σοφία λόγου] is a phrase which rejects the

6 Origen, PG 4.1.7.

7 George A. Kennedy *Classical Rhetoric and Its Christian and Secular Tradition from Ancient to Modern Times* (Princeton: Princeton University Press, 2nd rev. edn, 1983), p. 151. See also, Marshall, *Enmity in Corinth*, p. 389.

8 See Lars Hartman, 'Some Remarks on 1 Cor. 2.1-5', *SEÅ* 39 (1974), 109–120 (118, 120). Earlier, Weiss, *Der erste Korintherbrief*, p. 23, argued that Paul rejected the devices of rhetoric. Paul's aversion to rhetoric is assumed by Judge, 'The Reaction against Classical Education', 11. Pogoloff, *LOGOS AND SOPHIA*, p. 54, seems to agree with Judge's assessment.

9 Litfin, *Proclamation*, p. 207.

10 Ibid., pp. 247–50.

11 Winter, *Philo and Paul among the Sophists*, p. 141. See *idem* "Revelation versus Rhetoric: Paul and the First-Century Corinthian Fad," in *Translating Truth: The Case for Essentially Literal Translation* (Wheaton: Crossway, 2005), pp. 142–3.

discipline of what the Greeks called ῥητορική.'[12] Even Welborn, we have seen, agrees that σοφία in this context is a reference to rhetoric.[13]

Second, it is believed that Paul was accused by his opponents of not rising to the standards of what was regarded as persuasive speech. This is most clearly seen in 2 Cor. 10.10 and 11.6.[14] Based on this information, then, it is assumed that Paul presents a defense of his *modus operandi* in 1 Cor. 2.1-5.[15] The question arises, however, whether it is legitimate to import the exigencies that gave rise to the writing of 2 Corinthians into the writing of 1 Corinthians. Hans Dieter Betz has remarked that the situation has changed with 2 Corinthians and thus the nature of the issue regarding rhetoric had to be addressed differently in 1 and 2 Corinthians, namely in 1 Corinthians Paul criticizes the Corinthians for the kind of rhetoric they valued and points to himself as a model, but in 2 Corinthians it is Paul's own rhetoric that is under attack by being compared to that of the false teachers.[16] Winter also upholds the distinctions between the rhetorical situations of 1 and 2 Corinthians, but rightly emphasizes the continuity between the two epistles. He believes that the teachers (i.e., the super-apostles) appointed by the Corinthians had access to Paul's critique of the sophistic tradition. Thus, it seems that 'they ridiculed his performance as a public speaker by drawing on categories from his own *apologia* and critique of the sophistic tradition found in 1 Corinthians 1–4 and 9. Their criticisms can be recovered from 2 Cor. 10.10 and 11.6, and are supplemented by an allusion to his 'sophistic' attitude towards money (2 Cor. 12.16-18).'[17]

Thus, while the exigencies that gave rise to the writing of 1 and 2 Corinthians differ, it is better to qualify the distinction in terms of degree rather than nature of opposition. In other words, the issue of rhetorical eloquence is present in both letters though in different forms. In 1 Corinthians, Paul is the one critiquing the Corinthians' overemphasis on rhetorical skill in preaching, while in 2 Corinthians it is Paul who is accused of lacking such skill, because of the presence in the church of

---

12   Lim, "Not in Persuasive Words of Wisdom," 147.

13   Welborn, "On the Discord in Corinth," 102. See also Martin, *The Corinthian Body*, p. 47. Even Schmithals, *Gnosticism in Corinth*, p. 142, concedes that 1 Cor. 2.1-5 reveals a distinct constellation of rhetorical terms and allusions.

14   Ibid., p. 103. Cf. Thucydides 3.42.2-5. See also Judge, 'The Reaction against Classical Education in the New Testament', 13, and *idem* 'Paul's Boasting in Relation to Contemporary Professional Practice', 48. The Corinthians, thus, in 2 Corinthians could be said to have seen in these opponents of Paul the oratorical qualities which Paul lacked.

15   Cf. Dahl, 'Paul and the Church at Corinth according to 1 Corinthians 1.10-4.21', 321, 329.

16   Betz, 'The Problem of Rhetoric', p. 44. See also Barrett, 'Christianity at Corinth', 14.

17   Winter, *Philo and Paul among the Sophists and Theology According to the Apostle Paul*, pp. 142, 203–4. Pogoloff, *LOGOS AND SOPHIA*, p. 195, argues along similar lines.

rhetorically skilled teachers.[18] Thus the connection between the rhetorical situations of the two letters as related to sophistic rhetoric rests on reasonable grounds. Based on this connection, then, those who advocate that Paul rejects rhetoric in proclamation in 1 Cor. 2.1-5 find a proof of this in the accusations brought against Paul's lack of skill in speech as evidenced in 2 Cor. 10.10 and 11.6. Thus it is believed that the false teachers, aware of Paul's theological defense of his *modus operandi* (cf. 1 Cor. 2.1-5), seek to show that Paul's lack of eloquence in speech is not really a deliberate decision of Paul in order to align with his theological convictions, but rather that his deficiency in speech caused him to come up with a theology to justify it, which in turn would prove his lack of apostolic authority. Therefore, a brief analysis of the statements found in 2 Cor. 10.10 and 11.6 is necessary for an evaluation of whether Paul actually rejected rhetoric or not.

Paul's opponents in 2 Corinthians claimed that he was 'weak' in his stage presence (ἡ παρουσία τοῦ σώματος ἀσθενής) and 'contemptible' in his speech (ὁ λόγος ἐξουθενημένος, 10.10b), while Paul himself acknowledged that he was a 'layman' in speech (ἰδιώτης τῷ λόγῳ, 11.6). Winter, among others who believe that Paul rejected rhetoric, contends that all these statements have to do with what is known as 'rhetorical delivery' (ὑπόκρισις).[19]

The first assessment describes Paul's stage presence. The kind of bodily presence (ἡ παρουσία τοῦ σώματος) that Paul communicated precluded him from securing a large audience. Whether the weakness (ἀσθενής) of his stage presence had to do with some noticeable infirmity in his body,[20]

18   The difference is pointed out by D. A. Carson, D. J. Moo, and L. Morris, *An Introduction to the New Testament* (Grand Rapids: Zondervan, 1992), p. 279.

19   For the importance of 'delivery' in oratory in Second Sophistic see D. A. Russell, *Greek Declamations* (Cambridge: Cambridge University Press, 1983), p. 82. He is followed by Winter, *Philo and Paul among the Sophists*, pp. 213–20. See *idem* 'Is Paul among the Sophists?' *RTR* 53 (1994) 28–29; 32–33; and 'Philodemus and Paul on Rhetorical Delivery (ὑπόκρισις)', in *Philodemus*, 323–42. He is followed by Murray J. Harris, *The Second Epistle to the Corinthians: A Commentary on the Greek Text* (NIGTC; Grand Rapids: Eerdmans; Cambridge: Paternoster, 2005), p. 700. See also Timothy B. Savage, *Power through Weakness: Paul's Understanding of the Christian Ministry in 2 Corinthians* (SNTSMS, 86; Cambridge: Cambridge University Press, 1996), pp. 64–9.

20   According to the *Acts of Paul and Thecla 3*, 'Paul was a man of little of stature, bald-headed, with crooked legs, well-born, with eye-brows meeting and a long nose.' For the importance of the outward appearance in delivery see Epictetus, 'On Personal Adornment' (Περὶ καλλωπισμοῦ), 3.1.1-45, to which Winter, *Philo and Paul among the Sophists*, p. 222, makes reference. See also Epictetus, 'On the Calling of a Cynic' (Περὶ κυνισμοῦ), 3.22.86-89, quoted by David Garland, *2 Corinthians* (NAC, 29; Nashville: Broadman, 2001), p. 448. See also Marshall, *Enmity in Corinth*, pp. 333–4. Betz, 'Rhetoric and Theology', 41, however, by using the word σχῆμα in describing the nature of the 'weakness' seems to limit the reference only to his outward appearance. Martin, *The Corinthian Body*, pp. 53–4, also seems to limit the description to Paul's body. Augustine believed that Paul chose his name because the

with weakness with regard to his social status,[21] or with a feeble personality is not immediately clear.[22] Margaret Thrall thus may be right to state that, 'This expression is to be understood in a comprehensive sense, of the apostle's whole outward character and personality, not only his personal appearance in the narrower sense. It is worth noting, however, that physical appearance may have had some importance for the Corinthians.'[23] Generally speaking, then, ἀσθενής most likely describes an 'unimpressive' presence (including possibly physical infirmity, thus appearance), the reference being to 'one of the accepted qualifications for oratorical prowess.'[24] But what specifically was viewed as deficient in his personality and character to the point that it affected the success of his delivery (according to his opponents)? It could be his lack of firmness in administering discipline,[25] but it most likely refers to something related to his 'rhetorical delivery' such as self-confidence (i.e., *ethos*), but more will be said about this in our exegesis of 1 Cor. 2.1-5.

The second statement is also a reference to the issue of ὑπόκρισις. The

---

Latin adjective *paullus* means 'small, little', which would point to rhetorical piety. But see Murphy-O'Connor, *Paul*, p. 44. For critique see Ralph P. Martin, *2 Corinthians* (WBC, 40; Dallas: Word, 1986), p. 298. It is true that one meaning of the word ἀσθενής is to be 'sick', the opposite of which is ἰσχυρός – to be 'healthy' (cf. Louw-Nida, the semantic domains 79.62-79.69), but the contrastive ἰσχυρός in 2 Cor. 10.10a refers to Paul's letters, not to his body. The phrase probably means, cf. Winter, *Philo and Paul among the Sophists*, p. 222, that 'his presence constituted such a liability as to all but guarantee his failure as an effective public orator.'

21 Cf. Hock, *The Social Context of Paul's Ministry*, p. 60, argues that it refers to Paul's lowliness as an artisan, ἀσθενής being translated as 'insignificant.' Garland, *2 Corinthians*, p. 449, makes reference to Lucian, *The Dream*, 13. See however, Margaret E. Thrall, *A Critical and Exegetical Commentary on the Second Epistle of the Corinthians* (ICC, London: T&T Clark, 2000), 2.631, for a critique of this view.

22 Cf. Thrall, *Second Corinthians*, 2.631.

23 Ibid.

24 Cf. Harris, *Second Corinthians*, p. 699. See also BDAG 142, though this meaning is included under 'physical weakness.' It could have the sense of lacking presence. A search in *TLG* for the words παρουσ* and ασθεν* (* standing for any ending) at an interval of 5 words or less between the two words has resulted in the following relevant resources, excluding those writings quoting the verse: Josephus, *A.J.* 1.273.2; Alexander, *De an.* 170.19; Eusebius, *Comm. Ps.* 24.24.45; Basilius, *Ep.* 138.2.31; 162.1.18; 236.5.4; *Fide* 31.469.40; John Chrysostom, *De incomprehensibili dei natura* 1.152; *Exp. Ps.* 55.125.29; *Eclogae i-xlviii ex diversis homiliis* 63.634.41; Didymus Caecus, *Fragmenta in Psalmos* 701a.7; Proclus, *in Platonis Timaeum commentaria* 3.122.24; *De malorum subsistentia* 52.4. See Marshall, *Enmity in Corinth*, p. 385, who cites Plutarch, *Mor.* 7.B.

25 See Thrall, *Second Corinthians*, 2.632. She makes reference to Savage, *Power through Weakness*, pp. 64-9; and D. A. Black, *Paul, Apostle of Weakness: Astheneia and Its Cognates in the Pauline Literature* (AUSS, 7; New York: Peter Lang, 1984), p. 137, for similar understanding. Thus, a translation of ἀσθενής would be 'feeble' or 'puny'. Martin, *2 Corinthians*, p. 312, gives the meaning of 'retiring in the face of vigorous opposition'.

statement is a clearer reference to his speech (ὁ λόγος).[26] His opponents accused Paul of having a 'contemptible' speech, that is, his speech 'amounted to nothing' or 'was not worth listening to.'[27] In this sense, the critique may point out Paul's lack of eloquence or his contemptible rhetoric according to the sophistic standards of persuasive speech.[28] In other words, the critique referred more to the form (i.e., delivery) rather than the content. If that is the case, then Thrall raises a pertinent question: if his spoken discourse is deemed unsophisticated and ineffective from a rhetorical standpoint, then why is the contrast set between his speech and his letters? She contends: 'Perhaps a partial answer might be that Paul was somewhat deficient in the capacity for extempore oral rhetoric that was so much prized by the sophists.'[29] But in what consisted this deficiency? Was it his refusal to use rhetorical techniques in oral communication or, as Calvin put it, 'that he was deficient in that ornament and splendor of

26 Cf. Harris, *Second Corinthians*, pp. 699–700. See also John Calvin, *Commentary on the Epistles of Paul the Apostle to the Corinthians* (CC, 10.2; Grand Rapids: Eerdmans, 1999), p. 330. The question still remains, according to Thrall, *Second Corinthians*, 2.633, as to why his initial message was found persuasive and now it was deemed contemptible. She argues that the arrival of rhetorically trained teachers exacerbated the situation. The idea that Paul changed his approach or theology of preaching as a result of his apparent 'failure' in Athens, as, e.g., Frederik William Grosheide, *Commentary on the First Epistle to the Corinthians* (NICNT; Grand Rapids: Eerdmans, 1953), p. 59, asserts, is not reseasonable. See also Robertson and Plummer, *First Corinthians*, p. 31; George B. Caird, *The Apostolic Age* (London: Duckworth, 1955), p. 102, calls Athens 'the scene of Paul's disillusionment' which prompted 1 Cor. 2.1-5. See Jeffrey S. Lamp, 'Gospel and Rhetoric in 1 Corinthians 1–4: Ruminations over Implications for Christian Apologetics', in *ETSP* (Portland: Theological Research Exchange Network, microfiche, 1996), 9, n. 25, for contra arguments and further literature. See also Karl Olav Sandnes, 'Paul and Socrates: The Aim of Paul's Areopagus Speech', *JSNT* 50 (1993) 13–26.

27 For such meanings of the participle ἐξουθενημένος see Alfred Plummer, *A Critical and Exegetical Commentary on the Second Epistle of St Paul to the Corinthians* (ICC; Edinburgh: T&T Clark, 1915), p. 283, who rightly points to the chiasmus in the contrasted epithets, ἀσθενής being the antithesis of ἰσχυραί and ἐξουθενημένος of βαρεῖαι, the contrast being between the character of the letters and his personal character. See Louw-Nida, 88.195; BDAG 352. According to Winter, *Philo and Paul among the Sophists*, p. 223, 'the perfect participle may suggest that the problem could not be remedied.'

28 Cf. Harris, *Second Corinthians*, p. 700; Martin, *2 Corinthians*, p. 298. A search in *TLG* of the words λογ* and εχουθεν* at an interval of 5 or less word between the two words has resulted in the following relevant references, excluding those that quote the verse: Epiphanius, *Pan.* 3.303.12; Basilius, *Enarratio in prophetam Isaiam* 8.219.13; *De baptismo libri duo* 31.1533.39; Anna Comnena, *Alexias* 11.3.2.11; Theodorus, *Epistolae* 483.3; Eustathius, *Commentarii ad Homeri Illiadem* 4.740.15.

29 Thrall, *Second Corinthians*, 2.632. She follows Winter, *Philo and Paul among the Sophists*, pp. 214–16, 223. Winter cites Alcidamas, *On the Writers of Written Discourse or On the Sophists*, 9, 16, who noted that being a clever writer was no guarantee that one could speak well. Garland, *2 Corinthians*, p. 447, also cites Quintilian, *Inst.* 11.3.12-13. See also Harris, *Second Corinthians*, p. 700.

eloquence, which secures favor'?[30] Was it his accent or diction, or his grammatical slips?[31] Could it be that Paul's speech was not accompanied by the voice, gestures, posture, or attire, necessary for an accomplished orator of high status?[32] Or could it be that Paul refused to engage in the abusive rhetoric of boasting as the other teachers?[33] The answer depends, in our opinion, partly on one's view of Paul's childhood education – whether he was trained in Greco-Roman rhetoric or not – and on our interpretation of 1 Cor. 2.1-5, since Paul's opponents seem to have used his defense in that passage against him, issues that will be discussed below.

Thus, in our attempt to understand the way Paul was evaluated by the Corinthians, we can conclude that the description of Paul found in 2 Cor. 10.10b refers both to his bodily presence as well as to his speech. Both incurred disdain and despise from those who evaluated Paul according to what constituted a virtuoso orator. Thus, evaluated by the canon of ὑπόκρισις, Paul's oratorical performance has been found wanting.[34] But can this be true in light of the fact that his initial visit in Corinth did prove to be fruitful and his preaching persuasive? Though during his initial visit (cf. 1 Cor. 2.1) when he planted the church such rhetorical deficiency was less observable, once new rhetorically trained teachers came on the scene, his contemptible rhetoric came into more sharpness and caused the Corinthians to disdain him. His contemptible lack of eloquence, then, can be understood generally as weak delivery, or weak performance as a speaker. It is difficult, however, to determine specifically what made his delivery 'count for nothing'. Possibly, Paul's own evaluation may shed some light on the issue.

The meaning of the statement in 2 Cor. 11.6 – ἰδιώτης τῷ λόγω, which is Paul's self-description in terms of his rhetorical ability – depends on the

---

30   Calvin, *Second Corinthians*, p. 330. For the importance of eloquence, see e.g., Brian K. Peterson, *Eloquence and the Proclamation of the Gospel in Corinth* (SBLDS, 163; Atlanta: Scholars Press, 1998), pp. 59, 65.

31   Cf. Harris, *Second Corinthians*, p. 700, n. 181. See also Betz, 'Rhetoric and Theology', p. 42, for a similar possibility, and Anderson, *Ancient Rhetorical Theory and Paul*, pp. 278–9 (cf. Lucian, *Nav.* 2). On Paul's knowledge of Greek see below and Martin Hengel, *The Pre-Christian Paul* (London: SCM, 1991), ch. 2 where he argues that in Paul's family Greek was probably the main language, since his father was a Roman citizen. For the importance of correct Greek (ἑλληνισμός) as status mark that conferred prestige and power see Simon Swain, *Hellenism and Empire: Language, Classicism, and Power in the Greek World, AD 50–250* (Oxford: Clarendon, 1996), pp. 17–64.

32   For the importance of voice, gestures and posture see Quintilian, *Inst.* 11.3.12-14; 31.162-63; 33.52-55; 70.1-8; and 72.1-2, for such things as posture, hair trim, the way one walked or applauded, how one sneezed, and whether one scratched one's head or not. For these references I am indebted to Stowers, 'Social Status, Public Speaking and Private Teaching', 74, n. 84.

33   Cf. Savage, *Power through Weakness*, pp. 62–80.

34   See Martin, *2 Corinthians*, p. 298.

meaning of the key term ἰδιώτης. According to BDAG, the word means 'a person who is relatively unskilled or inexperienced in some activity or field or knowledge, *layperson, amateur* in contrast to an expert or specialist or any kind.'[35] Generally, then, the phrase means 'unskilled in speaking'. However, Winter, by making reference to Philo of Alexandria, notes that the term applies not only to those who have never been instructed in rhetoric, but also to 'those who are beginning to learn, those making progress and those who have reached perfection.'[36] So, is Paul an 'un-trained' speaker – i.e., never studied rhetoric – or a 'non-professional' speaker – studied rhetoric but chose not to make a living of it?

Winter argues that Paul was not only familiar with, for instance, forensic rhetoric, but also used it if need arose (cf. Acts 24), especially in his writings (e.g., Galatians).[37] He supports this argument by noting that 2 Cor. 11.6 presents a dichotomy (ἀλλ') between Paul's capacity as an orator (ἰδιώτης τῷ λόγῳ) and his knowledge of rhetoric ([ἰδιώτης] τῇ γνώσει).[38] He concludes thus that Paul was trained in rhetoric, that is, had the knowledge of rhetoric, but was not a professional since he eschewed rhetorical techniques in his delivery, though 'on occasion' he used them, presumably based on the verb in the third statement in this verse (i.e., Φανερώσαντες, 'revealing the knowledge').

Such an interpretation raises the issue of whether 2 Cor. 11.6 actually

---

35 BDAG 467. See Schlier, 'ἰδιώτης', in *TWNT*, 3.215-17, for the following references. Justin, *1 Apol* 1.39.3; 60.11; Josephus, *A.J.* 2.271; Schlier argues that the word gets its meaning usually from a contrast. E.g., layman in relation to the orator: Isocrates *Or.* 4.11; Aeschines *Ctes.* 1.7, 8; Hyperides, *Or.* 3.27; Lucianus, *Jup. Trag.* 27; or the philosopher or sophist: Aristotle, *Pol.* 2. 7, p. 1266a, 31; Philodemus Philosophus, Περὶ Παρρησίας, 51; Περὶ θεῶν, 1.25; Epictetus, *Diatr.* 2.12.2, 13.3; Chrysostom, *Or.* 12.17, 42.3, 47.8, 54.1; Xenophon, *Mem.* 3.7.7, 3.12.1. A search in *TLG* for the words ιδιωτ* and λογ* at an interval of 5 or less words between the two has confirmed this meaning of 'untrained'. See also Louw-Nida, 27.26. Τῷ λόγῳ is a dative of respect, indicating that in which Paul is unskilled, cf. Thayer, 297. Thus the translation would be 'layman with respect to speech'. AV translates 'rude in speech'. For ἰδιώτης with a genitive see Xenophon, *Oec.* 3.9 (ἰδιώτης ἔργου); Plato, *Prot.* 345a (ἰδιώτης ἰατρικῆς).

36 Winter, *Philo and Paul among the Sophists*, pp. 224–5, cf. 101–2; Philo, *Agr.* 159–60; Isocrates, *Or.* 15.201, 204. See also Martin, *The Corinthian Body*, pp. 48–9, who makes reference to *Against the Sophists* 14; and esp. Chrysostom, *Or.* 42.2-4. Note should be taken that the use of ἰδιώτης with the sense of untrained is predominant, while the sense of non-practicing trained orator is very rare. Also, Isocrates, *Or. 15,* gives the reason why the majority of those trained in rhetoric 'retire from their studies into private life': lack of natural gifts. See *contra* Anderson, *Ancient Rhetorical Theory and Paul*, p. 278, n. 7; and Lim, ' "Not in Persuasive words of Wisdom" ', 140.

37 Winter, *Philo and Paul among the Sophists*, pp. 225–8; *idem*, 'The Importance of *Captatio Benevolentiae* in Speeches of Tertullus and Paul in Acts 24.1-21', *JTS* 42 (1991) 505–31.

38 The dative τῇ γνώσει is a dative of reference and it points back to ἰδιώτης. Thus, Paul would say, according to Winter, that he does not lack the knowledge of rhetoric.

presents a contrast between the use of rhetoric and the knowledge of rhetoric: is Paul talking about knowledge of rhetoric or knowledge of a different kind? To answer this question we need to look at the second adversative (ἀλλ'). In this third statement (ἀλλ' ἐν παντὶ Φανερώσαντες ἐν πᾶσιν εἰς ὑμᾶς) Paul contends that he has displayed the γνώσεις of the previous statement. But if the nature of this 'knowledge' is rhetoric, then this contradicts Winter's assertion that Paul used his training in rhetoric 'on occasion' (e.g., to defend himself in court or in his writing), since Paul says that he used it ἐν παντί, ἐν πᾶσιν, εἰς ὑμᾶς, which most likely means that 'the depth of Paul's spiritual insight should have been clear to the Corinthians *in every dimension and detail of his ministry among them.*'[39] Thus, γνώσεις must refer to the 'knowledge of God' in a comprehensive sense already revealed to the Corinthians, rather than to 'knowledge of rhetoric.'[40]

This, however, does not necessarily mean that Paul had no knowledge of rhetoric; it simply means that Paul does not clearly say in this verse that he was trained in rhetoric. The most we can say from this verse and the use of ἰδιώτης is that Paul acknowledges to have been an amateur by the standards of rhetorical delivery, whether he was trained in it or not. The question of Paul's familiarity with the rhetorical expectations of an eloquent speaker still remains. Part of the claim that Paul rejected sophistic rhetoric in proclamation relies on a third assumption regarding Paul's education: Paul acquired the terminology and knowledge of rhetorical expectations from being trained in a Greco-Roman rhetorical school.[41] The place of such education is normally believed to be Tarsus. This is especially convenient in light of Strabo's characterization of the capital of Cilicia: 'There was so much zeal for philosophy and all the other aspects of education generally among the inhabitants that in this respect they surpassed even Alexandria, Athens, and any other place.'[42] Paul's education connected to Tarsus would thus say much about his familiarity with Greco-Roman rhetoric.

Much has been written on the 'Pre-Christian Paul', to borrow the title of Martin Hengel's work on the subject.[43] The issue that interests us here

---

39   Thrall, *Second Corinthians*, 2.677, quotes V. P. Furnish, *II Corinthians: A New Translation with Introduction and Commentary* (AB, 32A; Garden City, NY: Doubleday, 1984), p. 491 (emphasis added).

40   See John Chrysostom, *Sac.* 4.6.61-79.

41   E.g., Marshall, *Enmity in Corinth*, p. 400; Martin, *The Corinthian Body*, p. 67. Most scholars would not go so far as to claim that Paul received rhetorical education at a tertiary level. They are satisfied to affirm Paul's familiarity with rhetorical performance from attending a Greco-Roman elementary school.

42   Strabo, *Geogr.* 14.5.13, quoted by Hengel, *The Pre-Christian Paul*, p. 2.

43   See the more recent discussion by Richard H. Bell, *The Irrevocable Call of God: An Inquiry into Paul's Theology of Israel* (WUNT, 184; Tübingen: Mohr, 2005), esp. ch. 1 'Paul: A Hebrew of Hebrews', pp. 1–37.

is whether Paul grew up in Tarsus or Jerusalem and whether he received his education (at least elementary education) in his home town of Tarsus or whether he moved to Jerusalem early in his childhood. The key text in the debate is Acts 22.3.[44] The question of the place of Paul's 'upbringing' is dependent upon the punctuation of the verse and the semantics of ἀνατεθραμμένος and πεπαιδευμένος. First, should the phrase παρὰ τοὺς πόδας Γαμαλιήλ go with the preceding or with the subsequent statement?[45] Richard Bell has argued for following the majority under-standing of a break before the phrase, based on the stylistic feature of chiasm (i.e., A: ἀνατεθραμμένος B: δὲ ἐν τῇ πόλει ταύτῃ B': παρὰ τοὺς πόδας Γαμαλιήλ A': πεπαιδευμένος), with emphasis being placed on Paul's instruction (παιδεία) by one of the most prestigious Pharisees of the time.[46]

If this is the structure one adopts, then the second issue of the semantics of ἀνατεθραμμένος and πεπαιδευμένος points to a distinction between the two participles, as indicating two successive stages in life: one of 'upbringing', 'nurturing' (ἀνατεθραμμένος) at home followed by instruction (πεπαιδευμένος) 'at the feet' of Gamaliel.[47] Bell concludes: 'Since schooling started at the age of six to seven, his ἀνατροφή must have taken place before he was seven and therefore necessitated a move to Jerusalem at a very young age.'[48] If one adopts the Byzantine punctuation, followed

---

44 For a detailed analysis of this see Andrie B. Du Toit, 'A Tale of Two Cities: "Tarsus or Jerusalem" Revisited', *NTS* 46 (2000) 375–402. His article is a challenge to W. C. van Unnik's understanding of the verse presented in *Tarsus or Jerusalem. The City of Paul's Youth* (trans. G. Ogg; London: Epworth, 1962). Murphy-O'Connor, *Paul*, p. 33, n. 5, though sides with van Unnik's interpretation as the only valid one, still dismisses it on the basis that Luke is not historically credible.

45 The majority of the English Bible translations put the *caesura* before the phrase (e.g., ESV, NET, NIV, NAU, HCSB) following most modern text editions (e.g., UBS 3/4 and NA27) with the exception of NKJV which follows the BYZ punctuation. Among commentators who follow the 'traditional' break see e.g., F. F. Bruce, *The Book of Acts* (NICNT; Grand Rapids: Eerdmans, 1988), p. 414; and C. K. Barrett, *A Critical and Exegetical Commentary on the Acts of the Apostle* (ICC; Edinburgh: T&T Clark, 2004), 2.1029. See also Bell, *The Irrevocable Call of God*, p. 5, with a minor variation, following I. H. Marshall, *The Acts of the Apostles* (TNTC; Leicester: IVP, 1980), p. 354. Du Toit, 'A Tale of Two Cities', p. 384, follows the Byzantine punctuation, taking the phrase with the preceding participle verb ἀνατεθραμμένος.

46 Bell, *The Irrevocable Call of God*, p. 5.

47 See also Barrett, *Acts*, p. 1034; and John B. Polhill, *Acts* (NAC, 26; Nashville: Broadman, 1992), p. 457. BDAG 74, emphasizes the aspect of 'being reared' for ἀνατρέφω.

48 Bell, *The Irrevocable Call of God*, p. 7. In this he is in agreement with van Unnik, 'Tarsus or Jerusalem: The City of Paul's Youth', in *Sparsa Collecta: The Collected Essays of W. C. van Unnik (Part One)* (NovTSup, 29; Leiden: Brill, 1973), 259–320 (p. 301); and 'Once Again: Tarsus or Jerusalem', ibid., 320–27.

by Andrie B. Du Toit,[49] and takes the phrase παρὰ τοὺς πόδας Γαμαλιήλ with the participle ἀνατεθραμμένος, then both Paul's 'upbringing' and 'instruction' took place 'at the feet' of Gamaliel, thus implying a certain semantic overlap between the two participles, both pointing to Paul's schooling.[50] This, in turn, would suggest that though Paul was educated (i.e., both ἀνατεθραμμένος and πεπαιδευμένος referring to his education) in Jerusalem under Gamaliel, 'the upper limit of Paul's coming to Jerusalem could even be moved to his adolescent phase',[51] since only at that age one started his training under a rabbi.

The syntactical and semantic analysis of the verse shows the difficulty of making an absolute pronouncement about the time of Paul's move from Tarsus to Jerusalem upon which depends in part our ability to decide concerning Paul's knowledge of Greco-Roman rhetoric, though the weight of the argument seems to point to the reading of the majority: early move to Jerusalem.[52] Thus, the information must be corroborated with other evidences from the Pauline corpora that may be used to construct a picture of his acquaintance with sophistic rhetoric. We will leave for later the discussion of Paul's writing style, but for now we may focus on Paul's own perception of his upbringing and education as reflected in Phil. 3.5-6.[53]

Hengel has rightly noticed that from Paul's writings we get an unequivocal picture of the pre-Christian Paul as the Pharisee connected with Jewish Palestine and to whom Jerusalem seems to be more important

49   See his linguistic, rhetorical, and narratological arguments for such understanding in 'A Tale of Two Cities', 378–88.

50   See his evidence for a larger semantic range of ἀνατεθραμμένος, ibid., 379–83: e.g., Plato, *Theaet.* 172C; Isocrates, *Or.* 7.41; Josephus, *J.W.* 1.576, 2.101; *A.J.* 2.236. In light of his way of punctuating the text and of the broad semantic range of ἀνατεθραμμένος he asks: 'But is a statement implying that Paul's τροφή [strictly home upbringing] took place "at the feet of Gamaliel" not absurd, putting Gamaliel in fact in charge of a nursery school?' (385). This absurdity however is removed if the break is placed before the phrase aforementioned, the statement thus implying that Gamaliel was responsible only for his 'education' (παδεία).

51   Ibid., 388.

52   Acts 26.4 is another passage in Luke which depends for its meaning on the sense of one particle τε: 'All the Jews know my manner of life from my youth, which was from the beginning within my own nation, τε in Jerusalem.' If the particle has an explicative sense (i.e., 'namely', 'indeed') then Paul's move to Jerusalem must be placed very early in his childhood. See Bell, *The Irrevocable Call of God*, p. 36, n. 173. See also Polhill, *Acts*, p. 498; Barrett, *Acts*, p. 1150. If it functions merely as a conjunction (i.e., 'and'), then Paul's move to Jerusalem is rather late, interpreting 'my own nation' (ἐν τῷ ἔθνει μου) as referring to the Jews in Tarsus. See Du Toit, 'A Tale of Two Cities', 388–90.

53   For a detailed study of this passages in reference to Paul's education see Hengel, *The Pre-Christian Paul*, ch. 2, 'Upbringing and Education: Tarsus or Jerusalem?' 18–39, and the summary by Bell, *The Irrevocable Call of God*, pp. 11–16. Additional to this passage one may also consider 2 Cor. 11.21-22 and Rom. 9.3-5, 11.1.

than Tarsus, the place of his birth, of which we learn only from Luke.[54]
For instance, in Paul's autobiographical account in Galatians 1 and 2,
Tarsus plays no part, in complete contrast to Jerusalem. Nevertheless,
some have sought to argue, based on Gal. 1.22 ('And I was still unknown
to the churches of Judea that are in Christ'), that the pre-Christian Paul
had no connection to Jerusalem. But this is based on the faulty thinking
that Jerusalem was a small village where everybody knew everyone else.[55]
The best available text that can help one deduce the major influences on
Paul is Phil. 3.5-6.

In these verses, Paul lists seven things he was proud of – four privileges
which he inherited apart from his own act of will and three decisions he
took in his life as a Jew. Briefly, we can mention the significance of these
statements to our research into Paul's upbringing and education. The first
indicates that both his parents were Jews who observed the law strictly.
Second, neither he nor his parents were proselytes, but rather were Jews
by birth. Third, Saul/Paul belonged to the tribe of Benjamin which
inhabited Jerusalem at that time (cf. Neh. 11.7-9) and could trace his
genealogy all the way back to the first king of Israel, Saul. Presumably,
Paul/Saul was named after his most illustrious ancestor. Fourth, Paul
presents himself not as a Diaspora Jew speaking a foreign language.
Rather, he is a Hebrew-speaking Jew born of Hebrew-speaking parents.
Fifth, he was a Pharisee. Corroborated with Gal. 1.13-14, where Paul
characterizes his 'zeal for the traditions of the fathers' as 'advanced in
Jewish teaching' surpassing 'his contemporaries among his people', it is
hard not to place the pre-Christian Pharisee Paul in Jerusalem, particularly given that 'we know virtually nothing of a Diaspora Pharisaism.'[56]
This is strengthened by the seventh element in the list, which describes the
strict adherence to the Law, which was possible only in the Holy Land,
given the purity laws.[57] Bell concludes: 'In view of this, one has to place
Paul in the mainstream of Palestinian Judaism. Palestinian Judaism was
of course Hellenized. Paul like many Jews could speak and write fluent
Greek. But Paul was certainly not in the category of a thoroughly
Hellenized Jew like Philo of Alexandria.'[58]

Based on the information gathered from Luke and from Paul's own
presentation, then, we may conclude that the major influences on the pre-
Christian Paul were of a Palestinian Jewish nature. Both his upbringing
and education are heavily stamped by devotion to the 'traditions of the

---

54 Hengel, *The Pre-Christian Paul*, p. 1.
55 Ibid., p. 24.
56 Hengel, *The Pre-Christian Paul*, p. 31, where he quotes Günther Bornkamm, 'Paulus',
RGG 5 (1961) 168.
57 Ibid., p. 32.
58 Bell, *The Irrevocable Call of God*, p. 15.

fathers'. He was as Hebrew as one could get, which agrees with Luke's suggestion of an early move to Jerusalem. The question still remains, however, as to where Paul acquired the knowledge of Greek and of sophistic rhetoric to which he reacts in his Corinthian correspondence, if not from training in a rhetorical school (i.e., tertiary education). Or, do not his writings betray a thorough knowledge and use of rhetorical techniques? For instance, the 'Fool's Speech' of 2 Corinthians 10–13, though atypical of Paul's argumentation given the need to defend his authority by using the techniques of his opponents (i.e., boasting),[59] seems to belong to a person well versed in the techniques of persuasive artistry. Murphy O'Connor argues that Paul's 'conscious control of no use of rhetoric however collapsed in the heat of argument, and in the Fool's Speech deeply engrained qualities become evident.'[60] Christopher Forbes

59   Paul, in his foolish speech, intentionally does that which he judges to be inappropriate for proclamation. Even so, his speech in 2 Corinthians 10–13, though following the pattern of his opponents, distances from them by a clear emphasis on boasting in weakness. For a discussion of Paul's self-praise see Mario M. DiCicco, *Paul's Use of Ethos, Pathos, and Logos in 2 Corinthians 10–13* (MBPS, 31; Lewiston: Edwin Mellen, 1995), pp. 56–63. See Demosthenes' speech *De Corona* for possible parallelism. See also Margaret M. Mitchell, 'A Patristic Perspective on Pauline περιαυτολογία', *NTS* 47 (2001) 354–71. In this article, Mitchell discusses John Chrysostom's reference to Paul's 'speaking of himself' in his fifth oration *Laud. Paul.* in comparison to Plutarch's treatment of the same *topos* especially in his essay from *Mor.* entitled Περὶ τοῦ ἑαυτὸν ἐπαινεῖν ἀνεπιφθόνως. Though boasting was regarded as offensive or burdensome (ἐπαχθές βαρύς; Chrysostom, PG 22.1;38.4; Plutarch, *Mor.* 547D), as an expression of vainglory (φιλοτιμία; Chrysostom, PG 21.2; Plutarch, *Mor.* 540A), or madness (ἀπόνοια; Chrysostom, *Laud. Paul.* 5.13; Plutarch, *Mor.* 539C), Chrysostom, following Plutarch, argues that Paul's boasting was justified (cf. *Laud. Paul.* 5.15). See H. D. Betz, *Der Apostel Paulus und die sokratische Tradition* (BHT, 45; Tübingen: Mohr, 1972), pp. 74–89, for a similar conclusion. One should be quick however to analyze Paul's boasting in light of the conventionally accepted rhetorical techniques and conclude that he follows, for the parallelism could very well be a projection of Chrysostom's own rhetorical training. See Scott J. Hafemann, *2 Corinthians* (NIVAC; Grand Rapids: Zondervan, 2000), p. 423, n. 1, who follows Paul Barnett, *The Second Epistle to the Corinthians* (NICNT; Grand Rapids: Eerdmans, 1997), p. 494. Judge, 'Paul's Boasting in Relation to Contemporary Professional Practice', 37–50, argues that Paul is engaging in a careful *reductio ad absurdum* of rhetorical methods. See also Savage, *Power through Weakness*, pp. 62–4. Moreover, Marshall, *Enmity in Corinth*, pp. 353–64, in his discussion of self-praise and self-derision, points to the fact that there is no evidence in Greek and Roman authors of the kind of self-derision characterizing Paul. Not the least, self-derision was regarded as the worst form of praising oneself (cf. Quintilian *Inst.* 9.1.8; 11.1.21.22; 9.1.8). In conclusion, then, the most that can be said about Paul's boasting is that he is well aware of his opponents' methods of boasting, who are possibly rhetorically educated, and responds to such methods with self-derision. But it would go beyond evidence to claim that Paul's boasting in these chapters proves that he is rhetorically educated and follows the rhetorical convention of his day. For a balanced presentation on self-praise see D. E. Aune, 'Boasting', in *WDNTECLR*, 81–84.

60   Murphy O'Connor, *Paul: A Critical Life*, p. 51. He quotes Cicero who said of Plato 'It was when making fun of orators that he himself seemed to be the consummate orator' (*De Or.* 1.2.47).

concludes that, 'Whatever we have seen of Paul's rhetoric suggests a mastery and an assurance unlikely to have been gained without long practice, and possibly long study as well.'[61] David Aune, however, rightly disagrees: 'While there is no doubt that Paul was a victim of character assassination and had to defend himself in 2 Cor 10–13, there is nothing distinctive in that defense which suggests that he was drawing on what he had learned about ethos in his putative rhetorical education.'[62] The issue of Paul's literary style will be investigated later in this chapter, but concerning the issue of Paul's knowledge of Greek and rhetorical transaction, a couple of further possible answers may be given that could explain the similarities between Paul's argument and ancient rhetoric.

First, given the thoroughly Hellenized Jerusalem, it is possible that the Jewish synagogue adopted a discourse influenced by Greek rhetoric, since synagogue preaching was done in Greek. Based on this, Hengel concludes: 'It seems to me most plausible to suppose that Paul learned the basic insights of his indubitable rhetorical art, which is not orientated on classical literary models, through practical application in the Greek-speaking synagogues in Jerusalem.'[63]

Related to this background information is a second possible answer concerning Paul's knowledge of, and positive regard for, rhetorical transaction, namely that such knowledge finds its source in the Hebrew Scripture.[64] The Old Testament prophets evidence the use of rhetorical techniques, such as antithesis, hyperboles, enthymemes, etc., before they were prescribed in the ancient rhetorical handbooks, and Paul could have easily followed the model of the prophets.[65] Therefore, as Litfin rightly argues, 'to discover in Paul general features of communication which were discussed by the rhetoricians is by no means an automatic indication that the Apostle had embraced Greco-Roman rhetoric as such.'[66]

If this is the case, then, we can see why there would be some similarity between Paul's speeches (and those of the prophets) and ancient rhetoric. George Kennedy, for instance, notes that, 'The fundamental rhetorical technique of the Old Testament is assertion ... Authority is a nonartistic

61   Forbes, 'Comparison, Self-Praise and Irony: Paul's Boasting and the Conventions of Hellenistic Rhetoric', *NTS* 32 (1986) 1-30 (23).

62   Aune, 'Ethos', in *WDNTECLR*, 172.

63   Hengel, *The Pre-Christian Paul*, p. 58. See the entire ch. 4, 'Greek-Speaking Jerusalem and Greek Synagogue Education', 54–62, for evidences of a Hellenized Jerusalem. See also Bell, *The Irrevocable Call of God*, p. 36, and Judge, 'The Reaction against Classical Education in the New Testament', 9.

64   Cf. Bell, *The Irrevocable Call of God*, pp. 34–5.

65   See Kennedy, *Classical Rhetoric*, pp. 137–43, for other examples.

66   Litfin, *Proclamation*, p. 256.

analogy to ethos in classical rhetoric.'[67] But despite similarities, Kennedy is right to show the distinctions: 'In its purest form, Judeo-Christian rhetoric shows some similarity to philosophical rhetoric: it claims to be the simple enunciation of truth, uncontaminated by adornment, flattery, or sophistic argumentation; it differs from philosophical rhetoric in that this truth is known from revelation or established signs sent from God, not discovered by dialectic through human effort.'[68] Thus, in the Hebrew Bible the assertion of divine authority appeals to God's deeds and speeches in the past rather than to the speaker's ability to craft a credible and ordered presentation of a case and invent appropriate persuasive strategies. Paul, then, would be in continuity with such 'rhetoric', and one should not be pressed to argue that Paul employed the techniques of Greco-Roman rhetoric in his proclamation.[69]

But without getting too far ahead of ourselves in talking about Paul's written style, we may conclude that what we can learn from both Luke's and Paul's (self-) description in regard to his upbringing and education is that Paul's move to Jerusalem was most likely early in his childhood, so that the major influences on the pre-Christian Paul were of a Jewish nature, understanding that Jewish education at that time in Jerusalem was impacted by Hellenistic education.[70] We can also safely assume that, given the widespread practice of the sophists to declaim publicly, Paul, as any other citizen in the Roman Empire, would have been acquainted with the rhetorical flourish that such orators employed in their speeches in order to impress and persuade. That Paul presumably used such eloquence in his writings but not in his speech will be evaluated later in this chapter. For now it suffices to say with Litfin that,

> Our understanding of 1 Corinthians 1–4 requires us to assume on the part of the Apostle a certain limited understanding of the broad stance of Greco-Roman rhetoric, but only this and no more … We need assume of Paul nothing more than one would expect of an intelligent and literate man who was born a Roman citizen in Tarsus, spoke Greek, and lived and moved perceptively in the Hellenistic world of the first century, a world in which rhetoric and oratory were common features of daily life.[71]

---

67   Kennedy, *Classical Rhetoric*, p. 138.

68   Ibid., pp. 138–9.

69   For a critique of Kennedy's view of Christian rhetoric, see the article by John R. Levison, 'Did the Spirit Inspire Rhetoric? An Exploration of George Kennedy's Definition of Early Christian Rhetoric', in *Persuasive Artistry: Studies in New Testament Rhetoric in Honor of George A. Kennedy* (Duane F. Watson, ed.; JSNTSup, 50; Sheffield: JSOT Press, 1991), pp. 25–40.

70   Conzelmann, *1 Corinthians*, p. 246, may be too dogmatic in claiming that Paul was 'untouched by Greek education of his time.'

71   Ibid., pp. 137–9.

The view that Paul rejected (sophistic) rhetoric is thus based on the assumptions that Paul used terminology borrowed from the world of rhetoric in his presentation of his theology of proclamation, that he was accused of poor performance when judged against the conventional standards of persuasive rhetoric, and that he was familiar with rhetoric, possibly even undergoing education in rhetoric. The other two views which will be explained below are more of a response to this view or an attempt to reconcile the apparent discrepancy between Paul's written and oral communication.

Paul Does not Oppose Rhetoric

This view is expressed in various ways. Dean Anderson is among the most ardent proponents of the view that Paul is not against rhetoric. With this, Anderson takes an unusual stand against the notion of Paul's use of rhetoric: he denies both that Paul is using rhetoric, arguing that Paul's discourse shows poor style and rhetoric, and that he is trained in rhetoric. He states that 'Paul's characterization of his own preaching in 1 Corinthians 1–4 should not be interpreted against the specific background of Greco-Roman rhetorical theory.'[72] He bases his argument on his belief that '[t]hese chapters say virtually nothing concerning Paul's view on rhetorical theory and practice.'[73] We have already mentioned Anderson's critique of the former view in the previous chapter and Winter's response, so there is no need to repeat the arguments here. Suffice it to say that his view rests on the belief that the passages that present Paul's theology of proclamation (i.e., 1 Cor. 2.1-5) and the critique of Paul's oratorical performance (i.e., 2 Cor. 10.10 and 11.6) do not contain rhetorical terms or allusions. An evaluation of this view will have to await our in-depth exegesis of 1 Cor. 2.1-5 later in this chapter.

Most advocates of this second view, however, agree that Paul's writings present the reader with a proof of Paul's high rhetorical style, so that the issue of the apparent discrepancy between his letters and his speech requires explanation. One way to explain this is to argue that the Corinthians' critique of Paul does not revolve around his speaking style. Schmithals, for instance, states that 'the Corinthian judgment on the Pauline epistles, that they are weighty and impressive, makes us doubt even more that people in Corinth were critically occupied with Paul's language style and formal rhetoric.'[74] His solution is to suggest that Paul was regarded as lacking pneumatic presence, for which he was critiqued by the Gnostic Corinthians. We have already evaluated the alleged

72 Ibid., p. 276.
73 Anderson, *Ancient Rhetorical Theory and Paul*, p. 248.
74 Schmithals, *Gnosticism in Corinth*, p. 142.

Gnostic background for the Corinthian correspondence in Chapter 2 and have found it anachronistic.

Others agree, *contra* Anderson and Schmithals, that Paul's character-ization of his own preaching in 1 Cor. 2.1-5 contains rhetorical terms and allusions, but they disagree on Paul's rapport to rhetoric. We have already mentioned Smit's argument that passages such as 1 Cor. 1.18-31 and 2.6-16 'belong to the most rhetorical parts he has written and do not betray a single trace of his presumed aversion against rhetoric.'[75] In his view, then, οὐκ ἐν σοφίᾳ λόγου comes to mean 'not with rational, reasoning, logical wisdom', rather than 'not with rhetorical eloquence.' Thus, what Paul is against is not rhetoric but worldly argumentation. This does not mean that 1 Corinthians 1–4 does not contain rhetorical terms. On the contrary, presumably Paul purposely uses rhetoric.[76]

According to this logic, then, Paul, by using rhetorical terminology and argumentation approves of such practice, since he apparently does not speak against it in 1 Cor. 2.1-5. A similar view is adopted in a recent dissertation by Sojung Yoon, whose thesis is that 'it was the Corinthians who preferred spiritually inspired speech and thought that eloquent speech did not contain the power of the Spirit. Paul, then, was the person who favored rhetoric and was criticized by the Corinthians for his rhetorical skill.'[77] He bases his argument on the belief that the Corinthians could not have appreciated rhetoric since it is unlikely that they were rhetorically skilled, given their low level of education (cf. 1 Cor. 1.26). However, we believe he is unsuccessful in refuting the majority view explained in the previous chapter that the Corinthians were people with a hunger for status, which was manifested in their appreciation for rhetorical eloquence. The pervasive presence of public declamations also tells against his argument of the Corinthians' unfamiliarity with conven-tional rhetorical standards.[78]

Yoon is not the first to have argued that Paul in fact defended the use of rhetoric in preaching, though not in as sharp terms. John Levison, for instance, contends that 'though he [i.e., Paul] appears to reject rhetoric, he is in fact a masterful proponent of rhetoric.'[79] This view is ultimately based on the assumption that Paul's rejection of rhetoric is in itself a rhetorical *topos*, namely irony, a device meant to disarm one's opponents by arguing that one lacks eloquence, for the purpose of making his readers

75   Smit, 'Search for Coherence', 245.

76   See ibid., 247.

77   S. Yoon, '"Not in Persuasive Words of Wisdom"?: Paul's Rhetoric in 1 Corinthians 1.18-2.16' (unpublished doctoral dessertation, Graduate Theological Union, 2004), i.

78   See Hartman, 'Some Remarks on 1 Cor. 2.1-5', 120.

79   Levison, 'Did the Spirit Inspire Rhetoric', 40. See also Horsley, 'Wisdom of Word and Words of Wisdom in Corinth', 224, 230; Pogoloff, *LOGOS AND SOPHIA*, p. 136.

feel sympathetic to him and to his cause.[80] Dale Martin agrees with this when he states that 'Paul protests too much that he is not using rhetoric.'[81] He has gathered sufficient evidence to support the argument that rhetorical deprecation was common among the orators of the day.[82] E. A. Judge, for instance, states that 'one urbanely displayed one's skill by affecting the lack of it', a rhetorical *tropos* called *asteismos* or *prospoiesis*.[83] This device is allegedly used also by Paul here. Thus Martin concludes that 'Paul stands in a great tradition of rhetorical disavowals of rhetorical activity.'[84] Pogoloff, as we have seen in the previous chapter, agreeing that Paul uses irony, argues that Paul rejects not rhetoric, but the social values wedded to it.[85]

In this view, then (apart from Anderson's unusual stand that Paul says nothing about rhetoric and Smit's contention that Paul rejects argumentation by logical proof and not rhetoric), both Paul's rejection of rhetoric in 1 Cor. 2.1-5 and his acceptance of critique concerning his lack of eloquence in 2 Cor. 11.6, only appear so on the surface.[86] But in reality Paul is not only well acquainted with sophistic rhetoric, but he also uses it for purposes such as to defend his authority which was questioned by some in the Corinthian congregation.

Margaret Thrall comments on this possibility with regard to 2 Cor. 11.6 and rightly argues based on contextual information that '[t]his is probably to go too far, however. The context of the disclaimer (vv. 5, 6b, c) is surely to be understood seriously, rather than ironically. It is clear, moreover, from 10.10 that the Corinthians did regard Paul as in some sense oratorically incompetent, and would not themselves perceive any irony in what he says here.'[87] Likewise, E. A. Judge has gathered evidence from the

---

80 See Nils A. Rosaeg, 'Paul's Rhetorical Arsenal and 1 Corinthians 1–4', *Jian Dao* 3 (1995) 51–75, who claims that irony is the most acceptable suggestion. See also DiCicco, *Paul's Use of Ethos, Pathos, and Logos*, p. 24.

81 Martin, *The Corinthian Body*, p. 47. He adds: 'With all his decrying of the use of rhetoric, am I being cynical in insinuating that Paul is here more than anywhere using his own rhetorical training quite skillfully? Not at all' (p. 48).

82 Ibid., pp. 48–9. See Cicero, *De or.* 1.1.47, 1.31.137-1.32.145, 2.18.75-76, 3.19.70-73; Isocrates, *Or.* 8.38. See also Cicero, *Part. or.* 22; Quintilian, *Inst.* 4.1.8-9; Hermogenes, *Id.* 2.6.

83 Judge, 'Paul's Boasting in Relation to Contemporary Professional Practice', 37. See Chrysostom, *Or.* 42.3. Winter, *Philo and Paul among the Sophists*, 147–48, draws a parallel and contrast between Dio's apologia in *Or.* 47 and Paul's defense in 1 Cor. 2.1-5.

84 Martin, *The Corinthian Body*, p. 49.

85 Pogoloff, *LOGOS AND SOPHIA*, p. 121.

86 See Du Toit, 'A Tale of Two Cities', 397. Augustine, PL 4.7.15, also seems to take the form of Paul's sentence as concessive of debate, allowing a little room for doubt. As a result, Paul accepts the description only for the sake of debate.

87 Thrall, *Second Corinthians*, 2.675. Anderson, *Ancient Rhetorical Theory and Paul*, 278, n. 7, also rejects such a possibility.

Church Fathers with regard to such presumptions and has concluded that '[t]he verdict of the Fathers would be that Paul used no asteistic irony in admitting he was a layman in speech, but accepted the charge to confound it.'[88]

Timothy Lim also responds adequately to the alleged use of irony in 1 Cor. 2.1-5 concerning Paul's rejection of rhetoric. He rightly points to the impossibility of such an approach based on the flow of Paul's argument in the immediate context: 'It is unlikely that 1 Cor. 2.1-5 is a rhetorical strategy, whether as a tacit admission of the effectiveness of rhetoric or as an attempt to disarm his audience, for the use of a device wrought by human wisdom at this point in the letter would unravel the thematic development of 1.17-25 and 1.26-31, and would contradict his theology of the cross.'[89] As already explained in Chapter 1 of this work, Paul makes his first argument (i.e., 1 Cor. 1.18–2.5) in three successive steps. First (1 Cor. 1.18-23), he argues for God's *modus operandi* in the world in terms of the cross, a symbol of weakness and foolishness according to the values of the world. Second (1 Cor. 1.24-31), Paul exemplifies this apparent weakness and foolishness with the Corinthians' own low social status at the time of their conversion. In the third stage of his argument (1 Cor. 2.1-5), Paul gives his own example of his *modus operandi* with regard to his preaching. In order for his argument to function, his preaching must be characterized by the same counter-values as the social status of the Corinthians and God's *modus operandi* – weakness. Thus, if Paul's preaching is not 'weak', but persuasive (given the alleged use of irony), according to what was perceived as eloquent speech, then Paul's argument in this section is counterproductive. Thus, the thematic and logical flow of Paul's argument requires us to expect a sincere self-deprecation of Paul.

Therefore, Paul's rejection of rhetorical eloquence in preaching must be taken seriously, if the text refers to rhetoric. That Paul rejects argumentation by logical proof rather than rhetoric, according to Smit, seems to be a bit reductionistic. It seems that it is more accurate to think that logical argumentation is part of the art of persuasion, i.e., rhetoric, so that when Paul rejects rhetoric he also rejects the kind of argumentation that was considered eloquent. Charles Horne rightly argues that, 'the main thrust of Paul's statement [in 1 Cor. 2.2] is to disclaim any confidence in rhetorical phrases and rational demonstrations.'[90] But, regardless of what one thinks that Paul deems as inappropriate for preaching in 1 Cor. 2.1-5, one thing is certain: his statements in this section must be taken as sincere. The tendency to interpret Paul's

---

88 Judge, 'Paul's Boasting in Relation to Contemporary Professional Practice', 42.

89 Lim, '"Not in Persuasive Words of Wisdom"', 148, n. 29. See also Litfin, *Proclamation*, pp. 259–60.

90 Charles M. Horne, 'The Power of Paul's Preaching', *BETS* 8 (1965) 112.

statements as an example of irony seems to be driven by the difficulty of reconciling them with 1 Corinthians 1–2, which, in John Levison's view', [c]onstitutes a rhetorical *tour de force*.'[91] This apparent disparity will be discussed below, but for now we must seek to reach accurate exegetical conclusions by being faithful to the context as determinative of meaning, before we move to other larger issues. The question, as Levison presents it in light of the disparity between Paul's explicit rejection of rhetoric and his wholesale use of it is, 'Which aspect of this disparity represents Paul's viewpoint?'[92] While the advocates of this view prefer to side with Paul's literary practice and argue that Paul plays the role of an εἴρων, we have argued that Paul's argument in these opening chapters indicates that his deprecation of eloquence is necessarily sincere. Taking Paul's statements at their true face value is the most faithful reading of the text in its literary context.

Paul Is Ambivalent towards Rhetoric

This third interpretation of Paul's approach to rhetoric is in fact a variation of the previous views. If one is to take Paul's statements in 1 Cor. 2.1-5 seriously, then the question that some have rightfully raised is how Paul's rejection of rhetoric in preaching comports with his literary practice, which seems to be highly rhetorical or at least to be using rhetorical techniques (e.g., diatribe, antithesis, hyperbole). Is Paul disingenuous with his deprecation of rhetoric? The resolution to this question comes in various forms.

Some, for instance, see no problem in affirming the discrepancy between Paul's anti-rhetorical stance in his proclamation of the gospel and the style of his epistles. Jeffrey Lamp has argued that Paul used rhetoric in preaching to believers, but made a conscious decision (for theological reasons) not to employ rhetoric in his evangelistic and missionary contacts with unbelievers.[93] The reason this should not be regarded as inconsistency in Paul, Lamp contends, is because one should differentiate between the modes of discourse. He states: 'It appears that the spiritual condition of the audience determines Paul's approach in communicating the substance of the gospel. Evangelistic proclamation must be conducted in oratorically unadorned fashion, while exhortation or didactic discourse

---

91 Levison, 'Did the Spirit Inspire Rhetoric?', 36.

92 Ibid., 37.

93 Lamp, 'Gospel and Rhetoric in 1 Corinthians 1–4', 14–16. Witherington, *Conflict and Community in Corinth*, e.g., p. 123, seems to make this suggestion at different places in his commentary. See also A. Lynch, 'Pauline Rhetoric: 1 Corinthians 1.10-4.21' (unpublished masters dissertation, University of North Carolina, 1981), 46, cited in Winter, *Philo and Paul among the Sophists*, p. 227, n. 98.

to believers is open to a wider variety of rhetorical approaches.'[94] In other words, he suggests that the nature of the audience and the purpose of the discourse determines the form of one's discourse: if the audience was made up of unbelievers and the purpose was to evangelize them, Paul would have eschewed rhetoric from his preaching, but if the audience was made of believers and the purpose was to edify them, then Paul would have had no problem with using rhetorical techniques to persuade them.

While this may sound like a reasonable resolution, it seems to uphold a dichotomy that is hard to find in Paul. More will be said later in this chapter about the apparent discrepancy between Paul's written and oral speech, but suffice it to say here that Lamp's dichotomy seems to say that Paul believed that, while the Holy Spirit is responsible for engendering faith in the heart of the unbeliever, apart from the preacher's eloquence, the preacher is responsible, through his oratorical skill, to bring about conviction in the heart of the believer in a certain spiritual area. This, however, is inconsistent with Paul's affirmations in texts such as Phil. 3.15b ('And if on some point you think differently, that too God will make clear to you'), where Paul emphasizes the divine role in working conviction in the believer.

In the same category falls Witherington's claim that 1 Cor. 9.22 implies that Paul would use rhetoric to make a good first impression on rhetorically sophisticated audiences, such as the Corinthians.[95] Such a view, however, 'does not correspond with the complaints of the Corinthians.'[96]

Others seek to close the gap between the oratorical and literary practices of Paul and argue that Paul rejects only the use of the 'grand style', a florid and ornamental style associated with Asianism, as against the more 'plain style' associated with Atticism.[97] Michael Bullmore, for instance, argues that the debate between the two rhetorical styles was at home in first-century Corinth. He states: 'The debate concerned itself almost entirely with matters of style with the Atticists accusing the Asianists of stylistic frivolity and excess, and the Asianists responding by accusing the Atticists of stylistic dullness.'[98] Paul, then, allegedly reacts specifically against stylistic virtuosity as an illegitimate means of persuasion. Excess in style is regarded as inappropriate for the proclamation of

---

94   Ibid., 15.

95   Witherington, *Conflict and Community in Corinth*, p. 46, n. 139.

96   See Peterson, *Eloquence and Proclamation*, p. 65, n. 98.

97   See Witherington, *Conflict and Community in Corinth*, p. 392; and Bullmore, *St. Paul's Theology of Rhetorical Style*, 17 and 221. See also his description of Asianist and Attic rhetoric, and the debate between the two styles (pp. 90–113). See also Eduard Norden, *Die Antike Kunstprosa vom VI. Jahrhunderts vor Christus in die Zeit der Renaissance* (Darmstadt: Wissenschaftliche Buchgesellschaft, 1958; repr. Leipzig: B. G. Teubner, 1989), 507.

98   Bullmore, *St. Paul's Theology of Rhetorical Style*, p. 16.

the gospel, since it tends to overshadow the message, though eloquence seems to characterize Paul's writings.[99]

Timothy Savage is also ready to agree that 1 Cor. 2.1-5 presents Paul's rejection of rhetoric, but only a certain kind of rhetoric – the rhetoric of boasting. He contends: 'Paul is distancing himself from arrogant speech as well as abusive speech. This provides an even firmer basis for supposing that he is rejecting the vulgar rhetoric of his day and not the classical speech of the intellectual elite.'[100] The problem with such statement is that it reads 2 Cor. 10.1-11 into 1 Cor. 2.1-5 and fails to account for the rhetorical terms found in 1 Cor. 2.1-5 and the passage's larger context, where the issue seems to be that of establishing one's faith apart from logical argumentation and not that of establishing one's ethos through boasting of oneself, as we will argue later.

Another possibility has been suggested, namely that what Paul rejects is rhetoric that emphasizes form over content, or form as an end in itself. Horne asserts: 'The apostle certainly had no objection to persuasive words or logical thought per se, he was a master of both. The point is however, that he would not allow either to operate as ends in themselves but only as instruments to be employed under the guidance of the Spirit for the interpretation and communication of divine revelation.'[101] Thus, it is argued, Paul was willing to use rhetoric as means to enhance comprehension, but not for the purpose of, e.g., entertainment.

Augustine seems to fit in this category also.[102] In his writing *De Doctrina Christiana* Book 4, Augustine draws a distinction between three functions of eloquence according to rhetorical styles: the subdued style used to teach, the temperate style used to delight, and the majestic style used to move to action (cf. Cicero, *De or.* 21). Verbal ornaments were characteristic of both the temperate and the majestic styles, but the distinction, according to Augustine, consisted in the fact that the majestic style does not 'seek them if it does not need them. It is carried along by its own impetus, and if the beauties of eloquence occur they are caught up by

---

99   See DiCicco, *Paul's Use of Ethos, Pathos, and Logos*, p. 24.

100   Savage, *Power through Weakness*, p. 73.

101   Horne, 'The Power of Paul's Preaching', 113. See also Lim, 'Not in Persuasive Words of Wisdom', 149. See also Barrett, *First Corinthians*, p. 63; and Weiss, *Der erste Korintherbriefe*, pp. 49–50. The authors of the *Assembly Annotations* of 1688 also stated: 'Though the Apostle made little use of Oratory in his ordinary Discourses and Epistles, yet he knew how to use it to the Ends which he aimed at, *viz.* the Glory of God, and the good of Souls that were under his care. He did not turn Divinity into mere words and Rhetorical flourishes; yet he made use of these sometimes, as a *waiting Maid* to Divinity' (emphasis added), quoted by Hans Dieter Betz, *2 Corinthians 8 and 9: A Commentary on Two Administrative Letters of the Apostle Paul* (Hermeneia; Philadelphia: Fortress, 1985), p. 8.

102   See Judge, 'Paul's Boasting in Relation to Contemporary Professional Practice', 38–40.

the force of the things discussed and not deliberately assumed for decoration ... The appropriateness of the words [is] determined by the ardour of the heart rather than by careful choice.' (4.20.42). Augustine does not claim that Paul was an exponent of the majestic style, but he seeks to make Paul into a 'kind of professional in spite of himself', in the words of E. A. Judge.[103] Augustine states that where eloquence corresponds to the classical rules that is not by Paul's device but that these words 'spontaneously suggest themselves', because 'eloquence like an inseparable attendant, followed it [i.e., wisdom] without being called for.' (*tamquam inseparabilem famulam etiam non vocatam*, 4.6.10). In the same work (4.7.12) he states: 'Wisdom is his guide, eloquence his attendant.' Augustine, then, seems to agree that Paul rejected ornamentation for the sole purpose of pleasure, but makes an effort to justify eloquence in Paul based on his inadvertent use of σχήματα (the ornamental figures of speech). He states: 'Wisdom not aiming at eloquence, yet eloquence not shrinking from wisdom' (4.7.21). Augustine believes that Paul used different rhetorical styles depending on the end-result which he sought to bring about. Paul was not against rhetorical styles per se, only against their use when the purpose of the speech does not call for them, for instance, against using the temperate (ornamental) style in order to teach, since such style is appropriate only for the purpose of producing pleasure or holding attention. Thus Augustine believes that we find in Scripture, including Paul, all three rhetorical styles since the man of God is called to teach, delight, and persuade.[104]

Most of these various forms of the third view have in common an attempt to give an explanation to the apparent discrepancy between Paul's disavowal of rhetoric in preaching and his use of rhetorical techniques in his epistles, and therefore a final pronouncement concerning their validity will have to be postponed a little longer. For now, we must note that the overemphasis on style in all these views as against content in ancient rhetoric is exaggerated and reductionistic. The distinction between form and content that these scholars see in Paul is often compared with the debate between philosophers – who allegedly emphasized content – and

---

103   Ibid., 41.

104   *Contra* Litfin, *Proclamation*, p. 261, who claims that Paul rejects the rhetoric that attributes the speaker a role in persuasion. What he proposes in his monograph for further study is the argument that Paul would employ rhetorical techniques particularly for stage two in the process of communication – comprehension – but not beyond, for stage three – yielding.

rhetoricians – who allegedly emphasized style.[105] Paul would then resemble the philosopher who critiques the sophists' supposedly sole interest in style and form over truth and content.[106]

It is true that Plato, in his dialogue *Gorgias*, critiques the integrity of rhetoric brought to Athens by Gorgias in 427 BC. He argued that the orator was more concerned with being pleasant and entertaining than with communicating truth, accusing him of flattery (cf. 465c).[107] This accusation had become philosophical *topoi* for later critics of sophistry. But Plato also believed in a philosophically acceptable rhetoric. Pogoloff rightly states that the question for philosophy becomes not whether rhetorical expression should be eschewed in favor of philosophical content, but what kind of rhetoric is philosophically acceptable. Plato concludes that rhetoric is to be used for this one purpose always, of pointing to what is just ... [cf. 527c].'[108]

Aristotle (384–322 BC), Plato's pupil, while acknowledging the danger of rhetoric in the hands of the mere flatterer, wrote *Rhetorica* out of the conviction that that those speaking the truth have an obligation to be persuasive. In order to be persuasive, Aristotle pointed to the three forms of arguments (πίστις): ἔθος, πάθος, λόγος.[109] Thus, Aristotle envisioned

---

105   See e.g. Betz, 'The Problem of Rhetoric and Theology According to the Apostle Paul', p. 36. See also his monograph *Der Apostel Paulus und die sokratische Tradition* (BHT, 45; Tübingen: Mohr, 1972), esp. 47–69; and Malherbe, *Paul and the Popular Philosophers* (Minneapolis: Fortress, 1989), p. 68.

106   Edgar Krentz, '*LOGOS* OR *SOPHIA*: The Pauline Use of the Ancient Dispute between Rhetoric and Philosophy', in *Early Christianity and Classical Culture: Comparative Studies in Honor of Abraham J. Malherbe* (John. T. Fitzgerald, Thomas H. Olbnicht and L. Michael White, eds.; NovTSup, 110; Leiden: Brill, 2003), 282, sees Paul as engaging in the critique by philosophers of rhetoricians who have no concern for truth. For the discussion that will follow I am indebted to Pogoloff, *LOGOS AND SOPHIA*, esp. ch. 2, 'Form and Content in Classical Rhetoric', pp. 37–69. For more details on the history of ancient rhetoric in general, see Mark Harding, *Tradition and Rhetoric in the Pastoral Epistles* (SBL, 3; New York: Peter Lang, 1998), pp. 181–7; Kennedy, *Classical Rhetoric*, chs 3–5. *Contra* Anderson, *Ancient Rhetorical Theory and Paul*, p. 65, who follows Jacob Wisse, 'Welsprekendlheid en filosofie bij Cicero. Studies en commentaar bij Cicero, *De or.* 3.19-37a; 52–95' (i.e., unpublished dissertation, University of Amsterdam, 1994), 17, in arguing that the controversy between rhetoric and philosophy did not last beyond the forties of the first century BC, so that we should be cautious against referring Paul's negative comments on persuasion to a contemporary *philosophical* animosity to rhetoric.

107   J. D. Denniston, *Greek Prose Style* (Oxford: n.p., 1952), 12, quoted by Judge, 'Paul's Boasting in Relation to Contemporary Professional Practice', 42, says this about Gorgias: 'having nothing in particular to say, he was able to concentrate all his energies upon saying it.'

108   Pogoloff, *LOGOS AND SOPHIA*, p. 38. Plato develops his idea of a legitimate rhetoric in *Phaedr.* esp. 245–77.

109   Cf. Aristotle, *Rhet.* 1355a-56a.

the orator deliberating on his subject matter in a manner similar to the philosopher.

In Isocrates (436–338 BC), however, we find a consistent concern for the unity of form and content. He attacks those sophists who have no interest whatsoever in truth, but seek to make the worse appear the better (cf. *Or.* 13.9). Isocrates thus lays the foundation of rhetorical education, emphasizing the need of the orator to be involved in exhaustive education, including the study of philosophy, as well as a high moral character (cf. *Or.* 13.10-21). Isocrates summarizes his aim as cultivating the ability 'to think and speak well' (φρονεῖν εὖ καὶ λέγειν *Or.* 15.244).

Both Aristotle and Isocrates had great influence on the rhetoric of Paul's day expounded by Cicero and Quintilian. For Cicero (106–43 BC), the 'genuine orator' is one who has knowledge of all the issues of life, of which philosophy is one, 'inasmuch as that is the field of the orator's activity, the subject matter (*subiecta materies*) of his study' (*De or.* 3.15.54).[110] Thus, for him *res* (content) and *verba* (form) cannot be separated. He contends: 'Every speech consists of matter [*res*] and words [*verba*], and the words cannot fall into place if you remove the matter, nor can the matter have clarity if you withdraw the words ... It is impossible to achieve an ornate style without first procuring ideas and putting them into shape, and at the same time ... no idea can possess distinction without lucidity of style' (*De or.* 3.5.19, 24). Likewise, Quintilian (AD 40–95), in his *Institutio Oratoria*, argues for the unity of content and form: 'As to the material of oratory, some have asserted that it is speech (*oratione*) ... If ... we interpret "speech" as indicating the words (*verba*) themselves, they can do nothing unless they are related to facts ... The material of rhetoric is composed of everything (*omnes res*) that may be placed before it as a subject for speech' (2.21.1-4).

We see, then, that there is ample evidence to support the idea that rhetoricians were equally concerned for form and content, especially around the time of Paul's writing. It is true that their statements were apologetic and polemic, responding especially to the accusations of the philosophers that they were merely interested in appearance. However, the genuine sophist was regarded as equally concerned for truth and style. Thus, there existed a certain overlap between philosophy and rhetoric by Paul's time, especially in light of the fact that rhetoric became the subject matter of higher education. At the same time, we must be aware that the debate between philosophers and sophists never ceased. More import-

110   See Betz, 'The Problem of Rhetoric and Theology According to the Apostle Paul', pp. 30–2, on Cicero, where he states that Cicero attempted to bridge the gap between form and content by developing the concept of the *philosophus orator*, the *doctus orator*, indeed the *perfectus orator* (p. 31).

antly, the debate was more than over the issue of form and content. There were other criteria for distinguishing between the two groups.

The major criterion for evaluating rhetoric offered by philosophers was utility. From the perspective of the audience, the question was whether the art (τέχνη) was useful or harmful. From the perspective of the speaker, the question was whether he wished 'to be good or to be praised' (Epitectus *Ench.* 3.23.7: ὠφελῆσαι θώλεις ἢ ἐπαινεθῆναι).[111] A speech that was held for epideictic purposes rather than for the benefit of the hearer was considered harmful. We have already seen that eloquence was regarded as a means to status enhancement, so that rhetoric consisted in more than mere style; it evoked a whole world of social values.[112] It is in this respect that one can argue that Paul takes the side of the philosopher. If Paul rejected rhetoric, it was not just because it was empty flattery (though surely that was part of it), but because it was an avenue for boasting, which the cross precludes. Edgar Krentz concludes: 'He uses a *topos* known elsewhere as part of the philosophic tradition to reject rhetorical flourishes in favor of message whose content is Spirit driven. Having thus established his divine source, his pure message, and his lofty aims, Paul's rhetorical expression can only be for the benefit of his Corinthian audience.'[113]

Hans Dieter Betz, however, brings out the distinguishing factor between Paul and the philosophers of his day. He states: 'Here Paul clearly takes the side of the philosopher over against the orator, but his concerns are still different from those of the philosopher.' He continues: 'Wherein lies the power which makes Christian speech effective? Paul does not argue, as a philosopher would, that the power of speech which is really persuasive and does not make only empty promises comes from reason (that is, human reason argued by philosophical dialectic). The power coming to expression in the Christian kerygma is a divine power supplied by the spirit of God.'[114] Thus, while we may agree that Paul resembles the philosopher in his critique of the rhetorician, he is not identifying himself

111 See Krentz, '*LOGOS* OR *SOPHIA*', pp. 283–4. Krentz is however rightfully cautious not to argue that Paul claims to be a philosopher (p. 282).

112 Part of the personal gain that the sophist was expecting besides enhancing his status and increasing his honor was also financial gain. This was also a problem in Corinth (cf. 2 Cor. 2.17 'peddle the word of God for profit' – καπηλεύω), and therefore Paul sought to distance himself from patronage networks (cf. 1 Corinthians 9). See Winter, *Philo and Paul among the Sophists*, pp. 164–9; also Clarke, *Leadership in Corinth*, ch 3.

113 Krentz, '*LOGOS* OR *SOPHIA*', p. 290. Distinction must be made between two ways of defining benefit: one is the benefit in regard to status – worldly view – and the other is spiritual benefit in terms of faith – Paul's view.

114 Betz, 'The Problem of Rhetoric and Theology According to the Apostle Paul', p. 36.

with a philosopher.[115] He is neither a sophist nor a philosopher; he is a third kind of sage: a 'herald' of God's message, the reception of which is not the result of style nor argumentation but revelation (cf. 1 Cor. 2.6-16).[116]

We have seen, then, in this first section of the chapter, that there are basically three views concerning Paul and rhetoric: Paul against rhetoric, Paul indifferent to rhetoric, Paul ambiguous about rhetoric. Each view rests on certain assumptions concerning Paul's education, his use of allegedly rhetorical terms, the critique by his opponents, the characterization of his own preaching, and his literary practice. Of these, two major issues have come to the surface as in need of more study in order to determine with more accuracy Paul's stance towards rhetoric: (1) an exegesis of 1 Cor. 2.1-5 with special attention given to terms that presumably have a rhetorical background; and (2) a look into the issue of written and oral communication – similarities and differences.

The Rhetorical Nature of 1 Cor. 2.1-5

The issue that has preoccupied us in the first section of this chapter is whether Paul explicitly rejected rhetoric as appropriate for proclamation or not. The answer depends a great deal on the exegesis of 1 Cor. 2.1-5. The first step in reaching a conclusion has already been taken in the previous chapter where we concluded that a sophistic background is the most likely one for the concept of σοφία, given the thematic overview presented in chapter one of this work. It remains now to take a further step in our research and investigate the issue of the exact aspects in this sophistic tradition that Paul disavows, by a study of the terminology he uses here.

Bruce Winter's monograph on the Second Sophistic is helpful here. Despite Anderson's attempt to discard Winter's thesis, 1 Cor. 2.1-5 seems to be best interpreted from a rhetorical standpoint, and the terminology used here as being taken from the sophistic background.[117] Winter has aptly noticed that in 1 Cor. 2.1-5 (coupled with 1 Thess. 2.1-12) Paul presents himself in the opposite light from the sophists of his day. He has argued convincingly that in this text Paul describes his 'entry' into Corinth

---

115   Cf. Thrall, *Second Corinthians*, 2.617. *Contra* Betz, *Der Apostel Paulus und die sokratische Tradition*.

116   See Judge, 'The Reaction against Classical Education in the New Testament', 12.

117   Winter's analysis of the terms used by Paul in this text follows Lars Hartman's discussion of the vocabulary in light of the rhetorical tradition. See his 'Some Remarks on 1 Cor. 2.1-5', 116–19. *Pace* Krentz, *'LOGOS OR SOPHIA'*, p. 280.

(2.1, cf. εἴσοδον in 1 Thess. 2.1) in contrast to the conventions related to the initial arrival of a sophist in a city where he would declaim.[118]

Combined with an oration about his own renown called διάλεξις and an encomium to the city, the sophist would make use of Aristotle's three 'proofs' (πίστις) – ἦθος πάθος, and ἀπόδειξις – in order to impress and persuade.[119] The first, ἦθος, is the element in a speech which establishes the speaker's good character and credibility. The second, πάθος, refers to playing on the emotions of the hearer. The third, ἀπόδειξις, is a clear proof, a process of reasoning from what is certain in order to prove that which is uncertain. The key to a persuasive speech that combined these three elements was believed to be 'adaptation'. Adaptation to the expectations of the audience was determinative of the way the speaker would craft his message calculated to impress.

Duane Litfin has also convincingly shown that in Paul's time the public orators such as the sophists believed that the effectiveness of one's speech rested on the speaker. He was believed to be able to sway the feelings of his audience if he made a good impression of his own character by means of boasting and flattery and if he crafted his message in a manner that displayed an eloquent and ornamental style. He states: 'The message was the manipulated variable by which the equation was made to work, and it was up to the orator, by the sheer power of his rhetorical gifts, training and experience, to create a message that would do so.'[120]

Paul's rejection of the whole dynamic of sophistic rhetoric in his gospel proclamation can be seen in his recasting of the technical rhetorical terms in light of the dynamic of the cross. According to Winter, the three elements of communication mentioned above are reinterpreted by Paul, or as Judge asserts, Paul 'plunders the Egyptians', that is he empties the terms of their rhetorical meaning.[121] First, as far as the ἦθος is concerned, Paul refused to establish his reputation and superiority (ὑπεροχήν) in his first visit to Corinth.[122] In other words, contrary to the expectations from a public speaker, Paul consciously chose to dissociate from the speech and

---

118   In what follows I am indebted to Winter's *Philo and Paul among the Sophists*, pp. 143–64, and also 'The Entries and Ethics of Orators and Paul (1 Thess 2.1-12)', 55–74.

119   See Aristotle's discussion of these in his *Rhet.* 1.2.4. For a discussion of proof in Aristotle see Litfin, *Proclamation*, 76–78, and esp. DiCicco's detailed discussion of the three Aristotelian proofs in his *Paul's Use of Ethos, Pathos and Logos in 2 Corinthians 10–13*, pp. 36–77, 113–64, and 188–241 respectively.

120   See Litfin, *Proclamation*, pp. 207–8.

121   Judge, 'The Reaction against Classical Education', 11, quoted by Winter, *Philo and Paul among the Sophists*, p. 163.

122   For this understanding of 2.1 see *EDNT* 3.999; LSJ 1867; BDAG, 1034, category 1, 'I have not come as a superior person in speech and wisdom' (cf. *1 Clement* 57.2; Josephus, *A.J.* 9.3); Louw-Nida, 87.26, rightly include the meaning in the semantic domain pointing to 'high status or rank'. *Contra* Robertson and Plummer, *First Corithians*, p. 29; and Barrett, *First Corinthians*, p. 62, who connect ὑπεροχήν with καταγγέλλων and not with ἦλθον.

wisdom that marked the high-status people (e.g., sophists). Rather, the content of his speech – the cross – disqualified him as a high-status person.

Second, Paul refused to play on the emotions of the audience. This is clearly seen in his resort to proclaim a predetermined topic (λόγος) – Christ crucified – rather than to adapt for the purpose of wining the crowd over, which in turn would result in adulation for himself. Thus he came in 'weakness, fear, and trembling', qualities that are the antithesis of the confident speaker who stands over his audience and believes in his ability to manipulate his hearers.[123] These terms are in some sense taken over by Paul's opponents in 2 Cor. 10.10 to accuse him of an unimpressive and unforceful stage presence.[124] Winter then is right to state that in describing himself with these epithets, 'Paul portrays himself as one who is anti-ἦθος and anti-πάθος.'[125]

Third, in what is a clear reference to his dissociation from sophistic rhetoric, Paul refers to the source of his persuasive message as he uses terms such as πειθώ ἀπόδειξις, and δύναμις. Contrary to the contemporary sophists who believed that the persuasiveness of their declamations depended upon their oratorical skills, such as 'powerful eloquence' (δύναμις)[126] and 'clear proof' (ἀπόδειξις),[127] Paul bases the success of his first proclamation in Corinth on the 'demonstration' (ἀπόδειξις) provided

---

123   See Hartman, 'Some Remarks on 1 Cor. 2.1-5', 118. He quotes Quintilian's emphasis on the need for confidence (*fiducia*) (*Inst.* 12.5.1ff). See also Philostratus, *Vit. soph.* 519, where he describes the confidence of the sophist Scopelian.

Several ways were recommended by the ancient rhetorical handbooks for the stirring up of emotions, among which the most effective was considered visual imagery (*imago agens*) which was used for mnemonic purposes (cf. *Rhet. Her.* 3.16.29, 3.21.35; 3.22.35–37; Quintilian, *Inst.* 6.2.29; Cicero, *De or.* 2.87.358; Aristotle, *Rhet.* 1.2.4–6) and metaphors (cf. *Rhetorica ad Herennium* 4.34.45; Aristotle, *Poet.* 21.7; Quintilian, *Inst.* 8.6.19). Lanci, *Temple*, pp. 121–30, argues that Paul's use of the temple/community metaphor in 1 Corinthians 3 functions as an *imago agens*, seeking to stir up the emotions of the audience, thus making use of Aristotle's proof πάθος. Lanci calls the image of the temple 'an arresting image.' In light of our analysis of 1 Cor. 2.1-5, we are hesitant to agree with Lanci. For now we can say that Paul did use metaphors and images, but for different purposes: not to play on the emotions of his audience but for the purpose of comprehension and clarity. See Augustine, PG 4.10, who emphasizes the importance of perspicuity of style over eloquence when one seeks to teach.

124   See Marshall, *Enmity in Corinth*, p. 389.

125   Winter, *Philo and Paul among the Sophists*, p. 158. See also Hartman, 'Some Remarks on 1 Cor. 2.1-5'.

126   See the following references for a definition of rhetoric as δύναμις: Aristotle, *Rhet.* 1.2.2.1; Quintilian *Inst.* 2.15.2–4 (*vis persuadendi*); Chrysostom, *Or.* 33.3.

127   E.g., Quintilian *Inst.* 5.10.7; Cicero, *Acad.* 2.8; Diogenes Laertius, *Lives* 7.45; Epictetus 1.25.8; Plato, *Tim.* 40E, *Soph.* 265D, *Phaed.* 77c, cited by Lim, ' "Not in Persuasive Words of Wisdom" ', 147.

by the Spirit's powerful work.[128] Timothy Lim rightly says that 'by employing it with πνεύματος and δυνάμεως, Paul uses ἀπόδειξεις in a way which is different from and counter to the rhetorical meaning of the term.'[129] Thus, in contrast to the 'dynamic of rhetorical adaptation', Paul places the 'dynamic of the cross' and leaves the results to the Spirit. Paul does not take on the responsibility to create faith, but believes that proof (πίστις)[130] is provided by the δύναμις θεοῦ. Thus, as Winter concludes, 'where preaching was concerned, his [Paul's] overall strategy left no room for confidence in technical rhetorical devices.'[131]

128   John Chrysostom, PG 6.3, rightly believes that the gospel's glory is seen in the fact that it is preached without wisdom.

129   Lim, 'Not in Persuasive Words of Wisdom', 147.

130   See Winter, *Philo and Paul among the Sophist*, pp. 159–60, for πίστις as 'proof', as a rhetorical term. For this sense he makes reference to Acts 17.31. Winter is also right to see in the use of this term here a double-entendre, a meaning of both 'faith' and 'demonstration.' A search in the *TLG* database for the word πίστις has rendered results that point clearly to the meaning 'proof', such as: Aristotle, *Rhet.* 1355a.5; 1566a.27; 1394a.10; 1414a.36, b.8, 9. Even Philo in his religious writings uses the word πίστις with the meaning of 'proof'. See for instance *Opif.* 84.6; 93.1; 147.7; *Leg.* 3.208.4; *Sacr.* 34.6 ; *Post.* 97.4; *Abr.* 39.2; 141.1; 247.2; (exception is 268.2 where he speaks of the 'faith' of Abraham); *Ios.* 52.5; 158.6; *Mos.* 1.247.1; 1.261.1; 1.280.7; 1.298.4; 2.12.3, etc. Diodorus Siculus, *Bib. Hist.* 16.23.4.8 (translated 'pledge'). Dionysius Halicarnassus, *Ant. Rom.* 5.48.3.1; 7.29.4.3; in 5.69.1.8 translated 'credit'; in 6.83.3.12; 6.84.3.1; and 6.85.2.10 translated 'assurance'; *Dem.* 42.2 (translated 'argument'); *Thuc.* 47.12. Josephus, *J.W.* 1.601.2; *A.J.* 10.101.1 (translated 'pledge'). Athenagoras, *Leg.* 26.2.2.

131   Winter, *Philo and Paul among the Sophists*, p. 159. One is again confronted with an apparent contradiction: how can Paul say that he has not taken upon himself the responsibility to persuade when in other texts he explicitly states that his goal in preaching is to persuade (cf. 2 Cor. 5.11 – 'Knowing therefore the fear of the Lord, we persuade [πείθομεν] men …') and others describe his activity as that of persuasion (cf. Acts 18.4, 13; 19.8, 26; 28.23, 24)? The response, I believe, is in seeing a distinction between two kinds of persuasion: on the one hand, the sophists believed that the success of a speech rested on their shoulders; on the other hand, Paul sought to persuade his audience of the truth of his message, but did so with the understanding that it is the Spirit who convicts. See also Morna D. Hooker, 'A Partner in the Gospel: Paul's Understanding of His Ministry', in *Theology and Ethics in Paul and His Interpreters* (Eugene H. Lovering and Jerry L. Summey, eds.; Nashville: Abingdon, 1996), pp. 83–100.

In light of our contention that Paul did not rely on the 'demonstration' (ἀπόδειξις) used by the sophists in order to persuade, Paul's Areopagus speech seems to pose some problems. It seems that in Athens, which is paradigmatic of the gospel's encounter with surrounding culture, Paul did use an argumentation from generally accepted premises to less certain facts, something that we have shown him to reject in 1 Cor. 2.1-5. This is the view of W. L. Knox, *St. Paul and the Church of the Gentiles* (Cambridge: Cambridge University Press, 1939), p. 26. The question posed by the Areopagus speech is whether Paul adapted his message to his Hellenistic audience using the Hellenistic type of 'demonstration', seeking thus to become 'relevant' to the surrounding culture. Sandnes, for instance, in his article 'Paul and Socrates', argues that Paul used the rhetorical strategy of *insinuation* – a subtle and cryptic approach, an indirect way of attracting the attention of the audience, if necessary even by applying concealment, when facing a critical audience (cf. Cicero, *Inv.* 1.15-20 where he uses words like *dissimulatio, circumcitio,* and *obscure*; Quintillian, *Institutio Oratoria* 4.1.42-50). As such, Sandnes, *et al.*, argues that Luke presents here a 'clear comparison between Paul and Socrates' in their use of this rhetorical strategy as well as in other details of the speech (cf. Plato, *Apol.* 24B). Paul, Sandnes concludes, adjusts to the situation, following one of the basic principles of rhetoric – adaptation (cf. Quintillian, *Inst.* 11.1). Like Knox, Sandnes makes no reference to 1 Cor. 2.1-5 throughout his article. How should we then reconcile the two apparent contradictory approaches to preaching? First, we must take into consideration the two different genre: Acts is narrative and therefore descriptive, while 1 Corinthians is epistolary and therefore prescriptive. In this sense, Paul's statements in 1 Cor. 2.1-5 provide the interpretive grid for his speech in Acts 17, assuming that Luke records Paul's actual speech. On the importance of genre see E. D. Hirsch, *Validity*, ch. 3, 'The Concept of Genre'. Secondly, while this speech is 'the most important episode' of Luke's narrative of Paul's second mission (see J. A. Fitzmyer, *The Acts of the Apostles* [AB, 31; Garden City, NY: Doubleday, 1998], pp. 600, 613–17), Robert W. Wall, in his commentary *The Acts of the Apostles* (NIB 10; Nashville: Abingdon, 2002), p. 243, rightly observes that, 'The episode is important not because it evinces some missionary innovation or exposes a new angle of vision into Paul's mission. The pattern of Paul's missionary activity is being familiar.' See also R. C. Tannehill, *The Acts of the Apostles* (vol. 2 of *The Narrative Unity of Luke-Acts: A Literary Interpretation*; Minnesota: Fortress, 1990), 2.211-12, for similarities with the other speeches in Acts; and Polhill, *Acts*, p. 365, who argues that the speech in Lystra (14.15-18) is a précis of this speech. Thus, Barrett, *Acts*, 2.848, rightly states that 'there is nothing in vv 16–21, 34 that is in any way incredible', though he attributes Paul's address to Luke's editorial invention putting in Paul's mouth what had come to be accepted Christian approach to Gentiles. Therefore, the Areopagus speech is not unique or innovative in its methodology. Thirdly, Wall, *Acts*, p. 243, rightly argues that, 'The substance if not its [i.e., speech's] idiom is confirmed in general terms by Rom 1.18-32 and 1 Thess 1.9-10.' On this argument see also J. D. G. Dunn, *The Acts of the Apostles* (Valley Forge: Trinity, 1996), pp. 231–2; Ben Witherington, *The Acts of the Apostles: A Socio-Rhetorical Commentary* (Grand Rapids: Eerdmans, 1998), pp. 425–6; and Stanley Porter, *The Paul of Acts* (WUNT, 115; Tübingen: Mohr, 1999), pp. 141–9. *Contra* M. Dibelius, 'The Speeches in Acts and Ancient Historiography', in *Studies in the Acts of the Apostles* (Heinrich Greeven, ed.; New York: Scribner, 1956), pp. 71–2. Fourth, similarly, the content of the speech is biblical rather than philosophical. See Polhill, *Acts*, p. 370. Fifth, the use or non-use of the rhetorical proof Paul seems to reject in 1 Cor. 2.1-5 depends to some degree on the purpose of the Areopagus speech. Assuming that this is a faithful recording of Paul's actual speech and not merely Luke's editorial invention, the discussion is whether the speech should be rhetorically categorized as forensic/judicial or deliberative. While 'Areopagus' could be regarded both as a lecturing and declaiming place as well as the equivalent of a city council that would render verdicts upon debates with jurisdiction even in matters of religion, Polhill, *Acts*, p. 368, is right to see this speech as being similar to all the other councils in Acts. Paul was taken into custody (17.19, ἐπιλαμβάνομαι, cf. 21.30, 33, see BDAG 373) in order for him to defend his religious claims and authority to introduce foreign deities in the city of Athens (see B. Winter, 'On Introducing Gods to Athens: An Alternative Reading of Acts 17.18-20', *TynBul* 47 (1996) 71–90). It was not however a trial in any formal sense, since he was not formerly charged with any crime. In this sense, M. L. Soards, *The Speeches in Acts: Their Content, Context, and Concerns* (Lousiville: Westminster/John Knox, 1994), p. 96, is correct to refer to the rhetorical situation of Paul's speech as judicial while Paul's rhetorical motive is deliberative. This being the situation, Sandnes has argued that several rhetorical techniques are used in a deliberative speech, such as *insinuatio, captatio benevolentiae,* etc., allegedly

The succinct analysis of the terminology Paul uses in this passage has revealed that Paul is quite conscious of the kind of devices he repudiates in preaching. The constellation of these rhetorical terms and allusions in this passage supports our contention that Paul rejects sophistic rhetoric in proclamation. Paul takes such an anti-sophistic stand, he argues, not because he seeks to justify his 'weak' stage presence (as the 'super-apostles' will later claim) and thus to establish his ethos, but because his theology demands it. Hartman is correct when he states that, 'Paul may have cut a miserable figure as a preacher as measured by the standards of rhetoric, but he turns that into a reflection on how the contents of the message of the cross harmonized with the conditions of the message – and of the messenger.'[132]

Written and Oral Communication in Paul and His Culture

Our analysis of 1 Cor. 2.1-5 with a view toward the terminology used by Paul to describe his initial proclamation of the gospel in Corinth has

present also in Paul's Areopagus speech. But this is not so easily demonstrated. For instance, as Sandnes himself acknowledges, Paul already preached Jesus Christ and the resurrection as recorded in 17.18, so that his Areopagus speech is not a 'demonstration' *per se* from generally accepted facts to less accepted ideas, but it is a Christological focused speech throughout (cf. 1 Cor. 2.1). Paul's introduction of the resurrection in 17.31 does not take his audience by surprise as if this is the first time they heard Paul mention it. Christ is the main subject of his speech (*contra* Barrett, *Acts*, 2.825, who claims that, 'The Areopagus speech lacks the determining Christological factor'). Polhill, *Acts*, p. 379, states that, 'Paul's determination to preach the crucified Christ was only confirmed by his Areopagus experience.' Some have claimed that Paul uses the rhetorical technique of *captatio benevolentiae* in opening his speech with a characterization of his audience as δεισιδαιμονεστέρους. The word can have both a positive sense – very religious, pious, devout – or negative – very superstitious. BDAG 216 and Louw-Nida, 1.531 claim that Paul uses the term here in a positive sense. Werner Foester, 'δεισιδαίμων',in *TDNT*, 2.19, claims that the term is suited to be 'a general and supremely neutral expression for religion or piety.' If we take the description in a positive sense, then Paul could be seen as intending 'to elicit a positive impression' (see Wall, *Acts*, p. 246) by using the rhetorical technique of *captatio benebolentiae*. But Polhill, *Acts*, pp. 370–1, may be right here that, 'Paul deliberately chose the ambiguous word. For the Athenians it would be as commending their piety. For Paul who was already fuming at their idolatry, the negative connotation would be uppermost in his mind. By the end of the speech the Athenians themselves would have little doubt about Paul's real opinion of their religiosity.' Moreover, Ajith Fernando, *Acts* (NIVAC; Grand Rapids: Zondervan, 1998), p. 475, quotes Lucian saying: 'Complimentary exordia to secure the goodwill of the Areopagus court were discouraged.' In conclusion, Paul's alleged use of rhetorical techniques in his Areopagus speech rests on precarious evidence. It is better to see this speech as typical of his addresses to Gentile unbelievers and compatible with his statements in 1 Cor. 2.1-5. Porter, 'Paul of Tarsus and His Letters', 538, is rightfully cautious about analyzing Paul's speech in Acts 17 rhetorically: 'If anything, its rhetorical structure can only be analyzed as a speech preserved by the author of Acts. In this case, this speech, like all of the speeches in Acts does not necessarily provide direct access into Paul's rhetorical ability.'

132 Winter, *Philo and Paul among the Sophists*, p. 159.

confirmed our hypothesis that Paul repudiated the rhetorical techniques believed to be essential in securing a following. At least one other important issue remains to be discussed in order to firmly establish our hypothesis, namely whether there is a discrepancy between Paul's oral proclamation and his writings. This issue is particularly important since Paul's opponents in 2 Corinthians seem to accuse him of an inconsistency between his public appearance and his presence in letters (10.10). We will start with a discussion of epistolary genre in comparison to oral speech in antiquity, followed by an exegesis of the verse, and concluding with a discussion of Paul's literary style as measured by the standards of what was considered persuasive communication.

Written versus Oral Communication in Antiquity

The issue that we will seek to address in this section is how similar or how different were written speeches from oral declamations in Paul's time. Could it be that the reason why Paul's letters were perceived as 'weighty and impressive' in contrast to his own delivery was because of rhetorically trained 'messengers' Paul sent with his letters who were able to read and recite his letters in such a way as to add eloquence to them?[133]

Bruce Winter has pointed out the fact that there was a debate in ancient times between writing and extempore orators and that there was 'no guarantee that the clever writer could speak acceptably extempore.'[134] Most written speeches were destined for oral performance, either by the author or another reader,[135] but the extempore speakers were held in higher regard because of their spontaneity and ability to adapt to circumstances than those who read their speeches as recorded in Alcidamas' work *On the Writers of Written Discourse or On the Sophists* (23).[136] Neil O'Sullivan calls Alcidamas 'the great champion of

133 A similar question was raised by Judge, 'Paul's Boasting in Relation to Contemporary Professional Practice', 37.

134 Winter, *Philo and Paul among the Sophists*, pp. 205–6. History records a series of rhetors who wrote speeches but never performed before an audience for lack of skill in delivery and stage presence. See Winter, 'The Toppling of Favorinus and Paul by the Corinthians', in *Early Christianity and Classical Culture*, p. 295 and *idem., After Paul Left Corinth*, p. 35. Neil O'Sullivan, 'Written and Spoken in the First Sophistic', in *Voice into Text: Orality and Literacy in Ancient Greece* (Ian Worthington, ed.; Leiden: Brill, 1996), p. 127. For the 'uneasy marriage' between oral and written communication in Plato, see Harold Tarrant, 'Orality and Plato's Narrative Dialogues', in *Voice into Text*, pp. 128–47. For the public recital of literary works, esp. Xenophon's intention that his *Hellenica* be read in public, see Douglas Kelly, 'Oral Xenophon', in *Voice into Text*, pp. 150–63.

135 See Tarrant, 'Orality and Plato's Narrative Dialogues', p. 133, who gives the example of Euclides who arranged that *Theaetetus* be read by a slave.

136 Referenced by Winter, *Philo and Paul among the Sophists*, p. 205. He also recalls Dionysius Halicarnassensis, *Is*. 1, who explains that the reason why Isocrates refrained from public speaking was because he lacked 'the first and most important quality of a public

extemporaneous speech.'[137] The preference for extemporaneous speech was primarily the result of conceiving of oratory as more concerned with emotional impact and the manipulation of the feelings of an audience than with conveying the truth (3, 22, 34). As a result, flexibility, adaptability, and improvisation were crucial. Alcidamas inherited this preference for extemporaneous speech from his teacher Gorgias, the founder of the art of extempore oratory, who attacked the First Sophistic's interest in the written speech. Gorgias ridiculed especially Prodicus, because he delivered things which were 'stale and often repeated.'[138] Gorgias, however, emphasized the importance of καιρός, or the right moment. For him, language was not a fixed thing, but adaptable to the conditions of the moment.

It is such a debate that Winter believes to be reflected in 2 Cor. 10.10.[139] In other words, the Corinthians allegedly accused Paul of lack of adaptability to circumstances as far as his speeches were concerned when present with them. He was accused of lacking spontaneity and flexibility in language; he was not able to cope with sudden changes, but retreated when such exigencies occurred (cf. 2 Cor. 2.1). On the other hand, his letters were considered 'weighty and powerful', seemingly because those who carried his letters and read them aloud before the Corinthians were more skilled in rhetorical adaptability, thus being able to render Paul's message in letter-form in accordance with the standards of excellence of the time.[140] They would be able not only to read them eloquently, so the argument goes, but they were also able to comment on any issue that arose concerning the meaning of what Paul wrote.[141]

Such a reconstruction is based on the observation made above that written speeches were destined for oral performance, though the spontaneity of extemporaneous speech was preferred. It is largely accepted by scholars today that Paul's letters functioned as substitutes

---

speaker', the exhibition of 'self-confidence and a strong voice.' See also Quintilian, *Inst.* 11.3.12-13. For more details on the debate between the written speeches and extemporaneous speech see O'Sullivan, 'Written and Spoken in the First Sophistic', 115–27.

137   O'Sullivan, 'Written and spoken in the First Sophistic', 123.

138   This is recorded by Philostratus, *Vit. soph.* 482–83.

139   Winter, *Philo and Paul among the Sophists*, p. 205.

140   DiCicco, *Paul's Use of Ethos, Pathos, and Logos*, pp. 32–3, claims that, 'It is difficult to imagine that his most personal and emotionally filled letters, for example, the so-called "letter of tears," would have been randomly left to someone in the congregation to read in the same monotone one finds his letters still being read in church services to this day.'

141   See, e.g., Lamp, 'Gospel and Rhetoric in 1 Corinthians 1–4', 14; also Witherington, *Conflict and Community in Corinth*, pp. 36–45, 107, and 435. For the discussion that follows see esp. Richard F. Ward, 'Pauline Voice and Presence as Strategic Communication', *Semeia* 65 (1995) 95–107. Tarrant, 'Orality and Plato's Narrative Dialogues', p. 135, argues that, 'Early philosophic writers wrote in order to arouse admiration and curiosity; explanation was left for oral study.'

for oral communication. Richard Ward, for instance, rightly argues that '
[l]etters bore a kinship with oral messages' and that they were 'a major
way Paul overcame the separation from his churches.'[142] They seem to
have been read aloud in congregational meetings (cf. 1 Thess. 5.27 and
Col. 4.16) and thus through their oral performance 'Paul establishes a new
presence, that of Paul-in-the-letter, which, when embodied by the reciter,
gave Paul restored visibility in the community.'[143] Thus one may be right
in seeing letters as 'conversations in context',[144] 'long-distant oral
communication',[145] or 'one of the two sides of a dialogue.'[146] This has
been argued by various contributors to the volume *The Thessalonians
Debate*, whose primary purpose is to prove the legitimacy of rhetorical
criticism applied to Paul's letters, especially 1 Thessalonians. Raymond
Collins, for instance, rightly points to the functional similarity between 1
Thess. 4.9, 5.1, and 1.8c, where the verb 'speak' (λαλέω) is interchange-
able with the verb 'write' (γράφω). He then concludes that Paul's letters
should be regarded as 'speech acts.'[147] Collins argues all this for the
purpose of supporting his contention that it is legitimate to analyze letters
by the standard of rhetorical theory, since Paul composed his letters as
ancient rhetoricians composed speeches, the same rules applying for
both.[148]

142   Ward, 'Pauline Voice and Presence', 102. See also Martin, *The Corinthian Body*, p.
53, and Stanley Stowers, 'Greek and Latin Letters', in *ABD*, 4.290.
143   Ward, 'Pauline Voice and Presence', 103.
144   Witherington, *Conflict and Community in Corinth*, p. 35. See also Peterson, *Eloquence
and Proclamation*, p. 17, for support for the oral nature of letters in Cicero, *Fam.* 15.21.4, *Att.*
8.14, 9.10; Seneca, *Ep.* 75.1-2; and Quintilian, *Inst.* 9.4.19-20; 12.10.51. See also Ward,
'Pauline Voice and Presence', 95; and Pieter J. J. Botha, 'The Verbal Art of the Pauline
Letters: Rhetoric, Performance and Presence', in *Rhetoric and the New Testament,* 409–28.
See Abrahm J. Malherbe, ' "Seneca" on Paul as Letter Writer', in *The Future of Early
Christianity: Essays in Honor of Helmut Koester* (Birger A. Pearson, ed.; Minneapolis:
Fortress, 1991), p. 416, who makes reference also to Cicero, *Fam.* 12.30.1; Basil, *Ep.* 163.
145   Raymond F. Collins, ' "I Command that This Letter Be Read": Writing as a Manner
of Speaking', in *The Thessalonians Debate*, p. 332.
146   Demetrius, *Eloc.* 223. See also Pseudo-Libanius, *Epistolary Styles* 2, and Seneca, *Ep.*
75.1-2. See Malherbe, ' "Seneca" on Paul as Letter Writer', for more references.
147   Collins, ' "I Command that This Letter Be Read" ', p. 321.
148   Ibid., p. 337. See also Peterson, *Eloquence and Proclamation*, p. 19; Martin, *The
Corinthian Body*, p. 53. Frank W. Hughes, 'The Rhetoric of Letters', in *The Thessalonians
Debate*, p. 198, makes reference to Cicero's idea of a 'ready speaker' who 'will be able to take
the precepts from the three *genera* as they stand and make modifications from them to fit the
situation. ... Cicero portrays Catulus as saying that letters could use various rhetorical
features drawn from the conventional precepts about speeches.' See Cicero, *De or.* 2.49, who
argues that when official message must be sent to or from the Senate, and must be written in
an elaborate style, no other genus of rhetoric is needed, 'since the ability acquired by a ready
speaker, from the treatment of his other subjects and topics, will not fail him in situations of
that description.' He also mentions Demosthenes' *Epistle* 1 as a letter written according to
the standards prescribed by rhetorical theory (p. 199).

Our purpose here is not to evaluate the legitimacy of rhetorical criticism, though we have made comments on it throughout Chapter 1 of this work.[149] Our interest in mentioning the collected essays above is to support the idea that written speeches were very similar to oral communication; they are the one end of a telephone conversation.[150] The difference, however, between the two means of communication is that the oral communication had two more elements added to those of composing a letter: memory (μνήμη, *memoria*) and delivery (ὑπόκρισις, *pronunciatio*) added to invention (εὕρησις, *inventio*), arrangement (τάξις, *dispositio*), and style (λέξις, *elocutio*).[151] The argument of Winter, Ward, and others is that it was especially at the last stage that Paul was found wanting. Nevertheless, it is argued, Paul made up for this deficiency in sending his letters with rhetorically trained reciters.[152]

This behind the text reconstruction sounds convincing, but is the real issue in 2 Cor. 10.10 between the written and oral communication? Are Paul's opponents accusing Paul for lacking skills in extemporaneous speech, but are impressed by his letters because the 'reciters' of Paul's letters are 'naturally gifted' in rhetorical delivery? Initially, we could say that such an argument does not take into account the fact that Paul's 'weakness' in speech was a deliberate decision that he took for theological reasons as seen in 1 Cor. 2.1-5, so that sending a 'reciter' would render his earlier theological argument concerning delivery ineffective. But ultimately such questions can be answered only from a close exegesis of 2 Cor. 10.10 in its literary context.

An Exegesis of 2 Cor. 10.10a

In 2 Cor. 10.10 Paul records the critique that some in the Corinthian assembly were directing at him: 'His letters are βαρεῖαι and ἰσχυραί, but in person he is unimpressive and his speech amounts to nothing.' We have already discussed the second part of this critique that addresses the issue

149 See also Jeffrey A. D. Weima, 'What Does Aristotle Have to Do with Paul? An Evaluation of Rhetorical Criticism', *CTJ* 32 (1997) 458–68.

150 We agree more with Reed, 'The Epistle', 182, and Porter, 'Paul of Tarsus and His Letters', 584, who argue that 'the similarity is only functional, not formal.' Therefore, the application of rhetorical criticism to Paul's letters is less legitimate.

151 See, e.g., Hughes, 'The Rhetoric of Letters', 197; and DiCicco, *Paul's Use of Ethos, Pathos, and Logos*, p. 32.

152 Ward, 'Pauline Voice and Presence', 99–104, where he points to Quintilian's *Inst.*, for standards for oral performance of literature. See also DiCicco, *Paul's Use of Ethos, Pathos, and Logos*, p. 32. For this practice we have already pointed to Tarrant's article on Plato, 'Orality and Plato's Narrative Dialogues', p. 137. Winter, *Philo and Paul among the Sophists*, p. 220, referring to Plutarch, *Dem.* 9, reminds us of Demosthenes who hired an actor to help him with his delivery. *Contra* David Aune, *The New Testament in Its Literary Environment*, p. 159.

of his delivery (ὑπόχρισις). Paul, according to his critics, did not rise to the standards of a virtuoso rhetor. He lacked stage presence, that is, he was deficient possibly concerning his body, paralinguistic aspects, and/or his speech (e.g., figures of speech, accent, pronunciation). Nevertheless, his opponents seem to recognize in his letters (ἐπιστολαί) positive characteristics: βαρεῖαι and ἰσχυραί. The connotation of these two adjectives, however, needs clarification.

The first characteristic of his letters, according to Paul's opponents, is contained in the adjective βαρύς.[153] Eusebius, in his *Hist. eccl.* 7.5.1.12, uses this word as he writes: ἵνα μήτε μῆκος τῇ ἐπιστολῆς μήτε βάρος προσάψω τῷ λόγῳ.[154] It is clear in this quote that the word βάρος, though connected to λόγος, indirectly is a comment on ἐπιστολη, the sense being that of a 'burdensome letter', given its contents. If this is the connotation of the word in 2 Cor. 10.10, the opponents would make a negative statement concerning Paul's previous letters, namely that they are 'burdensome'.

Lexicons, however, attribute to the word βαρύς a range of meanings, from that of 'forceful', even 'violent',[155] to that of 'pertaining to being a

---

153   This adjective occurs five other times in the New Testament with meanings such as 'heavy' (metaphorical with reference to the law in Mt. 23.4), 'important' (Mt. 23.23), 'serious/ grievous' (with reference to complaints in Acts 25.7), 'difficult' (with reference to commandments in 1 Jn 5.3), 'fierce' (Acts 20.29). For these meanings see Timothy Friberg, Barbara Friberg, and Miller, *Lexicon*, 88; *EDNT* 1.200; Louw-Nida 1.732, 1.245, 1.626, 1.228. It appears 47 times in the LXX with similar meanings of 'heavy' (e.g., with reference to yoke in 2 Chron. 10.4 or metaphorical use in *3 Macc.* 5.47), 'powerful' (e.g., with reference to armies in Num. 20.20 where it is in conjunction with ἰσχυρᾷ), 'difficult' (e.g., with reference to a request in Dan. 2.11), 'burdensome' (e.g., Wis. 2.14), and 'violent' (e.g., *3 Macc.* 6.5). For these meanings see Johan Lust, Erik Eynikel, and Katrin Hauspie, *A Greek-English Lexicon of the Septuagint* (Stuttgart: Deutsche Bibelgesellschaft, 1996), 1.78. In the extra-biblical sources, the same connotations can be found: 'heavy' (e.g., Philo, *Her.* 146), 'burdensome' (e. g., Diodorus Siculus, *Bib. hist.* 13.20.1; 13.30.7), 'violent' (e.g., Plato, *Apol.* 23a), 'important' (e.g., Josephus, *A.J.* 19.326), etc. For more extra-biblical references see LSJ 308; *TDNT* 1.553-58; and BDAG 167.

154   This is the only relevant reference that has resulted from a search in the *TLG* database for the words βαρ* and επιστολ* at an interval of 5 or less words between the two in either order. We have excluded from the results the religious writings which quote the verse and therefore do not clarify the meaning, such as: Epiphanius, *Pan.* 2.486.2; John Chrysostom, PG 51.304.17; PG 61.383.44, 50 (12.272); 61.542.20 (12.375); 61.544.15 (12.377); 61.548.28 (12.380); Theodorus, *Epistulae* 297.2; John Damascene, PG 95.753.28; 95.756.48; Theodoretus, PG 82.436.42. We will comment on the meaning that the Church Fathers attributed to this verse below. Besides the reference in Eusebius, we have also come across other sources which contain the two words in proximity to each other, but the construction differs. See, for instance, Libanius, *Ep.* 1294.1.1 and Aelius Aristides, *Ars rhetorica* 1.2.2.5.2.

155   *TDNT* 1.556. Plummer, *Second Corinthians*, p. 282, mentions among possibilities the sense of 'tyrannical'.

source of difficulty or trouble because of demands made' (cf. 1 Jn 5.3),[156] and to that of 'weighty/grave' (presumably as in both Acts 25.7 and Mt. 23.23).[157] It can thus be observed that most lexicons believe that the word has some connection with the ethical demands that Paul placed on the Corinthians through his previous writings. In this sense, some in the Corinthian church believed that Paul came across in his writings as too demanding to the point that his ethical instructions were difficult to follow.[158] On the other hand, the critique could refer to Paul's previous letters which the Corinthians believed to be too 'severe'. Christopher Forbes has argued that the word denotes 'righteous indignation' which was usually the attitude of one being badly treated or of one whose achievements were credited to others (cf. Hermogenes, *On Rhetorical Forms* 2.8).[159] This would mean that some in the Corinthian congregation believed that Paul's tone in his letters was severe and stern (possibly characteristic of the letter mentioned in 2 Cor. 2.1-4, i.e., 1 Corinthians?), a tone that was characteristic of a bold speaker, not one who was weak and humble. According to these senses, then, the adjective is not a comment on Paul's letters' rhetorical prowess,[160] but on the fact that Paul's letters lay 'heavy' on the consciousness of the Corinthians. The phrase thus would communicate something negative, just as the second part of the critique concerning Paul's delivery.

Bruce Winter, however, disagrees with such connotations of the phrase ἐπιστολαὶ βαρεῖαι and believes that the comment must be referring to the positive rhetorical quality of Paul's letters.[161] He cites Hermes' statement found in Lucian (*Dialogues of the Dead* 373), that is, an injunction to a rhetorician (ῥήτωρ) embarking on the boat that takes the dead to Hades to throw away 'everything that makes his speeches heavy' (βάρη τῶν λόγων). Therefore he translates the phrase in 2 Cor. 10.10 as 'impressive/ weighty letters.' Winter may be right that the slogan is referring to something that is rhetorically impressive, but a closer look at the larger context of the statement in Lucian's *Dialogues* may confirm the critique

---

156 BDAG 167 and Louw-Nida 1.732. See also Furnish, *2 Corinthians*, p. 468, and Murray, *Second Corinthians*, p. 698.

157 LSJ 308.

158 Note should be made here of the fact that the reference is by no means to Peter's characterization of Paul's letters as δυσνόητά in 2 Pet. 3.16, which refers to theology rather than ethics.

159 Forbes, 'Comparison, Self-Praise and Irony: Paul's Boasting and the Conventions of Hellenistic Rhetoric', *NTS* 32 (1986) 1–30 (12–14, 16). Thrall, *Second Corinthians*, 2.629-30, disagrees.

160 See also Anderson, *Ancient Rhetorical Theory and Paul*, p. 278, n. 7.

161 Winter, *Philo and Paul among the Sophists*, pp. 208–9. For the rhetorical sense of 'impressive' see also Plummer, *Second Corinthians*, p. 282, who suggests it as one possibility; Marshall, *Enmity in Corinth*, pp. 384–8, who quotes Dionysius Halicarnassus, *Thuc.* 23.360.10; *Comp.* 11.37.16; *Dem.* 34.204.14.

brought up by R. D. Anderson, namely that 'Lucian engages in a metaphorical word-play.'[162] Hermes is in charge of making sure that all the dead who embark on the boat to Hades strip themselves of everything that is 'heavy luggage' and would sink the boat. Among the things considered 'heavy' are the playboy's beauty, kisses, and even skin, the soldier's trophy and honor, the athlete's fame and wreaths, the philosopher's flattery, vanity, gold, idle talk, and beard, and the rhetorician's endless loquacity, antitheses, balanced clauses, periods, and foreign phrases. All these things are considered 'heavy.' In contrast to the rhetorician's 'heavy' items, Hermes considers things such as 'plain speaking' (or frankness, παρρησίαν) as 'light and easy to carry' (κοῦφα καὶ πάνυ εὔφορα ὄντα). Thus, given this larger context, it is better to take the word βαρύς to actually mean physically heavy, understanding that the things the rhetorician (as well as are other people) is supposed to strip off do not have physical quality per se, but they do metaphorically in Lucian's *Dialogues*. So that when Lucian calls the speech heavy, the allusion is to everything that made a person a successful rhetorician in his lifetime, but now must be left behind as he makes his passage to Hades; they are luggage which is too heavy to carry.

Note should also be made of the fact that Winter points to a reference of the use of βαρύς not strictly with ἐπίστολη but with λόγος, though conceivably they could be used interchangeably, as argued above. A search in the *TLG* database for βαρύς defining λόγος has revealed a variety of senses: 'stern/grave',[163] 'offensive',[164] 'irksome',[165] 'important',[166] 'powerful/effective',[167] and also 'difficult' (cf. Dan. 2.11 LXX).

The linguistic evidence is thus scarcely decisive. The various possible senses is also confirmed by Cicero's use of the Latin word *graves* (Gr. βαρύς) in defining an *epistulam* (Gr. ἐπίστολη).[168] His use may be grouped under three connotations. First, the adjective βαρύς (lat. *graves*) when it defines the word ἐπίστολη (lat. *epistulam*), it can carry the meaning of 'serious.' In his *Epistulae ad familiares*, 2.4.1.6, Cicero writes, 'There remain two kinds of letters (*epistularum*) which have a great charm for me, the one intimate and humorous, the other austere (*severum*) and

---

162   Anderson, *Ancient Rhetorical Theory and Paul*, p. 278, n. 6.

163   See Plutarch, *Mor.* 68.F.10, and possibly Epiphanius, *Pan.* 3.150.3.

164   See Plutarch's *Mor.* 547.D.4, Dionysius Halicarnassus, *Ant. Rom.* 9.44.5.4; 10.5.1.8; Plato's *Leg.* 717.D.1.

165   Plato *Apol.* 37.D.1.

166   See Diodorus Siculus, *Bib. Hist.* 19.70.8.

167   Ibid., 29.21.1.8.

168   We have performed a search in the Latin texts contained in the *PHI-5* database. For the search we used the Vulgate translation of the verse, thus doing a search for *grav** and *epistul** within three lines of text. Marshall, *Enmity in Corinth*, p. 386, quotes Cicero, *De or.* 2.82.334.

serious (*grave*).' The same contrast between humorous and serious in describing a letter is found also in his *Quint. Fratr.* 3.2.29.3: 'He gave me your letter (*epistulam*) to read which he had only just received – and, upon my word, it was a clever mixture of grave (*gravem*) and gay (*suavem*) in the style.' In both these references the meaning of *graves* is that of 'serious', a style that Cicero thinks is appropriate when talking about 'public affairs' (*res publica*). If that is the sense preserved in Paul's letter, then it refers to the serious tone or style of Paul's previous letters.

But Cicero also uses the word *graves* with a second sense of 'important.' At least in two places in his letters he uses it in this way. In his *Att.* 1.13.1.7, he writes: 'They (i.e., letters) certainly provoke an answer: but I have been rather slow about sending one, for lack of a safe messenger. There are very few who can carry a letter of weight (*epistulam graviorem*) without lighting it by a perusal.' In the same letter, 4.16.1.5, he writes: 'The one (i.e., letter) that your guest M. Paccius delivered was of importance (*gravis*) and full of matter (*plena rerum*).' If Paul's opponents use the word with similar connotation, then they would agree that Paul's letters are quite important, referring to the weight of their contents.

The third connotation of the word *graves* present in Cicero's letters has more of a rhetorical quality, being used as a comment on the style of a letter. He writes in his *Quint. Fratr.* 1.2.13.2: 'The rest of that letter (*epistula*) was in stronger terms (*graviora*) than I could have wished – for instance your "keeping the ship on an even keel" and "dying once for all."' If this is the sense that some of the Corinthians attribute to Paul's letters then they could very well make a statement concerning Paul's literary style, possibly his use of figures of speech.

The use of βαρύς (and *graves*) in both ancient Greek and Latin literature has thus left us with a variety of possibilities for the meaning of βαρύς. Therefore, a final word concerning which of these meanings is implied in Paul's opponents' characterization of his letters must await the results of the study of the second adjective, a look at the interpretation of the verse in church history, particularly in the writings of the Church Fathers, and ultimately a reading of the slogan in its literary context.

The second adjective ἰσχυραί may aid us in our decision concerning the character of Paul's letters as commented on by his opponents.[169] Libanius, in *Ep.* 1162.1.2, directly associates the two words in what constitutes possibly the closest reference in meaning to 2 Cor. 10.10 in

169 Besides the obvious meaning of 'strong/vigorous' in the physical sense, the word (appearing 28 times in the New Testament) is used with the sense of 'severe/intense' (e.g., with reference to famine in Lk. 15.14), 'great' (e.g., with reference to status in Rev. 6.15), 'effective' (e.g., with reference to preaching – λόγος – in Acts 19.20), etc. See, e.g., BDAG 483, Louw-Nida, 1.680 ('powerful'), 1.686 ('intense'), 1.699 ('strong'), 1.737 ('great'). The same meanings of the word are found in LXX and extra-biblical literature. See LSJ 843; also Walter Grundmann, 'ἰσχυρός', in *TDNT*, 3.396-402.

ancient Greek literature.[170] He writes: τοῖς παρ' ἐμοῦ πρὸς τὸν ἄριστον Μαρκελλῖνον γράμμασι πρόσθες τι παρὰ σαυτοῦ καὶ ποίησον ἡμῖν ἰσχυρὰν τὴν ἐπιστολήν. The meaning of ἰσχυρὰν τὴν ἐπιστολήν is most likely that of a 'powerful letter'.[171] If this positive sense is also present in 2 Cor. 10.10, then Paul's opponents would suggest that his letters are powerful or impressive. Constantinus VII Porphyroge, in his *De insidiis* 36.35, mentions a letter from a mother to his son, which is said to contain an 'earnest' request, thus making the letter indirectly urgent and important, given its content.[172] If this is also the sense of ἰσχυρός in 2 Cor. 10.10, then the comment on Paul's letters means that they are intense, in the sense that their content is important and the injunctions earnest.

Most lexicons attribute the word ἰσχυρός in defining Paul's letters in 2 Cor. 10.10 the general meaning of 'strong/powerful',[173] but do not say anything about whether the adjective describes Paul's letters rhetorically or not. Liddell and Scott do not include the verse as a reference anywhere in their discussion of the word ἰσχυρός, but it could conceivably be grouped under the meaning of 'vigorous', speaking of literary style.[174] The word thus could be a description of stylistic qualities.[175]

Again, the question is whether the comment on Paul's letters as ἰσχυραί, is rhetorically focused referring to their powerful effect on his audience and vigorous style or whether the comment describes the intense tone of his letters. The linguistic evidence is again scarcely decisive. Nevertheless, the positive sense seems to be predominant.[176] The final answer, however, can be given only after an analysis of the immediate literary context in which the description appears.

170   We performed a search in the *TLG* database of the words ιοξυρ* and επιστολ* at an interval of 5 words between the two in either order, which has resulted in 13 references. This includes references in the Church Fathers who quote the verse. For these references see the previous *TLG* search for βαρ* and επιστολ*. We have also performed a search in *PHI-5* for *fort** and *epistul** within three lines of text, but with no results.

171   The same sense could be in Libanius, *Ep.* 1036.1.5.

172   See also BDAG 484. See Xenophon, *Cyr.* 3.3.48.8.

173   Grundmann, 'ἰσχυρός', in *TDNT*, 3.398; Louw-Nida, 1.699-700. Plummer, *Second Corinthians*, p. 282, suggests the possibility of 'violent'.

174   LSJ 843, where they refer to Dionysius Halicarnassus, *Comp.* 22. Winter, *Philo and Paul among the Sophists*, p. 209, picks up on this reference to argue that the slogan in 2 Cor. 10.10a says something about 'the style and the impact of Paul's letters.'

175   See also Marshall, *Enmity in Corinth*, p. 386. Marshall cites Dionysius Halicarnassus, *Thuc.* 55.417.17-18, who uses the word ἰσχυρός with the connotation of 'forceful.' Thrall, *Second Corinthians*, 2.630, seems to agree.

176   A search in the *TLG* database for ιοκυρ* and λογ* at an interval of 5 words or less has resulted in mostly uses with the meaning of 'weighty/strong/valid argument.' See, e.g., Plato, *Soph.* 241.C.9; Dionysius Halicarnassus, *Ant. Rom.* 11.35.1.2; Sextus Empiricus, *Pyrrhoniae hypostyposes*, 1.35.1; Epictetus, *Diatr.* 4.6.14.1.

A combination of the senses that have resulted from our investigation into the use of the two adjectives in describing letters lends at least two possible general alternatives: Paul's opponents could be saying either something positive, complimentary, or something negative, even contemptuous, when describing Paul in the letter.[177] Positively, Paul's opponents could be saying about Paul's letters that they are eloquent, impressive, powerful, effective, serious, vigorous, and/or important. Negatively, they could be saying that his letters are burdensome, forceful, offensive, stern, difficult, and/or irksome.

The two general possibilities are in fact seen also in the writings of the early Church Fathers. The negative aspect of these adjectives, particularly of βαρύς is emphasized in John Chrysostom's writings. In his *Homily I* on 2 Cor. 1.1, 4, he gives the phrase 'his letters are weighty' the meaning of 'when he is away he boasts greatly in what he writes.'[178] Chrysostom confirms this implied meaning in his *Homily XXI* on 2 Cor. 10.1, 2, where he states: 'For they said this, that "when he is present indeed, he is worthy of no account, but poor and contemptible; but when absent, swells, and brags, and sets himself up against us, and threatens"'.[179] Chrysostom, thus, believes that at least the meaning of βαρύς is a negative one, pointing to Paul's boasting in his letters. Augustine, however, reads into these terms positive connotations, namely rhetorical eloquence. He states: 'And certainly if we bring forward anything of his [Paul's] as a model of eloquence, we take it from those epistles which even his very detractors, who thought his bodily presence weak and his speech contemptible, confessed to be weighty and powerful.'[180]

We see thus in the early Church Fathers the same two general possible senses for the adjectives describing Paul's letters: negative or positive. It seems, however, that if the negative sense is accepted, then Paul's opponents would be saying about Paul in the letter that he is boastful, assertive, forceful, even threatening. If the positive prevails, then Paul's opponents would be agreeing that his letters are rhetorically eloquent, impressive, and effective. But the only way to determine the exact meaning of the statement about Paul's letters is to perform a study of the immediate context. In 2 Corinthians 10–13, Paul seeks to defend himself against the accusations of the 'super-apostles.' One such accusation, which he addresses in the first 11 verses of ch. 10, is that there is an

177   As far as we were able to find from a search in the *TLG* database, there were no instances of the two adjectives βαρ* and ισχυρ* occurring together to describe a letter, so that there is no exact parallel to the construction in 2 Cor. 10.10a in ancient Greek literature, thouth the two occur together in Chrysostom's *Or.* (i.e., 12.81.4 and 45.1.7) to describe other things.

178   John Chrysostom, PG 61.383.44-50 (12.272).

179   Ibid., 61.542.20 (12.375); See also 61.544.15 (12.377).

180   Augustine, PG 4.7.15.

inconsistency between Paul in the letter and Paul in the body, or Paul
when absent and Paul when present. As such, v. 10 is Paul's quote of what
some in Corinth were saying about him. This verse forms an *inclusio* with
v. 1,[181] where Paul hints at this accusation of 'two radically different
personae – "Paul the bold" and "Paul the timid." '[182]

It seems, from a close reading of the text, that the Corinthians' problem
with Paul had to do primarily with his 'weak' presence.[183] 'He was, as it
were, only a "paper" apostle', so the Corinthians claimed.[184] Paul himself
seems to accept the judgment concerning his letters, but does not fully
accept the judgment about the ineffectiveness of his presence.[185] This
means that the reason Paul brings up the issue of his letters is 'because in
the eyes of his critic(s) the effectiveness of his correspondence only serves
to throw into stronger relief the ineffectual impression he makes in
person.'[186] If that is the case, we begin to see which of the two possibilities
for the meaning of the adjectives characterizing Paul's letters emerges: the
positive, at least initially in the mind of his readers.[187] In fact, this is
required by the contrast expressed in the correlation (μέν δέ) of v. 10, if
the second part of the verse is a negative assessment of Paul when
present.[188]

He explains his 'weak' presence in two ways. First, he redefines
ταπεινός.[189] Paul argues that boldness should not be equated with
boasting as his opponents do, but true boldness, and for that matter

181   Murray, *Second Corinthians*, p. 698, points to the formula μὲν ... δέ in both v. 1 and
v. 10, but in a reverse order. He cites Philo's use of the contrast in *Her.* 29, in speaking of
Moses' confidence and boldness in approaching God mixed with humility. See also Thrall,
Second Corinthians, 2.602, for the similarity between 10.1 and 10.10 and the *inclusio*; also
Garland, *2 Corinthians*, p. 422.

182   Murray, *Second Corinthians*, p. 664. See also Plummer, *Second Corinthians*, p. 282;
Simon J. Kistemaker, *2 Corinthians* (BkNTC; Grand Rapids: Baker, 1997), p. 344; Ernest
Best, *Second Corinthians* (Interpretation; Louisville: John Konx, 1987), p. 96. See Murray,
Second Corinthians, p. 698, for a possible explanation.

183   Cf. Lim, ' "Not in Persuasive Words of Wisdom" ', 148, n. 30.

184   Garland, *2 Corinthians*, p. 432.

185   Ibid., p. 445; also Murray, *Second Corinthians*, p. 701.

186   Thrall, Second Corinthians, 629.

187   Malherbe, ' "Seneca" on Paul as Letter Writer', 417, rightly points to the ultimate
negative assessment even of Paul's letters.

188   This is more so since v. 10 is paralleled with v. 1 where the contrast is more obvious
between ταπεινός – negative – and θαρρῶ – positive. Murray, *Second Corinthians*, p. 700,
points to four contrasts. See BDF, 331–32 for the correlative construction (§447).

189   Notice that the Corinthians use the characterization of Paul as 'humble' in a
pejorative way – 'timid' (NIV). See Thrall, *Second Corinthians*, 2.602; also Garland, *2
Corinthians*, p. 429. Humility was regarded as a negative characteristic, unsuitable for one in
leadership in Greek society. See Walter Grundmann, ταπεινός, in *TDNT*, 8.1-4; Barrett, *2
Corinthians*, p. 247, citing Xenonphon, *Mem.* 3.10.5, for its rendering as 'self-abasement'. See
also Chrysostom, *Or.* 32.26-27.

confrontation (i.e., war), is expressed in 'meekness and gentleness', following the pattern of Christ (v. 1).[190] Thus, 'it is precisely in such "weakness" that he intends to engage in bold warfare ...'[191] In this, Paul again overturns the values of the world (cf. 1 Cor. 1.17-2.5) by appropriating his opponents' representation of him and giving ταπεινός a positive sense.[192] Thus, Paul's 'boldness takes an unexpected form' when present,[193] and in that respect somewhat different from the boldness in his writings, though he will surely show such boldness in the remaining of his *apologia*. Secondly, he is not only 'weak' when present because he follows the pattern set forth by Jesus Christ, but also because he has deliberately chosen to be so for the benefit of the Corinthians. The boldness is at times required by circumstances and is by no means Paul's preference (v. 2).[194] But under the present circumstance, he would rather be bold while absent so that when he is present he would not have to assume such a bold stance (cf. 1 Cor. 4.19-21; 1 Thessalonians 2).[195] As such, Paul 'is begging them not to compel him to abandon the Christ-like manner which he would wish to maintain towards them.'[196] Thus, only certain conditions require of him to be severe and bold. And since such exigencies have occurred, he promises that he will be bold in his next visit (v. 11).

What is important to observe is that, in the process of defending his 'weak' demeanor, Paul also redefines boldness, so that, even if he initially accepts the description of his letters as βαρύς and ἰσχυρός, for Paul these mean different things than they do for the Corinthians. Even from the onset (v. 1), Paul hints at the fact that the boldness of Paul in the letter is false, 'by not issuing a bold command but making an impassioned appeal (παρακαλῶ).'[197] Thus, even if the Corinthians see in these adjectives positive characteristics, such as being bold, assertive, powerful, even threatening, Paul sees in these adjectives negative connotations, since he does not wish to be perceived in letters the same way his opponents are in presence. Rather, he wants to be understood not as one who threatens and

---

190   For details see Garland, *2 Corinthians*, pp. 426–9. For the meaning of 'meekness' (πραΰτης) see, e.g., BDAG 861. For the meaning of 'gentleness' (ἐπιείκεια), see, e.g., BDAG 371.

191   Savage, *Power through Weakness*, p. 69. See also Marshall, *Enmity in Corinth*, pp. 374–5, where he associates such behavior with ὕβρις, characteristic of the superior social status people. See Lysias 24.15.

192   Thrall, *Second Corinthians*, 2.602, could be right that Paul's opponents had taken up Paul's own description in 7.6 for their own pejorative purposes and now Paul seeks to rehabilitate the term.

193   See Savage, *Power through Weakness*, p. 67.

194   See Calvin, *Second Corinthians*, p. 319.

195   See A. J. Malherbe, '"Gentle as a Nurse": The Cynic Background to 1 Thess 2', *NovT* 12 (1970) 203–17.

196   Thrall, *Second Corinthians*, 2.600.

197   Murray, *Second Corinthians*, p. 671.

demolishes through his letters, but as one who builds up. Therefore, he rejects any alleged inconsistency between what he is in person and what he is when away, and promises to show this consistency on his next visit.

But what qualities will he demonstrate in his next visit that will show consistency with the characteristics of his letters? These will be authority, boldness, severity, etc., but reinterpreted.[198] In other words, he will show again meekness and gentleness, for these are the true weapons that win a war. Consequently, his weak demeanor when present is the same as his boldness when absent; they are one and the same, and not opposite characteristics. It is power *through* weakness that Paul seeks. It is not power *and* weakness, as his opponents critiqued Paul to have depending on location. Neither is it power *apart* from weakness, as the 'super-apostles' claimed to have.

Giving a positive meaning to the adjectives, at least in the eyes of Paul's opponents, the question of the rhetorical aspect still remains. Are the Corinthians saying anything about the rhetoric of Paul's letters? In light of the exegesis of the text the answer should be both 'yes' and 'no'. It is 'no' in the sense that they are not referring in any way to the use of rhetorical features such as figures of speech, enthymemes, etc, in his letters as if such features were not part of Paul's speech when present. In other words, the positive characterization of Paul's letters from his opponents' perspective is not a comment on style. In this respect Schmithals is right: '... it is inconceivable that the style of the Pauline letters was in very serious contrast with that of his speech. But since the letters are just as vigorously praised for a certain matter as his speech is held in contempt for the same matter, Paul's style of language cannot possibly have been the basis for such divergent judgments ...'[199] But it is 'yes' in the sense that self-praise and boldness were rhetorical devices used by ancient rhetoricians in order to make their speeches persuasive.[200] In this sense, the discrepancy that the Corinthians perceived in Paul was really one between his behavior in person and the tone of his letters.[201]

Paul's Literary Style

We started this section of the chapter with questions concerning the alleged inconsistency between Paul in person and Paul in his letters. We

198   Thrall, *Second Corinthians*, 2.634, citing Furnish, *2 Corinthians*, p. 469, rightly points to the fact that while in v. 10 λόγος signifies Paul's spoken utterance, in v. 11 it refers to his letters.

199   Schmithals, *Gnosticims in Corinth*, p. 176.

200   For the rhetorical exercise of σύγκρισις see Marshall, *Enmity in Corinth*, pp. 53–5, 325–39.

201   Cf. Savage, *Power through Weakness*, p. 69. See also Marshall, *Enmity in Corinth*, p. 392.

have sought to show that the main thing the Corinthians were accusing Paul of lacking when present with them was boldness. It is this characteristic that they appreciated in Paul's letters and the lack of it when present that they disdained. This means that the apparent discrepancy between his letters and his speech is not that of use and rejection of rhetorical techniques, respectively. It was perceived to be between Paul the bold and Paul the timid. Both his demeanor and his speech when present were deemed contemptible by the contemporary standard of rhetorical delivery. The accomplished orator of the day communicated authority by his sheer presence and self-confidence when he opened his mouth to speak. Paul did not communicate any of these when he was with the Corinthians (cf. 1 Cor. 2.1-5). His delivery (ὑπόκρισις) has been found wanting. Paul, however, defended such 'weakness' by reinterpreting ταπεινός not as 'timidity' but as 'meekness and gentleness.' The issue, thus, seems to be more specific than that of lack of skills in extemporaneous speech.

To wrap up our discussion of written versus oral communication, however, we need to take a last look at Paul's literary style. If oral and written communication are not that different and if Schmithals is right that the distinction between Paul's letters and his speech is not that of rhetorical style, the question that we will seek to answer is whether Paul used rhetorical artifices both in his letters and his oral speeches. More specifically, how should we view the rhetorical quality of Paul's letters in light of contemporary rhetorical style? Did Paul use the same means of persuasion as his contemporaries? The only way to assess this is by an investigation into his literary style.

There are basically two opposing views.[202] The first view is of those who believe that Paul's literary style is of the highest quality. For instance, Andrie du Toit claims that, 'At times, it [i.e., literary embellishments] even reached impressive artistic heights.'[203] C. K. Barrett also comments that, 'On his own showing, Paul was not an impressive speaker, though this is a strange comment, for his writing, which always reads like speech, has (quite apart from its content) genuine eloquence, and for all its common touch and occasional Semitic structure rises to the heights of Greek prose.'[204] This they adduce from a cataloguing of all the rhetorical devices and figures of speech that Paul uses in different sections of his letters.[205] Once such a list is composed, they conclude that the very passage where

---

202   For a survey of different views on Paul's literary style around the turn of the twentieth century see Robertson, *Grammar*, pp. 1194–8. See also Hughes, 'The Rhetoric of Letters', 201–15, for a more comprehensive survey.

203   Du Toit, 'A Tale of Two Cities', 394.

204   Barrett, *First Corinthians*, p. 64.

205   See, e.g., du Toit, 'A Tale of Two Cities', 392–97, and Rosaeg, 'Paul's Rhetorical Arsenal and 1 Corinthians 1–4', 64–74. See also Wuellner, 'Greek Rhetoric and Pauline

Paul overtly rejects rhetoric (cf. 1 Cor. 2.1-5) 'itself is an excellent demonstration of Paul's own persuasive and rhetorical skills ...'[206] Therefore, the only logical ways to understand Paul's literary style are either that Paul is inconsistent, that he uses irony, that he is unaware when he uses such devices, or that he is naturally eloquent.

We have already shown how the first two options are not viable. Concerning the third possibility, Rosaeg writes: 'Paul never quotes Aristotle or any other authority on rhetoric, and if he applies rhetorical figures and techniques, he does not do it in an overt fashion. Apparently he is not especially aware of it nor deliberately planning it – quite the contrary he says in our text (1 Cor. 2.1-5) ... In contrast to contemporary orators, therefore, for Paul external rhetorical artifices were merely incidental.'[207] The fourth option seems to have been preferred by Augustine.[208] We have already presented his view explained in his *De Doctrina Cristiana*, Book 4. However, two quotes from his work are worth mentioning again. He states: '... the appropriateness of the words [is] determined by the ardour of the heart rather than by careful choice' (4.20.42), by this meaning that Paul used what Norden called a 'rhetoric of the heart.'[209] Augustine also claims that where eloquence corresponds to the classical rules that is not by Paul's device but that these words 'spontaneously suggest themselves', because 'eloquence like an inseparable attendant, followed it [i.e., wisdom] without being called for' (4.6.10). In the words of E. A. Judge, then, Augustine seeks to make Paul into a 'kind of professional in spite of himself.'[210]

Peter Marshall disagrees with such conclusions. He states: 'I suggest that terminology such as "coincidental" or "unconscious usage" or "naturally eloquent" no longer suffice to explain the rhetorical character of Paul's style.'[211] He prefers to compare Paul with another unconventional speaker, namely Cassius Severus.[212] We prefer, however, to state that the unique rhetorical quality of Paul's letters, as well as his speech, were a deliberate choice in light of his theology of the cross. Whether he

---

Argumentation', pp. 177–9, 188, where he argues that Paul consciously uses the rhetorical device of digression. See also Goulder, 'Σοφία in 1 Corinthians', 526, n. 26, for digression throughout the entire letter of 1 Corinthians.

206 Rosaeg, 'Paul's Rhetorical Arsenal and 1 Corinthians 1–4', 51.

207 Ibid., 60 and 61 respectively. Robertson, *Grammar*, p. 1197, seems to side with this view.

208 Judge, 'Paul's Boasting in Relation to Contemporary Professional Practice', 38–39.

209 Norden, *Die antike Kunstprosa*, pp. 502, 509 in du Toit 393. Krentz, '*LOGOS OR SOPHIA*', p. 288 also contends that Paul's rejection of sophistic rhetoric is similar to Sextus' and Philodemus' rejection of sophistic rhetoric in favor of 'natural rhetoric'.

210 Judge, 'Paul's Boasting in Relation to Contemporary Professional Practice', 41.

211 Marshall, *Enmity in Corinth*, p. 355.

212 For bibliography and characterization of Cassius Severus see ibid., 394.

was rhetorically trained, lacked the skill in extemporaneous speech, or was naturally gifted, is secondary. What is of importance is that Paul chose to write the way he wrote, and chose to speak the way he spoke, because of feeling theologically constrained to do so. He could have probably written and spoken differently, but the important fact is that he did not. Moreover, the success of his preaching is due not to his following a certain rhetorical convention, but on relying on the power of the Spirit (1 Cor. 2.5).

The second view concerning Paul's literary style is that he failed miserably to rise to the contemporary standards of literary style. The early Church Fathers are again the ones quick to notice this.[213] We have earlier quoted from John Chrysostom's *De sacerdotio* (PG 4.6.61-79), where he claims that by the classical standards of Greek rhetoric, Paul was embarrassingly unpolished and offered excuses for him. Judge also makes reference to the compiler of the apocryphal *Correspondence of Paul and Seneca* in which he deplored the artlessness and poverty of Paul's style. He even tells the story of Seneca presenting Paul with a manual to improve his style (*de verborum copia*, cf. *Ep.* 9).[214] Gregory of Nyssa also acknowledged the fact that Paul despised the ornamental figures of speech and presents him as one 'whose only ornament was truth', and for that reason 'both disdained himself to lower his style to such prettinesses, and instructs us also, in a noble and appropriate exhortation, to fix our attention on truth alone.'[215]

Several recent commentators seem to be in agreement with the Church Fathers. Adolf Deissmann, for instance, states that Paul does not write literary Greek according to the accepted Greek standards.[216] A little earlier than him, Eduard Norden found Paul's rhetoric sadly lacking: 'Paul is an author which [*sic*] I barely, with great difficulty, understand. This is clear to me for two reasons: First, his method of argumentation has a strange style; and second, his style, all things considered, is indeed unhellenic.'[217] Bruce Winter also points to the fact that 'Paul wrote in the

213 See again Judge, 'Paul's Boasting in Relation to Contemporary Professional Practice', 40–42. Besides the examples given below, see also Justin, *Apol* 14.5, where he makes a virtue of Jesus' and the apostles' lack of eloquence.

214 Ibid., 41. This is also mentioned by Du Toit, 'A Tale of Two Cities', 393. For more on Paul and Seneca see Malherbe, ' "Seneca" on Paul as Letter Writer', 414–21.

215 *Adv. Eunomium* 45.1.253B, referenced in Judge, 'Paul's Boasting in Relation to Contemporary Professional Practice', 41.

216 Adolf Deissmann, *Paul: A Study in Social and Religious History* (New York: Hodder and Stoughton, 1926), p. 42, n. 5, cited by Hengel, *The Pre-Christian Paul*, p. 95, n. 31. See also Margaret Thrall, *Greek Particles in the New Testament: Linguistic and Exegetical Studies* (Leiden: Brill, 1962), p. 9, cited by Winter, 'Revelation versus Rhetoric', 145.

217 Norden, *Die antike Kunstprosa*, p. 499, cited by Hughes, 'The Rhetoric of Letters', 202–3.

plain style of Greek that would have been judged as "unsophisticated" by rhetorical standards and "vulgar" in that it did not reflect classical learning and allusions.'[218]

E. A. Judge rightly points to the fact that such a negative assessment of Paul's literary style is unwarranted. Speaking of the Church Fathers, he contends that '[t]hey had lost sight of the fact that Paul was writing in the form of the language current amongst educated people in his day.'[219] In other words, they compared Paul's literary style to the standards presented in the rhetorical handbooks by Plato and Aristotle and not to those of his time. By the contemporary standards of rhetoric, then, Paul's letters would have been considered eloquent, but proposes that the final pronouncement be made by those trained in ancient literary style. Such study has been done to some measure by Janet Fairweather, a Cambridge classicist. She states: 'Paul had the ability to write better Greek but *chose not to*.'[220]

What, then, is one to make of Paul's literary style, which most likely parallels that of his oral communication? E. A. Judge proposes an alternative position to the two views presented above. We concur with his view and therefore we will cite him extensively here:

> Paul frequently denounces his opponents as sophists in the most pejorative sense, and in the same connection vehemently dissociates himself from their methods. Paradoxically, all of Paul's protests about not having professional qualifications or using the accepted methods of persuasion imply the opposite. They make it clear for one thing that he was himself attacked on the same charges that he brought against his competitors ... His direct renunciations of sophistry are explicitly made in order to cast the opprobrium of professionalism on to his opponents, and lead not to the claim that he was incompetent, but, ultra-sophistically, to the claim that his skill was by special endowment and, therefore, in fact superior to theirs. The final answer to this question lies, of course, in the literary appraisal of Paul's own work, which would easily demonstrate that his style possesses a versatility and force, unconventional maybe by the standards of the professional rhetoricians, but so effective as to rank him as an orator and writer of rare distinction.[221]

---

218 Winter, 'Revelation versus Rhetoric', 150. Earlier in the essay (p. 146) he makes reference to Janet Fairweather, 'Galatians and Classical Rhetoric: Part 1 and 2' *TynBul* 45 (1994) 1–38, and 'Galatians and Classical Rhetoric: Part 3', 45 (1994) 213–43.

219 Judge, 'The Reaction against Classical Education in the New Testament', 9.

220 See Fairweather, 'Galatians and Classical Rhetoric: Part 1 and 2' 1–38, and 'Galatians and Classical Rhetoric: Part 3', 213–43. The quote is from p. 236 (emphasis by author). She is cited by Winter, 'Revelation versus Rhetoric', 146.

221 Judge, 'The Early Christians as Scholastic Community', 135–36.

What Judge is saying, and we concur, is that though Paul's communication both in written and oral form was effective, its effectiveness is due not to the fact that Paul followed the conventional rhetorical rules for speech, but because of the superiority given by the Spirit of God. This is in fact what he argues in 1 Cor. 2.4-5: 'and my speech and my message were not in persuasive words of wisdom, but in demonstration of the powerful Spirit, so that your faith might not rest in the wisdom of men, but in the power of God.'

The issue of Paul's stance towards sophistic rhetoric has proved to be a difficult one. What we can say with certainty is that Paul rejected sophistic rhetoric, both in preaching and in writing, because it emptied the cross (1 Cor. 1.17). The rhetorical devices in his letters are not indications that he sought to follow the rhetorical conventions of his day, but most likely for the purpose of making his points clearer. Given the fact he wrote his letters in order to be read aloud and therefore heard, his letters do not differ much from his oral communication in terms of rhetorical devices. Neither should we see in Paul a deficiency with regard to extemporaneous speech for which he sought to make up by sending a reciter trained in rhetoric to read his letters. The distinction that his opponents perceived between his letters and oral communication had to do more with the tone of his communication: his letters portrayed a bold Paul while his presence communicated timidity, which he explains as intentional. It is in this respect, in the eyes of his opponents, that he did not rise to the standards of an accomplished orator.

The picture that 1 Cor. 2.1-5 presents of Paul agrees with this interpretation, as has been shown in our exegesis of the passage. Besides the intentional 'timidity' which characterized Paul when present in person, he also makes a statement concerning the method of presenting his predetermined message: devoid of persuasive words of wisdom. We have shown also that Paul's anti-sophistic stance was a matter of theology for him.

Paul's Apologia *in 1 Corinthians 1–4 and the Concept of* Paterfamilias

All things considered, one more issue needs to be addressed: the seeming apologetic nature of 1 Corinthians 1–4. More specifically, is Paul presenting his anti-sophistic stance by appeal to his theology of the cross as a way of re-establishing his authority (i.e., ethos) in the Corinthian community? The way we answer this question will contribute to our understanding of the parties and of the comparing of leaders that was taking place among the Corinthian Christians. Is Paul seeking to regain the following of the Corinthians presumably in light of the fact that his authority has suffered as a result of the coming on the scene of the more rhetorical Apollos? We know that in 2 Corinthians 10–13 Paul had to defend himself against the 'super-apostles', but can we say that in 1 Corinthians 1–4 his apostleship is also under attack, especially from those who were claiming allegiance to Apollos? The issue of Apollos will be discussed in Chapter 4, but Paul's alleged *apologia* will be addressed here, since it is related to his anti-sophistic stance.[222]

We have already alluded to the claim that this first rhetorical unit is an *apologia* of Paul's ministry. Some of the things that we have mentioned as in need of more discussion are as follows. First, we have introduced the idea that the father-figure imagery may be used by Paul as a metaphor that communicates authority. Second, in conjunction with this metaphor, Paul calls for imitation, allegedly, in order to establish his authoritative position in the Corinthian congregation. Third, it is assumed that Paul uses disguised speech (i.e., σχῆμα) in order to reassert his authority and at the same time to downplay Apollos', thus distinguishing his unique role in the church from all others.

First Corinthians 1–4 has been regarded as an *apologia* for Paul's ministry since N. A. Dahl's article 'Paul and the Church at Corinth according to 1 Corinthians 1.10–4.21,'[223] though he modified his view in a later edition of his article, stating that 'the characterization of 1 Cor. 1.10–4.21 as an apologetic section is one-sided and may be misleading.'[224] Though some have rightly accepted his modified view in believing that the unit only contains 'apologetic elements'[225] and therefore the situation of 2 Corinthians (esp. chs 10–13) differs from that of 1 Corinthians,[226] there is still a good number of scholars who follow his initial view.

The most thorough analysis of 1 Corinthians 1–4 as an attempt by Paul to re-establish his authority is in our view that of Charles A. Wanamaker.[227] The stated thesis of his article is to 'move Castelli's work forward by looking at the ways in which Paul's rhetoric in 1 Cor. 1.10–4.21 functions ideologically to reassert his power in the Corinthian

---

222   See, e.g., Litfin, *Proclamation*, p. 153.

223   1967; see esp. pp. 317, 321, and 329. This view was championed by Fee in his commentary *First Corinthians*, pp. 48–9. See also Hurd, *The Origin of 1 Corinthians*, pp. 111–13; and Fiorenza, 'Rhetorical Situation', 386–403; Smit, 'Search for Coherance', 250; and Vos, 'Die Argumentation des Paulus in 1 Kor. 1.10-3.4', 87–119.

224   Dahl, 'Paul and the Church at Corinth according to 1 Corinthians 1.10-4.21' (1977), p. 61, n. 50.

225   E.g., Winter, *Philo and Paul among the Sophists*, pp. 181–2, rightly points to the fact that 1 Corinthians 1–4 contains hortatory sections also, and that this passage is primarily a critique of the Corinthians rather than a defense.

226   See Betz, 'The Problem of Rhetoric and Theology According to the Apostle Paul', p. 44; Martin, *The Corinthian Body*, p. 52; and Dodd, *Paul's Paradigmatic "I,"* p. 44.

227   Wanamaker, 'A Rhetoric of Power', 115–37. See also Williams, 'The Terminology of the Cross', 677–92.

Christian community.'[228] This emphasis on power, Wanamaker contends, can be seen in each of the four sections of the first rhetorical unit. A synopsis of his argument will be presented here. Wanamaker, following Castelli, starts by contending that 1.17 'already places Paul in a privileged position of authority since he claims primary role in mediating the message of Christ crucified to the Corinthians.' [229] It is through this claim to the unique role as 'creator' of the community that Paul ideologically legitimates his authoritative position.

The first section his argument (1 Cor. 1.18–2.16) allegedly continues the argument by implying a 'narrative of origin', that is, the origin of the Corinthians' faith through the preaching of the gospel; not any version of the gospel, but Paul's version.[230] In this sense, it is believed that Paul uses the cross in the first building block (1 Cor. 1.18-25) as a rhetorical tool for the purpose of establishing his ἦθος.[231] The discourse of the cross functions as a foil against which Paul presents his authoritative position in the Corinthian assembly. Thus it is argued that Paul seeks to elevate himself over Apollos by use of disguised speech.[232] In the second building block (1 Cor. 1.26-31), it is contended that Paul 'allies himself with the socially disadvantaged in Corinth in an attempt to win their loyalty', since they are the majority in the Corinthian community.[233] In the third building block (1 Cor. 2.1-5) Wanamaker argues that Paul seeks to legitimate his *modus operandi* against the 'value system of the socially superior members of the community who almost certainly would have identified with and even approved of rhetorical sophistication ...'[234]

Wanamaker continues to make his argument by an analysis of the second section (1 Cor. 2.6-3.4) of the first rhetorical unit with a view to Paul's intent to reassert his authority. In the two building blocks of this section (1 Cor. 2.6-16 and 3.1-4) it is argued that Paul distinguishes himself from the Corinthians by characterizing himself as 'perfect' and the

---

228   Ibid., 116. He is referring to Elizabeth A. Castelli's work, *Imitating Paul: A Discourse of Power* (Louisville: Westminster/John Knox, 1991), where she argues that Paul's call for imitation in 4.16 is a clear indication of paternalism, authoritarianism, and manipulation, all under the disguise of a loving father.

229   Ibid., 124.

230   Ibid., 126. See also Carter, '"Big Men" in Corinth', 58; and Williams, 'The Terminology of the Cross', 688.

231   See esp. Williams, 'The Terminology of the Cross and the Rhetoric of Paul', 677, 683, 687, and 692.

232   See esp. Smit, 'Search for Coherance' 243–44. He contends that the verb ἀπόλλυμι in 1.18-19 is in fact an allusion to Apollos and his followers since the personal pronoun 'Απολλύων (as in Rev. 9.11) is often associated with the verb ἀπόλλυμι in ancient texts.

233   Wanamaker, 'A Rhetoric of Power', 127, citing Carter, '"Big Men" in Corinth', 61.

234   Ibid., 'A Rhetoric of Power', 128.

Corinthians as 'babies'.[235] Wanamaker contends: 'When 2.6-16 is read against the context provided by 3.1-4 it becomes clear that Paul has created a legitimating rationalization to explain his own position of dominance over the Corinthians ...'[236] In other words, the metaphors of 'mature' and 'babies' are regarded as functioning ideologically as a means by which Paul places himself in an authoritative position.

The third section of the argument (1 Cor. 3.5–4.5) likewise can be read as intended to covertly elevate Paul above the Corinthians, but more importantly, above the other teachers, especially Apollos. We have already argued that in the first building block (1 Cor. 3.5-17) Paul uses three analogies (i.e., land, building, temple) in order to prove the illegitimacy of human evaluation of teachers. Wanamaker and others go even farther to argue that in using metaphors to present himself and the other teachers, Paul, in a subtle way, allows for differentiations between himself and Apollos, placing Apollos and the other teachers (including the Corinthians) in a subordinate position.[237] He does this, allegedly, by pointing to at least three facts: he fulfilled the pioneering function in the originating of the Christian community as the one who planted and as the master builder; there will be distinctions in rewards; and those who destroy the temple founded by him will be destroyed.[238] In what is rightly regarded as a summary of Paul's argument (1 Cor. 3.18-25) in the first rhetorical unit, Wanamaker again sees another step in Paul's argument for his authority. He states that 'by accepting this unity, the community effectively subscribes to Paul's authoritative position as the architect of the community's unity, and therefore, the re-unification of the community re-inscribes Paul's own position of dominance within it.'[239] The third building block enforces Paul's authoritative position by pointing to the fact that he is outside the range of the Corinthians' competence to evaluate; he is above criticism.

235   We agree here with Wanamaker, 'A Rhetoric of Power', 128–29, n. 62, that the first person personal pronoun in 2.6-16 is a reference primarily to Paul and possibly the other teachers though with the practical potential of including all Christians. However we disagree that Paul uses such distinctions for the purpose of establishing his dominance over the Corinthians.

236   Wanamaker, 'A Rhetoric of Power', 129. See also Williams, 'The Terminology of the Cross', 690.

237   Cf. Stephan J. Joubert, 'Managing the Household: Paul as *paterfamilias* of the Christian Household Group in Corinth', in *Modelling Early Christianity: Social-Scientific Studies of the New Testament in Its Context* (Philip F. Esler, ed.; London: Routledge, 1995), 217; Williams, 'The Terminology of the Cross', 691; and Smit, 'Search for Coherance ', 250, n. 36, who follows Ker, 'Paul and Apollos', 96.

238   Wanamaker, 'A Rhetoric of Power', 131–33. See also esp. Ker, 'Paul and Apollos', 84–90; Hyldahl, 'Paul and Apollos', 68–82; Dickerson, 'Apollos in Acts and First Corinthians', 120; and Carter, '"Big Men" in Corinth', 59.

239   Wanamaker, 'A Rhetoric of Power', 134.

The final section (1 Cor. 4.6-21) is regarded as the clearest statement of Paul's alleged intent to reassert his authority. Eva Maria Lassen has pointed to the fact that the irony characterizing the first building block of this section (1 Cor. 4.6-13) emphasizes the inferior status and degrading treatment experienced by the father (i.e., Paul) while his children (i.e., the Corinthians) enjoyed the very best.[240] The distinction in status between Paul and the Corinthians is presented however in categories that associate Paul with those whom God chose (1 Cor. 1.27-28) and the Corinthians with those of high status (1 Cor. 1.26), pointing seemingly to Paul's superior position. If this is not clear enough, then, it is argued, Paul will overtly seek to establish his authoritative position by appeal to the father-figure imagery and the concept of imitation.[241] Wanamaker contends that by an appeal to a narrative of origin in which Paul is the 'begetter' of the community, he places himself in 'a unique position of unrivalled authority within the community in relation to other leaders whom he describes as mere παιδαγωγοί,' seemingly a subordinate role.[242]

Thus, it is in the use of the concept of *paterfamilias* that one most clearly perceives Paul's intention to exert authority over the Corinthians and present his authoritative position in the church above all the other teachers. This concept is believed to gather under its umbrella all that Paul has communicated in the first rhetorical unit: his appeal to the narrative of origins (1 Cor. 1.18–2.5); his distinction between the mature and the children (1 Cor. 2.6–3.4); his denying the Corinthians the right to judge the founder of the community (1 Cor. 3.5–4.5); and his injunction to imitation (1 Cor. 4.6-21). All these are believed to be inherent in the first century concept of *paterfamilias* and therefore a study of this concept, both in 1 Corinthians and in Paul's culture, is necessary in order to adequately evaluate the supposition that Paul seeks to reestablish his authority in 1 Corinthians 1–4.

Before we look at this important concept used by Paul in this final section, which offers the solution to the dissensions – imitation of Paul – it is important to see whether in fact Paul does aim at reasserting his authority all throughout the first rhetorical unit. It is not necessary to go into great detail in order to prove Wanamaker's argument invalid. We

240 Lassen, 'The Use of the Father Image in Imperial Propaganda and 1 Corinthians 4.14-21', *TynBul* 42 (1991) 127–36 (135–36).

241 For the idea that the concept of *paterfamilias* evokes authority, see, e.g., Joubert, 'Managing the Household', 213–23. For the idea of authoritarianism inherent in the concept of imitation see Castelli, *Imitating Paul*, pp. 100–3, 107–11.

242 Wanamaker, 'A Rhetoric of Power', 135. See also Fee, *First Corinthians*, p. 185; Fiorenza, 'Rhetorical Situation', 397; Trevor J. Burke, 'Paul's Role as "Father" to His Corinthian "Children" in Socio-Historical Context (1 Corinthians 4.14-21)', in *Paul and the Corinthians*, 108. See N. H. Young, '*Paidagōgos*' 150–70, for a discussion of παιδαγωγός in Paul's culture.

have already pointed out throughout the exegesis of 1 Corinthians 1–4 in Chapter 1 the theocentric/Christological stress in Paul's argument. There is clear evidence in these chapters of Paul's self-deprecation for the purpose of revealing the importance of God/Christ in the community's formation. His self-effacing cannot be regarded as a covert and subtle way of self-assertion, but should rather be taken at face value, namely as a sincere desire of Paul to point away from himself (and the other teachers) to God.[243]

For instance, in the first stage of his argument (1 Cor. 1.18–2.5), Paul clearly points to the triune God's central role in creating the Corinthian community: the message that saves is the message about the crucified Christ (1 Cor. 1.17-25); several times God is the subject of verbs that speak of his initiative in the salvation of the Corinthians (1 Cor. 1.26-31); and faith unto salvation is the result of the work of the Spirit (1 Cor. 2.1-5). In all this work of salvation, Paul is the mere herald of the message.[244]

Though in the next section (esp. 1 Cor. 3.1-4) he speaks of himself as 'mature' and the Corinthians as 'babies', his intention is not to elevate himself above the Corinthians, but rather to point to the Corinthians' spiritual condition as a dangerous one. Since in 2.6-16 Paul presents only two possible spiritual categories – believers and unbelievers based on their perception of the gospel – the Corinthians being fleshly find themselves in a dangerous condition spiritually – spiritual yet acting as unbelievers, as those who have not been enlightened by God. Thus, a central theme in 2.6-16 at least is that God occupies the central role in salvation, in that he is the one who enlightens men to salvation. The message of salvation is communicated by teachers such as Paul, but it is received only by revelation. Peter Lampe, thus, is on target when he states that '2.6-16 points out that "we preach *God's* wisdom, which *God* predestined" (2.7); "*God* revealed" (2.10) . . . and so forth. The word "God" occurs ten times in 2.6-16. Here we encounter the argument's point, and the polemic against the Corinthians. Facing the veneration of apostles, Paul calls out "God, God", not "Paul", not "Apollos", not "Cephas." '[245] By distinguishing between the 'perfect' and the 'babies', Paul is then seeking to make the Corinthians understand that their divisive spirit and preferences for teachers based on their eloquence of speech proves their worldly thinking, and is man-focused rather than God-focused.

That this is so is most clearly seen in the next section (1 Cor. 3.5–4.5). In this section, not only does Paul use metaphors to describe himself and the other teachers that are normally associated with low-status people, but he

---

243 For what follows see Dodd, *Paul's Paradigmatic "I"*, pp. 48–61.

244 See ibid., p. 53.

245 Lampe, 'Theological Wisdom and the "Word about the Cross"', 127 (author's emphasis).

also points to God's central role: *God* is the one who gives the teachers to the church; *God* is the only one who can create the church; *Christ* is the only foundation; *God* is the only one who will judge them; and all belong to *Christ/God*. Even when Paul speaks of himself as the one laying the foundation, he does not exalt himself since he performs his work 'according to the grace of God given to me.' Moreover, the metaphors he uses to describe himself and the other teachers are not to be thought as 'a covert jab at anyone else', for that would lead to a collapse of Paul's argument for unity, since he would be engaging in a practice he rejects.[246] Rather, his self-deprecation should be regarded as sincere, intended to point to God's significant role contrasted to his (and others') menial role.

This is the case also with the last section of the first rhetorical unit (1 Cor. 4.6-21). Like nowhere else before, Paul goes to great length to portray himself and the other teachers as the most despised people – 'the scum of the earth, the refuse of the world'. But in such conditions, they actually live out a cruciform life. It is this quality that Paul calls on the Corinthians to imitate.[247] When they learn to renounce all desires for fame and fortune – the 'benefits' that come with high status – they then will find the solution to their dissensions. Thus, Paul is not calling them to follow him per se, but to follow Christ.[248]

This quick survey of the first four chapters, then, shows what Paul's purpose truly is: not of reasserting his authority, but of elevating God's role in Christ. Brian Dodd rightly states: 'Throughout this opening section Paul depreciates himself for Christological emphasis, accepts the unity of the missionary workers in their gospel work, and stresses the cruciform nature of life in Christ, laying a foundation for his solution to the church problems.'[249] Paul's intentions are thus conciliatory, not authoritarian. Throughout 1 Corinthians 1–4, the emphasis is on the positive – unity – rather than the negative – polemic. Dodd is right that '[t]here is no direct evidence that Paul also responds to a challenge to his authority in 1 Corinthians.'[250] This is particularly seen in the fact that Paul is critical not only of his opponents but of his own adherents as well. Moreover, had his authority been questioned, no doubt that the Corinthians would not have asked for advice concerning the issues he responds to in 1 Corinthians

---

246 Ibid., 56.

247 Cf. Pickett, *The Cross in Corinth*, p. 59.

248 See Garland, *1 Corinthians*, p. 147; and Thiselton, *First Corinthians*, pp. 371–3.

249 Dodd, *Paul's Paradigmatic "I"*, p. 33.

250 Ibid., p. 40. See also Witherington, *Conflict and Community in Corinth*, p. 145. A more nuanced view is that of Winter, *Philo and Paul among the Sophists*, p. 182. See also Anderson, *Ancient Rhetorical Theory and Paul*, p. 275, who argues particularly against Litfin's contention that 1 Corinthians 1–4 is Paul's defense.

(cf. 11.2).[251] Not least, Paul writes to the whole church and not only to a certain party; his problem is with the Corinthians' high esteem of sophistic rhetoric in general that has led to preferences rather than the depreciation of his authority in their eyes as a result of the ministry of Apollos. Thus, Paul does not seek to secure a following, but ultimately to bring about unity.[252] This, in fact, was one of the responsibilities of a *paterfamilias*: the creation and maintenance of unity and peace within the household.[253]

Studies into the concept of *paterfamilias* have tended to overemphasize the aspect of authority and power (*patria potestas*) to the exclusion of any affections involved in a familial relationship.[254] But even though it is generally recognized that the *paterfamilias*, especially in the Roman society, was vested with authority, power, and control,[255] more recent scholarship has rightly construed a more balanced/moderate understanding of the concept, noting that in practice the *paterfamilias* rarely exercised his authority to its fullest extent.[256] Moreover, Andrew Clarke has rightly pointed out that the *potestas* was exercised in different ways over the father's offspring and his slaves.[257] Thus, in practice, the relationship between parents and children was characterized more than just by exercise of *potestas*; there was also mutual bond of *pietas* (respect) between the members of a family. In light of this, the question remains as to whether 'the authority which was customarily invested within the head of the

---

251   See Wire, *The Corinthian Women Prophets: A Reconstruction of Paul's Rhetoric* (Minnesota: Fortress, 1990), p. 46.

252   According to Welborn, 'A Conciliatory Principle in 1 Cor. 4.6', 320–46; and Mitchell, *Reconciliation*, pp. 199–200, 207–10, who read 1 Corinthians through the model of a classical oration περὶ ὁμονοίας in a political context, Paul exclusively pleads for unity.

253   See, e.g., Burke, 'Paul's Role as "Father" to His Corinthian "Children"', 107.

254   For a summary see Clarke, *Serve the Community of the Church*, pp. 86–101.

255   For instance, Lassen, 'The Use of the Father Image in Imperial Propaganda and 1 Corinthians 4.14-21', 129–33, points out that household metaphors were applied also to political positions of honor, particularly to emperors beginning with Augustus, who took upon themselves the title of *Pater Patriae* ('father of the fatherland'), cf. Eph. 3.14-15. See also Witherington, *Conflict and Community in Corinth*, p. 138.

256   The shift took place as a result of considering, besides the legal texts, social history, culture, and norms. See Clarke, *Serve the Community of the Church*, pp. 88–90, following Jane F. Gardner, *Family and Familia in Roman Law and Life* (Oxford: Clarendon, 1998), pp. 268–9. See also Lassen, 'The Use of the father Image in Imperial Propaganda and 1 Corinthians 4.14-21,' 128; Gardner 'The Roman Family: Ideal and Metaphor', in *Constructing Early Christian Families*, pp. 103–20; and Joubert, 'Managing the Household', 215.

257   Clarke, *Serve the Community of the Church*, pp. 90–5. He follows especially R. P. Saller, *Patriarchy, Property and Death in the Roman Family* (CSPESPS, 25; Cambridge: Cambridge University Press, 1994); *idem*, 'Corporal Punishment, Authority, and Obedience in the Roman Household', in *Marriage, Divorce, and Children in Ancient Rome* (B. Rawson, ed.; Oxford: Clarendon, 1991), pp. 144–65. See also Robertson, *Conflict in Corinth*, p. 62.

household [was] also dominant in the Christian congregation which met in his house.'[258]

Trevor Burke has recently done a thorough study of the metaphor of family. He lays the foundation of his methodology by rightly contending that,

> If metaphors are to be a useful means of communication 'the *person using the figure* and the *person ... hearing the words* [must] give the words the same content'. Thus, if Paul's usage of familial nomenclature is far removed from what was commonly associated with family members in antiquity, the correlation would be weak and the impact lessened and our findings rendered less useful.[259]

Burke then continues with pointing to a number of aspects of the parent-child relationship in antiquity, by reference to ancient texts. He identifies such elements as hierarchy (e.g., Aristotle, *Pol.* 1.3.2), authority (e.g., Aristotle, *Pol.* 1.13.6-7), imitation (e.g., Isocrates *Or.* 1.4.11), affection (e.g., Plutarch, *Frat. Amor.* 5.480C), and education (e.g., Plutarch, *De Lib.* 5.3E), as characterizing the parent-child relationship. Applying his findings to 1 Cor. 4.14-21, Burke contends that in order to bring about unity, 'Paul assumes a role similar to that of a *paterfamilias* in the ancient world who was responsible for exercising authority as well as maintaining order, peace, and concord within his own family. In brief, Paul here is about that business of household management.'[260] He sees in the use of the metaphor by Paul in 1 Cor. 4.15 all the above mentioned elements. Thus, Paul intends to establish his superordinate position in the Corinthian community and his authority over the church by calling his children to obey him through imitation, as a way of educating them.

Despite these similarities between the conventional understanding of a father-child relationship and Paul's use of the metaphor, Burke is careful to point to some important distinctions. First, he argues that, 'even though the apostle expected his Corinthian progeny to conform to his pattern, this ought not to be construed as a strategy of coercion or manipulation or authoritarianism on Paul's part. On the contrary ... Paul later sounds an important Christocentric note to inform his readers that to imitate him is merely to imitate Christ (11.1) whom he serves.'[261] Second, 'Paul's paternal role *vis-à-vis* his spiritual offspring is highly complex and variegated and should not be reduced to a *single* expression

258   Clarke, *Serve the Community of the Church*, p. 162.

259   'Paul's Role as "Father" to His Corinthian "Children"', 98, citing F. Lyall, *Slaves and Sons: Legal Metaphors in the Epistles* (Grand Rapids: Zondervan, 1984), p. 20.

260   Ibid., 107.

261   Ibid., 110. Contra Castelli, *Imitating Paul*, p. 101, and G. Shaw, *The Cost of Authority: Manipulation and Freedom in the New Testament* (London: SCM, 1983), p. 35.

of his hierarchical stance channeled through his call to imitate him.'[262] Thirdly, 'we should not assume an (over-simplistic) one-to-one correspondence between the social reality of a father in antiquity and Paul's metaphorical use of this term.'[263] Fourth, 'whilst his position as 'father' was a hierarchical one, there is a dialectic between this and the undoubted affection he also felt for his spiritual offspring.'[264] Thus, while Paul employs a metaphor that carries with it certain conventional and accepted perceptions, he does not mechanically employ it, but redefines it to fit his agenda as he presents the Christian community as a unique assembly.

We have already noted in Chapter 2 that some of the Corinthians were inclined to mistake their Christian assembly for other social networks to which they belonged, such as the household, and import their values into the structuring of their new Christian network. In this respect Paul seeks to affirm the fact that the Christian community has a unique identity, with a different set of values than those of the surrounding culture, with a particular structure, and therefore with redefined relationships among its members.[265]

If Paul seeks to redefine the system, then could it be that 'Paul's argument suffers an internal breakdown here because when he picks up the father image [evoking authority exclusively], he deflates the call to freedom and new possibilities that had not been an option for the poor, women, and slaves?'[266] Demetrius Williams aptly responds:

> Paul appears to aim at a redefinition of the father image. This means that his image as father is not based upon displays of power and authority. Unlike the Roman *paterfamilias* who would use his position to impose and support hierarchical social order, Paul as the Corinthians' 'father' makes a gentle appeal to them to imitate him (4.16). His model is based upon the cruciform pattern of the cross of Christ – the power of God for the establishment of the eschatological community.[267]

Andrew Clarke is particularly helpful in bringing out the similarities but also differences between the Christian assembly and the conventional household. First, he rightly observes that 'Paul certainly refers to himself as the father of the Corinthian community, but he also draws attention to

262 Ibid., 110, n. 43.
263 Ibid., 112.
264 Ibid., 113.
265 See for instance Wayne A. Meeks, *The Moral World of the First Christians* (London: SPCK, 1986), p. 139, referenced by Burke, 'Paul's Role as "Father" to His Corinthian "Children"', 95.
266 Williams, 'Paul's Anti-Imperial "Discourse of the Cross"', 821. This is the argument that Fiorenza, 'Rhetorical Situation', 386–403, makes.
267 Ibid., 821–2.

other significant householders in that community who were leading figures.'[268] The same is true concerning 1 Cor. 4.15: here 'he neither excludes the possibility of other "fathers" nor insists on being exclusively the one "father" of the *whole* church.'[269] Second, Paul offers other teachers as an appropriate model for emulation. Timothy, for instance, is presented by Paul 'as a means of reminding the Corinthians of what is appropriate behavior.'[270] Third, 'in contradiction to those models of leadership which were prevalent in Greco-Roman society, Paul's legitimation comes not from his own qualities which might have commanded respect, but rather he defers to Christ alone.'[271] Fourth, Paul does not describe himself in relation to the Corinthians exclusively in terms of parent/child relationship, which may evoke the idea of a superior/inferior relation, but also as a brother, that is, as an equal sibling.[272]

We may conclude, then, that the concept of *paterfamilias* carried with it various denotations, of which both authority and affection are part. When Paul uses the metaphor, however, he redefines it in light of the unique relationships that characterize the Christian community. And even if in the Roman mind, the concept evoked authority, in the case of Paul, it was modified by love.[273]

Conclusion

This chapter has been an important one in our process of determining Apollos' role in the dissensions in the Corinthian community. We have sought to determine Paul's stance towards sophistic rhetoric. Since we have shown that Paul brings together the themes of dissensions and wisdom in the first rhetorical unit and that the wisdom that the Corinthians valued was sophistic rhetoric, we have determined that Paul seeks to bring about unity by seeking to convince his readers that their love for rhetorical eloquence is contrary to the nature of the gospel. Therefore, Paul rejected sophistic rhetoric (both as a presentation and as argumentation), both in his preaching as well as in his writing. He rather prefers a humble stance, for in such way he embodies the weakness of the cross and allows God to retain the central role in salvation as he naturally deserves.

---

268 Clarke, *Serve the Community of the Church*, pp. 163, 217.
269 Ibid., p. 219. *Contra* Fee, *First Corithians*, p. 185.
270 Ibid., p. 221.
271 Ibid.
272 Ibid., p. 223. For more on this see Horrell, 'From ἀδελφόι to οἶκος θεοῦ', 303, and the discussion in Chapter 3.
273 Ibid., p. 222.

If such is Paul's stance towards rhetoric, we have also sought to evaluate the claim that Paul's self-deprecation as well as his role as a father for the Corinthians evokes authority, power, and control. We have seen that such an argument is incompatible with the theological/ Christological emphasis that is evident in the first rhetorical unit. Rather, being consistent with his use of other terminology and with his position towards cultural values, Paul redefines the concept of *pater-familias*, emphasizing affection towards the Corinthians in all his dealings with them.

In light of such conclusions, it remains to see in the next chapter where Apollos fits within the argument of 1 Corinthians 1–4. Is Apollos a teacher whose seeming rhetorical eloquence is downplayed covertly throughout Paul's argument?

4 APOLLOS' FUNCTION IN 1 CORINTHIANS 1–4

Introduction

This fourth chapter of the work will draw heavily on the research and conclusions reached in the previous chapters. We will seek to analyze how the information and conclusions reached so far bear on the subject of Apollos' function in 1 Corinthians 1–4 and his role in the dissensions, issues at which we have hinted all throughout this work. This is important since Apollos' name is mentioned six times in 1 Corinthians 1–4 out of eleven NT mentions. He is mentioned elsewhere only in 1 Cor. 16.12 and Acts 18.24-28, Tit. 3.13 giving no independent information and *1 Clem* 47.3-4 being wholly dependent on 1 Corinthians. Thus, information on Apollos always occurs in conjunction with the church in Corinth, and one inevitably wonders what Apollos' role was in the dissensions in the Corinthian *ecclesia*, how Apollos' name functions in Paul's argument for unity, and what kind of relationship did Paul and Apollos share. Before we address these issues, it may be helpful to summarize the findings so far.

After establishing the methodology underlying the research in this work, our purpose in the first chapter of this work was to determine the literary and thematic unity of 1 Corinthians 1–4. We sought to show how the themes of wisdom and dissensions, which are prominent in the first rhetorical unit, are interconnected by suggesting that worldly wisdom was the basic cause of the lack of unity in the Corinthian church. Paul thus warns the Corinthians of the illegitimacy of evaluating their teachers according to the world's norms and values, which, in his view, are overturned by the cross. Our exegesis of the text has also pointed to the nature of these dissensions: boasting in one teacher over against another. More specifically, it seems that some in the Corinthian *ecclesia* preferred Apollos over Paul, a preference that reflected their worldly perception of wisdom. Conceivably, some preferred Apollos, not only because they believed that he embodied the qualities of wisdom they so highly esteemed, but also because by association with him, they themselves would be considered wise.

If a worldly view of wisdom, which constituted a basis for boasting with one teacher against another, seems to be the root cause of dissensions in the Corinthian *ecclesia*, then in the second chapter we sought to determine the nature of this wisdom. We have argued that the most likely background for the concept of wisdom (i.e., σοφία) which Paul rejects in 1 Corinthians 1–4 is sophistic rhetoric. If that is the case, then this raises the issue of Apollos' function in the dissensions. Since his name becomes prominent in these chapters alongside that of Paul, and since Paul seems to insist on their collaboration against the partisan spirit, could it be that some in the Corinthian congregation preferred Apollos because he adopted a sophistic stance when he visited Corinth? Likewise, does Paul direct his critique of sophistic rhetoric against Apollos? Such questions become even sharper in light of the social background of the concept of σοφία that we conducted in the second chapter. We have shown how wise speech was regarded as a sign of high status, both of the one who employed it as well as of the one who associated with a rhetor. In other words, eloquent speech was a means to increase one's honor and to enhance one's status.

Since we have shown that the Corinthians inadequately viewed the Christian *ecclesia* as one relational network among other social or political networks to which they belonged, they were inclined to seek status and honor by association with a teacher whom they perceived would help them achieve just that. So, it is conceivable that their preferences for different teachers, especially Apollos, were based on these values, which Paul rejects by pointing to the unique identity of the Christian *ecclesia* as the temple of God. In other words, one could conceive that the dissensions were the result of Apollos' different *modus operandi* from Paul's. Their distinct *modus operandi*, judged against the backdrop of social values characterizing the larger society, has determined the Corinthians to esteem the two apostles in different ways. This could be supported further by the fact that the slogans of 1 Cor. 1.12 were most likely indicative of only two parties: Paul's and Apollos'. We concluded the chapter, however, by suggesting that the least we can say is that Apollos should not be held responsible for the dissensions, but the possibility that he indirectly contributed to the problematic situation by his *modus operandi* remains to be addressed in this fourth chapter.

In order to evaluate such a possibility we must determine whether there truly was a distinction between Apollos' and Paul's *modus operandi*. To this end, we devoted the third chapter to a discussion of Paul's stance toward sophistic rhetoric. Our research into statements concerning Paul and sophistic rhetoric in the Corinthian correspondence as well as an investigation of Paul' upbringing and education and his literary practice in comparison with his oral speech led us to believe that Paul rejects the whole dynamic of sophistic rhetoric. We argued, however, that this anti-sophistic stance should not be regarded as an attempt by Paul to reassert his authority over the Corinthians in light of the presumed loss of authority as a result of the appearance on the scene of the more rhetorical Apollos. This initial conclusion must be further investigated in this chapter.

Paul's relationship to Apollos, Apollos' function in 1 Corinthians 1–4, and consequently his role in the dissensions will thus be the focus here. We will seek to determine where Apollos fits into Paul's argument by surveying first the various opinions concerning the relationship between Paul and Apollos. Secondly, we will seek to understand the meaning of 1 Cor. 16.12, which seems to present a tension between the two, according to some interpreters. Third, we will investigate the issue of Apollos and rhetoric, where we will continue our discussion started in Chapter 2 concerning the information that Luke provides about Apollos particularly in ch. 18 of Acts. Paul's relation to Apollos, however, will have to be decided by a closer look at 1 Cor. 3.5–4.5, thus building on the exegesis of the text in chapter one and on the discussion of the alleged apologetic nature of the first rhetorical unit. Finally, one cannot pronounce a final judgment on the issue of Apollos and the Corinthians without a discussion of 1 Cor. 4.6 and the meaning of μετεσχημάτισα.

Paul's Relation to Apollos according to 1 Corinthians 1–4

There has been much discussion over the last two centuries concerning Apollos' role in the dissensions in the Corinthian *ecclesia*.[1] The views vary from those who claim that 1 Corinthians 1–4 is a polemic against Apollos and his followers to those who believe that Apollos had no role in the dissensions. For purposes of clarity, we will group the views under three rubrics: Paul and Apollos are rivals; Apollos unintentionally caused the problems in Corinth; and Paul's argument in 1 Corinthians 1–4 is against unnamed leaders, Apollos thus having no role whatsoever in the dissensions. These different views, as we will see, are heavily dependent upon one's view concerning the apologetic nature of 1 Corinthians 1–4 and the number and nature of parties, issues already discussed.

Paul and Apollos Are Rivals

According to several recent authors, it is believed that the dissensions in the Corinthian church were caused by Apollos, so that when Paul calls for unity he does it by construing his argument in 1 Corinthians 1–4 as a polemic against Apollos and his followers. Niels Hyldahl has been a

---

1   For a thorough survey of all the views and their advocates see Dickerson, 'Apollos in Acts and First Corinthians', 1–41.

strong advocate of this view in recent years.[2] He contends that 'Apollos was the person causing the troubles in Corinth which Paul had to face at the time of writing 1 Corinthians', though he is quick to state that 'there was no question of a party founded in Corinth by Apollos.'[3] He seeks to support his view with the following precarious arguments, which have already been addressed throughout this work and will not be rehearsed here. First, following Dahl's programmatic article, he fully agrees that Paul is contending with a single opposition front: against the non- or anti-Pauline parties, or more specifically against the pro-Apollos party. Therefore, in his view 1 Corinthians 1–4 is clearly an *apologia* in which Paul seeks to recover his authority lost as a result of Apollos' subsequent work in the Corinthian congregation. Second, he wrongly identifies the problems in the Christian *ecclesia* as being of a theological and doctrinal nature, more specifically a Philonic type of wisdom.[4] Third, he incorrectly reads the situation of 2 Corinthians into 1 Corinthians, thus identifying the 'super-apostles' of 2 Corinthians 10–13 with Apollos and his followers of 1 Corinthians, especially since Apollos' name is not mentioned at all in 2 Corinthians.[5]

Several recent scholars continue to maintain that Paul and Apollos are rivals and that Paul writes 1 Corinthians 1–4 as a polemic against Apollos and his party, but they present their case from a different angle. For instance, they work with the general agreement that there is a development of situation between the writing of 1 and 2 Corinthians, both letters responding to somewhat different exigencies. They also dissociate themselves from those who believe that Apollos introduced a Philonic type of wisdom in the Corinthian congregation, and are inclined to accept the rhetorical background for the concept of σοφία in 1 Corinthians 1–4. Notable among them are Donald Ker and Joop Smit, though Smit argues that σοφία λόγου refers to 'logical wisdom' rather than 'rhetorical skill'.

The very title of Ker's article – 'Apollos and Paul: Colleagues or Rivals'

2   See esp. his 'The Corinthian "Parties" and the Corinthian Crisis', *ST* 45 (1991) 19–32; and 'Paul and Apollos', 68–82, as well as his earlier 'Den korintiske situation – en skitse', *DTT* 40 (1977) 18–30. He is in agreement with the arguments of Sellin, 'Das "Geheimnis" der Weisheit und das Rätsel der "Christuspartei" ', 69–96, though Sellin seems to hold to a more moderate position allowing non-intentionality on the part of Apollos. See especially the arguments of Simone Pétrement, *A Separate God* (San Francisco: Harper, 1990), pp. 251–5. For a presentation and evaluation of this view see Dickerson, 'Apollos in Acts and First Corinthians', 17–19.

3   Hyldahl, 'The Corinthian "Parties" and the Corinthian Crisis', 21.

4   Following Sellin, Hyldahl, ibid., 24–26, argues that 'Apollos' *sofia*-movement is treated in 1 Corinthians in the same way as Paul treated the Judaizing movement in Galatians.'

5   See Hyldahl, 'Paul and Hellenistic Judaism in Corinth', in *The New Testament and Hellenistic Judaism* (Peter Borgen and Søren Giversen, eds.; Peabody: Hendrickson, 1997), 212; F. Watson, *Paul, Judaism and the Gentiles: A Sociological Approach* (SNTSMS, 56; Cambridge: Cambridge University Press, 1986), pp. 82–3.

– already suggests the direction in which he is taking his argument. His analysis of 1 Cor. 3.5-4.5, 4.6, 16.12, and Acts 18.24-28 leads him to conclude that the different styles of Paul and Apollos of doing ministry have placed the two into a 'strained relationship', so much so that Paul perceives Apollos as a rival in ministry. We will conduct an exegesis of these passages later in this chapter, but we should point to that fact that the emphasis of Ker's article is that Paul is antagonistic to Apollos in a *subtle* way. In other words, Ker comments, 'In a volatile situation open criticism of another can backfire.'[6] More specifically, the great following that Apollos won from among the Corinthians as well as his relationship with Aquila and Priscilla 'force Paul to present his case in a more irenic fashion than he otherwise would.'[7] Nevertheless, in his cautious exercise of language, Paul's main goal, according to Ker, is to undermine Apollos, 'the overall effect [being that of] cast[ing] Apollos into shadows.'[8]

Smit follows Ker in his argument that Paul addresses himself almost exclusively to the pro-Apollos group, so that Smit's thesis is to prove that what gives coherence to 1 Corinthians 1–4 is Paul's covert way of antagonizing Apollos and his followers. As already mentioned, the two major themes dominating the first rhetorical unit are wisdom and dissensions. Smit believes that 'the missing link connecting the two themes' is Apollos and his party so that the four slogans in 1 Cor. 1.12 'make known in covert terms that the adherents of Apollos are his principal target.'[9] He seeks to substantiate this claim by contending that Paul intentionally uses the participle οἱ ἀπολλύμενοι in 1 Cor. 1.18, 19 as an allusion to the adherents of Apollos, based on the lexical argument that the verb and the proper noun share the same root and are often associated.[10] That this may be the case also in 1 Corinthians 1–4, however, is a different issue. In order to prove this, one must at least show that Paul uses the rhetorical technique of 'covert allusion' throughout these chapters. We have already commented on this in Chapter 1, but a more detailed discussion especially of 1 Cor. 4.6 and the verb μετεσχημάτισα will be conducted at the end of this chapter. Both Ker and Smit would also have to prove that Paul is on defense in these chapters, something that has not been very convincing.

The claim that there is a 'strained relationship' between the two has been addressed many years before Ker and Smit advanced it. In his monograph on Apollos, Robert Wynne is careful to point to the fact that if Apollos was the cause of dissensions in the Corinthian congregation, it

6 Ker, 'Paul and Apollos', 84.
7 Ibid., 85.
8 Ibid., 96.
9 Smit, 'What is Apollos? What is Paul?', 244.
10 Ibid., 243–44. See, e.g., Rev. 9.11.

was more because 'the minds of a good many of these converts were of such imperfect grasp that they could not many of them fully appreciate Apollos without depreciating Paul', and not so much because there was some kind of rivalry between the two or that 'there was a jealousy or a suspicious dislike between the two.'[11] The problem was thus with the Corinthians and not with Apollos.[12] In spite of the fact that Apollos is not to be blamed, the issue of Apollos' role in the dissensions and Paul's focus on him in 1 Corinthians 1–4 still raises the question of whether there was a distinction between them in their *modus operandi*, a distinction that could have *unintentionally* led to dissensions.

Apollos' Unintentional Role in the Dissensions

If most scholars disagree with the suggestion that there might have been a rivalry between Paul and Apollos, some still contend that 1 Corinthians 1–4 is an *apologia* and that Paul addresses the pro-Apollos group that formed against the will of Apollos. Kuck raises the issue in a form of a question: 'If we can rule out personal opposition as the reason for Paul's discussion of Apollos, then does Paul single out Apollos because he unintentionally spawned a faction which is the main or only opposition to Paul in Corinth?'[13] He is right to observe that 'this is a harder question to answer with confidence,'[14] but there have been quite a few who have had no difficulty in connecting Apollos with the dissensions, though in a more indirect way. In other words, although Apollos is not to be held directly responsible for the dissensions, it is argued that his distinct *modus operandi* led unintentionally to the dissensions among the Corinthians given their penchant for worldly wisdom. Paul Barnett, for instance, expresses well the position of these scholars: 'It is not as though Apollos has set out to undermine or compete with Paul. Rather the problem lies with some of the Corinthians who have elevated Apollos above Paul while prompted to move off in unhelpful directions in the prizing of *sophia*-rhetoric and perhaps of the *pneumatika*.'[15]

The argument of Apollos' unintentional role in the dissensions is presented at least along two lines. First, Apollos is identified as more rhetorically eloquent than Paul. In light of this, it is argued that 'Paul's reminder that he preached "Christ crucified" but not in the "wisdom of speech" is most likely a corrective of the Corinthians' appreciation of

11   Wynne, *Apollos*, p. 46 and 68 respectively.
12   Cf. Litfin, *Proclamation*, p. 227.
13   Kuck, *Judgment*, p. 163.
14   Ibid.
15   Barnett, 'Paul, Apologist to the Corinthians', in *Paul and the Corinthians*, 319. See also Dodd, *Paul's Paradigmatic "I"*, p. 38, who follows Pogoloff, *LOGOS AND SOPHIA*; and Pickett, *The Cross in Corinth*, p. 51.

Apollos' recent ministry among them.'[16] Thus, as de Vos argues, 'the opposition to Paul in 1 Corinthians 1–4 appears to be based on his refusal to preach in a rhetorical/sophistic style. Given the obsession with rhetorical skill, eloquence and sophism at Corinth, it is likely that for many Christians it was an embarrassment to have Paul seen as their teacher.'[17] By contrast, at least in the minds of some Corinthians, Apollos fitted better the image of a sophist than Paul, 'which had the potential to affect severely the group's status.'[18] Litfin concludes: 'Hence, it is not only plausible but in fact likely that an unwitting contrast between the eloquence of Apollos and Paul would have triggered the sort of divisions we discover in rhetorically attuned Corinth.'[19]

Not only did the Corinthians appreciate the more eloquent Apollos, but second, it is also believed that those who most likely appreciated Apollos' eloquence in speech and despised Paul's deliberate anti-sophistic stance are the elite. They are the ones who regarded rhetoric as a status indicator so that when Paul, who was compared to a rhetor, took his anti-sophistic stance, he was perceived as one who lived below his expected status and was thus a basis for shame for the elite in the congregation.[20] Pickett is representative of this position when he states:

> It is likely that Paul was discredited for his weakness and shame. Conversely, Apollos was credited with possessing honor and power, the operative values of the privileged elite in the community. Apollos, in contrast to Paul, measured up to the ideal of a cultivated person current in Greco-Roman society ... The identification of Paul's opponents as members of a social elite further clarifies how Apollos whose rhetorical eloquence qualified him as a cultivated person in Greco-Roman society, served as a yardstick of Christian leadership for them. With the social values of honor and power as their criteria this dominant minority determined that Apollos more aptly exemplified an ideal of apostleship which was constructed on these values.[21]

16   Barnett, 'Paul, Apologist to the Corinthians', 316.

17   De Vos, *Church and Community Conflicts*, p. 219. He expresses the view of many, such as Chow, *Patronage and Power*, pp. 102–4; Marshall, *Enmity in Corinth*, pp. 339–41; Clarke, *Leadership in Corinth*, pp. 104–5; Litfin, *Proclamation*, pp. 153, 171, 188–93; Witherington, *Conflict and Community in Corinth*, p. 20.

18   De Vos, *Church and Community*, p. 220. See also, e.g., Savage, *Power through Weakness*, pp. 46–7; Witherington, *Conflict and Community in Corinth*, pp. 103–4. Litfin, *Proclamation*, p. 233, states: 'Paul did not suit their image of themselves while the erudite Apollos did.'

19   Litfin, *Proclamation*, p. 253. See also Winter, *Philo and Paul among the Sophists*, p. 179.

20   Cf. Martin, *Slavery as Salvation*, pp. 77–82; also Hock, 'Paul's Tentmaking and the Problem of His Social Class', 555–64; *idem The Social Context of Paul's Ministry*, pp. 60–4; Pogoloff, *LOGOS AND SOPHIA*, p. 152.

21   Pickett, *The Cross in Corinth*, p. 53 and 54 respectively.

The assumption that the dissensions were the unintentional result of a more eloquent Apollos who fared better with the hunger for honor and status of the elite in the Corinthian congregation has the benefit of reconstructing the rhetorical situation behind 1 Corinthians 1–4 in accord with the discussion we have carried in Chapters 1 through 3. For instance, it fits well with our exegesis of 1 Corinthians 1–4 in Chapter 2 and the conclusion we reached there that the major theme of this first rhetorical unit is that of dissensions caused by a worldly evaluation of teachers based on wisdom-criteria. The Corinthians seem to have evaluated their teachers according to the values of the world and what the world perceived as wisdom. It also has the benefit of taking into consideration the background of wisdom as sophistic rhetoric particularly related to speech as well as the social dimensions of the dissensions discussed in Chapter 2. In other words, the Corinthians had a high esteem of rhetoric as a status marker and were thus confusing the Christian ecclesia with other social networks to which they belonged. Lastly, it agrees with our conclusions in Chapter 3 that Paul opposes sophistic rhetoric in the proclamation of the gospel, both in speech as well as in writing.

Apart from these strengths, it seems that this view is heavily dependent on a rhetorical rendition of the description of Apollos in Acts 18.24-28 as ἀνὴρ λόγιος and δυνατός, and the belief that 1 Corinthians 1–4 is an *apologia* (or at least 2.1-5). The analysis of Luke's description of Apollos will have to await just a little longer till after our presentation of the third view concerning Paul's relation with Apollos and Apollos' role in the dissensions. Nevertheless, we may point to one possible weakness concerning the alleged Paul's self-defense and Apollos' unintentional role, namely, that it is hard to state, on the one hand, that Paul defends his preaching style with the word about the cross in 1 Cor. 2.1-5 and then, on the other hand, to state that Apollos is not directly responsible for the fact that the Corinthians appreciated more Apollos' style as different from that of Paul. In other words, the moment one claims that Paul reasons theologically for his *modus operandi* it is impossible to argue that a different *modus operandi* based on rhetorical conventions (i.e., that of Apollos) is acceptable, unless one believes that 1 Corinthians 1–4 is truly a polemic against Apollos, a conjecture that we have already shown to be implausible.[22] If the cross requires the style of one's presentation to be in weakness, devoid of rhetorical eloquence, as Paul's, it is impossible to see how the cross would allow for a style that is powerful, conforming to contemporary standards of an accomplished orator, allegedly as Apollos'.

---

22 Some have advanced the claim that Paul's choice not to use sophistic rhetoric in preaching the gospel was particular to his mission to Corinth, because of the Corinthians' penchant for rhetoric, but elsewhere he did use rhetoric in order to persuade. See, e.g., Litfin, *Proclamation*, p. 242.

If Paul, however, does not defend himself against the more highly esteemed Apollos, then it is very probable that their styles of preaching were not that different.[23] Consequently, the problem that Paul points to in 1 Corinthians 1–4 is the Corinthians' overvaluation of rhetorical style, rather than the distinction between himself and Apollos.[24] This will become clear in our exegesis of 1 Cor. 3.5–4.5 and will be confirmed by Luke's account of Apollos' ministry. For now, the least we can do is to agree with Pickett that, 'Paul nowhere implicates either of them [i.e., Apollos and Cephas] so there is no reason to assume that they were in any way responsible for the quarreling that occurred in their names.'[25]

Apollos' Neutral Role in the Dissensions

The question of why Paul would bring up Apollos' name in his discussion of dissensions that resulted from a worldly evaluation of teachers based on sophistic rhetoric has received yet another answer from Kuck, namely that 'Paul chose to speak about Apollos as one case in point, the most visible example of the absurdity of playing one Christian teacher against another.'[26] He continues:

> Paul singles out Apollos as a case in point, an example of how two of the teachers whom the Corinthians are using as mascots to promote themselves and berate others do in fact not behave that way to each other. Perhaps Paul chose Apollos precisely because, having been with Paul in Ephesus and having been mentioned in the Corinthian letter to Paul, he is the example Paul can use with the most effectiveness.[27]

The effectiveness of the use of Apollos' name in Paul's argument for unity can be seen from the fact that Paul chose to speak of collaboration with one who functioned more as an independent missionary. Barnett, for instance, is correct to observe that 'Apollos is a freer agent than Paul's more direct associates were',[28] never being admitted into the inner circle of the apostle's intimates nor ever functioning as a messenger or agent of Paul. From the information provided by Luke in Acts 18, one can conclude that Apollos was not a convert of Paul nor 'had [he] ever been subject to Paul's tutelage.'[29] This independent spirit, 'untrammeled and

---

23   *Contra* Pogoloff, *LOGOS AND SOPHIA*, p. 196; Litfin, *Proclamation*, p. 228; Mitchell, *Reconciliation*, p. 213; Winter, *Philo and Paul among the Sophists*, p. 183; who argue that Apollos is somehow associated with the issue of rhetoric in Corinth.

24   Cf. Munck, *Paul and the Salvation of Mankind*, pp. 143–9, summarized by Dickerson, 'Apollos in Acts and First Corinthians', 14. *Contra* Barrett, 'Christianity at Corinth', 4.

25   Pickett, *The Cross in Corinth*, p. 49.

26   Kuck, *Judgment*, p. 161.

27   Ibid.

28   Barnett, 'Paul, Apologist to the Corinthians', 318. See also Wynne, *Apollos*, pp. 62–3.

29   Ibid., 319. See also Kuck, *Judgment*, p. 162.

unguided by any earthly superior authority',[30] seems to be confirmed by
what we read in 1 Cor. 16.12, a passage we will analyze shortly. Thus,
using the independent Apollos as an example of unity and collaboration
would have had a greater rhetorical effect in teaching the Corinthians the
lesson of unity. According to this view, then, Apollos had absolutely
nothing to do with the dissensions in Corinth; he functions only as an
example. Those who caused the dissensions, it is believed, remain
unnamed.[31] In order to evaluate such a view, however, we will have to
await especially the discussion of 1 Cor. 4.6, since this view is heavily
dependent on the meaning of the verb μετεσχημάτισα, and the reference
to these unnamed teachers in the use of the indefinite pronouns ἄλλος,
ἕκαστος and τις in 1 Cor. 3.5-17.

The three views then differ based on the combination of several factors:
(1) whether Paul and Apollos are colleagues or rivals based primarily on 1
Cor. 3.5–4.5 and 16.12; (2) whether the issue is Apollos' rhetoric or not
based primarily on Acts 18.24-28; (3) whether Apollos played any role or
not in the dissensions based on 1 Cor. 4.6. According to the first view,
Apollos is associated with rhetoric, μετεσχημάτισα suggests in a covert
way that Apollos was the primary target of Paul's arguments, and
therefore a rival of Paul. The second view argues that though Apollos is
associated with rhetoric he is nevertheless an ally/colleague of Paul. The
third view believes that Apollos should not be associated with rhetoric
and, even if he is, Paul's mention of Apollos is for exemplary purposes, the
meaning of μετεσχημάτισα showing in a cryptic way that Paul has in
mind unnamed teachers. Thus, in order to determine Paul's relation to
Apollos and Apollos' role in the dissensions we turn now to an analysis of
1 Cor. 16.12, Apollos' rhetorical skill in light of Acts 18.18-24, and the
meaning of μετεσχημάτισα in 1 Cor. 4.6.

Paul's Relation to Apollos according to 1 Cor. 16.12

First Corinthians 16.12 plays an important part in determining the type of
relation shared by Paul and Apollos.[32] In this verse Paul states: 'Now
concerning (περὶ δὲ) our brother Apollos: I have strongly urged (πολλὰ
παρεκάλεσα) him to come to you with the brothers and it was simply not
the will (πάντως οὐκ ἦν θέλημα) that he come now, but he will come when
a good opportunity presents itself (εὐκαιρήσῃ).' Several issues must be

30 Wynne, *Apollos*, p. 62.

31 For the view that others than the ones named in the slogans are responsible for the
dissensions in Corinth, see De Vos, *Church and Community Conflicts*, p. 220; Baird, '"One
against the Other"', 123; and Clarke, *Leadership in Corinth*, p. 107.

32 For details and different views on Paul's relation with Apollos based on inferences
from this verse see Dickerson, 'Apollos in Acts and First Corinthians', 86–101.

clarified in this verse in order to determine what it tells us about Paul's relation to Apollos. As already mentioned, περὶ δὲ in 1 Corinthians usually introduces a new topic.[33] Ker, however, disagrees and contends that with this introduction 'Paul is responding to one of a number of items of concern that the Corinthians have expressed.'[34] If the initiative of Apollos' return does not come from the Corinthians, Ker argues, then it is difficult to understand why Paul would even raise it at all.[35] But if the request comes from the Corinthians, Ker argues, 'The fact that Paul postpones his response to this request until the very end of the letter, and then deals with it quickly, is significant. It may be that the return of Apollos was high on the Corinthian agenda.'[36] Those who associate Apollos with rhetoric could very well argue that the reason Apollos was so highly esteemed by the Corinthians and was wanted back was because of his rhetorical skill.[37] Garland, however, responds to such a conjecture by rightly asking the following: 'If Apollos was so prominent in the minds of the Corinthians and semi-independent of Paul, one wonders, why did they not write directly to Apollos instead of to Paul?' He responds: 'It may be the case that they made no inquiry about Apollos in their letter, and Paul simply anticipates their disappointment that Apollos had not returned and averts any suspicion that somehow he had prevented him from returning.'[38] Thus, not much should be made concerning this introductory formula.

Another issue that needs clarifying concerning the relationship between Paul and Apollos is that of the language of ἀδελφός which Paul uses to refer to Apollos. Ker contends again that this 'designation of Apollos sounds somewhat stark' when contrasted to 'Paul's commendatory language about Timothy, Stephanus, Fortunatus, and Achaicus.'[39] One wonders, however, whether such designation is 'stark' since Paul uses the same appellation in referring to his intimate co-workers even in the immediate context and 'refers to Timothy without *any* designation.'[40] Moreover, Thiselton notes that ' "brother" can include not only *friend*, but also *colleague, fellow Christian, co-worker*, or *associate*, and *which* is not specified.'[41] This is not to say that Apollos was part of Paul's inner

33 Mitchell, 'Concerning περὶ δὲ in 1 Cor', 229–56.
34 Ker, 'Paul and Apollos', 94. See also Robertson and Plummer, *First Corinthians*, p. 392; Fee, *First Corinthians*, p. 824; Barrett, *First Corinthians*, p. 391; and Barnett, 'Paul, Apologist to the Corinthians', 318.
35 Ker, 'Paul and Apollos', 94, n. 71. See also Fee, *First Corinthians*, p. 824.
36 Ibid., 94.
37 E.g., Witherington, *Conflict and Community in Corinth*, p. 313.
38 Garland, *1 Corinthians*, p. 761, following Schrage, *Der erste Brief*, 3.446.
39 Ker, 'Paul and Apollos', 95.
40 Garland, *1 Corinthians*, p. 762 (author's emphasis).
41 Thiselton, *First Corinthians*, 1333 (author's emphasis).

circle of colleagues, but neither was he a rival or antagonist of Paul.[42] This designation seems to point to the fact that there was no animosity between the two missionaries and that the designation should be taken at face value rather than conjure that the reference 'lacks any degree of Pauline personal warmth.'[43]

The third item that needs clarification is Paul's strongly urging Apollos to visit the Corinthians[44] and the reason he gives for Apollos' delay – 'it was simply not the will.'[45] Ker infers from this verse that, 'The very fact that Paul must urge Apollos to return rather than simply send him indicates that Paul recognized that Apollos was not under his authority. Apollos' resistance to Paul's urge to join others of his mission may indicate that he was cautious of becoming over-identified with it.'[46] Those who see in the Corinthian *ecclesia* an overvaluation of rhetoric and thus a higher esteem of Apollos reason that Apollos' reluctance to return may be due to the fact that his visit at this time could have led to exacerbating division in the church.[47] Ker, however, notes that in this case the wiser decision would have been for Apollos to 'accompany a clearly Pauline delegation, or indeed Paul himself, rather than opt out.'[48] Even so, Ker's suggestion that Paul's 'lack of further explanation leaves Apollos, not Paul, open to misunderstanding and criticism. . . . The overall effect [being] to cast Apollos into the shadows', thus undermining him,[49] goes beyond what the text allows us to state with confidence. Thus, as Garland

42 So Kuck, *Judgment*, p. 163.

43 Ker, 'Paul and Apollos', 76.

44 For the meaning of πολλά as 'strongly' or 'earnestly' rather than 'repeatedly' see Thiselton, *First Corinthians*, p. 1333; Garland, *First Corinthians*, p. 762; Louw-Nida 1.684 (78.3). *Contra* Collins, *First Corinthians*, p. 598.

45 Whose 'will' is referred to here (Apollos' or God's) is impossible to determine. Garland, *1 Corinthians*, p. 762, may be right in stating that, 'Paul may be deliberately ambiguous to avoid hurting feelings.' We incline, however, to believe that the reference is most likely to Apollos' will, given the context. See a different view in Paul Ellingworth and Howard A. Hatton, *A Handbook on Paul's First Letter to the Corinthians*, (USBHS: Helps for Translators; New York: UBS, 1995), p. 377.

46 Ker, 'Paul and Apollos', 95.

47 Cf. Calvin, *1 Corinthians* 10.2, p. 75. See also Robertson and Plummer, *First Corinthians*, p. 393; Barrett, *First Corinthians*, p. 392; Fee, *First Corinthians*, p. 824; Witherington, *Conflict and Community in Corinth*, pp. 87, 317; Thiselton, *First Corinthians*, p. 33; W. D. Thomas, 'New Testament Characters: Apollos', *ExpTim* 95 (1984) 245–246 (246).

48 Ker, 'Paul and Apollos', 96. *Contra* Fee, *First Corinthians*, p. 825, who comments that it would not have been wise to send Apollos, especially if Paul's authority suffered as a result of the more appreciated Apollos. See also Horrell, *The Social Ethos of the Corinthian Correspondence*, p. 113.

49 Ibid. The same negative tone is argued for also by Barnett, 'Paul, Apologist to the Corinthians', 318.

concludes, 'Since there is so little evidence to go on, caution is advised before giving free rein to the imagination.'[50]

In this sense, Fee draws out a more cautious conclusion from this verse. He states that 'this is sure evidence that Paul did not consider Apollos himself responsible for the trouble that is addressed in chaps. 1–4 … From Paul's point of view there is no rivalry between them.'[51] Barrett, though he disagrees with the view, comments that 'they may well be right who see in Apollos' disinclination to visit Corinth again a delicacy of sentiment that made him unwilling to appear even unintentionally in the character of a rival.'[52] In conclusion, this verse, if it says anything about the relation between Paul and Apollos, seems to speak of it in positive terms. It presents both Paul and Apollos as independent, on the one hand, yet mutually approving of each other's labors.[53] One cannot, however, conclude based on Apollos' inopportune time to visit the Corinthians that there was a tension between Paul and Apollos. Even so, the information in this verse is inconclusive for constructing a solid hypothesis concerning Paul's relation to Apollos. Apollos' role in the dissensions and his relation to Paul must remain vague, if limited to the information provided in this verse, and therefore we must look elsewhere for clues. One such text may be Acts 18.24-28.

Apollos' Rhetoric according to Acts 18.24-28

It is argued that Acts 18.24-28 provides that clearest information concerning the different *modus operandi* of Paul and Apollos in the Corinthian church, a difference that is believed to be the essential cause of dissensions to which Paul responds in 1 Corinthians 1–4.[54] The argument is that Luke describes Apollos as using words that have rhetorical connotations, such as ἀνὴρ λόγιος, and δυνατός, corroborated with the fact that Apollos is from Alexandria, known as a city of great education. We have already seen how inadequate the hypothesis is that Apollos' upbringing in Alexandria means that he exposed a Philonic type of wisdom since Philo himself was from Alexandria. Munck's observation is appropriate in putting an end to such suspicions:

> From the Alexandrian origin people draw conclusions about his philosophy and allegorizing; but they have firmly shut their eyes to the uncertainty involved in that method of drawing conclusions. One can quite well be a Jew and come from Alexandria without being

---

50 Garland, *1 Corinthians*, p. 762.
51 Fee, *First Corinthians*, p. 824. See also Kuck, *Judgment*, p. 163.
52 Barrett, 'Christianity at Corinth', 4. See also Wynne, *Apollos*, p. 47.
53 Cf. Wynne, *Apollos*, p. 71.
54 See, e.g., Litfin, *Proclamation*, pp. 240–2.

influenced by the allegorical interpretation of scripture and the Hellenistic Jewish philosophy that flourished in that city. ... As a rule it is rash to try to infer too much from the fact of a person's coming from a certain town. Nothing therefore can be quoted about Apollos to make it likely that he was striving for wisdom in the way that – as Paul thought – the Greeks strove for worldly wisdom.[55]

The question remains, however, as to whether Luke makes an effort to describe Apollos as not only trained in rhetoric but also employing it in his proclamation, thus indicating that his *modus operandi* was different from that of Paul. Pogoloff, for instance, states that, 'Although any speculation about Alexandrian origins is risky, we are on much firmer ground when we assume that any educated Alexandrian was well trained in rhetoric.'[56] Winter, likewise, gives a positive answer to his question: 'Is there evidence from the background and the *modus operandi* of Apollos to confirm that the congregational party spirit and desire to emulate former teachers had been culturally determined by the sophistic movement in that city?'[57] Winter is probably the most insistent on the fact that Apollos' description in Acts points convincingly to Apollos' skill and use of rhetoric in preaching, which forms the basis for the dissensions in Corinth.

Others are not so quick to accept such view. For instance, Litfin, who also argues for a rhetorical background to the dissensions in the Corinthian church, claims that 'Acts supplies inadequate grounds for concluding that Apollos depended upon the persuasive dynamic of Greco-Roman rhetoric in his preaching ... It would require moving beyond our evidence to conclude that Apollos depended in any full-fledged way in Corinth upon the dynamic of Greco-Roman rhetoric.'[58] Still, this does not exclude the possibility, according to some, that Apollos' description included 'at least a certain rhetorical ability.'[59]

Which of these views is correct: (1) Luke describes Apollos as a rhetorically skilled preacher who uses his skill in preaching, this leading to the dissensions in Corinth; (2) it is possible that the description of Apollos in Acts to have rhetorical connotations, but that says hardly anything

---

55   Munck, *Paul and the Salvation of Mankind*, pp. 143 and 144 respectively. See also Barrett, 'Christianity at Corinth', 4; Kuck, *Judgment*, p. 162; Barrett, *Acts*, 2.886 *Contra*, e.g., Barnett, 'Paul, Apologist to the Corinthians', 316.

56   Pogoloff, *LOGOS AND SOPHIA*, p. 181. Philo is a good example. See Pogoloff's references to J. Leopold, 'Philo's Knowledge of Rhetorical Theory', in *Two Treatises of Philo of Alexandria* (D. Winson and J. Dillon, Brown, eds.; JS, 25; Chico: Scholars Press, 1983), 129; Manuel Alexandre Jr., 'Rhetorical Argumentation as an Exegetical Technique in Philo of Alexandria', in *Hellenica et Judaica* (A. Caquot, M. Hadas-Lebel, and J. Riaud, eds.; Paris: Peeters, 1986), 21–25.

57   Winter, *Philo and Paul among the Sophists*, p. 177.

58   Litfin, *Proclamation*, p. 242. See also Ker, 'Paul and Apollos', 79.

59   Kuck, *Judgment*, p. 162, following Meeks, *Enmity at Corinth*, p. 61.

about the dissensions in Corinth; or (3) the terminology is not rhetorical and therefore has no bearing on the situation in the Corinthian congregation? In order to determine with precision which of these views is correct, we must carry out a study of the three phrases that describe Apollos' ministry in Corinth according to Luke: ἀνὴρ λόγιος, δυνατός, and ἐπιδείκνυμι.

The verb ἐπιδείκνυμι, according to several lexicons, is used in Acts 18.28 in a figurative sense meaning 'to prove, to demonstrate, or to show that something is true',[60] in our case by appeal to Scripture (διὰ τῶν γραφῶν). It is used usually in judicial rhetoric possibly as in Acts 25.7 where the verb is used in a legal context ('charges which they could not prove').

The adjective δυνατός, as we have already seen in our exegesis of 1 Cor. 2.1-5, can have the rhetorical meaning of 'powerful eloquence' especially in a context dealing with public speech, as is the case with Acts 18 describing Apollos' preaching.[61] Nevertheless, as we have argued in Chapter 2, that he was δυνατὸς ἐν ταῖς γραφαῖς does not single him out necessarily (especially in contrast to Paul), since preaching in the early church (cf. Acts) implied extensive knowledge of the Old Testament which served for proving the messianic character of Jesus.[62] The rhetorical connotations of these two terms thus allow the *possibility* of Apollos being described as a speaker that used the means of rhetorical persuasion known in his day. What seems to move the argument from the description of Apollos as merely allowing the possibility of rhetorical connotations to actually demonstrating it is the phrase ἀνὴρ λόγιος. According to Winter, for instance, 'the collocation [i.e., ἀνὴρ λόγιος] is clearly connected with rhetoric',[63] which would seem to indicate, he maintains, that 'Luke intends the reader to understand that Apollos is trained in rhetoric and makes use of it during his ministry in Corinth.'[64]

The description ἀνὴρ λόγιος usually means 'learned man' (cf. Plutarch, *Thes.* 3.2.7; Strabo, *Geogr.* 14.1.42.21), though it could also mean 'eloquent man' in a rhetorical context (cf. Plutarch, *Cic.* 49.5).[65] As we have argued in Chapter 3, tertiary-level education in Paul's day meant training in rhetoric.[66] Pogoloff then concludes: 'Given the context of

60 BDAG 370; Balz and Schneider, *EDNT*, 2.25; Louw-Nida 1.672 (72.5); LSJ 629.

61 See, e.g., Pogoloff, *LOGOS AND SOPHIA*, pp. 182–3.

62 Cf. Litfin, *Proclamation*, p. 242. So also Paul Ellingworth, *The Epistle to the Hebrews: A Commentary on the Greek Text* (NIGNT; Grand Rapids: Eerdmans, 1993), p. 21.

63 Winter, *Philo and Paul among the Sophists*, p. 178. He makes reference to Philo, *Cher.* 116; *Mut.* 220; *Post.* 53, 162; *Legat.* 142, 237, 310; *Mos.* 1.2, 23; *Virt.* 174; Plato, *Leg.* 656d, 799a, 819a.

64 Ibid., pp. 178, n. 171.

65 We performed a *TLG* search of the exact phrase ἀνὴρ λόγιος which resulted in a total of 15 references.

66 See Pogoloff, *LOGOS AND SOPHIA*, p. 181; and Barrett, *Acts*, 2.887.

preaching, Luke certainly seems to be referring to rhetorical ability.'[67] Litfin concurs when he states: 'It is undeniable that by this description Luke is seeking to emphasize the erudition of Apollos and in particular his eloquence and forcefulness as a speaker.'[68]

With this understanding of Apollos, Winter takes the leap and suggests that Apollos' rhetoric must have been the cause of dissensions in the Corinthian *ecclesia*. Dunn argues, 'It is an easy step of the historical imagination to identify those rebuked consistently throughout 1.17–3.23 for their false evaluation of wisdom and clever speech with Apollos or with an Apollos faction,'[69] and that is what Winter does. He states:

> The three terms [ἀνὴρ λόγιος, δυνατός, and ἐπιδείκνυμι] have rhetorical connotations, so that the Acts' account of Apollos would have conveyed to the readers that this Christian Jew from Alexandria depended on his rhetorical skill in his open συζήτησις with the Jews. Thus the rivalry in the congregation – which pitted Paul against Apollos – and Apollos' rejecting the request for his own return become clearer when seen against the latter's background.[70]

Given these descriptions of Apollos by Luke in Acts 18.18-24, it seems that we have only two options regarding their interpretation and implications for the Corinthian dissensions. First, one could infer with Winter and others from the rhetorical connotations of the terms used to describe Apollos' preaching ministry in Corinth that his distinct *modus operandi* that relied heavily on persuasion by means of sophistic rhetoric was the cause of dissensions among the Corinthian Christians. Especially the elite may have been attracted to Apollos' eloquent preaching, since this reflected their own status. Second, one could argue that even though such terms have rhetorical connotations, this would not imply that Apollos used the sophistic rhetoric against which Paul argues in 1 Corinthians 1–4.[71] That this second option is more viable is supported by the fact that Apollos' preaching is done in a Jewish, not a Hellenistic context, though we have argued that the average citizen of the Greco-Roman culture (including Jews) would have been familiar with sophistic rhetoric, especially public declamations. But Munck may be right that '[n]othing therefore can be quoted about Apollos to make it likely that he was striving for wisdom in the way that – as Paul thought – the Greeks strove for worldly wisdom.'[72] Moreover, there is no reason to doubt the

---

67   Ibid.

68   Litfin, *Proclamation*, p. 240.

69   Dunn, *1 Corinthians*, p. 30.

70   Winter, *Philo and Paul among the Sophists*, p. 178. See also Barnett, 'Paul, Apologist to the Corinthians', 325.

71   See esp. Litfin, *Proclamation*, p. 242.

72   Munck, *Paul and the Salvation of Mankind*, p. 144.

truthfulness of Luke's statement that Apollos 'was of great use (συνεβάλετο πολύ) to those [i.e., Corinthians] who by grace had believed' (Acts 18.27).[73] That Paul's and Apollos' *modus operandi* did not differ enough to cause the dissensions in the Corinthian church so that Paul had to argue against sophistic rhetoric (allegedly used by Apollos) is confirmed also by 1 Cor. 3.5–4.5 which describes the two missionaries in congenial terms though performing different functions in the church.

Paul and Apollos in 1 Corinthians 3.5–4.5

We have already conducted a detailed exegesis of 1 Cor. 3.5–4.5 in Chapter 1 of this work, so we will only summarize the important points here and move the discussion further by focusing on key issues in the text that have to do with the relationship between Paul and Apollos. According to our exegesis of the text, we have argued that Paul's purpose in this passage is to show the Corinthians how their teachers should be viewed properly, an issue that is closely related to the rise of dissensions. In the process of arguing for a proper evaluation of teachers, Paul makes several important observations.

First, he seeks to make it clear that the role of the judge is solely the prerogative of God, who will carry it out in the eschatological judgment. The Corinthians have no right to judge their teachers, Paul would argue, because the teachers are given by God, thus being accountable only to him as their employer. God will pass the final verdict and determine their pay and not the human public. Human evaluation is premature, πρὸ καίρου (1 Cor. 4.5). Thus, allegiance to human teachers based on worldly evaluation is misplaced; the Corinthians should instead be saying, 'We all belong to God.'

Second, Paul describes himself and the other teachers in servile terms, thus in contrast to the personality cult and the foolish veneration of the apostles as heroes by the Corinthians. Contrasted to the menial roles that the apostles have, Paul points to the superior and ultimate role of God in the formation of the community. Christ is the foundation, and everything else is secondary, though necessary.[74] By describing the teachers in such 'shameful' and 'despised' terminology, Paul seeks to take away from the Corinthians any grounds for boasting with them.

---

73 For the meaning of συνεβάλετο meaning 'contribute, help, give support' see the references in LSJ 1674: Antiphon 5.79; Plato, *Leg.* 905b; Demonsthenes 21.133; and BDAG 956: Philo, *Migr.* 219; Justin, *Didache* 46; Epitectus *Or.* 3.22.78; Josephus, *A.J.* 12.312; Tatian 24.1.

74 See Thiselton, *First Corinthians*, p. 310, quoted in Chapter 2.

Third, by implication, the teachers as servants of God are not only one but also equal, despite their distinct roles. This harmonious service to God undercuts the elevation of one over another. Kuck rightly draws out the implication: 'to latch onto the individual differences among the Lord's servants in an attempt to make the church a battleground for status is to overlook the fact that there is but one status in the church – servant of the Lord.'[75]

One question that we have raised concerning the equality yet distinction between roles in our exegesis of this passage and in our discussion of the supposed apologetic nature of Paul's argument in 1 Corinthians 1–4 is whether or not Paul seeks to covertly elevate himself above Apollos by assigning to himself the pioneering role of 'planting' and laying down the foundation as a 'skilled master builder'. Barnett may be quoted here as representative of those who give a positive answer to this question:

> The impact of 1 Cor 3–4 is twofold. On the one hand, Paul affirms that Apollos is with him both a συνεργός of God and a διάκονος 'through whom' the Corinthians have believed. Yet, on the other hand, there is not question that Paul has the priority over Apollos. In the agricultural image Paul planted and Apollos fulfilled the subsidiary role, watering. In the architectural image Paul is the foundation-layer but no role is attributed to Apollos. More to the point though they may have 'countless guides' Paul is their sole 'father.' In short, Paul is 'the planter,' 'the foundation layer' and 'the father' with Apollos playing a lesser role in each case. With great diplomacy Paul manages to relegate a subsidiary role to Apollos while not dis-affirming his ministry and thereby bringing continuing division in Corinth.[76]

It would seem, then, that by describing himself as the 'architect', Paul would subordinate all other roles under his. In order to answer this question we must first remember that Paul's emphasis is a theocentric one. According to Paul, what is crucial in the formation of the Christian community is not the preacher, but the one preached.[77] The Corinthians' problem was precisely the fact that they were thinking in terms of personalities (τίς) rather than functions (τί). Second, we have argued that Paul's purpose in this first rhetorical unit is not primarily apologetic but conciliatory; the imagery of the father is thus not used by Paul to reassert his authority. Third, the role of the ancient architect is an ambivalent one. Lanci rightly contends that the architect

---

75 Kuck, *Judgment*, p. 170.
76 Barnett, 'Paul, Apologist to the Corinthians', 317. See also Hyldahl, 'Paul and Apollos', 68–82; and Ker, 'Paul and Apollos', 75–97.
77 Cf. Garland, *1 Corinthians*, p. 115; Schrage, *Der erste Brief*, 1.298.

... was in control of the project in some respects, but was still a servant
of his patrons and donors. Paul never claims to be the founder or patron
of the community ... It is possible that Paul intends to claim a certain
special responsibility as the ἀρχιτέκτων ... Nevertheless ..., Paul is not
the designer of the structure, nor can he claim the status or influence of
a donor. The ambiguity of the architect's role, fits well the situation of a
missionary apostle ...[78]

Thus, it is inappropriate to draw conclusions of superiority based solely
on the meaning of 'master builder', since the emphasis in the context is on
God and his servants.[79] Moreover, the issue of Paul's superiority over
Apollos is drawn from a faulty understanding of the referent of the
indefinite pronouns in this text, an issue to be addressed shortly.

Another question we have raised in Chapter 1 is the purpose of the
distinction between construction materials and the outcome of the final
judgment. Since Paul makes a clear distinction between the quality of
materials (i.e., imperishable vs. perishable) that points to a distinction in
judgment (i.e., reward vs. barely saved and destroyed), one may infer that
Paul's purpose is to warn the teachers to watch how they build, since the
foundation is none other than Jesus Christ and the construction is none
other than the Temple of God in which the Holy Spirit dwells. There will
come a Day of reckoning, when the quality of their work will be tested by
fire to determine its compatibility with the enduring foundation, who is
Jesus Christ. He likewise warns the Corinthians of their secular perception
of the Christian *ecclesia*. Paul's emphasis is on the unique entity of the
Christian *ecclesia* as distinct from any secular and civic assemblies; it is
God's alternative to the secular Corinth. But the Corinthians were in
danger of reducing God's Temple to nothing but a means of enhancing
their personal status and increasing their own honor. Paul thus warns the
Corinthians against their destructive boasting in and evaluation of
teachers according to secular criteria of wisdom.

The warning implicit in Paul's discussion in this passage raises the
question of the identity of the ones to whom the warning is extended.
There are various opinions among commentators concerning the identity
of the person(s) behind the indefinite pronouns in these verses (i.e., ἄλλος
in v. 10; ἕκαστος in vv. 10, 13; and τις in vv. 12, 14, 15):[80] (1) Peter; (2)
Apollos and his followers; (3) unnamed teachers; or (4) the entire
Corinthian congregation. Goulder and Barrett are the main recent
advocates of the opinion that Paul has in view here Peter by the use of the

78 Lanci, *Temple*, p. 78.

79 The same is true regarding the planting and watering metaphors; see Dickerson,
'Apollos in Acts and First Corinthians', 113f.

80 See Dybvad, 'Imitation and Gospel in First Corinthians', 150–52, for different views
and their advocates.

indefinite pronouns.[81] Of course, much of the reason they propose such an interpretation is because of the belief that the background of the concept of σοφία is Hellenistic Jewish Wisdom, something that we have shown to be an inadequate explanation in Chapter 2. Following Barrett, Goulder argues that the 'another' who builds on the foundation laid by Paul is Cephas. He states: 'It has been thought [by Barrett] that there may be a polemical contrast here with claims that Cephas, as his name implies, was the true rock of the Church, with or without the support of Matt 16.18.'[82] He goes on to state that this is 'a plausible suggestion.' A plausible case could be made from the sequence of the names in 1 Cor. 3.22 – Paul, Apollos, Cephas – as being represented earlier in 1 Cor. 3.10 (Paul – laying the foundation), 1 Cor. 3.5-9 (Apollos – watering), and 1 Cor. 3.10-15 (Cephas – building upon the foundation).[83] The burden of the case, however, lies on the interpretation of the verb μετεσχημάτισα in 1 Cor. 4.6, and therefore a final response will have to await our study of the meaning of the word below. We may also point to the fact that the critique that follows against the view that Apollos is the referent is somewhat applicable to this view also.[84]

Ker is among the more recent advocates of the view that Paul constructs in this passage a polemic against Apollos and his followers,[85] but, as we have already mentioned, Paul is forced to do it in a more subtle way given the volatile situation. Thus, he argues, even though Paul may point to unity among himself and Apollos, 'this unity is not the last word'; distinction is.[86] The distinction is presumably seen in the various materials used for construction and in the wages they receive according to the labor of each. He also contends that 'it would make no sense to introduce a different personality here', since the discussion has been about Paul and Apollos.[87]

81 Goulder, 'ΣΟΦΙΑ in 1 Corinthians', 519; *idem, Paul and the Competing Mission at Corinth*, pp. 21–3; Barrett, *First Corinthians*, pp. 87–8; See also Bruce, *1 and 2 Corinthians*, p. 43.

82 Goulder, 'ΣΟΦΙΑ in 1 Corinthians', 519–20, referring to Barrett, *First Corinthians*, pp. 87–8.

83 Barrett, 'Cephas and Corinth'. Barrett also reads the Jewish dimension of the problems in 2 Corinthians into 1 Corinthians, something we have shown to be inappropriate given the distinct exigencies that led to the writing of the two letters. Goulder, *Paul and the Competing Mission in Corinth*, p. 17.

84 For a rebuttal of the proposal that this is a warning directed toward Peter, see Munck, *Paul and the Salvation of Mankind*, pp. 141–2.

85 Ker, 'Paul and Apollos', 84. See also Sellin, 'Das "Geheimnis" der Weisheit und das Rätsel der 'Christuspartei,' 75–76; and Smit, 'Search for Coherence' 242, who argues that priority in time means priority in status. See Hurd, *The Origin of 1 Corinthians*, p. 98, who also places a great emphasis on the chronological sequence.

86 Ibid., 86.

87 Ibid., 89. Thiselton, *First Corinthians*, p. 309, n. 54, seems to be sympathetic to the idea that the referent includes Apollos. He follows Grosheide, *First Corinthians*, p. 84.

One objection to such interpretation is actually acknowledged by Ker and those who see in these verses a polemic against Apollos, namely, that Paul speaks here in the present tense, thus it cannot refer directly to Apollos since he was already gone (nor to Cephas for that matter).[88] Thus Ker is somewhat willing to adjust his view and identify the referent with Apollos' supporters, though Apollos is still considered responsible for the divisions.[89] Schrage, however, states generally: 'Vor allem v. 12 zeigt, dass dabei nicht bloss Apollos oder gar Petrus, sondern jeder andere gemeint ist, der in den von Paulus gegründeten Gemeinden wirkt. Nicht von ungefähr folgt auf ἄλλος in v. 10 das allgemeine ἕκαστος.'[90]

The problem with those who limit the reference to a person, whether Apollos or Cephas, is that they tend to take v. 11 as a polemic, but as Kuck points out, 'in verses 11 and 12–15 Paul speaks only of those who build upon the one foundation not those who lay a different foundation.'[91] Thiselton also points to the fact that Paul and Apollos are spoken of in this text as 'perform[ing] complementary not competitive tasks.'[92]

It is harder to determine with precision which of the latter two views is more valid: unnamed teachers or the Corinthians. Hall may be right that '[t]he fact that ἄλλος and ἕκαστος are parallel words indicates that ἄλλος is used in a generic sense. It does refer to one particular other person but to other people in general,'[93] though he prefers to identify them with Apollos-type figures and with the 'super-apostles' of 2 Corinthians 10–13. Kuck also agrees with the generic sense, though he extends the reference to all the Corinthians. He states: 'It would seem that Paul in 3.10-15 is intentionally vague and expects his readers to apply what he says to all their teachers and in an extended sense to themselves as participants in God's work of building.'[94] If that is the case, the question is why Paul chose Apollos as his counterpart in this section and not the more

---

88   Ibid. See also Fee, *First Corinthians*, p. 136; Witherington, *Conflict and Community in Corinth*, p. 133; Hyldahl, 'Paul and Apollos', 72. Ker, 'Paul and Apollos', 89, takes the present to be a vivid present because Apollos will return (16.12) but, as Garland, *1 Corinthians*, p. 115, observes, this 'seems to be special pleading'.

89   See, e.g., Hyldhal, 'Paul and Apollos', 80.

90   Schrage, *Der erste Brief*, 1.295.

91   Kuck, *Judgment*, p. 172.

92   Thiselton, *First Corinthians*, p. 1332.

93   Hall, *Unity*, p. 8. Wolff, *Der erste Brief*, p. 71, urges also that 'Paul does not intend any specific person by ἄλλος.'

94   Kuck, *Judgment*, p. 172. Garland, *1 Corinthians*, p. 115, agrees: 'Paul is not aiming his remarks toward Apollos or any other apostle or their presumed supporters.' Fee, *First Corinthians*, pp. 138 and 139, seems to side with this position also. See also Dodd, *Paul's Paradigmatic "I"*, p. 57. *Contra* Ker, 'Paul and Apollos', 88, who thinks that this option 'is hardly possible since it would confuse the metaphor: the Corinthians can hardly be both the building and the builders.'

important figure, Peter. Litfin gives an initial answer that will have to be further explored shortly:

> With Christ the argument becomes grotesque while with Peter it becomes merely impossible to comprehend. The function of 3.18-21 with all its overtones of 1.18–2.5 would be unintelligible if it appeared in a section which centered upon a contrast between Paul and the former fisherman. In the argument of 3.4–4.5 as it stands, Apollos was the only plausible option.[95]

An initial response, then, to the referent of the indefinite pronouns, could be that they point to teachers other than Apollos, but there is no reason to assume that it excludes Apollos.[96] Those who tend to argue that the indefinite pronouns refer to unnamed teachers, possibly Apollos-type figures, usually base their view on the meaning of the verb μετεσχημάτισα and the interpretation of the verse. Therefore, we will turn last to an assessment of the meaning of μετεσχημάτισα and its importance for the discussion of Apollos and Paul in 1 Cor. 3.5–4.5.

The Meaning of μετεσχημάτισα *in 1 Corinthians 4.6*

First Corinthians 4.6 is a key verse for understanding Paul's argument in 1 Cor. 3.5–4.5 or even of the entire first rhetorical unit.[97] Unfortunately, two important statements in this verse (i.e., Ταῦτα δὲ μετεσχημάτισα εἰς ἐμαυτόν καὶ Ἀπολλῶν δι᾽ ὑμᾶς and ἵνα ἐν ἡμῖν μάθητε τὸ μὴ ὑπὲρ ἃ γέγραπται) 'have tended to conceal more than they reveal.'[98] In this verse Paul presents the purpose for which Paul's and Apollos' names were mentioned particularly in 1 Cor. 3.5–4.5: ἵνα μὴ εἷς ὑπὲρ τοῦ ἑνὸς φυσιοῦσθε κατὰ τοῦ ἑτέρου. Paul's discussion of himself and Apollos had been to deflating the Corinthians' boasting with teachers, which was the result of comparing one teacher against the other, leading thus to dissensions. Thus, even from this purposeful statement one can see that

---

95 Litfin, *Proclamation*, p. 228.

96 Cf. Dickerson, 'Apollos in Acts and First Corinthians', 117.

97 In Chapter 2 we argued that ταῦτα may refer to everything that has been said beginning with 1.10, but no doubt points back to at least the previous major section where Paul discusses the role of the apostles and the inappropriateness of judging their ministry. Regardless of how far the reference should be pushed, it is clear that 1.10-3.4 at least lays the foundation for what is said in 3.5-4.5, and therefore cannot be neglected. Fitzgerald, *Cracks in an Earthen Vessel*, p. 120, n 13; Dodd, *Paul's Paradigmatic "I"*, p. 45; Robertson and Plummer, *First Corinthians*, p. 80; Fee, *First Corinthians*, 165; Kuck, *Judgment*, pp. 210–11; Vos, 'Der μετασχηματισμός in 1 Kor 4.6', 154–72; and Wolff, *Der erste Brief*, p. 84, limit the reference only to 3.5-4.5. Most commentators however extend the reference all the way to 1.10. See, *inter alia*, Thiselton, *First Corinthians*, p. 348; and Fiore, '"Covert Allusion"', 94.

98 J. Ross Wagner, '"Not Beyond the Things which Are Written": A Call to Boast Only in the Lord (1 Cor. 4.6)', *NTS* 44 (1998) 279–87 (275).

Paul's intention in discussing himself and Apollos had not been in order to attack Apollos and his followers; it was rather for paraenetic purposes (δι᾽ ὑμᾶς – 'for your benefit').[99] If the purpose of using Apollos' name is thus not polemical but pastoral, the question remains as to how he uses the names. There are basically three views concerning the meaning of the verb μετεσχημάτισα:[100] (1) the rhetorical technique of 'covert allusion' – λόγος ἐσχηματισμένος; (2) 'to illustrate' or 'to exemplify'; and (3) the common usage of 'to change the form of something into something else'–'in place of'.

The first view has already been introduced in Chapter 1 of this work. There we pointed out that Fiore argues that the purpose of using such a rhetorical technique was for avoiding direct confrontation and public shaming of people of high status.[101]

The weakness of Fiore's argument, as we have seen, as well as of those who see in the use of the verb μετεσχημάτισα a reference to the ancient rhetorical device of λόγος ἐσχηματισμένος, is the fact that Paul speaks quite openly about the issue of divisions and directly critiques the Corinthians for their partisan spirit (cf. 1 Cor. 3.1-4). Moreover, 1 Cor. 4.6 seems to uncover that which Paul, allegedly, kept covered in order to avoid offending his listeners.[102] Thus, to say that Paul uses σχῆμα at first and then exposes his intention is to deny the very nature of such device. Paul may be indirect in 1 Cor. 1.18-2.16, but he is not using σχῆμα. Anderson is right to note that 'it is simply not enough to note that use is made of various figures in chapters one to four which *could* be used in a

---

99   Cf. Kuck, *Judgment*, p. 210.

100   For a survey of views see Thiselton, *First Corinthians*, pp. 348–51.

101   Fiore, '"Covert Allusion"', 89. For a discussion of this rhetorical device, see Quintilian, *Inst.* 9.1-2 who uses the phrase *solum schema*; Ps.-Demetrius, *On Style* 287–89; Philostratus, *Vit. soph.* 561; See also Fitzgerald, *Cracks in an Earthen Vessel*, pp. 224–6; Barrett, *First Corithians*, pp. 105–6; Heinrici, *Der erste Brief*, pp. 146–7. Fiore also claims that Paul uses such device not 'out of fear for his *asphaleia* (for he inevitably makes his charges clear), but out of *euprepeia* and with respect for the dignity of the persons charged with faults' (p. 95). See also Lampe, 'Theological Wisdom and the "Word About the Cross"', 117–31. The difference between Fiore and Lampe is that Fiore argues that the covert way of speech is seen in the use of figures of speech while Lampe suggests that the covert way is the indirect way of addressing the issue of divisions by addressing a secondary topic, namely wisdom. Both, however, claim that Paul is using the ancient rhetorical device. Others who agree with them are: F. H. Colson, 'Μετεσχημάτισα 1 Cor. 4.6', *JTS* 17 (1916) 379–84; Collins, *First Corinthians*, p. 176; Winter, *Philo and Paul among the Sophists*, pp. 196–8, builds on Fiore's article and argues that 'Paul mingles irony with this rhetorical device' (p. 197).

102   Vos, 'Der μετασχηματισμός in 1 Kor 4.6', also believes that if 4.6 refers to the putting on of a mask, it also takes off the mask, contrary to the nature of figurative language. Hall, *Unity*, p. 24, however objects in saying that Paul does not fully take off the mask in 4.6, since he still uses the indefinite terms ὁ εἷς and ὁ ἕτερος.

style of 'covert allusion'. It needs to be demonstrated that such figures are indeed used in this way.'[103]

Moreover, Fiore's argument is based on the use of the words σχῆμα and σχῆμα τίζω and not on the compound verb μετασχηματίζω.[104] As we will see, in its common use μετασχηματίζω never means 'to transform *something* by way of a (covert) figure' or 'to say something with the help of a figure of speech.'[105] When Quintilian speaks of the rhetorical technique to which Fiore makes reference, he uses the simple form σχηματίζω, where σχῆμα means 'figure of speech'. Had Paul used this form of the verb, he would have pointed back to the figures of speech he had used throughout the first four chapters, especially the figures of gardeners, builders, and stewards. This, in fact, is what Morna Hooker argues. She contends that '[i]t is the metaphor and not the outward appearance of Paul, which had been varied, and the εἰς indicates that the changing images have been applied to Paul and Apollos. The meaning seems to be: "I have applied these figures of speech to myself and Apollos." '[106] Hooker does acknowledge that this is an unusual meaning for the verb μετασχηματίζω, 'not used in this sense elsewhere', yet she believes that Paul's usage with this sense is legitimate, given the fact that σχῆμα and σχηματίζω can be used of figures of speech. But, as Anderson rightly argues, 'the prefix μετά implies a *change* from one form to another', where σχῆμα does not have the meaning of figure of speech.[107] Thus, if the basic meaning of the verb is 'to change' or 'to transform', the translation 'I have changed these figures of speech into Paul and Apollos' does not make sense.[108] The 'change' cannot be from metaphor to metaphor, but most likely from people to people.[109]

Given the uniqueness in ancient Greek texts of taking the verb μετασχηματίζω as referring to the rhetorical device of 'covert allusion' and the lexical distinction between σχηματίζω and μετασχηματίζω, it is

103   Anderson, *Ancient Rhetorical Theory and Paul*, p. 246.

104   See critique on this point by Kuck, *Judgment*, p. 211; and Anderson, *Ancient Rhetorical Theory and Paul*, p. 248. The argument is guilty of what James Barr, *The Semantic of Biblical Language*, p. 109, has called 'the root fallacy', that is, an attempt to discover the meaning of a word by studying the meaning of the root – which tells us more about its history than meaning – instead of looking at the contemporary usage of the word.

105   LSJ 1117 gives the meaning 'transfer as in a figure' without any references, though see Schneider, 'μετασχηματίζω', in *TDNT* 7.958 n. 9.

106   Morna D. Hooker, ' "Beyond the Things Which are Written"? An Examination of 1 Corinthians 4.6', *NTS* 10 (1963–64) 127–32 (131), thus transfers the meaning of σχηματίζω to μετασχηματίζω.

107   Anderson, *Ancient Rhetorical Theory and Paul*, p. 248.

108   Cf. Hall, 'A Disguise for the Wise: μετασχηματισμός in 1 Corinthians 4.6', *NTS* 40 (1994): 146.

109   *Contra* Fee, *First Corinthians*, pp. 166–7: Paul 'has gone from metaphor to metaphor'.

very improbable that Paul used the verb with the sense of 'covert allusion.'[110] It almost seems that the argument for such usage in 1 Cor. 4.6 provides a license 'to read between the lines' in 1 Cor. 3.5–4.5,[111] rather than taking Paul's argument about himself and Apollos at face value. This is what Ker and others seem to do, when they argue that the meaning of 1 Cor. 4.6 is that Paul *applied* the ταῦτα (i.e., the figures of speech in 1 Cor. 3.5–4.5) to himself and Apollos. Ker argues for such a meaning, we believe, because this is the only way he can maintain the alleged ranking between Paul and Apollos which he reads into Paul's argument in 1 Cor. 3.5-17.[112] But taking the verb μετασχηματίζω to mean 'apply' without implying some kind of 'change' is, as we will see, unique and therefore improbable. Moreover, our study of 1 Cor. 3.5–4.5 pointed to the need to take at face value Paul's argument for harmony between Apollos and him. To take the verb to mean what Ker argues would be to suggest that Paul was deceptive or at least disingenuous in his argument for unity in ministry with Apollos.

Despite these weaknesses, this view has the strength of giving the context a determinative role in interpretation. It especially gives due weight to the dominant figures of Apollos and Paul, particularly in ch. 3. Even if the verb makes little to no contribution to the context (since it is not taken to mean 'change'), this is in fact in agreement with a principle in semantics stated by Eugene Nida that '[t]he correct meaning of any term is that which contributes least to the total context, or in other terms, that which fits the context most perfectly.'[113] The emphasis then should be placed on maximizing the context, the implication being that Paul's and Apollos' names are not used merely as a smoke screen in the argument for unity, as is the case with the third view discussed below.

The second option for the meaning of μετασχηματίζω that has been suggested is that of 'to illustrate' or 'to exemplify'.[114] This view is based on the previous one, with the exception that it is not believed that Paul uses the verb as a reference to an ancient rhetorical device. This is a more loose

---

110 See also Héring, *First Corinthians*, p. 28, who believes that this view is 'unacceptable'.

111 See Schrage, *Der erste Brief*, 1.334, and Heinrici, *Dar erste Sendschreiben*, p. 147.

112 Ker, 'Paul and Apollos', 92.

113 Nida, 'The Implications of Contemporary Linguistics for Biblical Scholarship', *JBL* 91 (1972) 73–89 (86).

114 See Weiss, *Der erste Korintherbrief*, p. 101; Hans-Josef Klauck, *1 Korintherbrief*, (Wurzburg: Echter Verlag, 1984), p. 37, following Hans Lietzmann, *An die Korinther I & II* (HNT 9; Tubingen: Mohr, 1969), p. 19, who interpret the word to mean exemplification or instantiation (*exemplifiziert*); Conzelmann, *1 Corinthians*, pp. 85–6; Fee, *First Corinthians*, p. 167; *TDNT* 7.958, where Schneider discusses the verb under σχῆμα giving it the general meaning 'to express something in another than the expected or customary form'. The arguments that we will present here that are used to support this view are based on Vos' article 'Der μετασχηματισμός in 1 Kor 4.6', 154–72.

or catachrestic way of saying that Paul used the figures of speech in 1 Cor. 3.5–4.5 in order to be indirect.[115]

Johan Vos is the most recent proponent of this view.[116] In his opinion, the meaning of the verb μετασχηματίζω is a combination of two senses: one that denotes exemplification (*Exemplifikation*) – the transformation of a general statement into a particular statement – and the other that indicates the alternation of roles (*Rollenwechsel*). He finds support for the first meaning in Origen and Cyril of Alexandria and for the second in Athanasius.[117] David Hall has done a thorough evaluation of Vos' references and has rightly noted that Origen's exegesis is driven by his allegorical hermeneutic as well as by his tendency to generalize and actualize the teaching of Scripture, thus neglecting the historical context. It is no wonder, then, that Origen understood the verb to indicate an application of Paul's teaching to all generations.[118] Hall also notes that the verb μετεσχημάτισα is followed, not by εἰς ἐμαυτόν, but by ἐφ᾽ ἑαυτῷ in Cyril, phrases that differ in meaning. Therefore, he concludes, 'Cyril's words can scarcely be used as evidence to determine the meaning of what Paul wrote several centuries earlier.'[119] The passage from Athanasius is worth quoting here, since it parallels the phrase in Paul:

> It was not I who stopped them and made them ineffective but the Lord, who said, 'I beheld Satan fall like lighting from heaven.' But I, children, mindful of the words of the apostle, have transformed this into myself (μετεσχημάτισα ταῦτα εἰς ἐμαυτόν), so that you may learn not to give up in your spiritual discipline and not to be afraid of the manifestations of the devil and his demons.

According to Vos, Athanasius' statement speaks of an adoption of a role, namely that of an ἄφρων, given the larger context of the quotation.[120] Again Hall points to the preposition εἰς that governs a pronoun as indicative of the end product of the transformation.[121] As a result, Hall draws the conclusion that the meaning in Athanasius is that of attributing to oneself that which really belongs to another. Consequently, in 1 Cor.

---

115 Cf. *TDNT* 7.958.

116 Vos, 'Der μετασχηματισμός in 1 Kor 4.6', 154–72. Garland, *1 Corinthians*, p. 133, seems to adopt this view. See also Hall, *Unity*, pp. 19–25.

117 For his comments on Origen (the Greek text found in C. Jenkins, 'Origen on 1 Corinthians', *JTS* 9 [1908]: 231–47, 353–72, 500–14; *JTS* 10 [1909]: 29–51) and Cyril of Alexandria (PG 69.789A–D) see Vos, 'Der μετασχηματισμός in 1 Kor 4.6', 156, 163–64, and on Athanasius (PG 26.900A–4A) see p. 166, 172.

118 See Hall, *Unity*, pp. 20–1.

119 Ibid., p. 22.

120 Vos, 'Der μετασχηματισμός in 1 Kor 4.6', 166.

121 Hall, *Unity*, p. 23. For a more detailed presentation of the importance of the preposition εἰς in a construction see his 'Μετασχηματισμός in 1 Corinthians 4.6', 144 (cf. *4 Macc.* 9.22; 2 Cor. 11.13, 14). See also *TDNT* 7.957, n. 7.

4.6 it means that 'Paul was saying things about himself and Apollos which, though true, should really have been said about other people.'[122]

This takes us to the third view: the regular usage of 'to change the form of something into something else.' While the first two views seem to emphasize the immediate context as determinative of meaning, this view focuses on the basic or natural meaning of the verb, especially its current usage. This meaning is not only the one found in other biblical references (cf. Phil. 3.21; 2 Cor. 11.13, 14), but it was also the meaning given by the Church Fathers, including Crysostom (PG 61.23, 97), followed by Theodoret (PG 82.233) and Theophylact (PG 124.572) as they commented on 1 Cor. 4.6.[123] Chrysostom believed that the four parties mentioned in 1 Cor. 1.12 did not really exist and that Paul used these names instead of the real names for reasons of tact (PG 61.24). In modern times, this meaning can be found in the commentaries by Meyer and Roberson and Plummer. Robertson and Plummer, for instance, state: 'The meaning will be "I have transferred these warnings to myself and Apollos for the purpose of a covert allusion" … The μετασχηματισμός therefore consists in putting forward the names of those not really responsible for the στάσεις instead of the names of others who were more to blame.'[124] This view also has an overlap with the first and second view in that it contends that Paul uses his name and that of Apollos in a covert way, when in fact his problem is with other unnamed teachers in the Corinthian congregation.

Who are these unnamed teachers? Goulder and Barrett argue that the 'real issue was between the two of them [i.e., Paul and Apollos] and Cephas, but he has changed it to be as between himself and Apollos, for pastoral reasons.'[125] Barrett translates the statement as 'I have for your sake made these things *seem* to apply to Apollos and myself.'[126] Hall responds to such a claim by rightly pointing to what would be a surprising mention of Cephas alongside Paul and Apollos in 1 Cor. 3.22, if the issue was about Paul and Cephas as they argue. The mention of all three names, Hall argues, 'suggest[s] that the use of two names or three was of no

---

122 Hall, *Unity*, p. 23.

123 See also *4 Macc* 9.22; 1 Kgdms 28.8; Symmachus, *T. Reuben* 5.6; Josephus, *A.J.* 7.257, 8.267; Philo, *Aet. mund.* 79; *Legat.* 80, 346. These are referenced in Kuck, *Judgment*, p. 211, to mean 'physical transformation of appearance'. See also Hall, 'Μετασχηματισμός in 1 Corinthians 4.6', 143–44, for other references; *TDNT* 957; *BDAG* 641; for references in Church Fathers see Lampe, *Lexicon*, 861. See also Vos, 'Der μετασχηματισμός in 1 Kor 4.6', 162–63, who performed a *TLG* search for the phrase μετασχηματίζειν τι εἰς τινα and states that 'habe ich kein anderes Beispiel finden können' (n. 48).

124 Robertson and Plummer, *First Corinthians*, p. 81. See also Meyer, *First Corinthians*, p. 117, though his view has some variants.

125 Goulder, 'ΣΟΦΙΑ in 1 Corinthians', 519; *idem. Paul and the Competing Mission in Corinth*, p. 24; Barrett, *First Corinthians*, pp. 105–6.

126 Barrett, *First Corinthians*, p. 106 (emphasis added).

importance to his argument.'[127] Moreover, as we will argue later, it is
doubtful that Paul uses his name and that of Apollos merely for rhetorical
purposes, as a smoke screen, as it were. Paul clearly says that he
'transforms' these things to himself and Apollos not because he wants to
avoid a direct confrontation with Peter, but for the Corinthians'
benefit.[128]

Hall adopts a more general view of who these unnamed teachers are,
identifying them with Paul's opponents in 2 Corinthians. Following
Robertson and Plummer, he comments:

> If we translate in 4.6 according to the normal usage, Paul is referring to
> a transformation in his argument from statements about something or
> someone else into statements about himself and Apollos ... When Paul
> describes the relationship between himself and Apollos, what he is really
> concerned about is certain unnamed teachers who were at work in the
> church at Corinth, and competing for the allegiance of the church
> members.[129]

Hall appeals to a simple analogy, following Chrysostom, to explain his
rendering of Paul's statement in 1 Cor. 4.6:

> Paul illuminates Situation A (their existing situation – the presence in
> Corinth of rival wisdom-teachers) by an analogy with Situation B (the
> colleagueship of Paul and Apollos). The Corinthians are invited to
> discern for themselves the relevance of Situation B (which is described
> directly) to their own Situation A (which is alluded to indirectly).[130]

Chrysostom's view, followed by Hall, has the advantage of taking the verb
with its regular meaning.[131] Its weakness, however, is that it is believed
that Paul is confronted with opposition in 1 Corinthians from teachers
who should be identified with those in 2 Corinthians 10–13, something
that we have shown to be relying on shaky ground.[132] Moreover, the
problem was not so much with the teachers, though they are warned to
watch that the quality of their work be compatible with the foundation,
but with the Corinthians; all his argument is addressed not to the alleged
false teachers but to the Corinthians' desire to boast with one teacher
against another.[133]

Third, it has been pointed out that the argument in 1 Cor. 3.5-17 could

---

127 Hall, *Unity*, p. 146.
128 Dickerson, 'Apollos in Acts and First Corinthians', 106–7.
129 Hall, 'Μετασχηματισμός in 1 Corinthians 4.6', 144. See also *idem, Unity*, p. 5.
130 Ibid., 148.
131 Ibid., 149.
132 Hall, *Unity*, ch. 1. He rejects Vos' objection that Paul always confronts his opponents
openly.
133 Cf. Kuck, *Judgment*; and Litfin, *Proclamation*, pp. 221, 225, and 227.

not be applied to anyone else by Paul and Apollos. Hooker, for instance, argues that, 'He cannot have meant that his readers should understand in 1 Cor 4.6: "For Paul read X, and for Apollos substitute Y."'[134] Hall's response to this consists in pointing to the use of an analogy which contains an element of disguise: 'Paul's statements about himself and Apollos in 3.5-9 were plain statements about real people; but the implied reference was to the various church-builders whose work is analyzed in 3.10-20.'[135] Such a response, however, is unsatisfactory, since it is hard to completely exclude Paul and Apollos from the situation that had developed in Corinth, since the issue was both an overvaluation as well as an undervaluation of teachers when compared against each other. Thiselton also rightly comments that 'Chrysostom has already moved beyond the evidence in proposing that the names of Paul, Apollos, and Peter are fictional devices in 1.10-12 ...'[136]

In light of the weaknesses of each position, it is hard to determine the exact meaning of the verb. The verb certainly implies some kind of 'transformation' or 'transfer', but it may go beyond the evidence to suggest that there is a 'replacement'. What is needed, then, is a study of the current usage of the verb.

The verb μετασχηματίζω is used only three other times in the New Testament and all of them by the same author, Paul (2 Cor. 11.13, 14, 15; Phil. 3.21). In all occurrences the verb has its 'normal' meaning of 'to change the form of something into something else', whether the change is real or just a disguise.[137] In the contemporaneous extrabiblical literature of the first centuries BC and AD, the verb is used particularly by historians such as Diodorus Siculus, Josephus, and Plutarch and by philosophers such as Philo.

The historian Diodorus Siculus relates how a priest focuses in his education given to his sons on two subjects, geometry and arithmetic. In his argument for the need of knowledge in geometry, Diodorus gives the following explanation: ὁ μὲν γὰρ ποταμὸς κατ᾿ ἐνιαυτὸν ποικίλως μετασχηματίζων τὴν χώραν πολλὰς καὶ παντοίας ἀμφισβητήσεις ποιεῖ περὶ τῶν ὅρων τοῖς γειτνιῶσι (*Bib. Hist.* 1.81.6).

Philo, in writing to Gaius, rebukes him for illegitimately taking the insignia commonly used to adorn the images of the deities without

---

134 See Hooker, '"Beyond the Things Which are Written"'? 131. Fee, *First Corinthians*, p. 55, n. 37, also contends that the statements about Paul and Apollos in 3.5-9 are not 'in disguise' but are plain statement about real people.

135 Hall, 'Μετασχηματισμός in 1 Corinthians 4.6', 148.

136 Thiselton, *First Corinthians*, p. 350.

137 BDAG 641–42 gives the New Testament occurrences different semantic values. Phil. 3.21 is placed under the meaning 1 'to change the form of something'; 2 Cor. 11.15, 14, 13 under meaning 2 'to feign to be what one is not'; and 1 Cor. 4.6 under meaning 3 'to show a connection or bearing of one thing on another, to apply to'.

emulating their virtues. One such deity worthy of emulation is described in the following way: ... ὃ δὴ Παραδοξότατον ἦν, ἑνὸς σώματος οὐσίαν μετασχηματίζων καὶ μεταχαράττων εἰς πολυτρόπους μορφάς ... (*Legat.* 80.7). What is important to notice about this example and the previous one in Diodorus is that the verb μετασχηματίζω has the 'natural' meaning of 'changing the form of something into something else', with the specification that what changes is just the outward form; the essence remains the same.

The Greek historian Plutarch provides two relevant instances of the use of the verb. In writing about how people assume different positions at the dinner tables, he states: οὕτως ἡμῶν ἕκαστον ἐν ἀρξῇ μὲν ἐπὶ στόμα προνεύειν ἀποβλέποντα πρὸς τὴν τράπεζαν ὕστερον δὲ Μετασχηματίζειν ἐπὶ Βάθος ἐκ πλάτους τὴν κατάκλισιν (*Mor.* 680A). In writing about Zeus who "is not averse to changes" (μεταβολαῖς) he states: ἡ δ' ἐν ὡρισμένῳ πλήθει καὶ ἀριθμῷ κόσμων ἐπιμέλεια καὶ πρόνοια τῆς εἰς ἓν δεδυκυίας σῶμα καὶ πρόσηρτημένης ἑνὶ καὶ τοῦτο μετασχηματιζούσης καὶ ἀναπλαττούσης ἀπειράκις ἔμοιγε δοκεῖ μηδὲν ἔχειν ἀσεμνότερον μητ' ἐπιπονώτερον (*Mor.* 426.E). In both these examples the verb implies a real change on the outside.

Two examples come from the Jewish historian Josephus, both commenting on an Old Testament passage. The first one refers to Jeroboam sending his wife to consult the prophet Elijah: ἡ δὲ μετασχηματισαμένη, καθὼς αὐτῇ προσέταξεν ὁ ἀνήρ (*A.J.* 8.267). In commenting about David's sadness for his son Absalom's rebellion, Josephus reminds the readers of David's servants' advice to him to go to the gates and talk to people. Following their advice, Josephus states, μετασχηματίσας γὰρ ἑαυτὸν Δαυίδης καὶ ποιήσαι ἐπιτήδειον εἰς τὴ τοῦ πλήθους θέαν πρὸς ταῖς πύλαις ἐκάθισεν (*A.J.* 7.257). In both these examples the change is clearly that of appearance. More specifically, it is a change of clothes or facial expression.

These instances of the use of the verb in these authors point to two important aspects relevant for its use in 1 Cor. 4.6. First, the verb always refers to some kind of change in the appearance or form of something. The change can occur to people, whether it is their bodily position, clothing, or facial expressions, or to things such as the way a country or an object look. Second, when the change refers to a person's appearance, the change is into something new and is a real one. The person, however, remains the same; what changes is the outside. The change in appearance can be either for the purpose of disguise so that a person may be confused with a different one, as in the case of Jeroboam's wife, or it can be a change merely of clothes, such as the example of David, without any purpose of 'covering' anything. We may thus conclude based on these observations that the verb always implies some kind of outward change and that it never has the meaning of 'to apply' or 'to exemplify'.

This meaning of the verb in the current literature can easily be corroborated with the message of the immediate context of 1 Cor. 4.6. Both the determinative role of the context as well as the current usage of the verb are important in determining the meaning of the verb. Thus, what Paul is saying is that in 1 Cor. 4.6 he intends to change what has been said in order to apply to unnamed teachers – the 'natural' meaning of the verb, but at the same time Paul and Apollos are not excluded from the referent for that would go against the context. This is what Thiselton also believes as he combines different aspect of the meanings evaluated above. He states:

> I have allusively applied all this to myself and to Apollos' to convey precisely the balance between probability and openness latent in the Greek. Clearly the examples are *allusive* to those whom Paul does not mention by name; but it goes beyond the evidence to claim that Paul and Apollos themselves are necessarily only *ciphers of rhetorical fiction* whom Paul himself exempts from his own warnings. Indeed, his reference to his own self-knowledge or conscience (4.4) suggests the opposite. Mere *examples* undertranslates; *covert* rhetoric overtranslates; *allusive application* identifies the issue.[138]

Thus, we may conclude at least three things from our analysis of the verb. First, Paul and Apollos are certainly in danger of being evaluated by the Corinthians based on the Corinthians' high esteem of sophistic wisdom, which they saw represented in different ways in the two. Thus, at least the slogans connected to Paul's name and Apollos' in 1 Cor. 1.12 are real. Second, the verb μετασχηματίζω in 1 Cor. 4.6 seems to imply that Paul seeks to give a more general admonition to the Corinthians to do away with the personality cult. Thus, even though there may not have been an actual Cephas and Jesus party, these may be used as examples to point to the absurdity of the partisan spirit. Third, it does not follow from this that there were false teachers in the congregation who were competing for allegiance at the time of the writing of 1 Corinthians. The problem was solely with the Corinthians' comparing their teachers (especially Paul and Apollos) and pitting them against each other for the purposes of claiming allegiance to the one they thought would help them more effectively to enhance their status and increase their honor. What we see, then, in Paul's argument in 1 Corinthians 1–4 is a movement from a general discussion of σχίσματα (starting in 1 Cor. 1.10) to a particular σχίσμα (1 Cor. 3.4-17), and only to revert back to a discussion again of σχίσματα in general (starting in 1 Cor. 3.18). Given these arguments, Paul Ellingworth and Howard Hatton may be very close to what is Paul actually saying in this verse when they paraphrase Paul: 'In all that I have said up to now it may

138   Thiselton, *First Corinthians*, p. 351 (author's emphasis).

seem that I have been talking only about Apollos and myself; but what I have said can be applied more widely, namely to you readers'.[139]

Conclusion

This fourth chapter has sought to bring together the conclusions reached in the previous chapters and raise the question of Apollos' role in the dissensions as well as the function of his name in Paul's argument for unity. A definite answer to this question requires a discussion of several issues that we will seek to cover in this chapter.

We have concluded from an exegesis of 1 Cor. 16.12 that the information presented in this verse is far from clear, or at least allows for no definite pronouncements concerning Paul's relation to Apollos. The verse, nonetheless, seems to indicate that the two missionaries worked independently, but not necessarily in competition with one another, since Paul seems to use warm terms in referring to Apollos.

Whether Apollos and Paul had different *modus operandi* in their independent mission work in Corinth required an investigation of the information one finds in Acts 18.24-28. Our study of this passage led us to conclude that though it is possible that the terminology Luke uses to describe Apollos may have rhetorical connotations, there are no clear grounds for arguing that Apollos' *modus operandi* differed from Paul's to such a degree that he used sophistic rhetoric which Paul opposed in 1 Corinthians 1–4 and which led to the dissensions in the Corinthian assembly, especially since Apollos is presented as being of much help to the Corinthians.

This positive regard of Apollos by Luke is confirmed by Paul's non-polemical argument in 1 Cor. 3.5–4.5 as he mentions Apollos' name several times. A reading of the text at its face value forces us to believe that Paul describes Apollos in congenial rather than polemical terms, making thus the Corinthians responsible for the dissensions rather than Apollos.

That this is so was lastly corroborated by the study of the meaning of the verb μετεσχημάτισα in 1 Cor. 4.6. What we were able to say with certainty concerning its meaning is that Paul used himself and Apollos in his argument in the previous section, not just as examples or as an indirect way of referring to others, but that Paul and Apollos were themselves in danger of being evaluated according to worldly standards of wisdom. Thus the dissensions in the Corinthian church were not limited to preferences for Paul or Apollos, but neither did they exclude them.

---

139   Ellingworth and Hatton, *A Handbook on Paul's First Letter to the Corinthians*, p. 93, following somewhat Barrett, *First Corinthians*, pp. 105–6. Litfin, *Proclamation*, p. 227, is also close, though he still maintains a polemical argument against Apollos in 3.5-17.

5 SUMMARY AND CONCLUSION

Summary

The introduction presented the methodology followed throughout the work in assessing Paul's relationship to Apollos according to 1 Corinthians 1–4. We presented general guidelines for word studies to guard us from certain common exegetical fallacies by arguing that the meaning of a word is a combination of current usage and context. We also presented a defense of background studies by arguing that behind-the-text information is necessary for a 'thick' description of a text.

Chapter 1, then, presented an exegetical study of 1 Corinthians 1–4 for the purpose of discovering the thematic and literary unity of Paul's argument in this section of the letter. There we argued that Paul contends for unity in the Corinthian church by discussing the issue of wisdom, thus pointing to the central (theological) cause for divisions: a false perception of teachers based on a worldly understanding of wisdom. Paul sees as the cause of divisions a failure to grapple with the ethical implications of the cross: the cross overturns the cultural values.

Chapter 2 researched the background of wisdom in order to see what specifically divided the Corinthian Christian assembly. A survey of different views led us to believe that the most probable background for the concept of σοφία that does justice to the cumulative information available is sophistic rhetoric. Rhetorical eloquence in speech, as was seen, also carried with it certain social values, which seem to have been carried over from the surrounding culture into the Christian *ecclesia* and which led to dissensions. This socio-rhetorical background to the issue of dissensions raised then the issue of the nature and number of parties. What we were able to conclude with relative certainty was that (at least) Paul and Apollos were in danger of being thought of in competitive terms. Thus, the Corinthians' preference for a certain teacher against another was based on their evaluation of teachers in light of the values of the surrounding culture.

Chapter 3 analyzed Paul's stance toward sophistic rhetoric. From an analysis of Paul's upbringing and education, the opponents' critique of Paul's rhetorical delivery, as well as Paul's direct statements concerning his theology of proclamation, we concluded that Paul opposes the dynamic of sophistic rhetoric in the gospel presentation, both in oral and written form. He takes this anti-sophistic stance, we argued, as a function of his theology of the cross, and not, as some have argued, as a covert way of re-establishing his authority.

Chapter 4 sought to bring together the research conducted in the previous chapters in order to raise the question of Apollos' role in the dissensions in the Corinthian *ecclesia* as well as the part he plays in Paul's argument against dissensions in 1 Corinthians 1–4. The textual evidence available to us concerning Apollos led us to conclude that Paul does not construct a polemic against Apollos. Rather, Paul presents Apollos' ministry as complementary rather than competitive. If the evidence allows us to conclude anything about Apollos' ministry in Corinth, it is that he had a positive contribution to the Corinthians' spiritual growth. At fault for the dissensions, then, is not Apollos' style, as if it presented a major departure from Paul's *modus operandi*, but the Corinthians' high esteem of worldly wisdom.

Implications

This study into Apollos' ministry in Corinth and Paul's relationship to Apollos in light of Paul's stance toward rhetoric in 1 Corinthians 1–4 has led us to conclude that Paul and Apollos shared a congenial relationship. The detail of our study that has led us to conclude this bear several important implications. Three will be discussed here: methodological, biblical, and homiletical.

Methodological Implications

In our discussion of Paul's stance toward rhetoric in Chapter 3, we have concluded that Paul rejected the dynamic of sophistic rhetoric in the presentation of the gospel. We have also stated that the opponents' critique of Paul's stage presence in contrast to his presence in letters is not a reference to a lack of rhetorical devices in his speech, such as metaphors, enthymenes, etc. These are present in his letters and no doubt were means he used in his speeches for the purpose of conveying the gospel as clearly as possible. What his opponents perceived as inconsistency between his presence in body and presence in letters then is boldness or lack thereof. What Paul's opponents did not understand, however, was that Paul intentionally chose to be bold in letters so that he could be meek and less disciplinary when in their presence. In this way he sought to be more Christlike in his demeanor.

Thus, if Paul rejected not rhetorical devices but only the dynamic of sophistic rhetoric that believed that persuasion rests on the rhetor's oratorical abilities to adapt to his audience, then to what extent did Paul use the rhetorical techniques and devices described in the ancient rhetorical handbooks in his presentation of the gospel, particularly in its written form? More specifically, can we determine that Paul structured his letters according to the ancient rhetorical categories? Thus, is it legitimate to use rhetorical criticism in the interpretation of Paul's letters?

We have addressed this issue in several extensive footnotes throughout our work and we will only summarize the findings here. At least three topics must be clarified before we can make any claims concerning the legitimacy of analyzing Paul's letters through rhetorical criticism.[1] First, does Paul's education tell us anything about his ability to structure his letters according to ancient rhetorical categories? We have seen that Paul basically received Jewish education in Jerusalem though the Greco-Roman education and culture was so pervasive in his time that no doubt had significant influence on the Rabbinic thought. Also, we have seen that Paul's knowledge of sophistic conventions could have easily been learned from observation of the practices of public declamations of different sophists, something that was common knowledge since such practices were an important form of entertainment in antiquity. The question, though, is whether knowledge of sophistic rhetoric aquired from observation rather than training at the tertiary level provides sufficient evidence to suggest that Paul indeed used clear features of rhetoric in his writings. Stanley Porter has rightly pointed out that such argument is hardly plausible, since it 'overlooks the nature of rhetorical training and practice in the ancient world ... This training was intense and rigorous, as the handbooks attest, not the kind of thing that the vast majority had the luxury of time or of sufficient money to engage in.'[2] Paul's education in Jerusalem under a Rabbi, thus, seems to suggest that Paul would not have had the training necessary to use rhetorical categories learned only at the tertiary level in the Greco-Roman educational system.

Second, is there any overlap between the ancient epistolary and

---

1   The presentation here will be a combination of what we have already discussed at different points and Stanley E. Porter's position on the topic, with whom we agree to a great extent. His view is explained in several essays and articles: 'The Theoretical Justification for Application of Rhetorical Categories to Pauline Epistolary Literature', 100–22; 'Ancient Rhetorical Analysis and Discourse Analysis of the Pauline Corpus', in *The Rhetorical Analysis of Scripture: Essays from the 1995 London Conference* (Stanley E. Porter and Thomas H. Olbricht, eds; JSNTSup 146; Sheffield: Sheffield Academic Press, 1997), 249–74; 'Paul of Tarsus and His Letters', 533–85; 'Paul as Epistolographer *and* Rhetorician?' in *The Rhetorical Interpretation of Scripture: Essays from the 1996 Malibu Conference* (Stanley Porter and Dennis L. Stamps, eds.; JSNTSup, 180; Sheffield: Sheffield Academic Press, 1997), 222–48.

2   Porter, 'Paul as Epilolographer *and* Rhetorician?' 230. See also *idem*, 'Paul of Tarsus and His Letters', 562–64.

rhetorical categories that would legitimize the use of rhetorical categories in the writing of letters? It is very clear that the ancient rhetorical categories described in the handbooks were meant for speeches, both oral and written, and not for the writing of letters. Porter has rightly pointed out that 'epistolary theory only becomes a part of rhetorical theory much later than the composition of the New Testament' (i.e., Julius Victor, *Ars Rhetorica* 27; AD 4). This means that '[t]here certainly is no theoretical basis assumed or established for analyzing letters according to the categories of rhetoric.'[3]

We have argued that and important aspect of Paul's writings is the fact that his letters were meant to be read alound, which raises the question of whether Paul's letters should be considered in the same category as speeches, whether oral or written, which then in turn would justify the use of rhetorical criticism in analyzing the letter-speeches? This is an important question, since there were letters in antiquity that were rhetorical writings given an epistolary framework.[4] Jeffrey Reed has done some research into the ancient written speeches that present clear rhetorical influences, but has rightly pointed out that

> there appears to be a general principle that letters displaying rhetorical influence lack many of the optional epistolary formulas found in the personal letters (e.g., prayer, thanksgiving, disclosure formulas, closing greetings) – an observable difference between literary and personal letters. Conversely, letters replete with epistolary formulas lack full-blown rhetorical conventions. In sum, the rhetorical and epistolary genres may have been betrothed, but were never wed.[5]

3 Porter, 'Paul as Epilolographer *and* Rhetorician?' 232. For a more extensive argument see *idem*, 'The Theoretical Justification for Application of Rheotrical Categories to Pauline Epistolary Literature', 100–22; Reed, 'Using Ancient Rhetorical Categories to Interpret Paul's Letters: A Question of Genre', 294–314; *idem*, 'The Epistle', 186–92. S. K. Stowers, *Letter Writing in Greco-Roman Antiquity* (Philadelphia: Westminster, 1986), p. 52, observes that '[t]he letter-writing tradition was essentially independent of rhetoric... classification of letter types according to the three species of rhetoric only partially works.'

4 See, e.g., Anderson's discussion of several of these letter-speeches in his *Ancient Rhetorical Theory and Paul*, pp. 121–7. Among New Testament scholars who sought to place Galatians among the ancient Greek tradition letter-speech is H. D. Betz.

5 For examples of written speeches see Demosthenes, *Epistles* 1–4, who wrote speeches in the form of a letter only because he was in exile; Dionysius of Halicarnassus, *1–2 Amm.* These and other examples are discussed by Reed, 'The Epistle', 186–90. He concludes that despite the fact that letter writing was at least partly influenced by rhetorical conventions, the majority of ancient letters do not lend themselves to classical rhetorical analysis. Perhaps we should make here a distinction between private and official letters, only the latter presenting some traces of the influence of rhetorical categories. The question is whether Paul's letters paralles more closely the private or the official type of ancient letters. While the majority of scholars who analyze Paul's letters in light of ancient epistelography agree that he wrote in the style of the private letters, see M. Luther Stirewalt, Jr., *Paul, the Letter Writer* (Grand

Porter concludes in a similar way: 'Whereas there is merit in utilizing the categories of ancient rhetoric in discussion of ancient speeches, it cannot be shown that Paul's letters constitute examples of ancient speeches.'[6] This means that, since Paul's letters follow clearly the epistolographical categories (though Paul assumed freedom to adapt them), the influence of rhetorical categories is minimal.[7] This agrees with, for instance, Cicero's statement in *Fam.* 9.21.1: '*quid enim simile habet epistula aut iudicio aut contioni?*'

The most that can be claimed, then, concerning the relation between epistolary and rhetorical categories is that there are definitely functional similarities (e.g., influence at the level of style). This conclusion supports our contention that Paul's writings did not differ from his speeches in terms of the use of lack of use of rhetorical devices. What is less clear is that are also formal similarities to the point that it would justify the application of rhetorical criticism to the study of Paul's epistles whithout being an external, foreign imposition.[8]

Biblical Implications

We have seen that the argument that Apollos might have made use of the dynamic characteristic of sophistic rhetoric in his preaching in Corinth rests on speculative evidence. This has implications concerning the argument that Apollos might have been the author of the book of Hebrews. The first to advance such a proposal was Martin Luther.[9]

Several arguments have been advanced to support an Apollonian authorship of the epistle to the Hebrews, all based on inferences from Acts

---

Rapids: Eerdmans, 2003), for an argument that Paul wrote in the style of the official letters. The official letters seem to fit more easily in the category of written speeches, sent usually with an interpreter.

6   Porter, 'Paul as Epistolographer *and* Rhetorician', 233. *Contra* Kennedy, *New Testament Interpretation*, pp. 86–7.

7   See the well-taken point made by Porter, 'Paul as Epistolographer *and* Rhetorician', 230–31, that what we can state with certainty is that Paul wrote letters and this should be the starting point in the analysis of Paul's writings.

8   See ibid. 232–33.

9   See *LW* 8.178. Luther's proposal was supported by Théodore de Bèze and Philip Melanchthon. For nineteenth-century proponents see Craig R. Koester, *Hebrews: A New Translation with Introduction and Commentary* (AB, 36; New York: Doubleday, 2001), p. 44, n. 90. More recently, two commentators in particular have advocated Apollos' authorship of the book of Hebrews: C. Spicq, *L'Épître aux Hébreux* (EBib; Paris: Gabalda, 1952), 1.209-19; *idem*. 'L'Épître aux Hébreux, Apollos, Jean-Baptiste, les Hellénistes et Qumrân', *RevQ* 1 (1959) 365–90; followed by H. Montefiore, *A Commentary on the Epistle to the Hebrews* (BNTC; London: Black, 1964), pp. 9–11. For a critique see L. D. Hurst, 'Apollos, Hebrews, and Corinth: Bishop Montefiore's Theory Examined', *SJT* 38 (1985) 505–13. For a more recent advocate of an Apollonian authorship, see George H. Guthrie, 'The Case for Apollos as the Author of Hebrews', *F&M* 18 (2001) 41–56.

18.24-28. First, C. Spicq, among the more recent advocates, points to similarities between Hebrews and Philo of Alexandria that allegedly are consistent with the argument that Apollos was influenced by a Philonic type of wisdom and methods of interpretation since he was from Alexandria (Acts 18.24).[10] This argument, however, has been proven to be speculative in Chapters 2 and 4 of this work, since it is an argument from silence.[11] His Jewish origin from Alexandria does not necessarily imply that Apollos had been educated in the Philonic type of argumentation.

Second, Spicq has also observed that Luke presents Apollos as one who sought to prove from the Scriptures that Jesus was the Messiah (Acts 18.28), which may parallel the Christological arguments based on the Old Testament found in Hebrews.[12] We have, nevertheless, shown that such a description of Apollos is not a unique characteristic, but that this 'was the core of the primitive Christian kerygma.'[13]

Third, a less speculative argument is Spicq's observation that 'Apollos est à la fois *un érudit et un orateur*.' He continues: 'Qualités, si rarement réunies et qui traduisent de façon heureuse un des caractères les plus distinctifs de l'auteur de Hébr.'[14] The presence of rhetorical devices in Hebrews has been detected by many scholars and, since Apollos is described by Luke as an ανὴρ λόγιοις from Alexandria in Acts 18.24, presumably a reference to his rhetorical eloquence, it is easy to make the connection between Apollos and the author of Hebrews. Such argument is harder to refute, since we have shown that this description most likely is a reference to his rhetorical skill. Nevertheless, caution should be exercised in assuming that his Alexandrian origin implies that Apollos received his rhetorical education in Alexandria, known as an important center of education in ancient times.

What probably argues most convincingly against an Apollonian authorship of Hebrews (though we acknowledge this to be an argument from silence) is the fact that no Church Father identifies Apollos as the author of Hebrews; Luther was the first to suggest it. Thus, we conclude that most famous dictum of Origen on the issue of the authorship of Hebrews still stands: τίς δὲ ὁ γράψας τὴν ἐπιστολής, τὸ μὲν ἀληθὲς θεὸς οἶδεν.[15]

10   Spicq, *L'Épître aux Hébreux*, 1.209-10. See also Fitch, 'Paul, Apollos, Cephas, Christ', 21, for similar argument.
11   See Andrew H. Trotter, Jr., *Interpreting the Epistle to the Hebrews* (GNTE; Grand Rapids: Baker, 1997), p. 49.
12   Spicq, *Hébreux*, 1.213. See also Koester, *Hebrews*, p. 44.
13   Ellingworth, *Hebrews*, p. 21.
14   Spicq, *Hébreux*, 1.212.
15   Eusebius, *Hist. eccl.* 6.25.14. Cf. James Moffatt, *A Critical and Exegetical Commentary on the Epistle to the Hebrews* (ICC; Edinburgh: T&T Clark, 1957), xx.

Homiletical Implications

Our discussion and conclusion concerning Paul's rejection of the whole dynamic of sophistic rhetoric has important implications in the area of homiletics. If Paul deliberately adopted an anti-sophistic stance in his presentation of the gospel, how does that inform our preaching today?

Most books on sermon delivery assume a compatibility between Aristotelian rhetoric and Christian preaching, focusing thus on issues of speech communication. It is assumed that the responsibility of the preacher is to make use, for instance, of the three rhetorical 'proofs': ἦθος, πάθος, λόγος. We suspect that such assumptions are based on the belief that God uses human means to spread the gospel. While such belief is undeniably correct, the inference from this that our responsibility is to be accomplished speakers hardly has any biblical basis.[16] Several arguments support this.

First, in several extensive footnotes in the exegesis on 1 Cor. 2.1-5, we have sought to show that Paul's letters may be analyzed using rhetorical terminology such as the three proofs, but only with the understanding that Paul Christianized the terms. No doubt Paul believed in the importance of, for instance, the preacher's character, but to him the content of the gospel was central. Everything he did was for the sake of the gospel, so that even when people engaged in preaching with evil intentions, he was willing to overlook that as long as the gospel was proclaimed.

Second, the emphasis on the preacher's part in effecting salvation overlooks the biblical portrayal of the role of the preacher. Paul presents himself as a herald, whose responsibility is the placarding of the gospel. Paul's whole argument in 1 Cor. 1.17–2.5 is that the use of the 'wisdom of words' in preaching is incompatible with the message about the cross. Even more, rhetorical eloquence is counterproductive to the gospel, for it engenders a false and temporary faith, a faith that is the result not so much of the message proclaimed but of the way it is proclaimed. This, in turn, produces false assurance of salvation.

Third, last but not least, it neglects the theological principle that God's power is manifested through weakness. This is God's *modus operandi*. That the proclamation of the gospel is persuasive to some says nothing about the human vehicle through which the gospel is proclaimed, but says much about the Holy Spirit. There is something distinctive and unique about Christian proclamation that makes its persuasive power of a different order than other speeches, namely its divine source. That is why

---

16   This is not to deny the fact that the rhetorical handbooks were descriptive of what constituted persuasive speech, meaning that in a sense all speech is rhetorical and that some of the issues treated in these handbooks are characteristic of all speeches that make sense. Thus, we are referring here only to those rhetorical aspects that assume that man has the ability to persuade by the way he constructs and delivers the gospel.

Paul argues that the gospel makes sense only to those to whom the Spirit reveals it and it is communicated in spiritual words apart from human techniques. Our overemphasis on the human element in proclamation tends to neglect this theocentric emphasis and the mystery-nature of the gospel, aspects that are pervasive and preeminent in Paul's theology of preaching. Perhaps what is needed then today is a better grasp of a biblical theology of sermon delivery that emphasizes the divine, pneumatologic element in proclamation rather than the human.

Soli Deo Gloria!

BIBLIOGRAPHY

Aejmelaeus, L. *Schwachheit als Waffe: Die Argumentation des Paulus im Tränenbrief (2 Kor 10–13)*, PFES, 78. Göttingen: Vandenhoeck & Ruprecht, 2000.

Alexandre, Manuel, Jr. 'Rhetorical Argumentation as an Exegetical Technique in Philo of Alexandria', in *Hellenica et Judaica,* eds. A. Caquot, M. Hadas-Lebel, and J. Riaud, 13–27. Paris: Peeters, 1986.

Allo, E.-B. *Saint Paul. Première Épitre aux Corinthiens*. Paris: Gabalda, 2nd edn, 1956.

Anderson, R. Dean, Jr. *Ancient Rhetorical Theory and Paul*, CBET 18. Kampen: Kok Pharos, 1996; rev. edn 1999.

Aune, David E. *The New Testament in its Literary Environment*, LEC 8. Philadelphia: Westminster, 1987.

——. 'Boasting', in *WDNTECLR,* 81–84. Westminster: John Knox, 2003.

——. 'Ethos', in *WDNTECLR,* 172. Westminster: John Knox, 2003.

Bailey, Kenneth E. 'Recovering the Poetic Structure of 1 Cor. 1.17–2.2: A Study in Text and Commentary', *NovT* 17 (1975) 265–96.

——. 'The Structure of 1 Corinthians and Paul's Theological Method with Special Reference to 4.17', *NovT* 25 (1983) 152–81.

Baird, William. 'Among the Mature: The Idea of Wisdom in 1 Corinthians 2.6', *Int* 13 (1959) 425–32.

——. 'Review: *Wisdom and Spirit: An Investigation of An Investigation of 1Corinthians 1.18–3.20 against the Background of Jewish Sapiential Traditions in the Greco-Roman Period* by James A. Davis', *JBL* 106 (1987) 149–51.

——. '"One Against the Other": Intra-Church Conflict in 1 Corinthians', in *The Conversation Continues: Studies in Paul & John in Honor of J. Louis Martyn*, eds., Robert T. Fortuna and Beverly R. Gaventa, 116–36. Nashville: Abingdon, 1990.

Banks, R. '"Walking" as a Metaphor of the Christian Life: The origins of a Significant Pauline Usage', in *Perspectives on Language and Texts: Essays and Poems in Honor of Francis I. Andersen's Sixtieth Birthday*, eds. E. W. Conrad & E. G. Newing, 303–13. Winona Lake: Eisenbrauns, 1987.

Barbour, Robin S. 'Wisdom and the Cross in 1 Corinthians 1 and 2', in

Theologia Crucis-Signum Crucis: Festschrift für Erich Dinkler zum 70. Geburtstag, eds. Carl Andresen and Günter Klein, 57–72. Tübingen: Mohr, 1979.

Barclay, John M. G. 'Mirror-Reading a Polemical Letter: Galatians as a Test Case', *JSNT* 31 (1987) 73–93.

——. 'Thessalonica and Corinth: Social Contrasts in Pauline Christianity', *JSNT* 47 (1992) 49–74.

——. 'The Family as the Bearer of Religion in Judaism and Early Christianity', in *Constructing Early Christian Families: Family as Social Reality and Metaphor*, ed. H. Moxnes, 66–80. London: Routledge, 1997.

——. 'Poverty in Pauline Studies: A Response to Steven Friesen', *JSNT* 26.3 (2004) 363–66.

Barnett, Paul. *The Second Epistle to the Corinthians*, NICNT. Grand Rapids: Eerdmans, 1997.

Barnett, Paul W. 'Opposition in Corinth', *JSNT* 22 (1984) 3–17.

——. 'Paul, Apologist to the Corinthians', in *Paul and the Corinthians: Studies on a Community in Conflict. Essays in Honour of Margaret Thrall*, eds. Trevor J. Burke and J. Keith Elliott, NovTSup, 109, 313–26. Leiden: Brill, 2003.

Barr, James. *The Semantics of Biblical Language*. London: Oxford University Press, 1961.

Barrett, C. K. 'Christianity at Corinth', in *Essays on Paul*, 1–27. Philadelphia: Westminster, 1982.

——. 'Cephas and Corinth', in *Essays on Paul*, 28–39. Philadelphia: Westminster, 1982.

——. *The First Epistle to the Corinthains*, BNTC. Peabody: Hendrickson, 2nd edn, 1996.

——. *A Critical and Exegetical Commentary on the Acts of the Apostle*, ICC, 2. Edinburgh: T&T Clark, 2004.

Bartlett, Bill. 'Paul Planted the Seed, Apollos Watered, . . .but God Made It Grow', *Dialog* 30 (1991) 185–90.

Barton, George A. 'Some Influences of Apollos in the New Testament', *JBL* 43 (1924) 207–23.

Barton, Stephen C. 'Paul's Sense of Place: An Anthropological Approach to Community Formation in Corinth', *NTS* 32 (1986) 225–46.

——. 'Historical Criticism and Social-Scientific Perspectives in New Testament Study', in *Hearing the New Testament: Strategies for Interpretation*, ed. Joel B. Green, 61–89. Grand Rapids: Eerdmans, 1995.

Bassler, Jouette M. '1 Corinthians 4.1-5', *Int* 44 (1990) 179–83.

Baur, F. C. 'Die Christuspartei in der korinthischen Gemeinde, der Gegensatz des petrinischen und paulinischen Christenthums in der ältesten Kirche', *TZT* 4 (1831) 61–206.

Beekman, John, John Callow, and Michael Kopesec. *The Semantic Structure of Written Communication*. Dallas: Summer Institute of Linguistics, 5th edn, 1981.

Bell, Richard H. *The Irrevocable Call of God: An Inquiry into Paul's Theology of Israel*, WUNT 184. Tübingen: Mohr, 2005.

Belleville, Linda L. 'Continuity or Discontinuity: A Fresh Look at 1 Corinthians in the Light of First-Century Epistolary Forms and Conventions', *EvQ* 59 (1987) 15–37.

Best, Ernest. 'The Power and the Wisdom of God. 1 Corinthians 1.18-25', in *Paolo A Una Chiesa Divisa (1 Corinthians 1–4)*, ed. Lorenzo De Lorenzi, 9–39 SMBen. Roma: Edizioni Abbazia di S. Paolo fuori le mura, 1980.

——. 'Paul's Apostolic Authority?' *JSNT* 27 (1986) 3–25.

——. *Second Corinthians*, Interpretation. Louisville: John Knox, 1987.

Betz, H. D. *Der Apostel Paulus und die sokratische Tradition*, BHT, 45. Tübingen: Mohr, 1972.

——. *2 Corinthians 8 and 9: A Commentary on Two Administrative Letters of the Apostle Paul*, Hermeneia. Philadelphia: Fortress, 1985.

——. 'The Problem of Rhetoric and Theology According to the Apostle Paul', in *L'Apôtre Paul:Personalité, Style et Conception du Ministère*, ed. A. Vanhoye, 16–48. Leuven: Leuven University Press, 1986.

Bianchi, U., ed. *Le originin dello gnosticismo: Colloquio di Messina, 13–18 aprile 1966*, SHR, 12. Leiden: Brill, 1970.

Black, David Alan. *Paul, Apostle of Weakness: Astheneia and Its Cognates in the Pauline Literature*, AUSS 7. New York: Lang, 1984.

——. 'The Discourse Structure of Philippians: A Study in Textlinguistics', *NovT* 37 (1995) 16–49.

Bockmuehl, M. N. A. *Revelation and Mystery in Ancient Judaism and Pauline Christianity*. Tübingen: Mohr, 1990.

Botha, Pieter J. J. 'The Verbal Art of the Pauline Letters: Rhetoric, Performance and Presence', in *Rhetoric and the New Testament: Essays from the 1992 Heidelberg Conference*, eds. S. Porter and T. Olbricht, JSNTSup 90, 409–28. Sheffield: JSOT, 1993.

Borgman, Brian. 'Rethinking a Much Abused Text: 1 Corinthians 3.1-15', *R&R* 11 (2002) 71–93.

Branick, Vincent P. 'Source and Redaction Analysis of 1 Corinthians 1–3', *JBL* 101 (1982) 251–69.

Brant, Jo-Ann A. 'The Place of *Mimesis* in Paul's Thought', *SR* 22 (1993) 285–300.

Brown, Alexandra R. *The Cross and Human Transformation: Paul's Apocalyptic Word in 1 Corinthians*. Minneapolis: Fortress, 1995.

——. 'Apocalyptic Transformation in Paul's Discourse on the Cross', *Word & Word* 16 (1996): 27–36.

Brown, G. and G. Yule, *Discourse Analysis*. Cambridge: Cambridge University Press, 2nd edn, 1983.

Bruce, F. F. *I and II Corinthians*, NCB. Grand Rapids: Eerdmans, 1971.

——. *The Book of Acts*, NICNT. Grand Rapids: Eerdmans, 1988.

Bullmore, A. Michael. *St. Paul's Theology of Rhetorical Style: An Examination of 1 Corinthians 2.1–5 in Light of First Century Greco-Roman Rhetorical Culture*. San Francisco: International Scholars Publications, 1995.

Bultmann, Rudolf. 'Karl Barth, "Die Auferstehung der Toten"', in *Glauben und Verstehen: Gesammelte Aufsätze*, vol. 1. Tübingen: Mohr, 1961.

Bünker, M. *Briefformular und rhetorische Disposition im 1 Korintherbrief*, GTA, 28. Göttingen: Vandenhoeck & Ruprecht, 1983.

Burke, Trevor J. 'Paul's Role as "Father" to his Corinthian "Children" in Socio-Historical Context (1 Corinthians 4.14–21)', in *Paul and the Corinthians: Studies on a Community in Conflict. Essays in Honour of Margaret Thrall*, ed. Trevor J. Burke and J. Keith Elliott, NovTSup, 109, 95–114. Leiden: Brill, 2003.

Caird, George B. *The Apostolic Age*. London: Duckworth, 1955.

Callow, Kathleen. 'The Disappearing δέ in 1 Corinthians', in *Linguistics and New Testament Interpretation. Essays on Discourse Analysis*, eds. David Alan Black and David S. Dockery, 183–93. Nashville: Broadman, 1992.

Calvin, John, *Commentary on the Epistles of Paul the Apostle to the Corinthians* CC; Grand Rapids: Eerdmans, 1990.

Caneday, Ardel B. and Thomas R. Schreiner. *The Race Set Before Us: A Biblical Theology of Perseverance & Assurance*. Downers Grove: InterVarsity, 2001.

Carr, Wesley. 'The Rulers of This Age–1 Cor 2.6-8', *NTS* 23 (1976) 20–35.

Carson, D. A. *Exegetical Fallacies*. Grand Rapids: Baker, 1984.

Carson, D. A., D. J. Moo, and L. Morris, *An Introduction to the New Testament*. Grand Rapids: Zondervan, 1992.

Carter, Raymond F. '"Big Men" in Corinth', *JSNT* 66 (1997) 45–71.

Castelli, Elizabeth A. *Imitating Paul: A Discourse of Power*, LCBI. Louisville: Westminster/John Knox, 1991.

Chance, J. Bradley. 'Paul's Apology to the Corinthians', *PRSt* 9 (1982) 145–55.

Chow, John K. *Patronage and Power: A Study of Social Networks in Corinth*, JSNTSup, 75. Sheffield: JSOT Press, 1992.

Clark, D. L. *Rhetoric in Greco-Roman Education*. NY: Columbia University Press, 1957.

Clarke, Andrew D. *Secular and Christian Leadership in Corinth: A Socio-Historical and Exegetical Study of 1Corinthians 1–6*, AGJU 18. Leiden: Brill, 1993.

——. ' "Be Imitators of Me": Paul's Model of Leadership', *TynBul* 49 (1998) 329–60.

——. *Serve the Community of the Church: Christians as Leaders and Ministers, First-Century Christians in the Greco-Roman World*. Grand Rapids: Eerdmans, 2000.

Collins, Raymond F. *First Corinthians*, SP 7. Collegeville: Liturgical, 1999.

——. ' "I Command that This Letter Be Read": Writing as a Manner of Speaking', in *The Thessalonians Debate: Methodological Discord or Methodological Synthesis*, eds. Karl P. Donfried and Johannes Beutler, 319–39. Grand Rapids: Eerdmans, 2000.

Colson, F. H. 'Μετεσχημάτισα 1 Cor 4.6', *JTS* 17 (1916) 379–84.

Conzelmann, Hans. *1 Corinthians*, trans. J. W. Leitch; Hermeneia. Philadelphia: Fortress, 1975.

Cotterell, Peter and Max Turner. *Linguistics & Biblical Interpretation*. Downers Grove: InterVarsity, 1989.

Cousar, Charles B. '1 Corinthians 2.1-13', *Int* 44 (1990) 169–73.

——. 'The Theological Task of 1 Corinthians: A Conversation with Gordon D. Fee and Victor Paul Furnish', in *Pauline Theology, Volume 2: 1 & 2 Corinthians*, ed. David M. Hay, 90–102. Minneapolis: Fortress, 1993.

Cullmann, O. *Christ and Time*. ET London: SCM, 2nd edn, 1951.

Dahl, Nils A. 'Paul and the Church at Corinth According to 1 Corinthians 1.10-4.21', in *Christian History and Interpretation. Studies Presented to John Knox*, eds. W. R. Farmer, C. F. D. Moule, and R. R. Niebuhr, 313–335. Cambridge: Cambridge University Press, 1967.

——. 'Paul and the Church at Corinth according to 1 Corinthians 1.10-4.21', in *Studies in Paul: Theology for the Early Christian Mission*, ed. N. A. Dahl, 40–61. Minneapolis: Augsburg, 1977.

Davies, Rupert. *Studies in 1 Corinthians*. London: Epworth, 1962.

Davis, James. *Wisdom and Spirit: An Investigation of 1 Corinthians 1.18-3.20 against the Background of Jewish Sapiential Traditions in the Greco-Roman Period*. Lanham: University Press of America, 1984.

De Beaugrande, R. *Text, Discourse and Process: Toward a Multidisciplinary Science of Texts*, ADP, 4. Norwood: Ablex, 1980.

Deissmann, Adolf. *Light from the Ancient East: The New Testament Illustrated by Recently Discovered Texts of the Graeco-Roman World*, trans. L. R. M. Strachan. London, n.p., 1927.

——. *Paul: A Study in Social and Religious History*. New York: Hodder and Stoughton, 1926.

Denniston, J. D. *Greek Prose Style*. Oxford: n.p., 1952.

Derrett, J. Duncan M. 'Paul as Master-Builder', *EvQ* 69 (1997) 129–37.

De Saussure, Ferdinand. *Course in General Linguistics*. New York: McGraw-Hill, 1959.

DeSilva, David A. 'Let the One Who Claims Honor Establish That Claim in the Lord: Honor Discourse in the Corinthian Correspondence', *BTB* 28 (1998) 61–74.

——. *Honor, Patronage, Kingship & Purity: Unlocking New Testament Culture*. Downers Grove: InterVarsity, 2000.

——. 'Embodying the Word: Social-Scientific Interpretation of the New Testament', in *The Face of New Testament Studies: A Survey of Recent Research*, eds. Scott McKnight and Grant R. Osborne, 118–129. Grand Rapids: Baker, 2004.

De Vos, Craig S. *Church and Community Conflicts: The Relationships of the Thessalonian, Corinthian, and Philippian Churches with their Wider Civic Communities*, SBLDS, 168. Atlanta: Scholars Press, 1999.

Dibelius, M. 'The Speeches in Acts and Ancient Historiography', in *Studies in the Acts of the Apostles*, ed. Heinrich Greeven, 138–85. New York: Scribner, 1956.

DiCicco, Mario M. *Paul's Use of Ethos, Pathos, and Logos in 2 Corinthians 10–13*, MBPS, 31. Lewiston: Edwin Mellen, 1995.

Dickerson, Patrick Lynn. 'Apollos in Acts and First Corinthians'. Unpublished doctoral dissertation, University of Virginia, 1998.

Dodd, Brian. *Paul's Paradigmatic "I": Personal Example as Literary Strategy*, JSNTSup, 177. Sheffield: JSOT Press, 1999.

Douglas, Mary. *Natural Symbols: Explorations in Cosmology*. New York: Penguin, 2nd edn, 1973.

Dunn, James D. G. *First Corinthians*. NTG. Sheffield: Sheffield Academic Press, 1995.

——. *The Acts of the Apostles*. Valley Forge: Trinity, 1996.

Du Plessis, P. J. ΤΕΛΕΙΟΣ: *The Idea of Perfection in the New Testament*. Kampen: Kok, 1959.

Du Toit, Andrie B. 'A Tale of Two Cities: "Tarsus or Jerusalem" Revisited', *NTS* 46 (2000) 375–402.

Dybvad, Peter John. 'Imitation and Gospel in First Corinthians', Unpublished doctoral dissertation, Trinity Evangelical Divinity School, 2000.

Engsberg-Petersen, T. 'The Gospel and Social Practice according to 1 Corinthians', *NTS* 36 (1990) 557–84.

Ellingworth, Paul. *The Epistle to the Hebrews: A Commentary on the Greek Text*, NIGTC. Grand Rapids: Eerdmans, 1993.

Ellingworth, Paul and Howard A. Hatton, *A Handbook on Paul's First Letter to the Corinthians*, USBHS; Helps for Translators. New York: UBS, 1995.

Ellis, E. Earle. 'Paul and His Co-Workers', *NTS* 17 (1970–71) 437–52.

——. 'Traditions in 1 Corinthians', *NTS* 32 (1986) 481–502.

Eriksson, A. *Traditions as Rhetorical Proof: Pauline Argumentation in 1 Corinthians*, ConBNT, 29. Stockholm: Almqvist & Wiksell, 1998.

Esler, P. F., ed. *Modeling Early Christianity: Social-Scientific Study of the NT in its Context*. London: Routledge, 1995.

Evans, Craig A. 'How are the Apostles Judged? A Note on 1 Corinthians 3.10-15', *JETS* 27 (1984) 149–50.

Fairweather, Janet. 'Galatians and Classical Rhetoric', *TynBul* 45 (1994) 1–38, 213–43.

Fee, Gordon D. *The First Epistle to the Corinthians*. NICNT. Grand Rapids: Eerdmans, 1987.

——. 'Textual-Exegetical Observations on 1 Corinthians 1.2, 2.1, and 2.10', in *Scribes and Scriptures: New Testament Essays in Honor of J. Harold Greenlee*, ed. David Alan Black, 1–16. Winona Lake: Eisenbrauns, 1992.

——. 'Toward a Theology of 1 Corinthians', in *Pauline Theology, Volume 2: 1 & 2 Corinthians*, ed. David M. Hay, 37–58. Minneapolis: Fortress, 1993.

——. *God's Empowering Presence: The Holy Spirit in Paul's Letters*. Exeter: Paternoster and Peabody: Hendrickson, 1994.

Fernando, Ajith. *Acts,* NIVAC. Grand Rapids: Zondervan, 1998.

Fiore, Benjamin. 'The Function of Personal Example in the Socratic and Pastoral Epistles'. Unpublished doctoral dissertation, Yale Divinity School, 1982.

——. ' "Covert Allusion" in 1 Corinthians 1–4', *CBQ* 47 (1985) 85–102.

Fiorenza, Elisabeth Schüssler. 'Rhetorical Situation and Historical Reconstruction in 1 Corinthians', *NTS* 33 (1987) 386–403.

Fishburne, Charles W. '1 Corinthians 3.10-15 and the Testament of Abraham', *NTS* 17 (1970) 109–15.

Fitch, Walter Ogle. 'Paul, Apollos, Cephas, Christ', *Theology* 74 (1971) 18–24.

Fitzgerald, John T. *Cracks in an Earthen Vessel: An Examination of the Catalogues of Hardships in the Corinthians Correspondence*, SBLDS, 99. Atlanta: Scholars Press, 1988.

Fitzmyer, J. A. *The Acts of the Apostles*, AB, 31. Garden City: Doubleday, 1998.

Forbes, Christopher. 'Comparison, Self-Praise and Irony: Paul's Boasting and the Conventions of Hellenistic Rhetoric', *NTS* 32 (1986) 1–30.

——. 'Early Christian Inspired Speech and Hellenistic Popular Religion', *NovT* 28 (1986) 257–70.

Fowl, Stephen E. 'The Role of Authorial Intention in the Theological Interpretation of Scripture', in *Between Two Horizons: Spanning New Testament Studies & Systematic Theology*, eds. Joel B. Green and Max Turner, 71–87. Grand Rapids: Eerdmans, 2000.

Francis, J. '"As Babes in Christ" – Some Proposals regarding 1 Corinthians 3.1-3', *JSNT* 7 (1980) 41–60.

Freadman, Richard and Seamus Miller. *Re-thinking Theory: A Critique of Contemporary Literary Theory and an Alternative Account.* Cambridge: Cambridge University Press, 1992.

Fredrickson, David E. 'No Noose is Good News: Leadership as a Theological Problem in the Corinthian Correspondence'. *Word&Word* 16 (1996) 420–26: 465–72.

Friesen, Steven J. 'Poverty in Pauline Studies: Beyond the So-called New Consensus'. *JSNT* 26.3 (2004) 323–61.

Funk, Robert W. 'Word and Word in 1 Corinthians 2.6-16', in *Language, Hermeneutic, and Word of God: The Problem of Language in the New Testament and Contemporary Philosophy,* 275–305. New York: Harper & Row, 1966.

Furnish, Victor Paul. 'Fellow Workers in God's Service'. *JBL* 80 (1961) 364–70.

——. *II Corinthians: A New Translation with Introduction and Commentary*, AB, 32A. Garden City: Doubleday, 1984.

——. 'Theology in 1 Corinthians', in *Pauline Theology, Volume II: 1 & 2 Corinthians*, ed. David M. Hay, 59–89. Minneapolis: Fortress, 1993.

——. *The Theology of the First Letter to the Corinthians*, NTT. Cambridge: Cambridge University Press, 1999.

Gaffin, Richard B., J. 'Some Epistemological Reflections on 1 Cor. 2.6-16', *WTJ* 57 (1995) 103–24.

Gardner, Jane F. 'The Roman Family: Ideal and Metaphor', in *Constructing Early Christian Families: Family as Social Reality and Metaphor*, ed. H. Moxnes, 103–20. 'London: Routledge, 1997.

——. *Family and* Familia *in Roman Law and Life*. Oxford: Clarendon, 1998.

Garland, David E. 'Background Studies and New Testament Interpretation', in *New Testament Criticism and Interpretation*, eds. David Alan Black and David S. Dockery, 347–76. Grand Rapids: Zondervan, 1991.

——. *2 Corinthians*, NAC 29. Nashville: Broadman, 2001.

——. *1 Corinthians*. BECNT. Grand Rapids: Baker, 2004.

Gill, David W. J. 'In Search of the Social Elite in the Corinthian Church', *TynBul* 44 (1993) 323–37.

Gillespie, Thomas W. 'Interpreting the Kerygma: Early Christian Prophecy according to 1 Corinthians 2.6-16', in *Gospel Origins & Christian Beginnings: In Honor of James M. Robinson*, ed. James E. Goehring et al., 151–66. Sonoma: Polebridge, 1990.

Glancy, Jennifer A. 'Obstacles to Slaves' Participation in the Corinthian Church', *JBL* 117 (1998) 481–501.

Goulder, Michael D. 'Σοφία in 1 Corinthians', *NTS* 37 (1991) 516–34.

——. *Paul and the Competing Mission in Corinth*, LPS. Peabody: Hendrickson, 2001.

Grindheim, Sigurd. 'The Mystery in 1 Cor. 2.7', ETSP, 2001.

——. 'Wisdom for the Perfect: Paul's Challenge to the Corinthian Church (1 Corinthians 2.6-16)', *JBL* 121 (2002) 689–709.

Grosheide, Frederik William. *Commentary on the First Epistle to the Corinthians*, NICNT. Grand Rapids: Eerdmans, 1953.

Guthrie, George H. 'The Case for Apollos as the Author of Hebrews', *F&M* 18 (2001) 41–56.

Hafemann, Scott. *Suffering and the Spirit: An Exegetical study of II Cor. 2.14-3.3 within the Corinthian Correspondence*. Tübingen: Mohr, 1986.

——. 'Self-Commendation and Apostolic Legitimacy in 2 Corinthians', *NTS* 36 (1990) 66–88.

——. *2 Corinthians*, NIVAC. Grand Rapids: Zondervan, 2000.

Hagner, Donald A. 'The New Testament, History, and the Historical-Critical Method', in *New Testament Criticism & Interpretation*, eds. David Alan Black & David S. Dockery, 71–96. Grand Rapids: Zondervan, 1991.

Hall, David R. 'A Disguise for the Wise: μετασχηματισμός in 1 Corinthians 4.6', *NTS* 40 (1994) 143–49.

——. *The Unity of the Corinthian Correspondence*, JSNTSup, 251. London: T&T Clark, 2003.

Hanges, James C. '1 Corinthians 4.6 and the Possibility of Written Bylaws in the Corinthian Church', *JBL* 117 (1998) 275–99.

Hanson, Anthony Tyrrell, *The Paradox of the Cross in the Thought of Paul*, JSNTSS, 17. Sheffield: JSOT Press, 1987.

Harding, Mark. *Tradition and Rhetoric in the Pastoral Epistles*, SBL, 3. New York: Peter Lang, 1998.

Harland, Philip A. *Associations, Synagogues, and Congregations: Claiming a Place in Ancient Mediterranean Society*. Minneapolis: Fortress, 2003.

Harris, Murray J. *The Second Epistle to the Corinthians: A Commentary on the Greek Text*, NIGTC. Grand Rapids: Eerdmans, 2005.

Harris, R. 'Who Sent Apollos to Corinth?' *ExpTim* 11 (1916) 175–83.

Hart, J. H. A. 'Apollos', *JTS* 7 (1906) 16–28.

Hartman, Lars. 'Some Remarks on 1 Cor. 2.1-5', *SEÅ* 39 (1974) 109–20.

Hays, Richard B. 'Ecclesiology and Ethics in 1 Corinthians', *Ex auditu* 10 (1994) 31–43.

——. *First Corinthians*, Interpretation. Louisville: Knox, 1997.

——. 'The Conversion of the Imagination: Scripture and Eschatology in 1 Corinthians', *NTS* 45 (1999) 391–412.

——. 'Wisdom According to Paul', in *Where Shall Wisdom Be Found?*

Wisdom in the Bible, the Church and the Contemporary World, ed. Stephen C. Barton, 111–23. Edinburgh: T&T Clark, 1999.

Heinrici, Georg. *Der erste Brief an die Korinther*. Göttingen: Vandenhoeck, 1896.

Hengel, Martin. *Crucifixion in the Ancient World and the Folly of the Message of the Cross*, trans. J. Bowden. Philadelphia: Fortress, 1977.

——. *The Pre-Christian Paul*. London: SCW. 1991.

Héring, J. *The First Epistle of Saint Paul to the Corinthians*, trans. A.W. Heathcote and P. J. Allcock, London: Epworth. 1962. 2nd edn.

Herman, John D. 'Paul's Rhetoric of the Cross in 1 Corinthians 1–4'. Unpublished M. St. dissertation, Trinity Lutheran Seminary, 1993.

Herrmann, Léon. 'Apollos', *RSR* 50 (1976) 330–36.

Hiigel, John Lewis. 'Leadership in 1 Corinthians: An Exegetical Study in Paul's Ecclesiology'. Unpublished doctoral dissertation, Fuller Theological Seminary, 1999.

Hirsch, E. D. *Validity in Interpretation*. New Haven: Yale University Press, 1967.

Hock, Ronald F. 'Paul's Tentmaking and the Problem of His Social Class', *JBL* 97 (1978) 555–64.

——. 'The Workshop as a Social Setting for Paul's Missionary Preaching', *CBQ* 41 (1979) 438–50.

——. *The Social Context of Paul's Ministry: Tentmaking and Apostleship*. Philadelphia: Fortress, 1980.

Hollander, Harm W. 'The Testing by Fire of the Builders' Works: 1 Corinthians 3.10-15', *NTS* 40 (1994) 89–104.

Hooker, Morna D. 'Beyond the Things Which Are Written': An Examination of 1 Cor. 4.6', *NTS* 10 (1963–64) 127–32.

——. 'A Partner in the Gospel: Paul's Understanding of His Ministry', in *Theology and Ethics in Paul and His Interpreters*, eds. Eugene H. Lovering and Jerry L. Summey, 83–100. Nashville: Abingdon, 1996.

——. 'Hard Sayings: 1 Corinthians 3.2', *Theology* 69 (1966) 19–22.

Horne, C. M. 'The Power of Paul's Preaching', *BEIS* 8 (1965) 112.

Horrell, David G. *The Social Ethos of the Corinthians Correspondence: Interests and Ideology from 1 Corinthians and 1 Clement*, SNTIW. Edinburgh: T&T Clark, 1996.

——. 'Leadership Patterns and the Development of Ideology in Early Christianity', *SR* 58 (1997) 323–41.

——. 'From ἀδελφοί to οἶκος Θεοῦ: Social Transformation in Pauline Christianity', *JBL* 120 (2001) 293–311.

Horsley, Richard A. 'Pneumatikos vs. Psychikos: Distinctions of Spiritual Status among the Corinthians', *HTR* 69 (1976) 269–88.

——. 'Wisdom of Word and Words of Wisdom in Corinth'. *CBQ* 39 (1977) 224–39.

——. '"How Can Some of You Say that There Is no Resurrection?" Spiritual Elitism in Corinth', *NovT* 20 (1978) 203–31.

——. 'Gnosis in Corinth: 1 Corinthians 8.1-6', *NTS* 27 (1980) 32–51.

——. '1 Corinthians: A Case Study of Paul's Assembly as an Alternative Society', in *Paul and Empire: Religion and Power in Roman Imperial Society*, ed. Richard Horsley, 242–52. Harrisburg: Trinity Press International, 1997.

——. 'Building an Alternative Society: Introduction' to *Paul and Empire: Religion and Power in Roman Imperial Society*, ed. Richard Horsely. Harrisburg: Trinity Press International, 1997.

Howard, W. F. '1 Cor. 4.6; Exegesis or Emendation?' *ExpTim* 33 (1921–22) 479–8.

Hughes, Frank W. 'Rhetorical Criticism and the Corinthian Correspondence', in *The Rhetorical Analysis of Scripture: Essays from the 1995 London Conference*, eds. Stanley E. Porter and Thomas H. Olbricht, JSNTSup, 146, 246–61. Sheffield: Sheffield Academic Press, 1997.

——. 'The Rhetoric of Letters', in *The Thessalonians Debate: Methodological Discord or Methodological Synthesis?* eds. Karl P. Donfried and Johannes Beutler, 194–240. Grand Rapids: Eerdmans, 2000.

Humphries, Raymond A. 'Paul's Rhetoric of Argumentation in 1 Corinthians 1–4', Unpublished doctoral dissertation, Graduate Theological Union, 1980.

Hunter, Archibald Macbride. 'Apollos the Alexandrian', in *Biblical Studies: Essays in Honor of William Barclay*, ed. Johnston R. McKay, 147–56. Philadelphia: Wesminster, 1976.

Hurd, John C. *The Origin of 1 Corinthians*. Macon: Mercer University Press, 2nd edn, 1983.

——. 'Good News and the Integrity of 1 Corinthians', in *Gospel in Paul: Studies on Corinthians, Galatians, and Romans for Richard N. Longenecker*, eds. L. A. Jervis and P. Richardson, JSTNSSup 108, 38–62. Sheffield: Sheffield Academic Press, 1994.

Hurst, L. D. 'Apollos, Hebrews, and Corinth: Bishop Montefiore's Theory Examined', *SJT* 38 (1985) 505–13.

Hyldahl, Niels. 'Die Frage nach der literarischen Einheit des zweiten Korintherbriefes', *ZNW* 64 (1973) 289–306.

——. 'The Corinthian "Parties" and the Corinthian Crisis', *ST* 45 (1991) 19–32.

——. 'Paul and Apollos: Exegetical Observations to 1 Cor. 3.1-23', in *Apocryphon Severini Presented to Søren Giversen*, eds. Per Bilde, Helge Kjser Nielsen and Jørgen Podemann Sørensen, 68–82. Aarhus: Aarhus University Press, 1993.

——. 'Paul and Hellenistic Judaism in Corinth', in *The New Testament and Hellenistic Judaism*, eds. Peder Borgen and Søren Giversen, 204–16. Peabody: Hendrickson, 1997.

——. 'Den korintiske situation – en skitse', *DTT* 40 (1977) 18–30.

Johnson, E. E. 'The Wisdom of God as Apocalyptic Power', in *Faith and History: Essays in Honor of Paul W. Meyer*, eds. J. T. Carroll, C. H. Cosgrove, and E. E. Johnson, 137–48. Atlanta: Scholars Press, 1990.

Joubert, Stephan J. 'Managing the Household: Paul as *paterfamilias* of the Christian Household Group in Corinth', in *Modeling Early Christianity: Social-Scientific Studies of the New Testament in Its Context*, ed. Philip F. Esler, 213–23. London: Routledge, 995.

Judge, E. A. 'Early Christians as a Scholastic Community: Part II', *JRH* 1 (1960–61) 4–15; 125–37.

——. *The Social Pattern of Christian Groups in the First Century: Some Prolegomena to the Study of the New Testament Ideas of Social Obligations*. London: Tyndale, 1960.

——. 'Paul's Boasting in Relation to Contemporary Professional Practice', *ABR* 16 (1968) 37–50.

——. 'The Social Identity of the First Christians', *JRH* 11 (1980) 201–17.

——. 'Early Church Against Classical Education', *JCEd* 77 (1983) 11.

——. 'The Reaction against Classical Education in the New Testament', *JCEd* 77 (1983) 7–14.

——. 'The teacher as Moral Exemplar in Paul and in the Inscription of Ephesus', in *In the Fullness of Time: Biblical Studies in Honour of Archbishop Donald Robinson*, 185–201. Homebush West: Lancer, 1992.

Käsemann, E. 'Sentences of Holy Law in the NT', in *New Testament Questions of Today*. London: SCM, 1969.

——. *Perspectives on Paul*. Philadelphia: Fortress, 1971.

Keck, L. 'God the Other Who Acts Otherwise: An Exegetical Essay on 1 Cor. 1.26-31', *Word & Word* 16 (1996) 437–43.

Kelly, Douglas. 'Oral Xenophon', in *Voice into Text: Orality and Literacy in Ancient Greece*, ed. Ian Worthington, 150–63. Leiden: Brill, 1996.

Kennedy, George A. *New Testament Interpretation Through Rhetorical Criticism*. Chapel Hill: University of North Carolina Press, 1984.

——. 'Truth and Rhetoric in the Pauline Epistles', in *The Bible as Rhetoric*, ed. M. Warner, 195–202. London: Routledge, 1990.

——. *Classical Rhetoric and Its Christian and Secular Tradition from Ancient to Modern Times*. Princeton: Princeton University Press, 2nd rev. edn, 1983; Chapel Hill: University of North Carolina Press, 1999.

Ker, Donald P. 'Paul and Apollos–Colleagues or Rivals?' *JSNT* 77 (2000) 75–97.

Kistemaker, Simon J. *2 Corinthians*, BkNTC. Grand Rapids: Baker, 1997.

Klauck, Hans-Josef. *1 Korintherbrief. Wurzburg*: Echter Verlag, 1984.

Kleinknecht, K. T. *Der leidende Gerechtfertigte: Die alttestamentlich-*

jüdische Tradition vom 'leidenden Gerechten' und ihre Rezeption bei Paulus. WUNT 2/13. Tübingen: Mohr, 1984.

Kloppenborg, John S. and Stephen G. Wilson, eds. *Voluntary Associations in the Graeco-Roman World.* London and New York: Routledge, 1996.

Klutz, T. E. 'Re-Reading 1 Corinthians after Rethinking "Gnosticism"', *JSNT* 26 (2003) 193–216.

Knox, W. L. *St. Paul and the Church of the Gentiles.* Cambridge: Cambridge University Press, 1939.

Koenig, John. 'Christ and the Hierarchies in First Corinthians', *ATR* 11 (1990) 99–113.

Koester, Craig R. *Hebrews: A New Translation with Introduction and Commentary*, AB, 36. New York: Doubleday, 2001.

Koperski, Veronica. ' "Mystery of God" or "Testimony of God" in 1 Cor. 2,1: Textual and Exegetical Considerations', in *New Testament Textual Criticism and Exegesis: Festschrift J. Delobel*, ed. A. Denaux, 305–15. Leuven: Peeters, 2002.

Kovacs, Judith. 'The Archons, the Spirit, and the Death of Christ: Do We Need the Hypothesis of Gnostic Opponents to Explain 1 Corinthians 2.6-16?' in *Apocalyptic and the New Testament: Essays in Honor of J. Louis Martyn,* eds Joel Marcus and Marion L. Soards. JSNTSup, 24, 217–36. Sheffield: JSOT, 1989.

Krentz, Edgar. '*LOGOS* or *SOPHIA*: The Pauline Use of the Ancient Dispute between Rhetoric and Philosophy', in *Early Christianity and Classical Culture: Comparative Studies in Honor of Abraham J. Malherbe*, eds. John T. Fitzgerald, Thomas H. Olbricht and L. Michael White, NovTSup, 110, 277–90. Leiden: Brill, 2003.

Kuck, David W. *Judgment and Community Conflict: Paul's Use of Apocalyptic Judgment Language in 1 Corinthians 3.5-4.5*, NovTSup, 66. Leiden: Brill, 1992.

——. 'Paul and Pastoral Ambition: A Reflection on 1 Corinthians 3–4', *CTM* 19 (1992) 174–83.

Laeuchli, Samuel. *The Language of Faith: An Introduction to the Semantic Dilemma of the Early Church.* Nashville: Abingdon, 1962.

Lambrecht, Jan, S. J. 'The Power of God: A Note on the Connection between 1 Cor. 1.17 and 18', in *Collected Studies on Pauline Literature and on the Book of Revelation*, AnBib, 147, 35–42. Roma: Editrice Pontificio Istituto Biblico, 2001.

——. 'Paul as Example: A Study of 1 Cor. 4.6-21', in *ibid.*, 43–62.

Lamp, Jeffrey S. 'Gospel and Rhetoric in 1 Corinthians 1–4: Ruminations over Implications for Christian Apologetics', paper presented at the 47th National Conference. Portland: Theological Research Exchange Network, 1996. Microfiche (ETSP).

——. 'The Spiritual Christian: A Matter of Degree or Definition? (1 Cor.

2.6-3.4)', paper presented at the 48th National Conference. Jackson, MS.: Theological Research Exchange Network, 1997. Microfiche (ETSP).

——. *First Corinthians 1–4 in Light of Jewish Wisdom Traditions: Christ, Wisdom, and Spirituality*, SBEC, 42. Lewiston: Edwin Mellen, 2000.

Lampe, Peter. 'Theological Wisdom and the "Word about the Cross", The Rhetorical Scheme in 1 Corinthians 1–4', *Int* 44 (1990) 117–31.

Lanci, J. R. *A New Temple in Corinth: Rhetorical and Archeological Approaches to Pauline Imagery*. SBL, 1, New York: Peter Lang, 1997.

Lassen, Eva Maria. 'The Use of the Father Image in Imperial Propaganda and 1 Corinthians 4.14-21'. *TynBul* 42 (1991) 127–36.

Law, Robert. *The Tests of Life*. Edinburgh: n. p., 1909.

Legault, André. '"Beyond the Things which Are Written"', *NTS* 18 (1972) 227–31.

Leopold, J. 'Philo's Knowledge of Rhetorical Theory', in *Two Treatises of Philo of Alexandria*, JS 25, eds D. Winson and J. Dillon, Brown, 129–36. Chico: Scholars Press, 1983.

Levison, John R. 'Did the Spirit Inspire Rhetoric? An exploration of George Kennedy's Definition of Early Christian Rhetoric', in *Persuasive Artistry: Studies in New Testament Rhetoric in Honor of George A. Kennedy*, ed. Duane F. Watson, JSNTSup, 50, 25–40. Sheffield: JSOT Press, 1991.

Lewis, Harry Wayne. 'An Exegetical Study of the Pauline Concept of Sophia in 1 Corinthians', Unpublished doctoral dissertation, Southwestern Baptist Theological Seminary, 1982.

Lietzmann, Hans. *An die Korinther I & II*. HNT 9. Tubingen: Mohr, 1969.

Lightfoot, J. B. *Notes on the Epistles of Saint Paul from Unpublished Commentaries*. London: n.p., 1904.

Lim, Timothy H. '"Not in Persuasive Words of Wisdom, but in the Demonstration of the Spirit and Power"', *NovT* 29 (1987) 137–49.

Lindemann, Andreas. *Der erste Korintherbrief*. Tübingen: Mohr, 2000.

——. 'Die paulinische Ekklesiologie angesichts der Lebenswirklichkeit der christlichen Gemeinde in Korinth', in *The Corinthians Correspondence*, ed. Reimund Bieringer, 64–86. Leuven: Leuven University Press, 1996.

Litfin, Duane. *St. Paul's Theology of Proclamation: 1 Corinthians 1–4 and Greco-Roman Rhetoric*, SNTSMS, 79. Cambridge: Cambridge University Press, 1994.

——. 'Review: *St. Paul's Theology of Rhetorical Style: An Examination of 1 Corinthians 2.1-5 in Light of First Century Greco-Roman Rhetorical Culture* by Michael A. Bullmore', *JBL* 116 (1997) 569.

Louw, J. P. *Semantics of New Testament Greek*, SBLSS. Philadelphia: Fortress, 1982.

Lüdemann, Gerd. *Opposition to Paul in Jewish Christianity*. Minneapolis: Augsburg, 1977.

Lull, David J. ' "The Law was Our Pedagogue": A Study in Galatians 3.19-25', *JBL* 105 (1986) 481–98.

Lyall, F. *Slaves and Sons: Legal Metaphors in the Epistles*. Grand Rapids: Zondervan, 1984.

Lynch, A. 'Pauline Rhetoric: 1 Corinthians 1.10-4.21', Unpublished masters dissertation, University of North Carolina 1981.

Malherbe, Abraham. ' "Gentle as a Nurse": The Cynic Background to 1 Thess 2', *NovT* 12 (1970) 203–17.

——. *Social Aspects of Early Christianity*. Baton Rouge: Louisiana State University Press, 1977.

——. *Paul and the Popular Philosophers*. Minneapolis: Fortress, 1989.

——. ' "Seneca" on Paul as Letter Writer', in *The Future of Early Christianity: Essays in Honor of Helmut Koester*, ed. Birger A. Pearson, 414–21. Minneapolis: Fortress, 1991.

Mare, W. Harold. *1 Corinthians*. EBC 10. Grand Rapids: Zondervan, 1976.

Marshall, I. H. *The Acts of the Apostles*, TNTC. Leicester: IVP, 1980.

Marshall, P. *Enmity in Corinth: Social Conventions in Paul's Relations with the Corinthians*, WUNT, 2. Tübingen: Mohr, 1987.

Martin, Dale B. *Slavery as Salvation: The Metaphor of Slavery in Pauline Christianity*. New Haven: Yale University Press, 1990.

——. *The Corinthian Body*. New Haven: Yale University Press, 1995.

——. 'Review Essay: Justin J. Meggitt, Paul, Poverty, and Survival', *JSNT* 84 (2001) 51–64.

Martin, Ralph P. *2 Corinthians*, WBC, 40. Dallas: Word, 1986.

Meeks, Wayne A. *The First Urban Christians: The Social World of the Apostle Paul*. New Haven: Yale University Press, 1983.

——. *The Moral World of the First Christians*. London: SPCK, 1986.

Meggitt, Justin J. 'The Social Status of Erastus (Rom. 16.23)'. *NovT* 38 (1996) 218–23.

——. *Paul, Poverty, and Survival*. Edinburgh: T&T Clark, 1998.

——. 'Response to Martin and Theissen'. *JSNT* 84 (2001) 85–94.

Merklein, H. 'Die Einheitlichkeit des ersten Korintherbriefes', *ZNW* 75 (1984) 153–83.

——. *Der erste Brief an die Korinther. Kapitel 1–4*, ÖTNT 7/1. Gütersloh: Mohn, 1992.

Metzger, B. M. *A Textual Commentary on the Greek New Testament*. New York: UBS, 2nd edn, 1994.

Miller, Gene. 'Ἀρχοντων του Αιωνος τουτου–A New Look at 1 Corinthians 2.6-8', *JBL* 91 (1972) 522–28.

Mitchell, M. Margaret. 'Concerning περὶ δε/ in 1 Corinthians', *NovT* 31 (1989) 229–56.

———. *Paul and the Rhetoric of Reconciliation: An Exegetical Investigation of the Language and Composition of 1 Corinthians*. Tübingen: Mohr, 1992.

———. 'Rhetorical Shorthand in Pauline Argumentation: The Functions of "the Gospel" in the Corinthian Correspondence', in *Gospel in Paul: Studies on Corinthians, Galatians, and Romans for Richard N. Longenecker*, ed. L. A. Jervis and P. Richardson, JSNTSup, 108, 63–88. Sheffield: Sheffield Academic Press, 1994.

———. 'A Patristic Perspective on Pauline περιαυτολογία', *NTS* 47 (2001) 354–71.

Moffat, J. *A Critical and Exegetical Commentary on the Epistle to the Hebrews*, ICC. Edinburgh: T&T Clark, 1957.

Montefiore, H. *A Commentary on the Epistle to the Hebrews*, BNTC. London: Black, 1964.

Morris, Leon. *1 Corinthians*, TNTC. Grand Rapids: Eerdmans, rev. edn, 1987.

Moxnes, H. 'What is Family? Problems Constructing Early Christian Families', in *Constructing Early Christian Families: Family as Social Reality and Metaphor*, ed. H. Moxnes, 13–41. London: Routledge, 1997.

Mulholland, Robert. 'Sociological Criticism', in *New Testament Criticism & Interpretation*, eds. David Alan Black and David S. Dockery, 295–316. Grand Rapids: Zondervan, 1991.

Munck, Johannes. 'The Church Without factions: Studies in 1 Corinthians 1–4', in *Paul and the Salvation of Mankind*, 135–67. London: SCM Press, 1959.

Murphy-O'Connor, Jerome. *St. Paul's Corinth: Text and Acheology*. GNS, 6. Wilmington: Michael Glazier, 1983.

———. 'Interpolations in 1 Corinthians'. *CBQ* 48 (1986) 81–94.

———. *The Theology of the Second Letter to the Corinthians*. Cambridge: Cambridge University Press, 1991.

———. *Paul the Letter Writer*. Collegeville: Liturgical, 1995.

———. *Paul: A Critical Life*. Oxford: Clarendon, 1996.

Myrick, Anthony A. '"Father" Imagery in 2 Corinthians 1–9 and Jewish Paternal Tradition', *TynBul* 47 (1996) 163–71.

Neyrey, J. H. 'Body Language in 1 Corinthians: The Use of Anthropological Models for Understanding Paul and his Opponents', *Semeia* 35 (1986) 129–70.

Nida, E. A. 'Implications of Contemporary Linguistics for Biblical Scholarship', *JBL* 91 (1972) 73–89.

Norden, Eduard. *Die Antike Kunstprosa vom VI. Jahrhunderts vor Christus in die Zeit der Renaissance*. Darmstadt: Wissenschaftliche Buchgesellschaft, 1958; repr. Leipzig: B. G. Teubner, 1989.

Oakes, Peter. 'Constructing Poverty Scales for Graeco-Roman Society: A

Response to Steven Friesen's "Poverty in Pauline Studies"', *JSNT* 26.3 (2004) 367–71.

O'Brien, Peter T. *Introductory Thanksgivings in the Letters of Paul*, SNT, 49. Leiden: Brill, 1977.

O'Day Gail R. 'Jeremiah 9.22-23 and 1 Corinthians 1.26-31: A Study in Intertextuality', *JBL* 109 (1990) 259–67.

Offerman, H. 'Apollos, Apelles, Apollonios'. *LCR* 38 (1919) 145–50.

Oke, C. C. 'Paul's Method not a Demonstration but an Exhibition of the Spirit', *ExpTim* 67 (1955) 85–86.

Orr, William F. and James A. Walther. *First Corinthians*, AB, 32. New York: Doubleday, 1976.

Osiek, Carolyn. 'The Family in Early Christianity: "Family Values" Revisited', *CBQ* 58 (1996) 1–25.

O'Sullivan, Neil. 'Written and Spoken in the First Sophistic', in *Voice into Text: Orality and Literacy in Ancient Greece*, ed. Ian Worthington, 115–28. Leiden: Brill, 1996.

Painter, John. 'Paul and the Πνευματικοί at Corinth', in *Paul and Paulinism: Essays in Honor of C. K. Barrett*, eds. M. D. Hooker and S. G. Wilson, 237–50. London: SPCK, 1982.

Pearson, Birger Albert. *The Pneumatikos-Psychikos Terminology in 1 Corinthians. A Study in the Theology of the Corinthian Opponents of Paul and Its Relation to Gnosticism*, SBLNHS, 12. Missoula: Scholars Press, 1973.

——. *Gnosticism, Judaism and Egyptian Christianity*. Minneapolis: Fortress, 1990.

Penna, Romano. *Paul the Apostle: Wisdom and Folly of the Cross in a Theological and Exegetical Study*, vol. 2, trans. Thomas P. Wahl. Collegeville: Liturgical, 1996.

Peterlin, Davorin. 'Clement's Answer to the Corinthian Conflict in AD 96', *JETS* 39 (1996) 57–69.

——. 'The Corinthian Church Between Paul's and Clement's Time', *ATJ* 53 (1998) 49–57.

Peterson, Brian. K. *Eloquence and the Proclamation of the Gospel in Corinth*, SBLDS, 163. Atlanta: Scholars Press, 1998.

Pétrement, Simone. *A Separate God*. San Francisco: Harper, 1990.

Pickett, Raymond. *The Cross in Corinth: The Social Significance of the Death of Jesus*, JSNTSup, 143. Sheffield: Sheffield Academic Press, 1997.

Plank, Karl. *Paul and the Irony of Affliction*. Atlanta: Scholars Press, 1987.

Plummer, A. *A Critical and Exegetical Commentary on the Second Epistle of St. Paul to the Corinthians*, ICC. Edinburgh: T&T Clark, 1915.

Plummer, R. L. 'Imitation of Paul and the Church's Missionary Role in 1 Corinthians', *JETS* 44 (2001) 219–36.

Pogoloff, M. Stephen. *LOGOS AND SOPHIA: The Rhetorical Situation of 1 Corinthians*, SBLDS, 134. Atlanta: Scholars Press, 1992.

Polhill, John B. 'The Wisdom of God and Factionalism: 1 Corinthians 1–4', *RevExp* 80 (1983) 325–39.

——. *Acts*, NAC 26. Nashville: Broadman, 1992.

Porter, Stanley E. 'The Theoretical Justification for Application of Rhetorical Categories to Pauline Epistolary Literature', in *Rhetoric and the New Testament: Essays from the 1992 Heidelberg Conference*, eds. Stanley E. Porter and Thomas H. Olbricht, JSNTSup, 90, 100–22. Sheffield: Sheffield Academic Press, 1993.

——. 'Ancient Rhetorical Analysis and Discourse Analysis of the Pauline Corpus', in *The Rhetorical Analysis of Scripture: Essays from the 1995 London Conference*, eds Stanley E. Porter and Thomas H. Olbricht, JSNTSup, 146, 249–74. Sheffield: Sheffield Academic Press, 1997.

——. 'Paul as Epistolographer *and* Rhetorician?' in *The Rhetorical Interpretation of Scripture: Essays from the 1996 Malibu Conference*, eds. Stanley Porter and Dennis L. Stamps, JSNTSup 180, 222–48. Sheffield: Sheffield Academic Press, 1997.

——. 'Paul of Tarsus and His Letters', in *Handbook of Classical Rhetoric in the Hellenistic Period 330 B.C.-A.D. 400*, 533–85. Leiden: Brill, 1997.

——. *The Paul of Acts*, WUNT, 115. Tübingen: Mohr, 1999.

Proctor, John. 'Fire in God's House: Influence of Malachi 3 in the NT', *JETS* 36 (1993) 9–14.

Reed, Jeffrey T. 'Using Ancient Rhetorical Categories to Interpret Paul's Letters: A Question of Genre', in *Rhetoric and the New Testament: Essays from the 1992 Heidelberg Conference*, eds. S. E. Porter and T. H. Olbricht, JSNTSup, 90, 292–324. Sheffield: Sheffield Academic Press, 1993.

——. 'Modern Linguistics and the New Testament: A Basic Guide to Theory, Terminology, and Literature', in *Approaches to New Testament Study*, eds. Stanley E. Porter and David Tombs, JSNTSup 120, 36–62. Sheffield: Sheffield Academic Press, 1995.

——. 'Discourse Analysis as New Testament Hermeneutic: A Retrospective and Prospective Appraisal', *JETS* 39 (1996) 223–40.

——. *A Discourse Analysis of Philippians: Method and Rhetoric in the Debate over Literary Integrity*, JSNTSup, 113. Sheffield: Sheffield Academic Press, 1997.

——. 'The Epistle', in *Handbook of Classical Rhetoric in the Hellenistic Period 330 B.C.-A.D. 400*, 171–93. Leiden: Brill, 1997.

Reiling, J. 'Wisdom and the Spirit: An Exegesis of 1 Corinthians 2.6-16', in *Text and Testimony: Essays on New Testament and Apocryphal Literature in Honour of A. F. J. Klijn*, eds. T. Baarda and A. Hilhorst, 200–11. Kampen: J. H. Kok, 1988.

Reumann, J. 'Servants of God–Pre-Christian Religious Application of OIKONOMOS in Greek', *JBL* 77 (1958) 339–49.

——. 'οἰκονομία-Terms in Paul in Comparison with Lucan *Heilsgeschichte*', *NTS* 13 (1966/67) 147–67.

Robertson, A. T. 'Apollos the Gifted'. *BR* 6 (1921) 380–95.

Robertson, A. T. and A. Plummer. *A Critical and Exegetical Commentary on the First Epistle of St. Paul to the Corinthians*, ICC. Edinburgh: T&T Clark, 2nd edn, 1914.

Robertson C. K. *Conflict in Corinth: Redefining the System*, SBL, 42. New York: Peter Lang, 2001.

Rosaeg, Nils A. 'Paul's Rhetorical Arsenal and 1 Corinthians 1–4', *Jian Dao* 3 (1995) 51–75.

Ross, J. M. ' "Not above What is Written": A Note on 1 Cor. 4.6', *ExpTim* 82 (1971) 215–17.

Rosscup, James E. 'A New Look at 1 Corinthians 3.12 – "Gold, Silver, Precious Stones" ', *MSJ* 1 (1990) 33–51.

Ruef, J. *Paul's First Letter to Corinth*. Philadelphia: Westminster, 1971.

Russell, D. A. *Greek Declamations*. Cambridge: Cambridge University Press, 1983.

Saller, R. P. 'Corporal Punishment, Authority, and Obedience in the Roman Household', in *Marriage, Divorce, and Children in Ancient Rome*, ed. B. Rawson, 144–65. Oxford: Clarendon, 1991.

——. *Patriarchy, Property and Death in the Roman Family*, CSPESPS 25. Cambridge: Cambridge University Press, 1994.

Sanders, Boykin. 'Imitating Paul: 1 Cor. 4.16', *HTR* 74 (1981) 353–63.

Sandnes, Karl Olav. 'Paul and Socrates: The Aim of Paul's Areopagus Speech', *JSNT* 50 (1993) 13–26.

Savage, Timothy. B. *Power through Weakness: Paul's Understanding of the Christian Ministry in 2 Corinthians*, SNTSMS, 86. Cambridge: Cambridge University Press, 1996.

Schiefer Ferrari, M. *Die Sprache des Leids in den paulinischen Peristasenkatalogen*. Stuttgart: katholisches Bibelwerk, 1991.

Schmithals, W. *Gnosticism in Corinth: An Investigation of the Letters to the Corinthians*, trans. John E. Steely. Nashville: Abingdon 2nd edn, 1971.

Schnelle, U. *The History and Theology of the New Testament Writings*. London: SCM, 1998.

Schrage, Wolfgang. 'Das Verständnis des Todes Jesu Christi in Neuen Testament', in *Das Kreuz Jesu Christi als Grund des Heils*, eds. E. Bizer et al., STAEKU, 3, 49–90. Gütersloh: Mohn, 1967.

——. 'Leid, Kreuz und Eschaton. Die Peristasenkataloge als Merkmale paulinischer theologia crucis und Eschatologie', *ET* 34 (1974) 141–75.

——. 'Das apostolische Amt des Paulus nach 1 Kor 4, 14–17', in *L'Apôtre*

Paul: Personnalité, style et conception du ministère, ed. A. Vanhoye, 103–19. BETL, 73. Leuven: Leuven University Press, 1986.

——. *Der erste Brief an die Korinther: 1Kor 1, 1–6, 16*. EKKNT, 7/1. Zürich; Braunschweig; Neukirchen-Vluyn: Benziger Verlag; Neukirchener Verlag, 1991.

——. *Der erste Brief an die Korinther: 1 Kor 15,1–16,24*. EKKNT 7/3 (Zurich: Benzinger/Neukirchen-Vluyn: Neukirchener Verlag, 2001.

Schubert, Paul. *Form and Function of the Pauline Thanksgivings*, BZNW, 20. Berlin: Alfred Töpelmann, 1939.

Schütz, John Howard. *Paul and the Anatomy of Apostolic Authority*, SNTSMS, 26. Cambridge: Cambridge University Press, 1975.

Scroggs, Robin. 'Paul: ΣΟΦΟΣ and ΠΝΕΥΜΑΤΙΚΟΣ', *NTS* 14 (1967–68) 33–55.

Selby, Gary S. 'Paul, the Seer: The Rhetorical Persona in 1 Corinthians 2.1-16', in *The Rhetorical Analysis of Scripture: Essays from the 1995 London Conference*, eds. Stanley E. Porter and Thomas H. Olbricht, JSNTSup, 146, 351–73. Sheffield: Sheffield Academic Press, 1997.

Sellin, Gerhard. 'Das "Geheimnis" der Weisheit und das Rätsel der "Christuspartei" (zu 1 Kor 1–4)', *ZNW* 73 (1982) 69–96.

Sevrin, J. 'La Gnose à Corinthe: Questions de Méthode et Observations sur 1 Co 1,17–3,3', in *The Corinthian Correspondence*, ed. Reimund Bieringer, 121–39. Leuven: Leuven University Press, 1996.

Shanor, Jay. 'Paul as Master Builder: Construction Terms in First Corinthians', *NTS* 34 (1988) 461–71.

Shaw, G. *The Cost of Authority: Manipulation and Freedom in the New Testament*. London: SCM, 1983.

Silva, Moisés. *Biblical Words and Their Meaning: An Introduction to Lexical Semantics*. Grand Rapids: Zondervan, 1983.

Smit, Joop F. M. '"What is Apollos? What is Paul?" In Search for the Coherence of First Corinthians 1.10-4.21', *NovT* 44 (2002) 231–51.

——. 'Epideictic Rhetoric in Paul's First Letter to the Corinthians 1–4', *Bib* 84 (2003) 184–202.

Soards, M. L. *The Speeches in Acts: Their Content, Context, and Concerns*. Lousiville: Westminster/John Knox, 1994.

Sojung, Yoon. 'Not in Persuasive Words of Wisdom? Paul's Rhetoric in 1 Corinthians 1.18-2.16', Unpublished doctoral dissertation, Graduate Theological Union, 2004.

Spencer, William David. 'The Power in Paul's Teaching (1 Cor. 4.9-20)', *JETS* 32 (1989) 51–61.

Spicq, C. *L'Épître aux Hébreux*, EBib. Paris: Gabalda, 1952.

——. 'L'Épître aux Hébreux, Apollos, Jean-Baptiste, les Hellénistes et Qumrân', *RevQ* 1 (1959) 365–90.

Stanley, David. '"Become Imitators of Me": The Pauline conception of Apostolic Tradition', *Bib* 40 (1959) 859–77.

Sterling, Gregory E. ' "Wisdom among the Perfect:" Creation Traditions in Alexandrian Judaism and Corinthian Christianity', *NTS* 37 (1995) 355–84.

Still, E. Coye, III. 'Divisions over Leaders and Food Offered to Idols: The Parallel Thematic Structures of 1 Corinthians 4.6-21 and 8.1-11.1', *TynBul* 55 (2004) 17–42.

Stirewalt, M. Luther, Jr. *Paul, The Letter Writer*. Grand Rapids: Eerdmans, 2003.

Stowers, Stanley K. 'Social Status, Public Speaking and Private Teaching: The Circumstances of Paul's Preaching Activity', *NovT* 26 (1984) 59–82.

——. *Letter Writing in Greco-Roman Antiquity*. Philadelphia: Westminster, 1986.

——. 'Paul on the Use and Abuse of Reason', in *Greeks, Romans, and Christians: Essays in Honor of Abraham J. Malherbe*, eds. Dabid L. Balch, Everett Ferguson, and Wayne A. Meeks, 253–86. Minneapolis: Fortress, 1990.

——. 'Greek and Latin Letters', in *ABD*, vol. 4, ed. David Noel Freedman, 290–99. New York: Doubleday, 1992.

Strüder, Christof W. 'Preferences not Parties: The Background of 1 Cor. 1.12', *ETL* 79 (2003) 431–55.

——. *Paulus und die Gesinnung Christi: Identität und Entscheidungsfindung aus der Mitte von 1Kor 1–4*, BETL, 190. Leuven: Leuven University Press, 2005.

Stuhlmacher, Peter. 'The Hermeneutical Significance of 1 Cor. 2.6-16', in *Tradition and Interpretation in the New Testament: Essays in Honor of E. Earle Ellis for His 60th Birthday*, eds. Gerald F. Hawthorne and Otto Betz, 328–48. Grand Rapids: Eerdmans, 1987.

Swain, Simon. *Hellenism and Empire: Language, Classicism, and Power in the Greek World, AD 50–250*. Oxford: Clarendon, 1996.

Tannehill, R. C. *The Narrative Unity of Luke-Acts: A Literary Interpretation, vol. 2: The Acts of the Apostles*. Minnesota: Fortress, 1990.

Tarrant, Harold. 'Orality and Plato's Narrative Dialogues', in *Voice into Text: Orality and Literacy in Ancient Greece*, ed. Ian Worthington, 128–47. Leiden: Brill, 1996.

Terry, Ralph Bruce. *A Discourse Analysis of First Corinthians*, SILUTAPL, 120. Arlington: University of Texas at Arlington Press, 1995.

——. 'Patterns of Discourse Structure in 1 Corinthians', *JOTT* 7 (1996) 1–36.

Theissen, G. *The Social Setting of Pauline Christianity. Essays on Corinth by Gerd Theissen*, ed. and trans. John H. Schütz. Philadelphia: Fortress, 1982.

——. *Psychological Aspects of Pauline Theology*, trans. John P. Galvin. Philadelphia: Fortress, 1987.

——. *Social Reality and the Early Christians: Theology, Ethics, and the World of the New Testament*, trans. Margaret Kohl. Minneapolis: Fortress, 1992.

——. 'The Social Structure of Pauline Communities: Some Critical Remarks on J. J. Meggitt, Paul, Poverty, and Survival', *JSNT* 84 (2001) 65–84.

——. 'Social Conflicts in the Corinthians Community: Further Remarks on J. J. Meggitt, Paul, Poverty, and Survival'. *JSNT* 25 (2003) 371–91.

Thiselton, Anthony. 'Semantics and New Testament Interpretation', in *New Testament Interpretation: Essays on Principles and Methods*, ed. I. Howard Marshall, 75–104. Exeter: Paternoster, 1977.

——. 'Realized Eschatology at Corinth', *NTS* 24 (1978) 510–26.

——. *The Two Horizons: New Testament Hermeneutics and Philosophical Description with Special Reference to Heidegger, Bultmann, Gadamer, and Wittgenstein*. Grand Rapids: Eerdmans, 1980.

——. *The First Epistle to the Corinthians: A Commentary on the Greek Text*. NIGTC. Grand Rapids: Eerdmans; Carlisle: Paternoster, 2000.

Thomas, W. D. 'New Testament Characters: Apollos', *ExpTim* 95 (1984) 245–46.

Thrall, Margaret E. *Greek Particles in the New Testament: Linguistic and Exegetical Studies*. Leiden: Brill, 1962.

——. *A Critical and Exegetical Commentary on the Second Epistle of the Corinthians*, vol. 2, ICC. London: T&T Clark, 2000.

Trotter, Andrew H., Jr. *Interpreting the Epistle to the Hebrews*, GNTE. Grand Rapids: Baker, 1997.

Tuckett, Christopher M. 'Jewish Christian Wisdom in 1 Corinthians?' in *Crossing the Boundaries: Essays in Biblical Interpretation in Honour of Michael D. Goulder*, eds. Stanley E. Porter, Paul Joyce, and David E. Orton, BIS, 8, 201–20. Leiden: Brill, 1994.

——. 'Paul, Scripture and Ethics: Some Reflections', *NTS* 46 (2000) 403–24

Turner, Max. 'Historical Criticism and Theological Hermeneutics for the New Testament', in *Between Two Horizons: Spanning New Testament Studies & Systematic Theology*, eds. Joel B. Green and Max Turner, 44–70. Grand Rapids: Eerdmans, 2000.

Tyler, Ronald L. 'First Corinthians 4.6 and Hellenistic Pedagogy', *CBQ* 60 (1998) 97–103.

——. 'The History of the Interpretation of μὴ ὑπὲρ ἃ γέγραπται in 1 Corinthians 4.6', *ResQ* 43 (2001) 243–52.

Vanhoozer, Kevin J. *Is There Meaning in This Text? The Bible, The*

Reader, and the Morality of Literary Knowledge. Grand Rapids: Zondervan, 1998.

Van Unnik, W. C. *Tarsus or Jerusalem. The City of Paul's Youth*, trans. G. Ogg. London: Epworth, 1962.

——. 'Tarsus or Jerusalem: The City of Paul's Youth', and 'Once Again: Tarsus or Jerusalem', in *Sparsa Collecta: The Collected Essays of W. C. van Unnik*, NovTSup 29, 259–320; 320–327. Leiden: Brill, 1973.

Verheyden, J. 'Origen on the Origin of 1 Cor. 2,9', in *The Corinthian Correspondence*, ed. Reimund Bieringer, 491–511. Leuven: Leuven University Press, 1996.

Vos, Johan S. 'Der μετασχηματισμός in 1 Kor. 4.6', *ZNW* 86 (1995) 154–72.

——. 'Die Argumentation des Paulus in 1 Kor. 1.10-3.4', in *The Corinthian Correspondence*, ed. Reimund Bieringer, 87–119. Leuven: Leuven University Press, 1996.

Wagner, J. Ross. ' "Not Beyond the Things which are Written": A Call to Boast Only in the Lord (1 Cor. 4.6)', *NTS* 44 (1998) 279–87.

Walker, William O., Jr. '1 Corinthians 2.6-16 A Non-Pauline Interpolation?' *JSNT* 47 (1992) 75–94.

Wall, Robert W. *The Acts of the Apostles*, NIB, 10. Nashville: Abingdon, 2002.

Wanamaker, Charles A. 'Epistolary vs. Rhetorical Analysis: Is a Synthesis Possible?' in *The Thessalonians Debate: Methodological Discord or Methodological Synthesis?* eds. Karl P. Donfried and Johannes Beutler, 255–86. Grand Rapids: Eerdmans, 2000.

——. 'A Rhetoric of Power: Ideology and 1 Corinthians 1–4', in *Paul and the Corinthians: Studies on a Community in Conflict. Essays in Honour of Margaret Thrall*, eds. Trevor J. Burke and J. Keith Elliott, NovTSup 109, 115–38. Leiden: Brill, 2003.

Ward, Richard F. 'Pauline Voice and Presence as Strategic Communication', *Semeia* 65 (1995) 95–107.

Watson, Duane F. 'Paul's Boasting in 2 Corinthians 10–13 as Defense of his Honor: A Socio-Rhetorical Analysis', in *Traditions as Rhetorical Proof: Pauline Argumentation in 1 Corinthians*, ConBNT 29, ed. Anders Eriksson, 260–75. Stockholm: Almqvist & Wiksell International, 1998.

Watson, Francis. *Paul, Judaism and the Gentiles: A Sociological Approach*, SNTSMS, 56. Cambridge: Cambridge University Press, 1986.

——. 'Christ, Community, and the Critique of Ideology: A Theological Reading of 1 Corinthians 1.18-31', *NThT* 46 (1992) 132–49.

Weima, Jeffrey A. D. 'What Does Aristotle Have to Do with Paul? An Evaluation of Rhetorical Criticism', *CTJ* 32 (1997) 458–68.

Weiss, Johannes. *Der erste Korintherbrief*. Göttingen: Vandenhoeck & Ruprecht, 2nd rev. edn, 1910.

——. *Das Urchristentum*, ed. R. Knopf. Göttingen: Vandenhoeck & Ruprecht, posthumously published in 1917.

Welborn, L. L. 'A Conciliatory Principle in 1 Cor. 4.6', *NovT* 39 (1987) 320–46.

——. 'On the Discord in Corinth: 1 Cor. 1–4 and Ancient Politics,' *JBL* 106 (1987) 85–111.

——. 'The Identification of 2 Corinthians 10–13 with the "Letter of Tears" ', *NTS* 37 (1995) 138–53.

——. *Politics and Rhetoric in the Corinthian Epistles*. Macon: Mercer University Press, 1997.

——. 'Μωρὸς γένεσθω: Paul's Appropriation of the Role of the Fool in 1 Corinthians 1–4', *BibInt* 4 (2002) 420–35.

——. *Paul, the Fool of Christ: A Study of 1 Corinthians 1–4 in the Cosmic-Philosophic Tradition*, JSNTSup 293. London: T&T Clark, 2005.

Widmann, M. '1 Kor 2.6-16: Ein Einspruch gegen Paulus', *ZNW* 70 (1979) 44–53.

Wilckens, Ulrich. *Weisheit und Torheit: Eine exegetisch-religionsgeschich-tliche Untersuchung zu 1Kor 1 und 2*, BHT, 26. Tübingen: Mohr, 1959.

——. 'Das Kreuz Christi als die Tiefe der Weisheit Gottes: Zur 1 Kor. 2,1–16', in *Paolo a una Chiesa Divisia*, SMBen, ed L. de Lorenzi, 43–81. Rome: S. Paolo, 1980.

Williams, Demetrius K. 'The Terminology of the Cross and the Rhetoric of Paul', SBLSP 37 (1998) 677–99.

——. 'Paul's Anti-Imperial "Discourse of the Cross": The Cross and Power in 1 Corinthians 1–4.' SBLSP 39 (2000) 796–823.

Williams, H. H. Drake, III. *The Wisdom of the Wise: The Presence and Function of Scripture Within 1 Cor 1.18-3.23*, AGAJU, 49. Leiden: Brill, 2001.

Williams, Michael. *Rethinking "Gnosticism": An Argument for Dismantling a Dubious Category*. Princeton: Princeton University Press, 1996.

Wilson, R. ML. 'How Gnostic Were the Corinthians?' *NTS* 19 (1972) 65–74.

——. 'Philo of Alexandria and Gnosticism', *Kairos* 14 (1972) 213–19.

——. 'Gnosis at Corinth', in *Paul and Paulinism: Essays in Honor of C. K. Barrett*, ed. M. D. Hooker and S. G. Wilson, 102–14. London: SPCK, 1982.

Winter, W. Bruce. ' "If a man does not wish to work…": A Cultural and Historical Setting for 2 Thessalonians 3.6-16" '. *TynBul* 40 (1989) 303–15.

——. 'Civil Litigation in secular Corinth and the Church: The Forensic Background to 1 Corinthians 6.1-8', *NTS* 37 (1991) 559–72.

——. 'The Importance of the *Captatio Benevolentiae* in the Speeches of Tertullius and Paul in Acts 24.1-21', *JTS* 42 (1991) 505–31.

——. 'The Entries and Ethics of Orators and Paul (1Thess 2.1-12)', *TynBul* 44 (1993) 55–74.

——. 'Is Paul among the Sophists?' *RTR* 53 (1994) 28–38.

——. 'On Introducing Gods to Athens: An Alternative Reading of Acts 17.18-20', *TynBul* 47 (1996) 71–90.

——. *After Paul Left Corinth: The Influence of Secular Ethics and Social Change.* Grand Rapids: Eerdmans, 2001.

——. *Philo and Paul among the Sophists: Alexandrian and Corinthian Responses to a Julio-Claudian Movement.* Cambridge: Cambridge University Press, 1997. Grand Rapids: Eerdmans, 2nd edn, 2002.

——. 'The Toppling of Favorinus and Paul by the Corinthians', in *Early Christianity and Classical Culture: Comparative Studies in Honor of Abraham J. Malherbe*, eds. John T. Fitzgerald, Thomas H. Olbricht and L. Michael White, NovTSup, 110, 291–306. Leiden: Brill, 2003.

——. 'The "Underlays" of Conflict and Compromise in 1 Corinthians', in *Paul and the Corinthians: Studies on a Community in Conflict. Essays in Honour of Margaret Thrall*, eds. Trevor J. Burke and J. Keith Elliott, NovTSup, 109, 139–56. Leiden: Brill, 2003.

——. 'Philodemus and Paul on Rhetorical Delivery (ὑπόκρισις)', in *Philodemus and the New Testament World*, eds. John T. Fitzgerald, Dirk Obbink, and Glenn S. Holland, NovTSup, 111, 323–42. Leiden: Brill, 2004.

——. 'Revelation versus Rhetoric: Paul and the First-Century Corinthian Fad', in *Translating Truth: The Case for Essentially Literal Translation*, 135–50. Wheaton: Crossway, 2005.

Wire, Antoinette Clark. *The Corinthian Women Prophets: A Reconstruction of Paul's Rhetoric.* Minnesota: Fortress, 1990.

Witherington, Ben, III. *Conflict and Community in Corinth: A Socio-Rhetorical Commentary on 1 and 2 Corinthians.* Grand Rapids: Eerdmans, 1995.

——. *The Acts of the Apostles: A Socio-Rhetorical Commentary.* Grand Rapids: Eerdmans, 1998.

Wolff, C. *Der erste Brief des Paulus an die Korinther*, THKNT, 7. Leipzig: Evangelische Verlagsanstalt, 1996.

Wright, Arthur. 'Apollos: A Study in Pre-Pauline Christianity', *ExpTim* 9 (1897–98): 8–12.

Wuellner, Wilhelm 'Haggadic Homily Genre in 1 Corinthians 1–3', *JBL* 89 (1970) 199–204.

——. 'The Sociological Implications of 1 Corinthians 1.26-28 Reconsidered', in *SE* VI, ed. E. A. Livingstone, 666–72. Berlin: Akademie,1973.

——. 'Greek Rhetoric and Pauline Argumentation', in *Early Christian*

Literarure and the Classical Intellectual Tradition: In Honorem Robert M. Grant, ThH, 53, eds. William R. Schoedel and Robert L. Wilken, 177–88. Paris: Beauchesne, 1979.

——. 'Paul as Pastor: The Function of Rhetorical Questions in First Corinthians', in *L'Apôtre Paul:Personalité, Style et Conception du Ministère*, BETL, 73, ed. Albert Vanhoye, 46–77. Leuven: Leuven University Press, 1986.

——. 'Where is Rhetorical Criticism Taking Us?' *CBQ* 49 (1987) 41–54.

Wynne G. Robert. *Apollos or Studies in the Life of a Great Layman of the First Century*. London: SPCK 1912.

Yinger, K. I. *Paul, Judaism, and Judgment according to Deeds*, SNTSMS, 105. Cambridge: Cambridge University Press, 1999.

Young, Norman H. '*Paidagōgos:* The Social Setting of a Pauline Metaphor', *NovT* 29 (1987) 150–76.

Yoon, Sojung. '"Not in Persuasive Words of Wisdom"? Paul's Rhetoric in 1 Corinthians 1.18-2.16', Unpublished doctoral dissertation, Graduate Theological Union, 2004.

Zaspel, Fred G. 'The Apostolic Model for Christian Ministry: An Analysis of 1 Corinthians 2.1-5', *R&R* 7 (1998) 21–34.

INDEX OF BIBLICAL CITATIONS

INDEX OF OTHER CITATIONS

Index of Authors